Earth, Water, Air and Fire
Studies in Canadian Ethnohistory

David T. McNab,
editor for Nin.Da.Waab.Jig.

Wilfrid Laurier Un

Publication of this book was made possible in part by a grant from Nin.Da.Waab.Jig., the Walpole Island Heritage Centre, of the Walpole Island First Nation and the support of the Department of Indian Affairs and Northern Development.

We acknowledge the support of the Canada Council for the Arts for our publishing program.

We acknowledge the financial support of the Government of Canada through the Book Publishing Industry Development Program for our publishing activities.

Canadian Cataloguing in Publication Data

Main entry under title:

Earth, water, air and fire : studies in Canadian ethnohistory

Proceedings of a conference held May 12-14, 1994, in
    Bkejwanong, Ont.
Includes bibliographical references and index.
ISBN 0-88920-297-4

1. Indians of North America – Canada – Congresses.
I. McNab, David T., 1947-   .   II. Nin.Da.Waab.Jig. (Group).

E78.C2E27 1998   971′.00497   C98-930431-0

Copyright © 1998
WILFRID LAURIER UNIVERSITY PRESS
Waterloo, Ontario, Canada   N2L 3C5

Cover design by Leslie Macredie based on an original illustration created by Teresa A. Altiman for this book

Printed in Canada

To
the citizens of
Bkejwanong

Contents

Introduction

David T. McNab

On 12-14 May 1994 Nin.Da.Waab.Jig. organized, in partnership with Wilfrid Laurier University, the Laurier III conference called Earth, Water, Air and Fire: Worlds in Contact and Conflict: A Conference on Ethnohistory and Ethnology. The participants gathered at the Walpole Island Day School and Study Centre at Bkejwanong. At Highbanks, on Walpole Island, stands Nin.Da.Waab.Jig., the Walpole Island Heritage Centre. Nin.Da.Waab.Jig., which means "those who seek to find," epitomized, more than anything else, the intent of this conference.

The papers and the ensuing discussions represented a sharing of ideas, of values and, above all, of work in various stages of progress. The conference was cross-cultural and interdisciplinary. Aboriginal and non-Aboriginal people exchanged their ideas from a variety of approaches—from Aboriginal oral traditions to Aboriginal studies, art, law, history, folklore and anthropology.

The citizens of Bkejwanong acted as hosts for the conference and, through Nin.Da.Waab.Jig., did all the local organization work to make the event a success. They participated fully in the conference proceedings and helped to make the conference an unforgettable and significant historical event for all the participants. Significantly, Nin.Da.Waab.Jig. then generously agreed to sponsor the publication of a selection of the papers presented at Laurier III, in partnership with Wilfrid Laurier University Press.

Notes to the Introduction are on p. 6.

The conference presenters outlined their research on applied and diverse aspects of ethnohistory in Canada. The focus was broad, covering Eastern Canada, Ontario, the Prairies, British Columbia and the North. The papers addressed diverse themes and highlighted the extensive variations in First Nations communities right across this country. In this respect, the papers cut across, and sometimes contradicted, the grain of conventional thought in government policy making. No longer can "Indians" be seen superficially through the lenses of nineteenth-century racial constructs. Too often in the past they have been misrepresented by politicians and bureaucrats as simply "good" or "bad," depending on how willing they were to collaborate with governments. Nor can they be perceived only in terms of government policies designed by white bureaucrats to better the condition of the First Nations. Twenty years ago the research emphasis was concentrated on methodology, abstract arguments and definitions. Now, the approach is much more holistic and differentiated, as the title of this book illustrates—*Earth, Water, Air and Fire*—the four elements comprising the Aboriginal world.

Earth, Water, Air and Fire was deliberately chosen as the title for the conference and this work as a way of reflecting the holistic worldview of Aboriginal people. This decision allowed for the creation of a barometer of what was happening to Aboriginal scholarship over the last decade, and especially after Oka. It also enabled the organizers to cast a large net to see what was happening in the fields of ethnology and ethnohistory in the 1990s. What emerged were papers on applied research that highlighted the strengths and diversities of Aboriginal communities and the initiatives of their citizens.

It is to be hoped that this applied approach will, through the publication of this book, provide policymakers with new ethnohistorical knowledge. It may be too sanguine to hope that this information will be used by politicians and bureaucrats in their work on the plethora of practical issues confronting Aboriginal people in Canada as we approach the twenty-first century. Yet, as we saw in the summer of 1990, we cannot afford conventional thinking any longer. We cannot afford the several hundred million dollar cost of another resistance movement like Oka. There are alternatives, and they must be considered.

Earth, Water, Air and Fire is a selection of papers and communications from Laurier III. Not all of the conference presenters chose to submit written papers or their oral communications after the conference ended. Those who did agreed to share their research and to allow their work to be published by Wilfrid Laurier University Press, in partnership with Nin.Da.Waab.Jig. Nin.Da.Waab.Jig. thanks all of the contributors for their generosity and kindness in making this book possible. The presentations in the communications sessions were not intended to be formal academic papers. These are identified in this Introduction. Nevertheless, some have been substantially rewritten and updated since they were first presented at Bkejwanong in the spring of 1994.

The significance of this Nin.Da.Waab.Jig. publication is in the emphasis that it gives to First Nations' perspectives on Earth, Water, Air and Fire and the potential influence of these perspectives on non-Aboriginal research. To be sure, First Nations oral traditions are a "cultural tool, the First Nations' way of knowing and understanding themselves and others."[1] *Earth, Water, Air and Fire* reflects the diversity and complexity of Aboriginal studies. It also highlights how difficult it is to write about ethnohistory and ethnology. It is significant to recognize how prominent and active Aboriginal citizens have been in their own present and past.

Earth, Water, Air and Fire has been divided into five parts. The first part provides two Aboriginal perspectives. The remaining four parts are organized by geographic area, as follows: Bkejwanong; Atlantic Canada—the Mi'kma'ki and the Mi'kmaq Nation; Ontario: Sovereignty, History and Law; the North, Gender and Aboriginal Governance. In addition, there is a brief Retrospect on the conference and on the significance of *Earth, Water, Air and Fire*.

The first part is intended to provide Aboriginal perspectives on Earth, Water, Air and Fire. The first article, by Dean Jacobs, our host for the conference and the executive director of Nin.Da.Waab.Jig., introduces us to Bkejwanong and the richness of the Walpole Island First Nation community. "Bkejwanong—'The Place Where the Waters Divide': A Perspective on Earth, Water, Air and Fire" highlights the meaning of these four elements as the theme. Our special banquet speaker on Friday evening was Olive Patricia Dickason. Professor Dickason, who became a member of the Order of Canada in 1996, provided the conference with a thought-provoking speech on "Art and Amerindian Worldviews." Her paper combines all four elements of the natural world and is a thoughtful synthesis of Aboriginal art and the larger worldviews that are part of it.

Part II focuses on the history of Bkejwanong and its people—a world of conflict and resistance. In "'Water Is Her Life Blood': The Waters of Bkejwanong and the Treaty-Making Process," I examine the treaty-making process as part of the relationship of Bkejwanong to the outside world, literally a meeting ground of water and fire.[2] The history of Bkejwanong has been enormously influenced by its strategic location in the Great Lakes and by the waters that surround the community. Water was and is truly the lifeblood of the people. Water cannot be neglected as a significant and formative factor in Aboriginal history. In her paper " 'Under the Earth': The Expropriation and Attempted Sale of the Oil and Gas Rights of the Walpole Island First Nation during World War I," Rhonda Telford demonstrates that First Nations land rights are not limited to the surface of the earth, but also include mineral and sub-surface rights. Telford shows that Aboriginal people were involved in activities under the earth, and that they resisted the federal government when it attempted to expropriate oil and gas rights from the Walpole Island and Sarnia First Nations by the use of the *War Measures Act* in 1918. The Reverend Jim Miller of St. John the Baptist Anglican Church, Walpole Island, now retired, presented his paper, entitled "The Reverend Simpson Brigham (1875-1926): The Worlds of Henry Ford and Simpson Brigham Collide." Miller illustrates the significance, and some of the problems, of conflict between two disparate worlds in the early twentieth century, as epitomized by Simpson Brigham and Henry Ford. The focus of this paper is on the surface of the Earth—commercial agriculture in the early twentieth century.

Part III concerns the history of Mi'kma'ki and the Mi'kmaq in the north Atlantic in the nineteenth century. The focus of this section is on Earth and Water. Janet E. Chute, an anthropologist at Dalhousie University in Halifax, shows that fishing and fishing places were a primary component of the Mi'kmaq economy and society. Chute's paper, entitled "Mi'kmaq Fishing in the Maritimes: A Historical Overview," greatly adds to our understanding of the complexity and the bounty of Mi'kmaq life. The second is a communication of research in progress by Theresa Redmond; " 'We Cannot Work Without Food': Nova Scotia Indian Policy and Mi'kmaq Agriculture, 1783-1867," focuses on successful Mi'kmaq forays into agriculture at a time when the Earth was being taken from them by white settlers. In "Glooscap Encounters Silas T. Rand: A Baptist Missionary on the Folkloric Fringe," Thomas S. Abler, an anthropologist at the University of Waterloo, uses a biographical focus to explore Rand and the history of Rand's collection of Mi'kmaq legends as well as the influence of his ethnological writings on the Mi'kmaq.

Part IV is about sovereignty, history and law in what is now Ontario. Drawing on new and old sources, and reinterpreting white settler history, these papers break new ground. In "Colonizing a People: Mennonite Settlement in Waterloo Township," E. Reginald Good critically reviews the microhistory of Mennonite settlement in part of southwestern Ontario. Sidney L. Harring's paper, "The Six Nations Confederacy, Aboriginal Sovereignty and Ontario Aboriginal Law: 1790-1860," uses new archival and legal sources. A lawyer and legal historian at the City University of New York Law School, Harring concludes that nineteenth-century court rulings demonstrate the unequal character of Canadian law for Aboriginal people. The effects are still being felt by Aboriginal people today. In Elizabeth Graham's communication, "The Uses and Abuses of Power in Two Ontario Residential Schools: Mohawk Institute and Mount Elgin," she has used Aboriginal oral testimony as well as written sources to illustrate the workings of the residential school system and its horrific social and cultural effects on Aboriginal citizens. The final article in this section is a study of Aboriginal sovereignty in Northern Ontario in the late twentieth century. Bruce W. Hodgins is a historian from Trent University and formerly director of the Frost Centre for Canadian Heritage and Development Studies in Peterborough, Ontario. In "The Crown Domain and the Self-Governing Presence in Northern Ontario," he illustrates how the federal and provincial governments have continually tried to ignore or to obliterate the Aboriginal presence in Ontario's Northland. In spite of some recent government initiatives, this has been a tragic story of the taking of treaty and reserve lands. Hodgins also emphasizes that the Aboriginal presence is increasing in the North through various First Nation initiatives in the areas of Aboriginal governance and land and treaty rights.

Part V concerns the Canadian North, Gender and Aboriginal governance. Heather Rollason examines an old source of our knowledge about Aboriginal women and their history in her communication, "Some Comments upon the Marked Differences in the Representations of Chipewyan Women in Samuel Hearne's Field Notes and His Published *Journal*." Rollason, an MA graduate of Trent University[3] and now a PhD candidate at the University of Alberta, critically compares the *Journal* of Samuel Hearne with his field notes, attempting to provide a more balanced perspective on Aboriginal women in the late eighteenth century. "Is This Apartheid? Aboriginal Reserves and Self-Government in Canada, 1960-82" was the most controversial paper presented at the conference. In it, Joan G. Fairweather of the National Archives of Canada challenges the notion that Canada's Aboriginal policy is a form of apartheid. She concludes that Canada's Aboriginal policy, at least since 1960, was not based on apartheid as the term was used in the South African colonial context. However, it cannot be denied that the apartheid-like effects of the *Indian Act*, i.e., the actual administration of the reserve system and the fact that Aboriginal citizens were not persons and could not vote prior to 1960, existed in Canada since the nineteenth century. "The Sechelt and Nunavut Agreements: Evolutionary and Revolutionary Approaches to Self-Government," by Cameron Croxall and Laird Christie of Wilfrid Laurier University, argues that the Sechelt municipal-style, self-government approach is derived from the *Indian Act* and that it is an evolutionary approach to Aboriginal governance in southern British Columbia. In contrast, the situation of Nunavut is portrayed as a revolutionary approach that has been derived from the Nunavut comprehensive land claim settlement agreement.

In the Retrospect, "A Meeting Ground of Earth, Water, Air and Fire," I attempt to bring together the diverse themes of the conference and this work. This is a stocktaking of where we have come from, and where we are headed, as we approach the twenty-first century. The Aboriginal concepts of Earth, Water, Air and Fire may become a useful perspective in our understanding of Aboriginal history. We must never forget that Aboriginal history is and always has been vibrant within Aboriginal communities. This history has been until recently "invisible to the Canadian mainstream," and the reason for this failure has been a "want of looking—more accurately, a want of listening, because the singular source for Aboriginal perspectives on history is oral tradition."[4]

Finally, it is hoped that *Earth, Water, Air and Fire: Studies in Canadian Ethnohistory* will encourage us to continue to share our research and our scholarship. It is both vital and necessary that ethnohistorians, whether Aboriginal or non-Aboriginal, carry on both the spirit and the objectives of Nin.Da.Waab.Jig.—those who seek to find.

Notes

1 See David McNab and S. Dale Standen, eds., with an "Introduction," *Gin Das Winan: Documenting Aboriginal History in Ontario*, Occasional Papers of The Champlain Society, no. 2 (Toronto: The Champlain Society, 1996).

2 Richard White, *The Middle Ground: Indians, Empires, and Republics in the Great Lakes Region, 1650-1815* (Cambridge: Cambridge University Press, 1991).

3 It should be noted that this communication is based on Rollason's MA thesis, "Studying under the Influence: The Impact of Samuel Hearne's *Journal* on the Scholarly Literature about Chipewyan Women" (Trent University, 1995).

4 McNab and Standen, eds., *Gin Das Winan: Documenting Aboriginal History in Ontario*.

Part I

Aboriginal Perspectives

1

Bkejwanong—"The Place Where the Waters Divide": A Perspective on Earth, Water, Air and Fire

Dean M. Jacobs

The purpose of this paper is to provide a perspective on Bkejwanong and ourselves—the Walpole Island First Nation citizens. In our language we know our lands and waters as Bkejwanong, which means in English "the place where the waters divide." We are pleased and proud to invite you as visitors to our Homeland.[1] I want you to remember that we are still here in our Territory and to tell you what this means to us. This has always been a special place.

Our present-day community is nestled between Ontario and Michigan at the mouth of the St. Clair River. The modern delta emerged only 6,000 years ago. We are part of Earth, Water, Air and Fire. We are timeless. Furthermore, we are here and we are not going away. Bkejwanong is a meeting ground and a place of sacred fire. So if you want to share with us, as a visitor to Turtle Island, you must make an effort to understand us and our ways and our stories—Gin Das Winan—which is our way of knowing and understanding our history.

To understand the Aboriginal concept of history as well as our sense of place is a significant part of knowing Aboriginal people and their history. White visitors to our sacred place, like yourselves, have not always

Notes to chapter 1 are on p. 19.

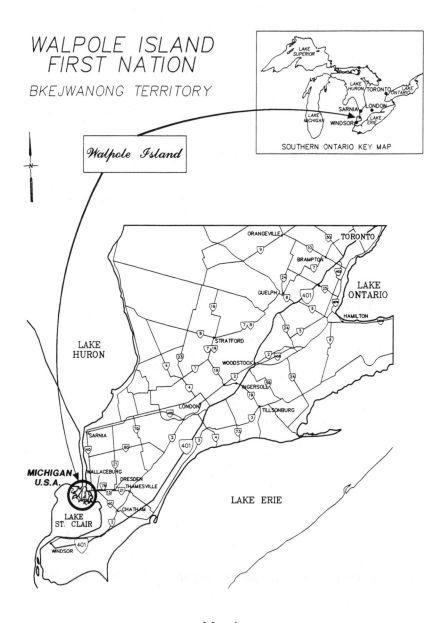

Map 1

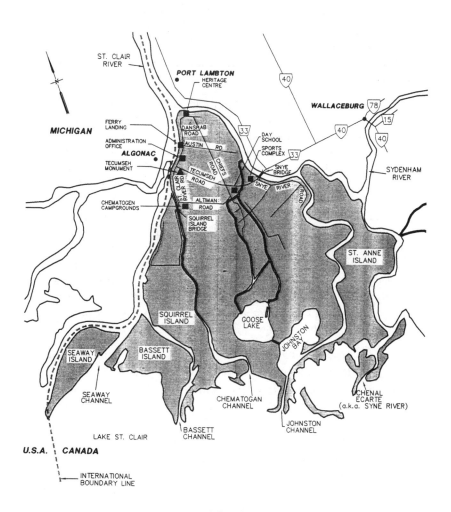

Map 2

shown sensitivity to, or comprehended, the meaning of our place.[2] Our hereditary chief Begigishigueshkam explained this fact to the superintendent of the Indian Department, Samuel Peters Jarvis, when he visited our lands and waters in September 1839, now more than one hundred and fifty years ago. We explained the significance of the history of our lands and waters to him:

> [W]e have no records of ancient treaties to refer to, we have no books handed down to us by our ancestors to direct us in our speech; we have but our hearts and the traditions of our old men; they are not deceitful.
>
> Father when the White Elk [Alexander McKee] finding that our Fathers were growing poor and wretched in the vicinity of the Long Knife brought them up to the Island on which you now find us, he lept from his Canoe with a lighted Brand in his hand and after having kindled the first Council Fire which had ever shone upon it, he gave it to them forever.
>
> "Remain my children"; said he, "do not desert the abode to which I have brought you & never shall any one molest you. Should any persons come to ask from you a part of these lands, turn from them with distrust and deny them their request. Never for a moment heed their voice and at your dying day instruct your sons to get theirs, teach them as generation succeeds generation to preserve intact their inheritance and poverty shall be unknown to them."[3]

But Jarvis failed to understand our words. He came to hunt for sporting purposes and to exploit our resources. Moreover, he never fulfilled his solemn promises to us to protect Bkejwanong. And he never returned.

Today our lands and waters still remain intact and unceded. To us they are sacred. They are our spiritual Mother. They remain a place of Fire. We are spiritual beings. As such, our sources of life are all around us—the four elements of Earth, Water, Air and Fire.

This notion has been well expressed by one twentieth-century Aboriginal writer, N. Scott Momaday, in his autobiographical and highly reflective work, *The Names*. Within the circle of life and history, he has written, time does not, in one sense, exist:

> I have no notion of time; the moment does not exist for me as time, but it exists only as pain or puzzlement, perhaps a sound, a word. What I shall come to know as time is now an imperceptible succession of colours, of dawns and dusks, mornings and afternoons, a concentration of days into one day, or is it simply the inside of eternity, the hollow of a great wing.[4]

Twenty years ago Momaday remarked that there are many ways to tell stories—to recall the names and history—whether that history be oral or written.[5] Our name for our history comes from our word for stories:

Gin Das Winan. This is one of the ways in which we keep ourselves and our understanding of our history alive.[6]

Place is not only important, it is all-encompassing. It is Earth, Water, Air and Fire. It is something to be respected and honoured. For without these elements we will weaken and then die culturally and physically.

We tell stories about our Territory, our lands and our waters, the plants and the animals. For example, there is the story of the creation of Bkejwanong—the soul of Indian Territory—one of the sacred places and a place of Fire. It is also a place where the story is told of the muskrat who helped create our world of Turtle Island when it was all covered with water:

> To this day, the ancestors of our brother, the muskrat, have been given a good life. No matter that marshes have been drained and their homes destroyed in the name of progress, the muskrats continue to multiply and grow. The Creator has made it so that muskrats will always be with us because of the sacrifice that our little brother made for all of us many years ago when the Earth was covered with water. The muskrats do their part today in remembering the Great Flood; they build their homes in the shape of the little ball of Earth and the island that was formed from it.[7]

Bkejwanong is our world as we know and understand it.

The citizens of the Walpole Island First Nation, also known as the Council of Three Fires, the Ojibwa, Potawatomi and Ottawa Nations, have protected and conserved Bkejwanong since time immemorial. This is understood, and told, from the perspective of the First Nation, by our Elders. They tell us who we are and, in spiritual terms, what the land means to our people. We have used our lands and waters and have shared in the harvesting of the land for thousands of years. Our people and our land will continue for thousands of years. The primary objective of the Walpole Island First Nation is spiritual—to protect the land—our Mother Earth.

This is for us a sacred trust, a trust to protect the land. The continuity and integrity of our lands are important to our survival as an Indigenous people. The Walpole Island First Nation citizens have used all parts of the land within Bkejwanong on an everyday basis. Some parts of Bkejwanong have been taken up and used by private interests or governments for other purposes, oftentimes without consultation with us, much less with our permission. This violates our sense of sharing and of mutual respect.

Generations of First Nation members have used the land and have shared in its bounty and its uses. The significance of the oral history and the prehistory of the Walpole Island First Nation must be understood today from our perspective, and its impact cannot be ignored. Our traditions and our culture cannot be ignored.

The integrity of Bkejwanong must be respected and maintained for future generations. This involves management and control through Aboriginal governance, including protection for the land and its uses wherever they may be within our Territory. To this end, there must be protection and conservation of the flora and fauna, of village sites and former village sites, of natural heritage sites, of traditional historical sites, of sacred burial places, as well as protection of the environment.

Our Aboriginal and treaty harvesting rights of the Walpole Island First Nation citizens must be respected and protected. Those harvesting rights include hunting, fishing, trapping and all manner of harvesting and gathering activities. They include, but are not restricted to, the harvesting of maple sugar, nuts, herbs, sweet grass for ceremonial purposes and medicines to make our people well. These would also include gathering activities related to traditional ceremonies, subsistence, barter and commerce and commercial activities for subsistence, all of which have been recognized by Canadian courts over the past two decades, within Bkejwanong.

Our lands and waters remain unceded. Aboriginal title and rights have always been a primary concern of the Walpole Island First Nation. The land provides meaning and significance to our lives and protects our Aboriginal title. The Walpole Island First Nation has chosen to safeguard and to protect Aboriginal title by using the concept of self-determination and by insisting on the principle of mutual respect through various means of peaceful resistance in negotiations with the Crown. In the treaty-making process, Aboriginal title has also been reaffirmed. We have successfully resisted the attempted intrusions on our lands and have kept Bkejwanong safe and secure. It has been kept together to this day.

The Creator made us responsible for the natural world. As its caretakers, we see protection of the land as fundamental; it is a major tool of Aboriginal governance. Aboriginal governance does not need to be "granted" through government policy or by legislation, for it is there and has always existed. What is needed is the legal recognition of the constitutional fact of Aboriginal governance within the Confederation of Canada. We will then be sovereign and will truly be in a nation-to-nation relationship with the rest of Canada. This recognition, and with it, mutual respect, was removed by the federal government and effectively foregone, without the consent or consultation with the Aboriginal Nations at Confederation in 1867. Land and a land base are significant, but they are not the only components of Aboriginal governance and management. The people and the land are one, and Aboriginal governance is what binds them together to provide shape and form and substance.

Our economy was once bountiful and rich and complex. It was based on a variety of activities which included but was not restricted to hunting, fishing, trapping and the planting of corn, as well as gathering activities, including the making and trading of maple syrup. These activities had many dimensions, which included a substantial trading component and many commercial activities. Our Territory was also at the crossroads of many Aboriginal Nations and European empires. It has had many military and trade advantages. Our Territory has always been a strategic place.

Bkejwanong has been occupied by Aboriginal people for thousands of years. It is today home to more than 3,000 Ojibwa, Potawatomi and Ottawa. Having a common heritage, we formed the Three Fires Confederacy—a political and cultural compact that has served us well.[8]

The "Island" is blessed with a unique ecosystem, including 6,900 hectares of the most diverse wetlands in all of the Great Lakes Basin. Actually, Walpole Island consists of six islands, with Walpole being the largest. The land portion of the "reserve" contains a total of 58,000 acres. I use the term "reserve" advisedly because in fact Walpole Island has never been founded, legislated, established, set apart or surveyed as a "reserve." Walpole Island has the distinction of being "unceded territory." This fact, together with its natural and human resources, makes Walpole Island a very special place.

Walpole Island is also known for its rare flora and fauna. Our local economy is highly diverse and rich. It is dependent on the bounty and fruits of the land.[9] Our lands and waters still support recreation and tourism. Hunting, fishing and trapping is a multimillion dollar industry in our community. We are the southernmost reserve in Canada. Citizens of our First Nation still support their families through hunting, fishing, trapping and guiding activities. These traditional activities are central to our economic base and cultural integrity.

Our second-largest industry is still agriculture. Today, nearly 12,000 acres are under cultivation, with cash crops such as corn and soybeans grown. Collectively, we farm 4,400 acres under a co-operative we call

Tahgahoning ("garden," in English) Enterprise. To give you an idea of the size of our farm operation in the early 1980s we purchased the world's largest corn picker. At that time, there were only a handful of these monsters in North America. Ours was the first in Canada.

Through the centuries we have resisted attempts by white people to change our spiritual values and our way of life. We have tried to protect Earth, Water, Air and Fire for our children and our grandchildren. There have been many misconceptions by white people about us and futile attempts by missionaries and government officials to change and assimilate us.[10]

In 1965, Walpole Island expelled the last Indian agent, the first reserve to do so in Canada, thus opening the door to our modern era of self-government. More than thirty years ago, we started at zero level.

We replaced the Indian agent with one of our own citizens,[11] and now bureaucracy is our third largest industry. Today this sector of our workforce numbers well over two hundred. It is what you might call a growth industry. I confess that I am one of those bureaucrats, as part of Nin.Da.Waab.Jig. at the Walpole Island Heritage Centre. Nin.Da.Waab.Jig. means "those who seek to find" in our language. This phrase captures the essence of our work. It can further be described as co-operative, community-based research.

However, all is not right in kitigan ("our garden," in English)—in our paradise. Today our lands and waters are under siege. Walpole Island has been subjected to pollutants for decades. First, upstream is Canada's major petrochemical and refining region, called "Chemical Valley." Between 1974 and 1986, a total of thirty-two major spills, as well as hundreds of minor ones, involved ten tonnes of pollutants. Since 1986, the Ontario Ministry of the Environment has recorded an average of one hundred spills per year. A decade later, this number is now only beginning to decline. But the prophecy of the seventh fire is over and, in 1998, the balance has now shifted in our favour, as has been foretold.

Second, passing ocean-going freighters are a constant reminder that a "*Valdez*-type" disaster is possible. As it is, these ships are to blame for introducing the menacing and resilient zebra mussels to Lake St. Clair and our wetlands. Purple loosestrife is another prolific foreign invader crowding out everything in its path. If only we could train the zebra mussels to eat purple loosestrife.

Third, significant agricultural run-off of pesticides and fertilizers is a major non-point pollution source. Our once-popular beaches are closed for weeks on end because of high levels of bacteria. And last, dredging of contamination sediments in the surrounding waters poses yet another serious environmental problem.

Environmental degradation has significant implications for our wildlife and its habitat, our human health and well-being. It determines our water quality and whether we can safely drink the waters of Bkejwanong. It affects our economic development. This effect is cumulative and complex. For example, our economic activities depend to a large degree on the viability of our natural resource base. This, in turn, affects tourism.

The beauty as well as the spirit of Bkejwanong are found in our natural resources and in us. Clearly, our First Nation faces a great deal of stress. Yet our everyday life continues. The people of Walpole Island view our lives in a spiritual, holistic and dynamic way. We have a keen sense of place and community that is perhaps unrivalled in this part of the country. Our Homeland is all we have ever known. It is important for all of us to understand how this fits into our perspective and scheme of life.

Our story is also shared by First Nations from coast to coast. It can best be summarized as follows:

> For Aboriginal people, traditional belief is often expressed by using the circle to represent life. Our life goal can be described as follows: we did not inherit a legacy from our ancestors. We hold it in trust for our future generations.

Aboriginal people have their own history, their own cultures. They have retained values, traditions and knowledge that are integral to living in harmony with nature and the natural world, which encompasses Earth, Water, Air and Fire. We have a close relationship with the land and its resources, which have survived, relatively intact, through centuries of colonization. Those who earn part or all of their livelihood through trapping and other harvesting activities develop a detailed knowledge of wildlife populations and local environmental conditions, which is of value to resource monitoring and management as well as conservation. This traditional ecological knowledge gives Aboriginal people the authority to speak on behalf of the land and to make decisions about the disposition and use of local resources. Also, it avoids and mitigates natural resource exploitation.

Aboriginal people have much to teach the wider population of Canada and North America about living in harmony with nature and in community with other people. Our Elders know our lands and our waters. They will continue to share that knowledge with scientists of

Eurocentric inclinations. But the latter have to be ready and well prepared to listen to our ideas and our voices. Through knowledge comes first understanding and then wisdom. A strong feature of our cultures is an emphasis on community, on sharing resources through good and bad times, and on group decision making through consensus. The preservation of the unique cultures of Aboriginal people and the sharing of their knowledge are therefore an important part of our sustainable life strategy. For this reason, one of the indicators of overall sustainability should be the well-being of Aboriginal communities.

Recently, there have been a few signs that the balance may be shifting in our favour, from exploitation to sustainablity. For example, in 1995 our community was the recipient of a major international award, the "We the Peoples: 50 Communities Award."[12] We have now been recognized by the United Nations, on its fiftieth anniversary, as one of fifty communities around the world demonstrating, among other achievements, our commitment to environmental issues. This international recognition comes from our exemplary record in environmental research and sustainable development advocacy. In particular, the award is for the leadership role which our community has taken in combining traditional and non-traditional environmental knowledge as the basis for "interacting effectively with the non-indigenous population and western environmental scientists to everyone's mutual benefit." This is a sign of a true meeting ground of ideas.

In these ways, we are continuing to make our own history within the circle of life; metaphorically speaking, within the "hollow of a great wing." Our lands and the waters, their meaning and context, are important in understanding our history. Without it, you will not understand our customs, our language and our laws. The significance of Aboriginal places—their customs and cultures—needs to be better understood.

Historians trained in the European tradition have understood the significance of visiting the place of the battle site before understanding and interpreting the written documents. But they and their documents do not always see us, much less know us. It is important to see a historical event, indeed, all of history, in a holistic way,[13] which is the way we view our lands and waters. The spiritual world of a place[14] is much more than land—it is Earth, Water, Air and Fire. It is both our strength and the source of our well-being. It is our soul.

Notes

1 See Dean Jacobs, "'We have but our hearts and the traditions of our old men': Understanding the Traditions and History of Bkejwanong," in David McNab and S. Dale Standen, eds., with an "Introduction," *Gin Das Winan: Documenting Aboriginal History in Ontario*, Occasional Papers of The Champlain Society, no. 2 (Toronto: The Champlain Society, 1996), pp. 1-13.

2 For other examples see ibid.

3 Samuel Peters Jarvis Papers, Metropolitan Toronto Reference Library, Baldwin Room, S 125, B57, July-September 1839, pp. 373-83. See also Jacobs, "'We have but our hearts and the traditions of our old men': Understanding the Traditions and History of Bkejwanong."

4 N. Scott Momaday, *The Names*, Sun Tracks, An American Indian Literary Series, vol. 16 (Tucson and London: The University of Arizona Press, 1976), p. 6.

5 Ibid., "Prologue," p. 1.

6 See Nin.Da.Waab.Jig., *Walpole Island: The Soul of Indian Territory* (Walpole Island, ON, 1987), and Jacobs, "'We have but our hearts and the traditions of our old men': Understanding the Traditions and History of Bkejwanong."

7 Edward Benton-Banai, *The Mishomis Book: The Voice of the Ojibway* (St. Paul, MN: Red School House, 1988).

8 Nin.Da.Waab.Jig., *Walpole Island: The Soul of Indian Territory*, especially pp. 1-26.

9 For an excellent description of the Walpole Island First Nation Territory see Fred Coyne Hamil, *The Valley of the Lower Thames, 1640-1850* (Toronto: University of Toronto Press, 1951), pp. 4-6.

10 Jacobs, "'We have but our hearts and the traditions of our old men': Understanding the Traditions and History of Bkejwanong."

11 Mr. Edsel Dodge who replaced the last Indian agent is now one of our Elders and a member of Nin.Da.Waab.Jig.'s Heritage Committee.

12 This award was presented to us in New York in September 1995.

13 See, for example, one of the first environmental histories by European-trained and educated Simon Schama, *Landscape and Memory* (Toronto: Random House of Canada, 1995).

14 See Basil Johnston, *The Manitous: The Spiritual World of the Ojibway* (Toronto: Key Porter Books, 1995).

2

Art and Amerindian Worldviews

Olive Patricia Dickason

The connection between worldviews and art in pre-contact tribal societies is so close that they can be regarded as two aspects of the same reality. Worldviews express people's perceptions of the universe and its powers. Art in its many aspects, both performing and visual, played an essential role. In tribal societies, art is more than paintings, sculpture, literature, music, song and dance, ritual or architecture, although it is all of these things, and a wide range of others as well. In examining the relationship between worldviews and art, it will be necessary to first of all survey briefly how the Amerindians saw the cosmos and their place within it.

Cosmic Curiosity

Amerindians, no less than peoples in other parts of the world, were intensely interested in their origins, their relationship with the cosmos and the natural surroundings in which they lived. Their curiosity about living things, and indeed in all things around them, ranged far and wide. Beyond this keen and continuous observation lay mythic thought, which reached—and still reaches—conclusions that cannot be verified by experience, but which are essential for the completion of human-kind's self-image. Amerindians perceived the universe as an intricate meshing of personalized powers, great and small, beneficial and danger-ous, whose equilibrium was based upon reciprocity. Just as there was no

---

Notes to chapter 2 are on pp. 29-31.

clear division between humans and animals, and each could sometimes assume the form of the other, so were spirits intimately connected with the physical world, and could take its forms, both animate and inanimate. Major creator spirits in North America were Hare, Crow-Raven, Coyote and Spider.[1]

For Amerindians, spirits revealed the true nature of the world around us; they did not have the concept, as Western thought did, of a split between a world of spiritual plenitude and a world of material imperfection.[2] Another difference was in the conception of time, which for Amerindians was a recurring cycle that passed through well-defined stages, and for Europeans was linear, with a beginning and an end. In one aspect, Amerindians and Europeans shared a common characteristic: their worldviews, while stable, were not static, although essentials persisted in the midst of changing conditions and new influences. Since oral societies see the revelations of the spirits as a continuous process rather than being fixed in time, they are somewhat more flexible in this regard than literate societies that fix the word in writing.

In oral traditions, harmony was of the utmost importance, but its maintenance was by no means automatic, as the demands of life could make it necessary to break the rules.[3] Hence the importance of the trickster, who could be an individual, but who could also be an aspect of the Creator, perhaps in the form of the figures already noted—Coyote, Hare, Spider or Crow-Raven. Laughter, humour and irony permeated trickster's shenanigans.[4] This figure was a buffer between the ideal of peaceful co-operation and the violence that could result from confrontations with malevolent, destructive forces.

All living beings were related—indeed, were "people," some of whom were human—and had soul-forms.[5] So did some objects that the Western world considers to be inanimate; for instance, certain stones, under certain conditions, could be alive or inhabited by minds.[6] According to the Ojibwa, some stones can roll of their own volition, and shamans can carry on conversations with them.[7] The Sto:Lo of British Columbia, a Salishan people, thought that certain "transformer" rocks were actually "men in stone." In their belief, being turned into stone was the fate of chiefs who did not share their wealth with the people.[8]

Art's Mythic Origins

This diversity arising out of essential unity was mirrored in myths, which explained and communicated patterns of relationships. Claude Lévi-Strauss went so far as to assert that Amerindian mythologies are all essentially one, all solidly founded in nature.[9] This is not to say, however, that the same myths were to be found among all peoples; quite the contrary, endless series of adventures involving a large range of characters ensured wide variation in details.[10] Nor was the symbolism uniform; in fact, it could be highly individualistic. Yet consistency was still to be found, principally in underlying themes and structural relationships—in other words, in fundamental patterns. This was particularly evident in storytelling, so important for revealing the interconnecting patterns of spiritual and material worlds, which provided keys for defining peoples' perceptions of themselves. This is what history still means to Amerindians today, in contrast to the European concept of history as a series of events that relates only indirectly, if at all, to basic universal relationships.

From the need to understand and to communicate fundamental patterns flowed the importance of art. In the words of Carl Jung (1875-1961),

> Great art till now has always derived its fruitfulness from myth, from the unconscious process of symbolization which continues through the ages and, as the primordial manifestation of the human spirit, will continue to be the root of all creation in the future.[11]

Symbolic figures that crop up the length and breadth of the Americas include supernatural birds that make thunder, the world tree, dwarves who live on odours, the trickster, and the sky twins personifying creative and destructive forces. The twins represented the duality and ambiguity of nature that has continually fascinated Amerindians. This multiplicity of forces and forms was reflected in the leashed vitality particularly evident in Northwest Coast art, and in the interweaving of animal and human forms.[12]

Art as "Control-Power"

Art, far from being considered as an entity in itself, was conceptualized in terms of process, a form of "control-power," aimed at communicating with, and evoking the co-operation of, plant and animal spirits. This was particularly true of shamanic art, where the creative act in itself was frequently of overriding importance.[13]

In other words, art was an active agent, not just something to be passively enjoyed. As is well known, Amerindians have no word for "art," nor did they have the concept of art for art's sake; when they painted or sculpted, it was for a particular purpose, not just to create a beautiful object. On the other hand, the more technically perfect the object created, and the more beautiful, the better chance it had of achieving its purpose. Art's intermediary role between the spiritual and material worlds was nowhere better illustrated than in the power accorded to the word—in storytelling, in poetry, in song. The Amassalik Inuit of East Greenland use the same word for "to breathe" and "to make poetry"; its root means "life force." Among the Salish the loss of a power song—considered to be personal property—was tantamount to losing one's soul.[14]

Relating to the Universe

Rituals, although closely connected with myths, tended to be both more conservative as well as more demanding in their requirements for exact observance. They were also more varied in their realization; besides relying heavily upon the performing arts, they used other forms of artistic expression, such as costumes, masks and various types of instruments. In fact, rituals have been called an early form of theatre; the Kwak'waka'wakw ceremonies illustrate this particularly well. While there were a variety of reasons for holding rituals, a principal one was the preservation and revitalization of a community's life forces, which meant that such events were usually held during winter, when those forces were at their most vulnerable; or, when the rites were held for individuals, during times of transition (such as puberty) or bereavement. The Iroquois, on the other hand, institutionalized life-negating forces in their Society of Faces (also known as the Society of Wooden Faces and the False Face Company), one of their three medicine societies. In these ceremonies, members wore the famous false face masks, in this case those representing the Bad Spirit, and replicated some of his acts in order to turn them, as in a mirror, back upon themselves, and so nullify their effects. The Zuni took still another approach, and sought to recreate the middle place where life forces are balanced, thus neutralizing malevolent powers.[15]

One of the most important of rituals was the widely popular ball game, which could also be played as a sport; every city in Mesoamerica, every pueblo in the US Southwest, had its ball court. Without such formality, versions were played in the forests of the North and even in the Arctic. As ritual, the game was played to divine the purpose of the gods. As such, it had to be played in a certain way, in which the ball became a metaphor for the sun or other heavenly body and replicated its movements. The symbolism of this was so serious that the captain of the losing team could be beheaded. Keeping the cosmos in tune—and keeping in tune with the cosmos—was not a matter to be taken lightly. Today the ball game has lost its cosmic connections, but even in its secularized forms such as baseball, football or hockey, it is a major player in a world dominated by economics.

On a personal level, relationships with spirits were achieved through dreams and visions, to which much importance was attached. The experiences were intensely personal, as they took the individual into a direct relationship with spirits without the benefit of intermediaries. These experiences could also be innovative as new revelations could, and sometimes did, replace established traditions. In other words, revelation was more important than fixed tradition. Vision quests were undertaken at puberty, with attendant purification rites involving prayer and fasting, among other things. Purification in order to gain spirit power could be undertaken at other times as well; thus, a person could end up with several spirit helpers, each with its own particular expertise. It is thought that much of the rock art that is found throughout the Americas is associated with these occasions. The connection between an individual and his spirit helper could become so close that the latter was in effect an alter-ego. If the helper died (spirits were not necessarily immortal), the person also died.

Technology's Contribution

The technology that aided in facilitating these interactive relationships in practical terms was, of course, vitally important. The simplicity of Stone Age tool kits should not be allowed to obscure the complexities of the cosmologies; nor should it be forgotten that in the final analysis, it is the touch of the hand that counts with art, not technological sophistication. Anthropologist Robin Ridington has made the point that Amerindian technology consisted of knowledge rather than tools;[16] technology is only one means by which humans relate to the cosmic cycle. For example, the overriding importance of maintaining harmony was reflected even in the plans of villages and encampments (not to mention the cities and temple complexes to the south) with their celestial orientations and emphasis on centres rather than boundaries. Even the way that shadows fell during the day or during the year could be incorporated into building designs and layouts, which then served as sorts of astrological calendars. The huge temple mounds of southern North America and Central America recreated the Sacred Mountain; it has been hypothesized that in building these monuments the people accepted the centralized authority needed for their construction through a sense of mission or a sense of obligation. These enormous structures allowed for only just enough usable space for ceremonials and rituals, and, in some cases, for tombs. The time and effort they called for was in the service of harmonizing the human world with that of the gods. The high degree of artistry that resulted was not for art's sake, or even for that of beauty; the aesthetic standards of Western civilization did not apply, although many of their works, such as the architecture and sculpture of the Maya, are beautiful by any standard. As indicated earlier, whether constructing buildings, chipping arrowheads, weaving textiles or painting ceramics, the aim was to make the objects pleasing to the spirits. The workmanship that was deemed appropriate often went far beyond the demands of simple utility. Where Europeans used metals for tools and weaponry, Amerindians used them mainly to express their sense of cosmological order, as well as for personal adornment and to denote status. For example, for Peruvians, gold was "the sweat of the Sun" and silver "the tears of the Moon."[17] They liked to work with these metals in sheets, which they manipulated into desired forms, with particular attention to surfaces and colour. In this way they emphasized their otherworldly connotations. When casting three-dimensional pieces, they used the lost-wax process. Copper, besides being used ceremonially, also served mundane purposes; on the Northwest Coast, copper worked into the form of shields represented wealth. Workaday materials in the Americas were stone, bone, wood, fibre and ceramics, although copper and copper alloys were also in use in certain areas.[18]

The otherworldly qualities of shiny metals, crystals, quartzite and certain types of shells, and the unevenness of their natural distribution, ensured a lively trade in such items the length and breadth of the Americas. These were among the items which Europeans, not understanding their spiritual significance, would later refer to as "trinkets." The wampum of the East Coast, dentalia and abalone of the West Coast

all had spiritual connotations that made them highly prized for ceremonials, diplomatic exchanges and personal adornment. Beads had the
added advantage of being in the form of berries, reputed to have extraordinary curative powers.[19] On this otherworldly base, and with the
help of Amerindian trade networks, Europeans would build commercial
empires.

Shamans as Artists

Not surprisingly, the most respected leaders were also shamans
(medicine men, sometimes women), individuals who had special abilities
for communicating with the non-material world, and whose skills
included balancing and harmonizing cosmic forces.[20] Although every
man and woman had the ability to make some contact with spirits, special powers were limited to a few. Principal duties of shamans were to
prevent and cure disease. They were also able to locate and "call" game
(on the Plains this would become particularly important when the herds
were decimated), divine the whereabouts of missing persons, guide individuals through difficult transitional periods and prophesy. Some
shamans could change into animal forms, and take spirit trips, which
called for an altered state of consciousness—a special metaphysical equilibrium. To achieve such feats, shamans had to have the required performing skills, as well as the art objects that were their indispensable
tools; both performing and visual arts were essential to the successful
fulfilment of the shamans' role. These accoutrements not only aided the
shamans' transition to the realm where they could communicate directly
with the spirit powers, they also provided the record to recreate that
contact as necessary.[21]

Into the Contemporary World

In today's market-driven society, art has undergone a profound change of purpose: instead of being a facilitator of cosmic relationships, it now defines humans in a human world. How does the
public see that world, and what images will it buy? Imagery plays a crucial role, indicating as it does what others think about Aboriginals, and
what Aboriginals think of themselves. In the case of Canada's Amerindians, the fact that today many of them are city dwellers has not altered
their self-image of belonging to the land, of being part of the regions
where they were born—their deep sense of place. The popular non-

Amerindian stereotype perceives Aboriginals not so much in terms of place, as in terms of time: Canada's First Nations are a people of the past, in tune with nature rather than with the technological present. This perception strongly influences what the buying public will accept as Aboriginal themes. Despite such difficulties, the arts provide Aboriginal peoples with an important means of asserting themselves, of creating, as it were, their own cultural self-portrait. It is not that influencing the spirits is no longer necessary, but that the human imperative has intervened. Without a clear and unequivocal self-statement, to which society in general will pay attention, the Aboriginal vision risks fading into insignificance. Therein lies the challenge: to reassert valued traditional principles in such a way that they will be pertinent in a fundamentally changed world. As one Amerindian artist put it, "The only way tradition can be carried on is to keep inventing new things."[22]

This new ethos valorizes the personal, rather than the collective, vision. It is a first-person perception of the Aboriginal identity as it expresses itself in the midst of swirling technological and commercial forces. To put this another way, the contemporary Aboriginal artist signs his work, something that his pre-contact predecessors never did. The Haida artist Charles Edenshaw (ca. 1839-1920) was one of the first to respond to these challenges by producing art for sale. His miniature totem poles in argillite, in particular, were an instant success with collectors, and established a tradition in Northwest Coast art that is still flourishing.[23] His designs, however, remained within the prescribed system.[24]

More radical and consequently more innovative has been the response of Ojibwa Norval Morrisseau, widely recognized as the father of contemporary Amerindian art. He defied taboos by visually reinterpreting sacred cultural motifs and making them available to the general public.[25] Still another response has been to synthesize Native and non-Native styles, as Daphne Odjig has done with Picasso and Matisse, in order to strengthen Aboriginal images.[26] Newspaper clippings, excerpts from the *Indian Act*, Aboriginal rock art, and snippets of photographs are only a small sampling of the unlikely ingredients that Jane Ash Poitras uses to create her vision of today's Aboriginal persona. George Littlechild has found his answer in flat planes of colour. Alex Janvier, for his part, has in a sense reinvented traditional concepts with his curvilinear compositions sweeping out from the centre into the four sacred directions. He reinforces their symbolism by a traditional use of colour. One of the most powerful affirmations of a traditional vision in modern technological terms is Bill Reid's monumental sculpture, *The Spirit of Haida Gwaii*.[27] Cast in bronze, it recreates a group of thirteen human, animal and bird figures interacting with each other as they head into the unknown in a Haida canoe, under the guidance of Chief Kilstlaai, wrapped in the skin of the mythical sea wolf and holding a speaker's staff that tells the Haida story of creation. The sculpture stands in front of the Canadian Embassy in Washington, DC. A second casting, under the name of *The Jade Canoe*, was purchased by the Vancouver Airport Authority for $3 million, and stands in the airport's concourse. In spite of the variety of themes and styles in these images, they are all powerfully Aboriginal, proud reassertions of the continuing pertinence of ancient conceptualizations. They dramatically illustrate the essential role of the arts in mediating between traditional values and contemporary realities.

There is more to it than that, however. In the international world, the image of Canada is, to a surprising extent, defined by her Native artists. Their works are displayed in Canadian embassies because they are so distinctive and recognizably Canadian. It is the artists of our First Nations, not to mention the Inuit, who are identifying and capturing the spirit of the Canadian persona, born of the interaction of ancient tradition and contemporary forces.

Notes

1 Jordan Paper, *Offering Smoke: The Sacred Pipe and Native American Religion* (Edmonton, AB: University of Alberta Press, 1988), p. 62.

2 Åke Hultkrantz, *Native Religions in North America* (New York: Harper & Row, 1987), p. 24.

3 This section is one of several scattered throughout the paper that are drawn from Olive Patricia Dickason, *Canada's First Nations: A History of Founding Peoples* (Toronto: McClelland and Stewart, 1992). Not all of them are credited. This particular section comes from p. 80.

4 Paul Radin, *The Trickster* (New York: Schocken, 1972), p. xxiv. The northern Cree versions of the trickster, Wisahkecahk (Wee-suck-a-jock, among other spellings), in his many aspects is examined by Jennifer S.H. Brown and Robert Brightman in *"The Orders of the Dreamed": George Nelson on Cree and Northern Ojibwa Religion and Myth* (1823; reprint St. Paul, MN: Minnesota Historical Press, 1988), pp. 128-36.

5 Jay Miller, "People, Berdaches, and Left-handed Bears," *Journal of Anthropological Research*, 38, 3 (1982): 274-87. See also Colin Scott, "Knowledge Construction Among Cree Hunters: Metaphors and Literal Understanding," *Journal de la Société des Américanistes*, 75 (1989): 193-208, particularly pp. 194-95. Stephen A. McNeary discusses these beliefs as expressed by the

Tsimshian in "Image and Illusion in Tsimshian Mythology," in Jay Miller and Carol M. Eastman, eds., *Tsimshian and Their Neighbors of the North Pacific Coast* (Seattle and London: University of Washington Press, 1984). See also the description of the Amerindian estimation of the reasoning capacity of beavers in *Nouveaux Voyages de Mr. le Baron de Lahontan dans l'Amérique septentrionale*, 2 vols. (The Hague: Honoré Frères, 1703), pp. 155-59. The Jesuits observed that Amerindians considered all souls—minds—to be immortal, whether human or otherwise (Reuben Gold Thwaites, ed., *Jesuit Relations and Allied Documents*, 73 vols. [Cleveland: Burrows Bros., 1896-1901], vol. 6, pp. 175-77).

6 A. Irving Hallowell, "Ojibway Ontology, Behavior and World View," in Stanley Diamond, ed., *Culture in History: Essays in Honor of Paul Radin* (New York: Brandeis University Press, 1960); reprinted in A.I. Hallowell, *Contributions to Anthropology* (Chicago: University of Chicago Press, 1976). See also Catharine McClellan, *My Old People Say: An Ethnographic Survey of Southern Yukon Territory*, 2 vols. (Ottawa: National Museum of Man, 1975), pp. 86-88.

7 Hultkrantz, *Native Religions in North America*, p. 23.

8 Brian Swarbrick, "A 9,000-Year-Old Housing Project," *Alberta Report*, 18, 34 (1991): 50-51. One such rock near Mission, BC, is known as Hatzic Rock. A longhouse excavated on the site has been radiocarbon dated to 9,000 years ago.

9 Claude Lévi-Strauss, *The Jealous Potter*, translated by Bénédicte Chorier (Chicago and London: University of Chicago Press, 1985), p. 59.

10 Lévi-Strauss has explored the general nature of these myths in *The Jealous Potter*. A study of the myths of a particular group, the Ojibwa of Big Trout Lake in Canada's subarctic, showing their relationship to Amerindian myths as a whole, is that of Emmanual Désveaux, *Sous le signe de l'ours* (Paris: Éditions de la Maison des Sciences de l'Homme, 1988). Nicolas Denys describes Indian love for storytelling in *The Description and Natural History of the Coasts of North America (Acadia)*, edited by William F. Ganong (Toronto: The Champlain Society, 1908), pp. 418-19. Recently, Canadian publishers have produced a spate of books recounting tales of Elders.

11 Carl Jung, "The Undiscovered Self," in *The Collected Works of C.G. Jung*, 20 vols. (New York: Pantheon, 1964), vol. 10, p. 303.

12 Katharine Kuh, "The First Americans as Artists," *Saturday Review*, 4 September 1971, pp. 44-45.

13 Marcilene K. Wittmer, "Art and Shamanism," *Ontario Indian*, 4, 8 (1981): 36-41, at 36. This article originally appeared in *Native Arts/West*.

14 Dickason, *Canada's First Nations: A History of Founding Peoples*, pp. 66-67.

15 Sam D. Gill, *Native American Religions: An Introduction* (Belmont, CA: Wadsworth, 1982), p. 22.

16 Robin Ridington, "Technology, World View, and Adaptive Strategy in a Northern Hunting Society," *Canadian Review of Sociology and Anthropology*, 19, 4 (1982): 469-81.

17 *Sweat of the Sun: Gold of Peru* (Edinburgh: City of Edinburgh Museum and Art Gallery, 1990). This is the catalogue for an exhibition of the same name.

18 Izumi Shimada and John F. Merkel, "Copper Alloy Metallurgy in Ancient Peru," *Scientific American*, 265, 1 (July 1991): 80-86.

19 Christopher L. Miller and George R. Hamell, "A New Perspective on Indian-White Contact: Cultural Symbols and Colonial Trade," *The Journal of American History*, 73, 3 (1986): 311-28.

20 A study of the shaman as artist can be found in Peter T. Furst, "The Roots and Continuities of Shamanism," *artscanada*, combined issue numbers 184-87 (December 1973/January 1974): 33-60. The entire issue is devoted to shamanism and the arts; its general title is *Stones, Bones and Skin: Ritual and Shamanic Arts*.

21 Wittmer, "Art and Shamanism," p. 38.

22 Carole Henderson Carpenter, "Form and Freedom: Art and the Northwest Coast," *The Canadian Forum*, 57, 673 (1977): 25-77, at 27.

23 Leslie Drew and Douglas Wilson, *Argillite Art of the Haida* (Vancouver, BC: Hancock House, 1980), in particular chap. 12, pp. 97-105.

24 Bill Holm, *Northwest Coast Indian Art: An Analysis of Form* (Seattle and London: University of Washington Press, 1971), p. 24.

25 Elizabeth McLuhan and Tom Hill, *Norval Morrisseau and the Emergence of the Image Makers* (Toronto: Published for the Art Gallery of Ontario by Methuen, 1984).

26 In the literary world, this blending of styles is a feature of the writings of N. Scott Momaday, 1968 Pulitzer Prize winner; a good illustration of this is *The Names* (New York and London: Harper & Row, 1976).

27 Odjig is Potawatomi, Poitras is Cree, Janvier is Chipewyan and Reid is Haida. Except for Janvier, they all have a white admixture.

Part II

Bkejwanong Territory

3

"Water Is Her Life Blood": The Waters of Bkejwanong and the Treaty-Making Process

David T. McNab

The story of water is a significant one for Aboriginal Nations. It is one of profound importance, of nourishment of the land, of creation and purification:

When Ah-ki' [the Earth] was young, . . . the Earth had a family. Nee-ba-gee'-sis [the Moon] is called Grandmother, and Gee-'sis [the Sun] is called Grandfather. The Creator of this family is called Gi'tchie Man-i-to [the Great Mystery or Creator].

The Earth is said to be a woman. In this way it is understood that woman preceded man on the Earth. She is called Mother Earth because from her come all living things. Water is her life blood. It flows through her, nourishes her, and purifies her.[1]

The story of the water is the story of beauty and peace and life. It is the beginning and the end of life. It provides an essential base for the First Nations' economy and their trade as well as food and an abundance of natural resource wealth.

The complete story of water has not been told in the white man's history.[2] To be sure, much has been written on the uses of the water, particularly for fishing. But, until recently, this has been told almost solely

---

Notes to chapter 3 are on pp. 56-63.

from the perspective of the written record and from the uses put to it by non-Aboriginal people.[3] Apart from Richard Bartlett's path-breaking legal study *Water Rights in Canada*, relatively little has been written on the history of water or, to give but one example, on the relationship between water and the treaty-making process.[4]

And yet a few perceptive people have observed its importance within the Bkejwanong Territory, "the place where the waters divide."[5] In July 1836, the Irish-born feminist traveller Anna Brownell (Jameson) Murphy, the wife of the attorney general for Upper Canada,[6] described part of Bkejwanong during her "summer rambles":

> Leaving the channel of the river and the cluster of islands at its entrance, we stretched northwards across Lake St. Clair. This beautiful lake, though three times the size of Lake Geneva, is a mere pond compared with the enormous seas in its neighbourhood. About one o'clock we entered the river St. Clair, (which, like the Detroit, is rather a strait or channel than a river,) forming the communication between Lake St. Clair and Lake Huron. Ascending this beautiful river, we had, on the right, part of the western district of Upper Canada, and on the left the Michigan territory. The shores on either side, though low and bounded always by the line of forest, were broken into bays and little promontories, or diversified by islands, richly wooded, and of every variety of form. The bateaux of the Canadians, or the canoes of the Indians, were perpetually seen gliding among these winding channels, or shooting across the river from side to side, as if playing at hide-and-seek among the leafy recesses. Now and then a beautiful schooner, with white sails relieved against the green masses of foliage, passed us, gracefully curtseying and sidling along. Innumerable flocks of wild fowl were disporting among the reedy islets, and here and there the great black loon was seen diving and dipping, or skimming over the waters. As usual, the British coast is here the most beautiful and fertile, and the American coast the best settled and cleared. Along the former I see a few isolated log-shanties, and groups of Indian lodges; along the latter, several extensive clearings, and some hamlets and rising villages.[7]

The citizens of Bkejwanong have always lived by and from the waters of their Territory. It is their life blood. On what is now seen, by some, to be the Canadian side, it extends from Lake Erie in the south to Lake Huron northward. It includes the watershed of Lake St. Clair and the Thames River as well as the St. Clair and Detroit Rivers. Bkejwanong is truly a place of water. Here the muskrats live and the fish and the fowl have been bountiful. In addition, it is a protected place. It is a sacred place. It is the soul of Indian Territory[8] as well as the heart and the heartland of Aboriginal North America.

The people of Walpole Island have used their waters within Bkejwanong for many purposes. Their treaties reflect this fact as well as their tenacity regarding Aboriginal title and rights. Fishing, hunting and gathering activities are an essential ingredient of their Aboriginal land rights and are also primary parts of their culture and their heritage. They hunt on the marshlands, a rich, sustainable resource. They developed traditional ways to sustain their fishery resource for many purposes, including personal, communal and ceremonial uses, for barter, for trade and other forms of commerce. Today their natural resources remain a primary component of their culture and heritage as well as their diverse economy.[9]

This paper examines the history of the waters of Bkejwanong as reflected through the treaty-making process with the Crown. These treaties include the framework of Gus Wen Tah, the Covenant Chain of Silver, the Treaty of Montreal of 6 September 1760, the Treaty of Detroit of 1761, the Treaty of Niagara of 1764, the Treaties of Detroit of 1764 and 1765, the Treaty of Lake Ontario (at Fort Ontario, now Oswego, New York) of 1766, Treaty #2, or the McKee Treaty, of 1790, the Simcoe Treaty of 1794, the St. Anne Island Treaty of 1796, among others. All of these treaties were negotiated and agreed to at significant places of water, for example, the St. Lawrence, Niagara, Oswego, Detroit, Thames, Chenail Ecarte and St. Clair Rivers, Lakes Ontario, Erie, St. Clair and Huron. Water and water rights were then, as now, a significant part of the way of life and the history of the people of Bkejwanong, the Walpole Island First Nation.[10]

The history of the Walpole Island First Nation includes their oral tradition,[11] the stories which are, in their language, Gin Das Winan.[12] Near the end of his illustrious career, Sir William Johnson, the superintendent of Indian Affairs, understood the significance of this oral tradition when, in 1768, he observed that "on the Contrary every thing was Conducted Rather with too much rapidity on which head I must Remarke that whosoever has any affairs to transact with Indians must know their forms and in some measure comply with them, and to our Ignorance, negligence and Hauteur in these points we must attribute the little esteem they have for us."[13] The oral tradition is a holistic view of history within circles of time. It is a way of knowing and understanding.[14]

The European historian Simon Schama has remarked on this relationship in his masterful and thought-provoking historical work, *Landscape and Memory*.[15] Schama argues effectively that the relationship between the two is significant, revealing "the richness, antiquity, and the complexity of our landscape tradition, to show just how much we stand to lose. Instead of assuming the mutually exclusive character of Western culture and nature, I want to suggest the strength of the links that have bound them together."[16] Rather than being separate cultural categories, landscape and memory are, in fact, inseparable. Aboriginal oral tradition sees humankind, as one with, and inseparable from, nature. Without "pen or ink," First Nations remember and understand their internal and external landscapes, using their oral traditions and their stories.

The oral tradition is also spiritual.[17] It tells us that the Council Fires of the Ojibwa were the meeting grounds or places where the Councils were held and where the treaties were made. This concept is very different from the Eurocentric notion of the "middle ground."[18] Basil Johnston has highlighted these differences in his work *Ojibwa Ceremonies*, in which it is clear that a treaty in the Ojibwa language meant "The Council Zuguswediwin," or "The Smoking of the Pipe."[19]

These stories from the oral tradition are also remembered and read in wampum belts or other Aboriginal "books" of recording the past, such as rock paintings or birchbark scrolls.[20] The oral tradition can sometimes be supplemented by the written record.[21] Sometimes, the oral tradition has been, in part, written down.[22] The treaties are not only the oral tradition and written word; they also include the use of wampum belts.[23]

One of the treaty papers from the Bkejwanong oral tradition that has been written down is entitled "Treaties between the Whites and Indians, of Chippewa, Ottawa, and Pottawatomie Tribes":

> In 1629 the English attempted to occupy the Valley of the St. Lawrence, but were opposed and driven out by the French, in cooperation with the Iroquois. Not until 1745 did the English again appear. At this time English traders from Pennsylvania established a trading station at old Fort Sandowski [Sandusky], and there made a treaty with the three tribes, concerning trade. Here the English remained until driven out by the French in 1753 [1653?]. In 1670 the French concluded a friendly treaty with the Three Tribes covering trading regulations between them. The principal French Trading Station in this region at that time was located on the left bank of the Detroit River, at the place now called Sandwich. All of the supplies for these Trading Stations came through Montreal.
>
> Then followed the French and English war which ended in 1759, and a short time later a treaty of peace was concluded at Montreal [the Treaty of Montreal of 6 September 1760].[24]

In 1818 Envoys representing England and the United States met the Three Tribes at Andarding [Anderdon or Amherstburg] in conference on the subject of the protection of game for the Indian, at which time it was agreed that only those whites holding licenses would be permitted to hunt and fish and that the fees accruing should all be paid over to the Indians. Since 1822 when these first licenses were issued, there has been no distribution of the funds thus accrued and at this time (1929) the aggregate amount of the hunting and fishing licenses fees collected by the Provinces and by the several states should doubtless and does represent a very large amount of money, all of which belongs to the Indians as per the treaty.

In Jay's Treaty of 1794 between England and the United States, the right of all Indians to free passage across the border by land or water for all times was officially recognized by both nations. These rights were confirmed in an explanatory article the two Governments concluded at Philadelphia on May 4th, 1796.

The Indians of the Three Tribes feel that they possess a valid grievance and many claims against the Canadian Government and of the United States because of the complete failure of the latter to observe the obligations of these old treaties, and they cannot but recognize the difference in the treatment of the Oklahoma Indians by the United States Government and that accorded the Three Tribes on Walpole Island to whom treaty obligations are held as sacred and as inviolate as they should be by the Canadian or Dominion Government and the United States Government.[25]

The Treaty of Montreal of 1701 ratified the peace between the French Crown and the First Nations that was established in September 1700. This occurred before the Treaty of Albany of 1701. The Treaty of Montreal also stated that "[the French Crown] recommending you, whenever you meet with each other, *to act as brothers and to agree together as regards hunting*, so that no disturbance may occur, and this peace may not be troubled."[26]

The British Imperial government, including the Indian Department, recognized that these Council meetings were, in fact, treaties. Wampum belts were exchanged, written and other records of the treaties were kept. For example, in his letter to the Lords of Trade in London on 28 September 1765, Johnson remarked on the Treaty of Detroit of 1765:

On Mr Croghan's arrival at Detroit he had a Treaty with all the Western League, who were assembled before his arrival, and by the Light in which he placed affairs effectually settled their minds & dissolved the Legue lately formed by the French with the Eighteen Nations, and he is now on his way to this place, after whose arrival I shall be enabled to transmit your Lordships the whole of his Transactions and the present state of Indian Affairs in that Country.[27]

In his letter to Thomas Aston Coffin, dated 5 January 1795, Joseph Chew, the secretary of the Indian Department later described these treaties, as they were understood by Sir William Johnson as well as by Alexander McKee, Chew's superior, who was then effectively the head of the Indian Department:

> Sir William Johnson who perfectly understood Indians and when they paid him friendly visits was Very free and merry with them; at the Time he held councils with them or had business of consequence to settle was particularly Ceremonious and transacted matters with much solemnity, at these Times though he was allowed to understand the Mohawk Language better than any other person and acquainted with that of several other Nations he always employed interpreters, who sometimes he was obliged to Correct, and I have heard some of them were under oath on particular occasions to interpret according to the best of their knowledge, at the Treaty of Fort Stanwix in 1768 all the Councils were opened and held with great Ceremony and Solemnity, and as much so as possible when the treaty was closed the Deed Signed and The Territory Ceded paid for; nothing can be more proper than delivering the Indians a Copy of the Deed and a Plan of the Lands purchased from them, this they will lodge with that nation intrusted with matters of that sort Belts of Wampum Speeches &tc. and may be seen at any time by all the nations; it will be the means of their young men knowing what their Chiefs have done and prevent Jealousies and Complaints.[28]

Likewise, Chew wrote to Coffin on 10 August 1795 on the significance of the wampum belts to record the treaties:

> They [the wampum belts] being the only means they have of rewording or Remembering their Transactions how far their request should be Complied with I am at a loss to say—I have seen very few Belts in Sir John Johnsons office, when ever one was delivered to Sir William Johnson a Label was put to it mentioning the occasion of it being delivered and the Vole. [Volume] of Record & page where the Speech was Recorded that was made on the delivery, those Belts have shared the fate of so many of Sir William Johnsons Very particular Transactions with Indians.[29]

The Walpole Island First Nation treaty-making process has a long history that was recorded in wampum belts, oral tradition and in the written record of Europeans.

The Two Row Wampum symbolized the Covenant Chain of Silver and what it represented in the relationship between the British Imperial government and the Aboriginal Nations: namely, Peace, Respect and Trust.[30] The Covenant Chain dates back to the mid-seventeenth century to a treaty signed between the Haudenosaunee and the British Crown at Albany, in present-day New York State on 24 September 1664. The treaty stated that the British Crown, replacing the relationship that the Aboriginal Nations formerly had with the Dutch, would provide "the Indian Princes" and "their subjects" with the same goods and trade "in the future" as they had had with the Dutch.[31] This treaty laid the framework for the relationship between the British Imperial government and the Aboriginal Nations that was embodied in the symbol of the Covenant Chain of Silver.[32]

The Covenant Chain was continually renewed by both the British Crown and the Aboriginal Nations.[33] Johnson observed its history and significance[34] in 1748:

> Brethren of the Five Nations
> I will begin upon a thing of long standing, our First Brothership. My reason for it is, I think there are several among you who seem to forget it; It may seem strange to you how I a Foreigner should know this, But I tell you I found out some of the old Writings of our Forefathers which was thought to have been lost, and in this old valuable record I find, that our first Friendship Commenced at the Arrival of the first great Canoe or Vessel at Albany, at which time you were much surprized but finding what it contained pleased you much, being Things for your Purpose. . . . After this was agreed on and done you made an offer to the Governor to enter into a Bond of Friendship with him and his People which he was so pleased at that he told you he would find a strong Silver Chain which would never break, slip or Rust, to bind you and him in Brothership together, and that your Warriors and ours should be as one Heart, one Blood &tc. and that what happened to the one happened to the other. After this firm agreement was made our Forefathers finding it was good and foreseeing the many Advantages both sides would reap of it, Ordered that if ever that Silver Chain should turn the least Rusty, offer to slip or break, that it should immediately be brightened up again, and not let it slip or break on any account for then you and we were both dead.[35]

Seven years passed and again the representatives asked Johnson for the written record of their agreements. The Seven Years' War (1755-63) was soon to commence. Once more the British Imperial government required the military support of the Aboriginal Nations to maintain its strategic position against the French Empire in North America.[36] Johnson replied, as follows, on 23 June 1755:

Behold Brethren these great books, 4 folio volumes of the records of Indian Affairs which lay upon the table before the Colonel. They are records of the many Solemn Treaties and the various Transactions which have passed between your Forefathers and your Bretheren the English, also between many of you here present & us your Bretheren now living.

You well know and these Books testifie [testify] that it is now almost 100 years since your Forefathers and ours became known to each other [meaning the Treaty of Albany of 1664]. That upon our first acquaintance we shook hands & finding we should be useful to one another entered into a Covenant of Brotherly Love & mutual Friendship. And tho' we were at first only tied together by a Rope, yet lest this Rope should grow rotten & break we tied ourselves together by an Iron Chain. Lest time or accidents might rust & destroy this Chain of Iron, we afterwards made one of Silver, the strength & brightness of which would subject it to no decay. The ends of this Silver Chain we fix't to the Immoveable Mountains, and this in so firm a manner that no mortal enemy might be able to remove it. All this my Brethren you know to be Truth. You know also that this Covenant Chain of Love & Friendship was the Dread & Envy of all your Enemies & ours, that by keeping it bright & unbroken we have never spilt in anger one drop of each other's blood to this day. You well know also that from the beginning to this time we have almost every year, strengthened & brightened this Covenant Chain in the most public & solemn manner. You know that we have become as one body, one blood & one people. The same King our common Father, that your enemies were ours that whom you took into your alliance & allowed to put their hands into this Covenant Chain as Brethren, we have always considered and treated as such.[37]

Bkejwanong was protected by the Crown, as part of the larger "Indian Territory" in the Royal Proclamation of 1763. The Aboriginal title and rights of the Walpole Island First Nation to its Territory were reaffirmed and protected as part of the "Indian Territory" by the Royal Proclamation of 1763.[38] The waters of Bkejwanong were part of the Indian Territory, if not the most important part. The waters were protected under Gus Wen Tah, the Covenant Chain of Silver.[39]

The significance of the Covenant Chain of Silver cannot be underestimated in terms of the Aboriginal Nations' waters, lands and sovereignty. Johnson highlighted its magnitude in 1764:

[A]s I know it has been verry customary for many People to insinuate that the Indians call themselves Subjects, although I am thoroughly convinced they were never so called, nor would they approve of it. Tis true that when a Nation find themselves pushed, their Alliances broken, and themselves tired of a War, they are verry apt to say many civil things, and make

any Submissions which are not agreable to their intentions, but are said
meerly to please those with whom they transact Affairs as they know they
cannot enforce the observance of them. But you may be assured that none
of the Six Nations, Western Nations [including the Western Confederacy]
&ca. ever declared themselves to be Subjects, or will ever consider themselves in that light whilst they have any Men, or an Open Country to
retire to, the very Idea of subjection would fill them with horror.[40]

Johnson understood the significance of Aboriginal sovereignty in the
mid-eighteenth century.

Johnson, moreover, was aware of the solemnity and the ceremony
involved in the treaty-making process. He observed in the same speech
that

Indeed I have been just looking into the Indian Records, where I find in
the Minutes of 1751 that those who made ye Entry Say, that Nine different Nations acknowledged themselves to be His Majesty's Subjects, altho'
I sat at that Conference, made entrys [entries] of all the Transactions, in
which there was not a Word mentioned, which could imply a Subjection,
however these matters (notwithstanding all I have from time to time said
on that subject) seem not to be well known at home, and therefore, it may
prove of dangerous consequence to persuade them that the Indians have
agreed to things which (had they even assented to) is so repugnant to their
principles that the attempting to enforce it, must lay the foundation of
greater Calamities than has yet been experienced in this Country.

It is necessary to observe that no Nation of Indians have any word
which can express, or convey the Idea of Subjection, they often say, 'we
acknowledge the great King to be our Father, we hold him fast by the
hand, and we shall do what he desires' many such like words of course,
for which our People too readily adopt & insert a Word verry different in
signifiation [signification], and never intended by the Indians without
explaining to them what is meant by a Subjection.

Imagine to yourself Sir, how impossible it is to reduce a People to
Subjection, who consider themselves Independant thereof by both Nature
& Scituation, who can be governed by no Laws, and have no other Tyes
among themselves but inclination, and suppose that it's explained to them
that they shall be governed by the laws liable to the punishments for high
Treason, Murder, Robbery and the pains and penaltys on Actions for
property or Debt, then see how it will be relished, and whether they will
agree to it, for without the Explanation, the Indians must be Strangers to
the Word, & ignorant of the breach of it.[41]

One of the first treaties with the British Imperial government was
the Treaty of Montreal of 6 September 1760.[42] This treaty occurred near
the end of the Seven Years' War (1755-63) which culminated in the

defeat of France in 1763. However, the Aboriginal Nations who fought in that European war were not conquered by the British Imperial government.[43] The Walpole Island First Nation's oral tradition is, in part, that the Treaty of Montreal of 1760 was a significant historical event which

> provided for the French occupancy of the Province of Quebec, and the English occupancy of Ontario, reserving to the Three Tribes a strip of ground, 66 ft. wide on each side of all rivers, 16 ft. wide on each side of all creeks and 99 feet wide along the shores of all lakes and around all lands entirely surrounded by water, also the use of all lands not fit for cultivation, and the right to hunt and sell timber in any forest, and to fish in any waters, also reserving to the Indians all stone, precious stones, and minerals. These strips of land were intended as a permanent inheritance to the Three Tribes, where they could camp and abide while fishing and trapping and cultivating the soil.[44]

Captain John Knox (?-1778),[45] of the English army, in his journal of the military campaigns in North America, noted, on 25 May 1760, that there was a request for a treaty from the First Nations with the Governor James Murray. Knox wrote that "Several tribes of Indians have sent a deputation to the Governor to treat for peace."[46] On 5 September 1760, Governor James Murray entered into a treaty with the Huron of Lorette, which provided them with the "protection" of the British Crown and that "henceforth no English Officer or party is to molest or interrupt them in returning to their settlement at Lorette and they are received upon the same terms with the Canadians, being allowed the free Exercise of their Religion, their Customs and liberty of trading with the English Garrisons recommending it to the Officers commanding the posts to treat them kindly."[47] In his journal entry of 5 September 1760, Murray wrote that at Longueil "two nations of Indians, of Hurons and Iroquois, came in & made their Pace [peace], at the same time Three of Sir William Johnstons Indians came in wth a letter from General Amherst, wch I immediately answer'd."

Although Murray's journal entry of 6 September 1760 is silent on the Treaty of Montreal,[48] Captain Knox vividly recorded the event in his journal:

> Brigadier Haviland has reduced fort Chambli, where he found some of our brass field-pieces; the van of his corps arrived yesterday at Longueuil, and they report that Sir William Johnson, with a large body of Indians, computed at fourteen hundred, will be there this day from General Amherst's army. Eight Sachems, of different nations, lately in alliance with

the enemy, have surrendered, for themselves and their tribes, to General Murray: These fellows, after conferring with his Excellency, and that all matters had been adjusted to their satisfaction, stepped out to the beach opposite to Montreal, flourished their knives and hatchets, and set up the war-shout; intimating to the French, that they are now become our allies and their enemies. While these Chieftains were negociating a peace. . . . [49]

The Treaty of Montreal was also noted by Johnson in the summer of 1761 at Niagara:

Altho I did myself the honour of writing your Exclly [Excellency] the 24th inst. [Instant, 24 July 1761] by one of the traders, I would not let slip so favourable an opportunity as this of Coll [Colonel] Eyres return, to inform you that since my last, I had a meeting with several chiefs of the Chipeweigh [Chippewa] Nation & some Mississage's [Ojibwa Nation]. . . . But I plainly discover an universal Jealousy and uneasiness amongst those of every Nation, on account of the hasty steps they look upon it we are taking towards getting possession of their overall Countrys & which uneasiness I am certain will never subside whilst we encroach within the limits which you recollect have been actually put under the King's protection in the year 1726 and continued to them by him, and his successors ever since, as well as positive orders sent to the Governor by his Late Majesty not to allow any of his Subjects settling thereon; with which they were then made acquainted—which your Excellency in your Speech of 22d April 1760 delivered by General Monckton was pleased to promise to secure to them, and to prevent any person whatsoever from settling, or even hunting thereon, but that it should remain—their absolute property.[50]

The Royal Proclamation would also reaffirm that the Walpole Island First Nation Territory was "their absolute property." The latter clearly included the waters of their Territory.

Subsequently, Johnson travelled to Detroit, arriving on 4 September 1761.[51] At that Council fire he made a treaty concerning, among other matters, Aboriginal trade as well as regulations for that trade:

Brethren
With this belt In the name of his Britannick Majesty, I strengthen and renew the antient [ancient] Covenant Chain formerly subsisting between us, that it may remain bright and lasting to the latest Ages, earnestly recommending it to you, to do the same, and to hold fast thereby as the only means by which you may expect to become a happy & flourishing people. *Gave the Belt of the Covt. [Covenant] Chain containing 20 Rows.* . . .

Brethren
I can with Confidence assure you that it is not at present, neither hath it been his Majestys intentions to deprive any Nation of Indians of their just

property by taking possession of any Lands to which they have a lawfull claim, farther than for the better promoting of an extensive commerce, for the security and protection of which (and for the occupying of such posts as have been surrendered to us by the Capitulation of Canada). Troops are now on their way; I therefore expect that you will consider and treat them as Brethren, and continue to live on terms of the strictest friendship with them and as I now declare these his Majestys favourable intentions to do you justice, I expect in return that nothing shall on your parts be wanting to testify the just Sense which you all conceive of his Majesty's favour, and of your earnest desire to live with the British subjects on the terms of friendship and alliance—
Gave a belt of 7 Rows

. . . Brethren of the several Nations here assembled
Tho' the management of your Affairs is the province allotted to me by his Majesty, I am no less bound by inclination than by duty to serve you, and so long as you shall pay a strict adherence to every part of the present treaty, I shall esteem all your Nations as our true and natural Allies, treat with you independent of any other Nation, or Nations of Indians whatsoever, and use the utmost Exertion of my abilities in the promoting of your interest and welfare. . . .

It gives us great satisfaction to hear that the King has no intentions to deprive us of our Lands (of which we were once very apprehensive) and as to the Troops who are now going to the distant posts, we are well pleased therewith, and hope they will look upon and treat us as Brethren, in which light they shall always be esteemed by us—as we are determined to live on the best terms with them—
A belt. . . .

The Speaker having ended—Macatepilesis a Speaker for the Ottawas, arose, and after going through all the ceremony of Condolance as the Hurons had done he proceeded as follows

Brother Warraghiyagey [Sir William Johnson]
. . . Brother
I speak on the part of all our confederacy here present, who are charmed with the speech which you made to them Yesterday, & determined to act for the future agreable thereto, and to make all Nations of Indians acquainted therewith, even to the setting of the Sun, and with the great work which you have now executed, whereby you have established tranquillity throughout the Land, and made the Roads, and the Waters of our Lakes, smooth and passable which were before rough and dangerous—
A belt. . . .

Brethren
I give you thanks for all the assurances you have made of remaining firm in your resolutions of abiding by the present treaty, and promising to com-

municate your intentions to all the other Nations, as also for your present-
ing the Calumet of peace, and the bunch of Green Wampum, as proofs of
the truth of what you had sayed; and I sincerely wish that the Chain of
friendship together with these your resolutions may remain entire and
unbroken for ever on your parts, which I am confident it must whilst you
regard your own peace and welfare, and the friendship of the English, so
long therefore as you pay a strict attention thereto, you may depend on
our preserving the Chain entire, bright, and unsullied, and that we shall
afford you all the Protection, friendship, and reasonable indulgences to
which your conduct shall intitle you—

The Conference then ended. . . . [52]

The Treaty of Detroit of September 1761, under the Covenant Chain,
was significant, involving, among other matters, peace and friendship,
Aboriginal Lands and Waters, Trade as well as Regulations for this
Trade, Presents from the King's Bounty, blacksmiths and agricultural
implements. These solemn promises of Johnson would be reaffirmed, on
behalf of the Crown, in subsequent treaties.

In July 1764 the Western Confederacy met with Johnson at
Niagara. Other Aboriginal Nations were also present at this large gather-
ing. At that time Johnson told them, among other things, that their
Territory, including their waters, was reaffirmed and protected by the
Crown. He presented them with "the great Covenant Chain, 23 Rows
broad & the year 1764 worked upon it." This belt has been kept by the
Aboriginal Nations.[53]

At Detroit, on 7 September 1764, Colonel John (Jean-Baptiste)
Bradstreet (1714-74)[54] also met the "Western Nations" in a "Congress"
"held with the Chiefs of the Ottawas [Ottawa], and Chippaweigh
[Ojibwa] Nations." This treaty served to reinforce and to reaffirm the
Crown's solemn promises at the Treaty of Niagara, earlier that same
summer:

Wassong [also Wasson (ca. 1730-90)[55]] Chief of the Chippaweighs
[Chippewa or Ojibwa] Spoke as follows—

. . . Wasong [Wasson] then Spoke on a green Belt.

Brother.

I beg you would hearken to Wassang, Attawaky, Shamindawa, Outawang,
Butawang, Apockess, and Abbetts. Last Year God forsook us. God has now
opened our Eyes, and we desire to be heard. 'tis [It is] God's will our
hearts are altered. 'twas [It was] God's Will you had such fine Weather to
come to us. It is Gods Will also that there shall be Peace, and Tranquility
all over the face of the Earth, and of the Waters. . . . [56]

On 27 August to 4 September 1765, an ancient Council Fire was lit at Detroit. Over the course of the week, a treaty was negotiated between the Crown represented by Colonel George Croghan,[57] deputy superintendent for Indian Affairs, representing Johnson, and the Western Nations, or Confederacy. Chief Pontiac was their spokesman:[58]

Septbr 2d [1765] The Chiefs of the Wyondatts [Wyandot] or Huron, came to me & said they had spoke last Summer [the Treaty of Niagara of July 1764] to Sir Willm Johnson at Niagara about the lands, on which the French had settled near Detroit belonging to them, & desired I would mention again to him, they never had sold it to the French, & expected their new Fathers the English would do them justice, as the French were become one People with us. A Belt.

4th Pondiac [Pontiac] with several chiefs of the Ottawas, Chippawaes [Chippewa or Ojibwa] & Potowatamies likewise complained that the French had settled part of their country, which they had never sold to them, & hoped their Fathers the English take it into Consideration, & see that a proper satisfaction was made to them. That their Country was very large, & they were willing to give up such part of it, as was necessary for their Fathers the English, to carry on Trade at, provided they were paid for it, & a sufficient part of the Country left them to hunt on.[59]

In his letter to the Lords of Trade in London on 28 September 1765, Johnson reported that

On Mr Croghan's arrival at Detroit he had a treaty with all the Western League, who were assembled before his arrival, and by the Light in which he placed affairs effectually settled their minds & dissolved the Legue lately formed by the French with the Eighteen Nations, and he is now on his way to this place, after whose arrival I shall be enabled to transmit your Lordships the whole of his Transactions and the present state of Indian Affairs in that Country.[60]

The following year Johnson met with Chief Pontiac and the representatives of the Western Confederacy of Nations at Lake Ontario (Fort Ontario near present-day Oswego, New York). Specific reference to water is found in this treaty in connection with trade and trading rights:

[Chief Pontiac is the speaker.]
Father. We thank you for the goodness you have for us in sending plenty of Merchandise to Detroit this will be a great means of promoting a good understanding between us as it will enable us, as we shall always have it in our power, to clothe our Children well. We likewise heartily thank you for not letting the Traders to straggle through the Woods to our Villages, but to trade only at the Posts under the Inspection of the Commissary (at the

different Posts, that causes great mischief for them to be able to go through the Villages) and if they came up their Rivers they shall be protected (meaning the Commissary of the Different Posts). It was not prudent to let them ramble where they pleased but as you have settlements there will be no danger along the Waters to the Forts and there we shall be fairly dealt with.

A Belt of 6 Rows[61]

Johnson died eight years later and thereafter things began to fall apart.[62] Treaty documents were seemingly lost during the American Revolution and by the 1790s the treaties themselves were forgotten. In the years that followed, the Crown failed to keep the solemn promises that Johnson had made on its behalf in the years 1760-66.

Meanwhile, on 19 May 1790 Treaty #2, also known as the McKee Treaty, was entered into by the Crown and the Walpole Island First Nation at Detroit.[63] Gifts from the Western Confederacy were transferred into unfulfilled promises, alienation of Aboriginal lands and, according to the Crown's later interpretation, outright land surrenders.[64] It is clear from the geographic description in Treaty #2 that the waters of Bkejwanong were not included or referred to in the document.[65] Two years later, in July 1792, the Crown's representatives reaffirmed water and water rights in the Gun Shot Treaty.[66]

Both the land and the water cannot be alienated; it can only be shared. Water was not to be sold; it was too important to the traditional way of life. It was to be protected or the land and the people would die, culturally and then physically.[67]

Again, in 1796, water and water rights were not for sale. The solemn commitments of the Crown recorded at the Council Meeting of 30 August 1796 constitute the written terms of the Treaty of St. Anne Island. Water rights were once again reaffirmed as part of Bkejwanong.[68]

The oral tradition of the Walpole Island First Nation, as has been written, reaffirmed the St. Anne Island Treaty in 1835 and 1839:

> Father—Whenever the white people make a treaty with us they can write it down when they wish to know what was done for years before they can turn to their papers then our laps are always open to them—now we think that our father below had been looking over his papers; thinks of forgotten children again and wishes to hear from them.

> Father—When we were created we were made without those advantages; we have no pen or ink to write, we have nothing but a little piece of flesh called a heart, to remember by, and we wish to relate to you the old Speech made to our fathers, by our Great father over the waters—This has been told us by our fathers who are dead.

Father—When the White People first came among us, they were received by us with friendship, we joined hands, they were lashed together strongly, they called us their children, and said that we should remain so; this we were told by our fathers, and we hope that you still remember it—

Father—The first white father that we had was the King of the french when you came he walked off—you reached out your hands to us, we took it, you told us that you made the same things that our other father did, that you would do as by us as he did, that you had no desire to make us poor; but to do us good and that you would give us all that he did—

Father—The first place that we met was at Detroit, you then told us that our great father below would send us the things we needed and that we should never want. Moreover, you told us that it was a great distance to bring provisions across the great waters, but if we would agree to give you a piece of land, you would raise provisions and that we would never go hungry, we gave you the lands and that place was Malden; When you received this land, you were glad, and Said that you could set down among us and be happy that you could raise off, of that land the white things they call dollars and with them you would make us happy—that you would never be tired of giving us the things which we wanted and that our friendship should remain forever or as long as the world should stand.

Father—You then told us that we thought that by giving you this land that it would make our wives and children poor; and assured us that it would not be so, you said that you only wanted the soil that you could not take a gun, on your shoulder, and hunt the game as you Indians do, but we can raise our living ourselves, and the land only is ours, but not the game. . . .

Father—When he [Alexander McKee] came to see us on St. Ann's [St. Anne] Island down Baldoon [Chenail Ecarte] River, he built a fire in front of his red children and said, "I do not build this fire before you to take the land from you; it is the fire of friendship. The brands are so strongly put together, that no man can part them, asunder and no person shall extinguish it."

Father—When we surrounded the fire of friendship that he had kindled, he again told us that the land was to remain ours—that he did not tell us this of himself but it came from our father over the great waters—that the word which he now spoke was heard by him who made us and would be sent to our great father over the waters, and as some of our young men were not present they might come whenever they please and enjoy all that was promised us, and again told us that this land should forever belong to the three tribes—Moreover, he told us that this land is good; even the marshes will yield you peltry, the great river is full of living animals for your use, and the Prairies will give you something, therefore, keep it for the use of your three tribes and never part with it.

Father—He moreover told us that the land we had gave him was of a great benefit to him; if you attempt to come upon it we would tell you to stand aside—now your marshes are as good to you as the land is to us, if any of our people come to take your game, make a strong arm against them, let us know, and we will prevent it—therefore, keep this place for yourselves and children—Father—He again told us that some of his young men, might come and fancy this good land of yours; but do not sell it, do not give it away, but keep it for the benefit of your children. . . .

Father—Since that great fire which was the fire of friendship was made we hope it will never go out, but some of your people are endeavouring to put it out. The vessels come with the things, for us as they did to our fathers but we receive no notice of their coming, no word is sent to us as it was before, we only hear it from report; we come in sight of the place where the goods are, we see our young men climbing out of the windows of the house, we return empty away, sorrowful, ashamed, and dejected, and our wives and children remain, naked. Now we hope you will attend to this for us or we shall think that you neglect us.[69]

A similar reaffirmation came as a speech of the Indian Chief Begigishi-gueshkam[70] to Colonel Jarvis on Walpole Island, September 1839.

Father we are rejoiced to see you for the first time among us.

Father give me your hand and accept the welcome of this string of Wampum.

Father listen to my voice and complaints as your fathers did in days of yore to mine, and I will not detain you long for I know that it is many days since you left your home and that you have travelled far—

Father we have no records of ancient treaties to refer to, we have no books handed down to us by our ancestors to direct us in our speech; we have but our hearts and the traditions of our old men; they are not deceitful.

Father when the White Elk [Alexander McKee] finding that our Fathers were growing poor and wretched in the vicinity of the Long Knife brought them up to the Island on which you now find us; he lept from his Canoe with a lighted Brand in his hand and after having kindled the first Council Fire which had ever shone upon it, he gave it to them forever.

"Remain my children"; said he, "do not desert the abode to which I have brought you & never shall any one molest you. Should any persons come to ask from you a part of these lands, turn from them with distrust and deny them their request. Never for a moment heed their voice and at your dying day instruct your sons to get theirs, teach them as generation succeeds generation to preserve intact their inheritance and poverty shall be unknown to them. Tell them as I tell you now never to forsake the Allegiance of their Great British Father, tell them to aid him in all his wars with the bad Long Knife who tho' [though] a giant in stature & in strength must ever succumb before the Red Coat."

"Adieu my children I now leave you to enjoy your new lands. May you dwell upon them in happiness and in plenty. More would I do for you but my arms are weak, & short, & I cannot reach for you all the goods that I could wish."

Father such were the words of the White Elk. You find us still the same as the old men that he addressed faithful and ready in our Allegiance to our Great Mother but in all other respects alas how altered. Our lands have passed from our hands into those of the rapacious Squatter, the Clearings we had made have been torn from us to yield their crops to new masters—There is hardly a foot of ground that we can call our own or tread secure from the threats & ill deeds of these men. One hundred of our pigs have been destroyed, our dogs have been shot at the very doors of our Lodges, our Horses have been stolen from us.

And the superintendent of Indian Affairs, Samuel Peters Jarvis, replied, in part, that

Children
I will convey to your great Father in Toronto the words which have fallen from the lips of your Chief. He will be pleased to hear such sentiments of devoted affection and Loyalty to the British Government—Your great Mother the Queen will likewise be rejoiced to hear that her Red children are grateful for the beautiful supply of presents which she sent to them from across the Great Salt Lake.

This Island which the White Elk brought you upon, and which he promised should be reserved for your benefit, will not be taken from you. It was unwise for you to allow so many white settlers to come among you, and wrong to allow any belonging to the Country of the Long Knives. Such people cannot be your friends.

I will endeavour to have the worst of them turned away, and those that remain shall, be made to contribute to your comfort and support.[71]

In the years that followed, the Walpole Island First Nation kept the Covenant Chain of Silver bright and untarnished. They continued to reside in their traditional places at the confluence of the waters of Bkejwanong and moved seasonally to obtain the abundance of the natural resources from the waters of Bkejwanong. These places included, for example, the reserves at Walpole Island, Chenail Ecarte and the ancient village of Kitigan on the banks of Big Bear Creek, among other locations. They also continued to occupy and use all of their Territory, including the Lake St. Clair and the St. Clair, the Chenail Ecarte Rivers, the reserve of that name and its waters, among other places, in their seasonal round of traditional activities.[72] And yet encroachments by white settlers continued from governments and settlers from both the east and the west.

In 1807 the Walpole Island First Nation entered into a treaty, again at Detroit, with the government of the United States. In this treaty, the waters on the American side of the international boundary, as well as some lands in Michigan, were to be shared with white people. A number of reserves along the St. Clair River and Lake St. Clair were excepted from this treaty. However, the uses of these waters was not relinquished by this treaty. For example, fishing rights remained. No islands were surrendered.[73]

During the War of 1812-14, along with the famous role played by Tecumseh, the Walpole Island First Nation defended the "Indian territory" against another American invasion, assisting in the defence of Upper Canada and thereby the maintenance of it as a colony within the British Empire for their British allies. Yet that War changed fundamentally the military balance in British North America. The American threat was effectively removed and the Aboriginal Nations were, from the perspective of the British Imperial government, no longer required as military allies. After the War, the British Imperial government gave them medals and gave their waters and lands to the white settlers for little or no consideration. And yet they continued to remain as allied Nations. The British Imperial government did not leave Penetanguishene until 1834 and did not leave Fort Malden until the mid-nineteenth century.

The peace, called the Treaty of Ghent, signed on Christmas Eve 1814, ended the conflict between Britain and the United States. Although the situation of the Aboriginal Nations was well known and was widely discussed by the plenipotentiaries of the treaty, the negotiations themselves did not include the Aboriginal Nations. This had long-term, unfortunate consequences, since the treaty provided for the settlement of the boundary questions between the two countries. This resulted in the survey of the boundary thereafter, and by the late 1820s in the loss of part of the Walpole Island Reserve, for example, Harsen's Island in Lake St. Clair, without a treaty being signed for the islands.[74]

With the passing of the Johnson, Elliott and McKee families from power within the department by the 1820s, the First Nations found it to be a struggle to remind the Crown of its treaty promises. One example is the speech of 1815 at St. Anne Island. Its words are a constant reminder of how fragile that relationship really is and how strong the Covenant Chain has been for the Aboriginal Nations.[75]

In the years from 1815 to 1850, British and American emigrants arrived in Upper Canada to settle and take the waters and lands of the Aboriginal Nations, often without regard for the precise terms of the Royal Proclamation of 1763 and in the treaties. But the people of Walpole Island did not forget the solemn terms of their treaties. They continued to protect their lands and their waters.

Yet the Crown demanded more and more land for white settlement in Upper Canada. To this end, the Treaty of Amherstburg was made at the Council Meeting of 16 October 1818.[76] This treaty was made between the Crown and the Ojibwa Nation (then known as the Chippewa Nation, part of the Council of Three Fires, the Walpole Island First Nation). The Council Meeting was held at Amherstburg, which is located south of Windsor. Amherstburg is part of the Anderdon Reserve, which was established under Treaty #2, or the McKee Treaty, entered into in May 1790.[77] The treaty arrangements provided for the reaffirmation of First Nation Aboriginal title and land and water rights.[78]

Water was not an issue in the Treaty of Amherstburg. It was understood by all concerned that water would continue to remain part of the Aboriginal title and rights. Moreover, the treaty area specifically did not include waters; nor did it include the surrender or the relinquishment of water rights. Since these matters were not explicitly referred to, the First Nations understanding was that their Aboriginal title as well as water rights remained intact. Moreover, the Crown made a solemn promise at the treaty negotiations that never again would the Crown seek to obtain any additional lands and waters. The reserves, which were excepted from the treaty area, were never "augmented." Less land was provided than that promised by the Crown in the Treaty of Amherstburg. The reserves were also to continue forever. The Crown promised never to ask the Aboriginal Nations to share more lands. These solemn promises were not kept.

On 5 August 1867, about one month after the Confederation of Canada, the ancestors of the Walpole Island First Nation wrote a "memorial" to the governor general of Canada. This memorial was reiterated in a further petition to the superintendent and deputy superintendent of Indian Affairs, dated 14 November of that same year. The Walpole Island First Nation stated in both memorials that they were the "rightful proprietors of the Peninsula between Lakes Huron, St. Clair and Erie," including their waters, the lakes, the islands in them and the connecting waters within that Territory. This memorial, and another one in 1869, were presented to the governor general of Canada to reaffirm the Walpole Island First Nation's relationship with the Crown.

There is no evidence that the Crown, as represented by the governor general of Canada or any other official representing the Crown, has ever responded to these memorials. However, in internal Department of Indian Affairs reports in 1869-70, officials of the Crown, notably William Spragge, deputy superintendent general of Indian Affairs, acknowledged the validity of the Aboriginal title and the rights to the waters and the lands of Bkejwanong without apparently communicating these views to the people of Walpole Island.[79]

Since the 1870s the Walpole Island First Nation has vigorously protected its waters and marshes. Through the negotiation of various leases, the First Nation asserted its rights and title to the waters and marshlands, and determined to protect the resources on them. In doing so, it resisted the intrusion in its affairs of the Indian agent and "Headquarters," the Department of Indian Affairs in Ottawa, the prime minister of Canada and non-Indian users of the marshlands. It successfully negotiated leases directly with private interests, on its own initiative. These leases were in their long-term interests.

The leasing of the waters and the marshlands by the Walpole Island First Nation was a significant departure from the nineteenth-century treaty-making process. Yet, at the same time, it was wholly consistent, as we have seen with the Walpole Island First Nation position on their waters and water rights within the framework of the Covenant Chain and the treaty-making process. In reaffirming water rights as well as Aboriginal title, it provided an alternative to the federal government's extinguishment policy towards land and treaty rights.

The solemn treaty promises have not been fulfilled to this day, despite official pronouncements by the federal government since the resistance movement at Kanesatake in the summer of 1990. The Crown's relationship with the Aboriginal Nations has been put into jeopardy and severely damaged. The Covenant Chain, always unbroken, has not been "recast," but it has been tarnished and bent.[80]

Many of their waters have been taken over by the white settlers in the twentieth century. Commercial and then sports fisher have destroyed the fish and the valuable fishery. The commercial fishery was closed in 1970 as a result of mercury pollution. Governments have sanctioned pollution of the waters by private industry in the twentieth century. The quality of the waters on the lakes and the rivers has deteriorated. Spills from Chemical Valley are still almost a daily occurrence today. Pollution from the effects of the St. Lawrence Seaway continues to damage the waters and the natural resources in the St. Clair River and Lake St. Clair, part of the Bkejwanong Reserve. The struggle to stop this destruction continues as the twenty-first century approaches.

In 1766 Johnson asked the Western Confederacy to keep the Treaty of Lake Ontario "fresh in their memories."[81] Oral tradition is a powerful tool. Unlike the written record, it cannot be lost as books or papers are misplaced or forgotten. Moreover, Aboriginal people remember. Their history is not one of books or of writing: "We have no words of ancient treaties to refer to, we have no books handed down to us by our ancestors to direct us in our speech; we have but our hearts and the traditions of our old men; they are not deceitful."[82]

"We have but our hearts" and our "traditions." One of these traditions is the story of the waters of Bkejwanong and the treaty-making process. This is a theme worthy of exploration, indeed of critical examination, for ethnohistorians. The subject has been neglected. It is essential for understanding Aboriginal history, and, for that matter, in writing an environmental history of Canada. In this sense, this is the beginning of the story of water; it is not the end. "Water is her life blood," for without water, Mother Earth will not survive. Without water, and Mother Earth, the people of Bkejwanong will not survive.

Notes

1 Edward Benton-Banai, *The Mishomis Book: The Voice of the Ojibway* (St. Paul, MN: Red School House, 1988), pp. 1-2.
2 There is no history of water, ice or snow in Canada from the perspective of the European written tradition. There are only regional histories of the uses of the waters or legal studies—see, for example, Claude Thibault, comp., *Bibliographia Canadiana* (Toronto: Longman Canada Limited, 1973), pp. 625-28. See also Frederick Hamil's *The Valley of the Lower Thames* (Toronto: University of Toronto Press, 1951). Hamil pays special attention to the waters of the Thames River and its tributaries. However, more attention is being paid to the significance of the water in recent years—for example, Barry M. Gough, *Gunboat Frontier* (Vancouver, BC: University of British Columbia Press, 1984), shows the conflict on the waters between the gunboats of the Royal Navy and the Aboriginal Nations in the Pacific Northwest. The Aboriginal people, of course, have their own "history" of their waters—for example, see Louis Miranda and Philip Joe, "How the Squamish Remember George Vancouver," in Robin Fisher and Hugh Johnston, eds., *From Maps to Metaphors: The Pacific World of George Vancouver* (Vancouver, BC: University of British Columbia Press, 1993). See also Charles E. Cleland, *Rites of Conquest: The History and Culture of Michigan's Native*

Americans (Ann Arbor: University of Michigan Press, 1992), and Dianne Newell (on Aboriginal fishing in British Columbia), *Tangled Webs of History: Indians and the Law in Canada's Pacific Coast Fisheries* (Toronto: University of Toronto Press, 1993).

3 On the subject of the significance of the oral tradition see also Olive Patricia Dickason's "Art and Amerindian Worldviews" in this volume (pp. 21-31).

4 See, for example, Robert Doherty, *Disputed Waters, Native Americans & the Great Lakes Fishery* (Lexington, KY: University Press of Kentucky, 1990). Laurence Hauptman has done some work on the use of the waters for the St. Lawrence Seaway, which spans both sides of the Canadian-American international border, in his *The Iroquois and the New Deal* (Syracuse, NY: Syracuse University Press, 1981). For Canadian work, see the publications by Leo Waisberg, Victor Lytwyn and Tim Holzkamm on fishing in the Treaty #3 area. Since this paper was presented in 1994 Lytwyn has provided a different perspective of water in his "Waterworld: The Aquatic Territory of the Great Lakes First Nations," in David McNab and S. Dale Standen, eds., with an "Introduction," *Gin Das Winan: Documenting Aboriginal History in Ontario*, Occasional Papers of The Champlain Society, no. 2 (Toronto: The Champlain Society, 1996), pp. 14-22. This paper fails to put water into the context of the Covenant Chain of Silver or the totality of the treaty-making process under it. The only work on Aboriginal people, water and water rights which covers all of Canada, and only from a legal perspective, is Richard H. Bartlett's *Aboriginal Water Rights in Canada: A Study of Aboriginal Title to Water and Indian Water Rights* (Calgary, AB: The Canadian Institute for Resources Law, The University of Calgary, 1988).

5 Geographically, this Territory roughly includes much of the lands and the waters in present-day southwestern Ontario as well as the southern part of the state of Michigan.

6 Clara Thomas, "Anna Brownell (Jameson) Murphy," in *Dictionary of Canadian Biography*, vol. 8: *1851-1860* (Toronto: University of Toronto Press, 1985), pp. 649-51.

7 Anna Jameson, *Winter Studies and Summer Rambles in Canada* (London: Saunders and Otley, 1838; reprint in Coles Canadiana Collection, Toronto: Coles Publishing Company, 1970, 1972), vol. 3, pp. 5-6.

8 Nin.Da.Waab.Jig., *Walpole Island: The Soul of Indian Territory* (Walpole Island, ON, 1987), especially pp. 1-26. Bartlett has observed that there are three legal sources of Aboriginal rights to water: (1) Aboriginal title, (2) treaties and (3) riparian rights which flow from reserve land ownership under English common law. See his *Aboriginal Water Rights in Canada*, pp. 1-6. Aboriginal title and rights to water also are protected under Section 35(1) of Canada's Constitution as "Existing Aboriginal and Treaty Rights." The latter is significant for federal and provincial legislation (which is often in direct conflict with Aboriginal water rights) since most waters in Canada have not been the subject of a treaty.

9 Nin.Da.Waab.Jig., *Walpole Island: The Soul of Indian Territory*, pp. 1-26.

10 For these treaties see the following: Treaty of Niagara, 9-14 July 1764, *The Papers of Sir William Johnson*, prepared for publication by Milton W. Hamilton, vol. 11 (Albany, NY: University of the State of New York, 1953), pp. 262-333; Treaty of Detroit, 27 August-4 September 1765, in E.B.

O'Callaghan, ed., *Documents Relative to the Colonial History of the State of New York*, vol. 7 (Albany, NY: Weed, Parsons, 1856), pp. 775-88; letter, Sir William Johnson to the Lords of Trade, Plantations General Papers, vol. 25 (K. 7), Johnson Hall, 16 November 1765 (the enclosure, containing the Treaty of Detroit, is with this letter); "Journal of Colonel Croghan's Transactions with the Western Indians," Plantations General Papers, vol. 25; "Journal & Transactions of George Croghan Esqr Deputy Agent for Indian Affairs with the several Indian Nations on his Journey to the Illinois as delivered by him to Sir William Johnson Baronet on his return" (the treaty is on pp. 782-84); Treaty of Lake Ontario, 22-30 July 1766, National Archives of Canada (NAC), Record Group 10, vol. 1829, pp. 1-36; O'Callaghan, ed., *Documents Relative to the Colonial History of the State of New York*, vol. 7, pp. 854-67; "Proceedings of Sir William Johnson with Pondiac and other Indians," Plantations General Papers, vol. 26, Treaty #5; Proceedings at a Congress with Pondiac [Pontiac, War Chief of the Ottawas, b. ca. 1712-25, d. 1769] & Cheifs [Chiefs] of the Ottawas, Pautawattamies [Potawatomi], Hurons and Chippawaes begun Tuesday, 23 July 1766. See also Julian Gwyn, "Sir William Johnson," in *Dictionary of Canadian Biography*, vol. 4: *1771-1800* (Toronto: University of Toronto Press, 1979), pp. 394-98.

11 On Iroquoian oral tradition see Mary A. Druke, "Iroquois Treaties: Common Forms, Varying Interpretations," in Francis Jennings, ed., *The History and Culture of Iroquois Diplomacy: An Interdisciplinary Guide to the Treaties of the Six Nations and Their League* (Syracuse, NY: Syracuse University Press, 1985), pp. 85-98.

12 These stories have also been known as *aewitchigun* (or *auwaetchigum*), meaning stories akin to parables, which are told by its citizens (Nin.Da.Waab.Jig., *Walpole Island: The Soul of Indian Territory*, pp. 1-26). On the stories see Basil Johnston, *Ojibwa Ceremonies* (Toronto: McClelland and Stewart, 1982), pp. 155-75, and his recent *The Manitous: The Spiritual World of the Ojibway* (Toronto: Key Porter Books, 1995), pp. xi-xiii, 1-7, as well as Cleland, *Rites of Conquest*, pp. 1-10.

13 *The Papers of Sir William Johnson*, prepared for publication by Milton W. Hamilton, vol. 6 (Albany, NY: University of the State of New York, 1928), letter, Johnson to Henry Moore, 20 September 1768, Fort Stanwix, pp. 398-404.

14 In the oral traditions, landscape, or Mother Earth, including water, is inseparable with the memory of that landscape. On this subject and land rights see David T. McNab, "Making a Circle of Time: The Treaty-Making Process and Aboriginal Land Rights in Ontario," in *Co-existence? Studies in Ontario-First Nation Relations* (Peterborough, ON: Frost Centre for Canadian Heritage and Development Studies, Trent University, 1992), pp. 27-49.

15 Simon Schama, *Landscape and Memory* (Toronto: Random House of Canada, 1995), pp. 3-19.

16 Ibid., p. 14.

17 Basil Johnston, *The Manitous: The Spiritual World of the Ojibway* (Toronto: Key Porter Books, 1995), pp. xi-xiii, 1-7.

18 See Richard White, *The Middle Ground: Indians, Empires, and Republics in the Great Lakes Region, 1650-1815* (Cambridge: Cambridge University Press, 1991).

19 Johnston, "The Council Zuguswediwin," in *Ojibwa Ceremonies*, pp. 155-75. Johnston, an Aboriginal person from Cape Croker, is a noted Ojibwa historian, formerly with the Department of Ethnology in the Royal Ontario Museum, who has published widely on the history and culture of the Ojibwa Nation. He has also written on the Ojibwa treaties and their understanding of them.

20 RG 8, "C" Series, British Military and Naval Records, National Archives of Canada, Ottawa, Manuscripts Division, Microfilm Reel #C-2848, vol. 248, letter, Joseph Chew to Thomas Aston Coffin, 10 August 1795, pp. 255-57. See also Joan Vastokas, "History without Writing: Pictorial Narratives in Native North America," in McNab and Standen, eds., *Gin Das Winan: Documenting Aboriginal History in Ontario*.

21 See, in the Iroquoian context, Druke, "Iroquois Treaties: Common Forms, Varying Interpretations," especially pp. 85-98.

22 Nin.Da.Waab.Jig. files, Norman Miskokomon Treaties Paper, "Treaties between the Whites and Indians, of Chippewa, Ottawa, and Pottawatomie Tribes," 1929.

23 In the Iroquoian context treaties have been defined by William N. Fenton in his article, "Structure, Continuity, and Change in the Process of Iroquois Treaty Making," in Jennings, ed., *The History and Culture of Iroquois Diplomacy*, pp. 3-36. The Walpole Island First Nation's views on treaties were different than that of the Iroquois, noted above by Basil Johnston in his description of the Council, "The Smoking of the Pipe" or Treaty. See also Druke, "Iroquois Treaties: Common Forms, Varying Interpretations," pp. 85-98.

24 John Thompson, "The Treaties of 1760," *The Beaver*, 76, 2 (April/May 1996): 23-28. It is noteworthy that Thompson observes that there was another treaty on 6 September 1760. However, he provided no details of it in this article.

25 Nin.Da.Waab.Jig. files, Norman Miskokomon Treaties Paper, "Treaties between the Whites and Indians, of Chippewa, Ottawa, and Pottawatomie Tribes," 1929. I wish to express my thanks to the late Norm Miskokomon for sharing this paper with me in 1994. See also my "'The Promise that He Gave to My Grand father Was Very Sweet': The Gun Shot Treaty of 1792 at the Bay of Quinte," Research Note, *The Canadian Journal of Native Studies*, 16, 2 (1996): 293-314.

26 See E.B. O'Callaghan, ed., *Documents Relating to the Colonial History of the State of New York: Procured in Holland, England and France*, by John Romeyn Brodhead, vol. 9 (Albany, NY: Weed, Parsons, 1855), pp. 722-25. A recent book by Ian K. Steele of the University of Western Ontario (*Warpaths: Invasions of North America* [New York: Oxford University Press, 1994]) succinctly and accurately provides the European context for these treaties on pp. 148-49. On p. 149, "Figure 8," Steele has an illustration of a wampum belt from the McCord Museum of Canadian History in Montreal which is "said to represent a clause from the 'Great Peace' between the Five Nations and the French, 1701."

27 O'Callaghan, ed., *Documents Relating to the Colonial History of the State of New York: Procured in Holland, England and France*, vol. 9, pp. 765-67, letter, Sir William Johnson to the Lords of Trade, Plantations General Papers, vol. 25 (K. 6), Johnson Hall, 28 September 1765.

28 NAC, RG 8, "C" Series, Microfilm Reel #C-2848, Vol. 248, letter, Joseph
    Chew to Thomas Aston Coffin, 5 January 1795, pp. 1-3a.
29 Ibid., pp. 251-57a. Many of the written records from the Johnson family
    have recently (1997) been purchased by the National Archives of Canada.
30 I am indebted to Mr. Paul Williams for drawing this to my attention. See also
    his "The Chain" (unpublished LLM thesis, Osgoode Hall Law School,
    1982).
31 The written documents relating to the Covenant Chain of Silver can be
    found in O'Callaghan, ed., *Documents Relative to the Colonial History of
    the State of New York*, vol. 7; and *The Papers of Sir William Johnson*, pre-
    pared for publication by Milton W. Hamilton, vol. 1 (Albany, NY: University
    of the State of New York, 1953). See also Williams, "The Chain"; and
    Gwyn, "Sir William Johnson," pp. 394-98.
32 RG 8, "C" Series, British Military and Naval Records, National Archives of
    Canada, Ottawa, Manuscripts Division, Microfilm Reel #C-2848, vol. 248,
    pp. 1-3a.
33 *Anishnabek News*, 1995. Beyond this reference, there are some in the Abo-
    riginal oral tradition. For example, the Elders and others at Rama have a
    very clear remembrance of this treaty passed down from generation to gener-
    ation. The citizens of Rama recall that "After their [the French and English]
    night on the plains of Abraham they sat down together to make a peace
    treaty. Our nation was present and we have a wampum belt that was made
    during the ceremony. It has three persons standing beside each other. The
    Indian is in the middle holding one hand with the British and holding one
    hand with the French. This belt describes how the French, the British and
    the Indian Nations would live in harmony side by each. Each of the three
    nations would make their own rules or laws. They each would keep their
    own religions, languages, their own systems of government, and other insti-
    tutions as needed. They would travel on three separate paths or in three sep-
    arate canoes. They would go into the future as brothers. Each would move
    ahead in harmony, side by each and, if necessary, lend a hand to help if
    asked. They would go into the future as equals, with no one ahead and no
    one behind. They especially liked the new phrase they made: Three 'distinct'
    nations."
34 Gwyn, "Sir William Johnson,"pp. 394-98.
35 *The Papers of Sir William Johnson*, vol. 1, pp. 158-59.
36 Steele, *Warpaths: Invasions of North America*, especially chap. 4, pp. 59-79.
    On this period see Colin G. Calloway, *Crown and Calumet: British-Indian
    Relations, 1783-1815* (Norman, OK: University of Oklahoma Press, 1987),
    and the same author's recent *The American Revolution in Indian Country:
    Crisis and Diversity in Native American Communities* (Cambridge: Cam-
    bridge University Press, 1995).
37 National Archives of Canada (NAC), RG 10, vol. 1822, p. 35.
38 Royal Proclamation of 1763, 7 October 1763, in Ian A.L. Getty and
    Antoine S. Lussier, eds., *As Long as the Sun Shines and the Water Flows: A
    Reader in Canadian Native Studies* (Vancouver, BC: University of British
    Columbia Press, 1983), pp. 29-37.
39 National Archives of Canada (NAC), RG 10, vol. 1822, p. 35.

40 *The Papers of Sir William Johnson*, vol. 11, pp. 395-96. See also Gwyn, "Sir William Johnson."

41 *The Papers of Sir William Johnson*, vol. 11, pp. 395-96.

42 See *The Papers of Sir William Johnson*, prepared for publication by Milton W. Hamilton, vol. 3 (Albany, NY: University of the State of New York, 1953), pp. 237, 267-75; and NAC, Claus Family Papers, MG 19, vol. 1, pp. 7-8, Microfilm Reel #C-1478.

43 Steele, *Warpaths: Invasions of North America*, especially chap. 4, pp. 59-79.

44 Nin.Da.Waab.Jig. files, Norman Miskokomon Treaties Paper, "Treaties between the Whites and Indians, of Chippewa, Ottawa, and Pottawatomie Tribes."

45 C.P. Stacey, "John Knox," in *Dictionary of Canadian Biography*, vol. 4: *1771-1800* (Toronto: University of Toronto Press, 1979), pp. 415-16.

46 A.G. Doughty, ed., *An Historical Journal of the Campaigns in North America: For the Years 1757, 1758, 1759, and 1760 by Captain John Knox*, 3 vols. (Toronto: The Champlain Society, 1914-16), vol. 2, p. 453.

47 Ibid., p. 517. This treaty is known today as the Murray Treaty of 5 September 1760, which was entered into at Longueil, Montreal. It was this treaty that was the subject of the Supreme Court of Canada judgment in the Sioui case in 1990, in which case the Supreme Court found in favour of the Huron of Lorette.

48 Ibid., vol. 3, pp. 330-34.

49 Ibid., vol. 2, pp. 515-17, 583.

50 RG 10, Indian Affairs Records, Microfilm Reel #C-1221 and #C-1222, "Copy of Sir William Johnson Letter to Genl [General] Amherst Dated Niagara July 29, 1761," vol. 6, ff. 75-77.

51 Ibid.

52 RG 10, Indian Affairs Records, Microfilm Reel #C-1222, vol. 6—the Treaty of Detroit of 1761 is on pp. 100-26.

53 Treaty of Niagara, 9-14 July 1764, in *The Papers of Sir William Johnson*, vol. 11, pp. 262-333.

54 W.G. Godfrey, "John Bradstreet," in *Dictionary of Canadian Biography*, vol. 4: *1771-1800* (Toronto: University of Toronto Press, 1979), pp. 83-87.

55 Harry Kelsey, "Wasson," in ibid., vol. 4, pp. 761-62.

56 *The Papers of Sir William Johnson*, vol. 11, pp. 349-51.

57 There is no biography for Croghan in the *Dictionary of Canadian Biography*. However, see Louis Chevrette, "Pontiac," in *Dictionary of Canadian Biography*, vol. 3: *1741-1770* (Toronto: University of Toronto Press, 1974), pp. 525-31.

58 Ibid. See also Helen Hornbeck Tanner, ed., *Atlas of Great Lakes Indian History* (Norman, OK: University of Oklahoma Press, 1987), p. 52.

59 The Treaty of Detroit, 27 August-4 September 1765, in O'Callaghan, ed., *Documents Relative to the Colonial History of the State of New York*, vol. 7, pp. 775-88.

60 Ibid., letter, Sir William Johnson to the Lords of Trade, Plantations General Papers, vol. 25 (K. 6), Johnson Hall, 28 September 1765, pp. 765-67.

61 Treaty of Lake Ontario, 22-30 July 1766, National Archives of Canada (NAC), Record Group 10, vol. 1829, pp. 1-36. Another later copy of this

treaty, which, according to this document, was held at "Ontario," is in O'Callaghan, ed., *Documents Relative to the Colonial History of the State of New York*, vol. 7, pp. 854-67, entitled "Proceedings of Sir William Johnson with Pondiac and other Indians," Plantations General Papers, vol. 26, Treaty #5]. This latter document is noted to be "a true copy of Sir William Johnsons Transactions at Ontario compared with the Records." However, the location is not given in it.

62 Nin.Da.Waab.Jig., *Walpole Island: The Soul of Indian Territory*, pp. 1-26.

63 Reginald Horsman, "Alexander McKee," in *Dictionary of Canadian Biography*, vol. 4: *1771-1800* (Toronto: University of Toronto Press, 1979), pp. 499-500.

64 The best examples are Pelee and Bob Lo Islands, both of which are currently the subject of land claims before the federal government. Neither of these islands has ever been ceded or surrendered.

65 Treaty #2 (otherwise known as the McKee Treaty of 1790), 19 May 1790, in Canada, *Indian Treaties and Surrenders* (Ottawa, ON: Queen's Printer, 1891; reprint Saskatoon: Fifth House Publishers, 1992), vol. 1, pp. 1-5.

66 McNab, " 'The Promise that He Gave to My Grand father Was Very Sweet': The Gun Shot Treaty of 1792 at the Bay of Quinte," pp. 293-314.

67 Nin.Da.Waab.Jig., *Walpole Island: The Soul of Indian Territory*, chaps. 1 and 2, pp. 1-26.

68 Ibid. The copy of the document quoted here is from RG 10, vol. 785, pp. 181477-80.

69 National Archives of Canada (NAC), RG 10 (RG 10), Indian Affairs Records, vol. 58, pp. 59778-81.

70 Donald B. Smith, "Bauzhi-geezhig-waeshikum (Pazhekezhikquashkum, Pechegeecheqquistqum, Beyigishiqueshkam)" (ca. 1841-42), in *Dictionary of Canadian Biography*, vol. 7: *1836-1850* (Toronto: University of Toronto Press, 1988), pp. 54-55.

71 Samuel Peters Jarvis Papers, Metropolitan Toronto Reference Library, Baldwin Room, S 125, B57, July-September 1839, pp. 373-83.

72 Nin.Da.Waab.Jig., "Enaaknigewinke geeshoog Treaty Making 1790-1827," in *Walpole Island: The Soul of Indian Territory*, chap. 3, pp. 17-26.

73 Treaty of Detroit, 1807.

74 Treaty of Ghent, 1815. See also, for its effect on the Walpole Island First Nation, 1987, Nin.Da.Waab.Jig., "Enaaknigewinke geeshoog Treaty Making 1790-1827," in *Walpole Island: The Soul of Indian Territory*, chap. 3, pp. 17-26.

75 See David T. McNab, " 'What Liars those People Are': The St. Anne Island Speech of the Walpole Island First Nation given at the Chenail Ecarte River on August 3, 1815," *Social Sciences and Humanities Aboriginal Research Exchange*, 1, 1 (Fall-Winter 1993): 10, 12-13, 15.

76 I would like to thank Elder Charles Shawkence, the Chief of Kettle Point First Nation for many years, for drawing my attention to the Treaty of Amherstburg of 1818.

77 Nin.Da.Waab.Jig., *Minishenhying Anishnaabe-aki, Walpole Island: The Soul of Indian Territory*, especially pp. 1-26; and Treaty #2 (otherwise known as the McKee Treaty of 1790), 19 May 1790, in Canada, *Indian Treaties and*

Surrenders, vol. 1, pp. 1-5. The historical details of the First Nation understanding of this treaty can be found in the following: Upper Canada Land Petitions, 1797, Bundle A, 1796-1840, Petition of Sarah Ainse, NAC, Public Records Division, RG 1, L 3, Vol. 3, A Bundle 4, 1796-98, #45, pp. 45c-45d (Microfilm Reel #C-1609).

78 The Claus Family Papers are in the NAC, Manuscripts Division, MG 19, F 1, vol. 11, pp. 94-96 (Microfilm Reel #C-1480). It should be highlighted that even though waters were included in these so-called "surrenders," the subject was not even raised, much less discussed at their council meetings. The federal government's official history of the treaty-making process with the Council of Three Fires (as set out in Canada, *Indian Treaties and Surrenders*, vol. 1) is also in error since it provided only for minimum legal conveyance of lands without recognition of the treaty-making process.

79 "Memorial of the Chippeway, Potawatomy and Ottawa Indian Nations of Walpole Island, Touching their Claim of the Huron Reservation, Fighting and Bois Blanc Island" to Lord Monck, Governor General of Canada, 5 August 1867, hand delivered by William N. Fisher at Ottawa, Nin.Da.Waab.Jig. files; and "Memorial," Walpole Island First Nation, to Sir John Young, Governor General of Canada, 30 May 1869, NAC, RG 10, vol. 787, pp. 12-20 (Microfilm Reel #C-13499).

80 David McNab, "The Walpole Island Indian Band and the Continuity of Indian Claims: An Historical Perspective," Walpole Island: Nin.Da.Waab.Jig., Occasional Papers, 1985.

81 Treaty of Lake Ontario, 22-30 July 1766, National Archives of Canada (NAC), Record Group 10, vol. 1829, pp. 1-36.

82 Samuel Peters Jarvis Papers, Metropolitan Toronto Reference Library, Baldwin Room, S 125, B57, July-September 1839, pp. 378-80. A copy is also in Nin.Da.Waab.Jig.'s files.

4

"Under the Earth": The Expropriation and Attempted Sale of the Oil and Gas Rights of the Walpole Island First Nation during World War I

Rhonda Telford

Introduction

Anishinabe First Nations in southwestern Ontario, where most of Ontario's oil and gas fields are located, never relinquished subsurface or submarine rights through treaties or other agreements with the Crown. Oil, gas and other minerals under the ground and under the land beneath the water on reserves and in shared Territories (also called treaty areas) remain Aboriginal property. These minerals are and have always been the property of the Ojibwa (Chippewa), Ottawa and Potawatomi Nations of southwestern Ontario.

During World War I, Duncan Campbell Scott, the deputy superintendent general of Indian Affairs, artificially manufactured conditions

Notes to chapter 4 are on pp. 76-79.

that allowed the federal government to use the federal *War Measures Act* to expropriate oil and gas resources on the Walpole Island Reserve. The government was unable to carry out actual expropriation because of strong and continuous Aboriginal resistance. The First Nation protest was successful and defeated the actions of the federal government. These deeds shed new light on Aboriginal resistance movements and their leadership. They also illustrate the workings of the federal Department of Indian Affairs [hereafter DIA] under the *Indian Act* and the "narrow vision" of Duncan Campbell Scott.[1] These government actions are a warning, indicating how easily Ottawa can override citizens' rights, through orders-in-council under the *War Measures Act* or other legislation.

This was not the first time government took oil-bearing lands from the Walpole Island First Nation without authorization. Colonial authorities had illegally sold the 400-acre Enniskillen Reserve in which Walpole Island, Sarnia, Kettle Point and Stoney Point First Nations had interests. These Nations purchased the reserve in 1841 and 1842 with their own money for $750. The sale of this land was a by-product of Canada's first oil boom and is still the subject of a long-standing land claim.

While oil and gas are recognized as important resources in Northern Ontario today, their importance for Southern Ontario is less well known. Yet during World War I, these subsurface Aboriginal resources were seen to be of national interest. Their geographic location would have made the transportation and distribution of oil and gas easier and cheaper.

Aboriginal protest against federal actions during World War I indicates that Native people have always viewed their subsurface rights, and oil and gas in particular, as significant natural resources. The Walpole Island First Nation has never relinquished ownership of subsurface or submarine rights, either in their reserves, in their unceded Lands or in their ceded Territories by treaty. All of this belies the impression that First Nations do not have Aboriginal Title and Rights, control over, interest in, or treaty rights to such resources. The subsurface and the submarine are part of the traditional economy and culture of First Nations, part of their conception of the Earth.

Traditional Aboriginal Knowledge and Use of Oil

Native peoples tapped oil from wells and collected seepage oil from the surface of the land and water. Aboriginal peoples probably knew about and collected oil from the time they first encountered seepages from the earth and on the surface of the water. Charles Robb, a geologist and engineer for the Montreal Mining Company, writing in 1861, maintained that Native peoples in his present-day Pennsylvania in the US and in Enniskillen Township in southwestern Ontario had also tapped oil from wells, noted the existence of ancient wells:

> The early French settlers, and the Indians of western Pennsylvania, were aware of their [petroleum springs] existence, and made use of their products. Old oil vats and oil wells have been discovered, affording undoubted evidence of human works of great antiquity; and in Enniskillen, the great centre of the oil spring region in Canada, deers' horns, and pieces of timber bearing the marks of the axe, have been dug up from considerable depths below the surface, in what appear to have been old wells.[2]

Robb, unfortunately, did not estimate the antiquity of these wells. Nevertheless, Aboriginal people have refined and commercially sold oil to whites since at least the 1600s. The Seneca, for example, were selling oil-medicine to the whites at exorbitant prices by 1627.[3]

The Ojibwa and Delaware had long-standing knowledge and use of such oil, which they collected from pools along the Thames River near Moraviantown in Zone Township and the Bear and Black Creeks in Enniskillen Township. In February of 1793, Ojibwa from the Bear Creek settlement informed Lieutenant Governor John Graves Simcoe of an oil seepage on the Thames River in their hunting grounds.[4] This party of Ojibwa would likely have included, among other families, members of the Miskokomon family who resided at Bear Creek. The Miskokomons are of the Bear clan and would have been likely to encounter non-Natives, since part of their responsibility to the community was policing or patrolling their territory. The Ojibwa teacher Edward Benton-Banai asserts that another major responsibility of the Bear clan was making medicine. This clan in particular spent a great deal of time "close to nature" because of its policing duties. Thus, they also gained extensive knowledge of plants and other natural materials, including oil, which were used to make medicine for the community.[5]

One such medicine was that made from oil, collected by placing a blanket over the surface of the water. After the water and oil were absorbed, the blanket was wrung into a bowl and the oil skimmed, bottled and sold as a medicine.[6] This was likely one of the first occasions on which Aboriginal people shared the location of oil, a sacred medicine, with the English.

The Ojibwa around Black Creek shared their medicinal knowledge with the first settlers arriving in the early 1830s.[7] Their information led provincial authorities to examine Enniskillen Township in 1832, but they did not discover the gum beds that stretched over half an acre in a densely treed swamp.[8]

The Moravian-Delaware people on the Thames River had knowledge of and medicinal use for seepage oil, which they collected and sold. The Delaware preserved and retailed such oil in the United States prior to their arrival in Canada about 1800. On the Muskingum River, in Pennsylvania, white consumers paid four guineas (or $20) a quart for the Aboriginal medicine.[9] In 1844, at Fairfield on the Thames, the Moravian mission in Canada, they sold it at three dollars a gallon (or seventy-five cents a quart). Seepage oil and water were collected in kettles and the water boiled off. The oil was "preserved" and used externally for a variety of ailments, including sprains, rheumatic pains, toothaches and headaches. This medicine was also taken internally.[10]

Oil was a sacred medicine for Aboriginal people in southwestern Ontario. The waters and lands from which it sprung commanded respect and protection. It was the southwestern Ojibwa and Delaware who first drew the attention of the whites to the oil and gas potential under Aboriginal Territory. First Nation revelations of the precise locations of oil seepages on land and water led the whites to "discover" the vast oil and gas fields of southwestern Ontario. But Native people were the original discoverers of this oil and gas and the first people to have sacred and commercial uses for the substance.

Government Appropriation and Expropriation of Oil and Gas

Provincial investigations in the 1850s led to the oil boom at Oil Springs in 1857 and 1858, the first in the world for commercial purposes. That boom was eclipsed by a second at Petrolia, partially triggered when colonial authorities illegally authorized developers to remove oil from the Enniskillen Reserve belonging to the Walpole Island, Sarnia, Kettle Point and Stoney Point First Nations. In 1858, the Indian agent held a council with only the Sarnia First Nation to obtain its consent to the sale of the Enniskillen Reserve. The council allegedly agreed, but no formal surrender for the land was ever secured by the Department. Beyond this, it is not clear that the agent specifically asked for subsurface rights. At most, the council allegedly agreed to share the land only, but not the mineral rights. The Walpole Island, Kettle Point and Stoney Point First Nations were not consulted or informed at the time. This action was illegal under the rules of the Royal Proclamation of 1763, the Crown Instructions of 1794 to Sir John Johnson and the treaties.

This was not the last time the Canadian government acted improperly in connection with the oil and gas resources of the Walpole Island First Nation. In February of 1918, Imperial Oil informed the DIA of its desire to explore for oil and gas on the Walpole Island Reserve.[11] In May, the Reverend Simpson Brigham, one of the earliest Aboriginal people to be ordained an Anglican deacon and then priest, and certainly the first such person from Walpole Island, tried to influence his people to lease oil rights at a vote.[12]

It is not known what other economic issues Brigham, involved himself in since 1899 when he was assigned to the Anglican Church on Walpole Island.[13] His reasoning for pushing the surrender of oil and gas rights seems to have been that he anticipated the federal government would take them anyway if First Nation consent was not obtained.[14] Canada had behaved this way in the past when it forced the Walpole Island First Nation to endure an unwanted survey of its islands. To facilitate this action, Ottawa changed the *Indian Act* in 1898 by order-in-council so that the survey of reserves could be carried out without First Nation consent.

Simpson Brigham came from a long line of "runners," or messengers, stretching back at least to the Treaty of 1827.[15] As a runner, or messenger, his duty was to carry messages and to mediate relations between his people and the whites. In order to carry out his responsibilities he had to educate himself. At that time, his only choice was to become a minister. Christianity itself was not his primary concern—it was, he believed, the means by which white people would respect him and listen to him. Brigham often used his position to explain traditional Ojibwa ways to white people so that they would see the intrinsic value in Aboriginal culture. The non-Native separation of the spiritual, social and economic realms is an unnatural one for Aboriginal people to make. Thus, Brigham did nothing "wrong" when he mixed spiritual and economic issues.[16]

Brigham's position as a runner meant he often had to place himself in awkward situations and make difficult decisions. He was obligated to put himself between both worlds to try and bring harmony between the Nations while still upholding the strongest possible position for his people.[17] This is what he tried to do during World War I at the oil and gas vote. He appears to have believed that the chief and council would be able to control the terms of lease because "the oil companies were falling all over each other to make concessions to them."[18]

This, however, must not have been the perception of the majority of the First Nation citizens. The outcome of the vote, 105 against and 11 for, was overwhelmingly negative.[19] In addition, the chief and councillors were also against such a surrender. The proposition was rejected because the Walpole Island First Nation was unable to adequately control the terms of the lease and did not trust the DIA to conclude a satisfactory arrangement.[20] Brigham failed to bring a solution to this issue, which ended as he predicted it would. Soon after the failed vote, the Department took extraordinary steps to procure oil and gas rights.

D.C. Scott was under pressure from Arthur Meighen, minister of the Interior (also superintendent general of Indian Affairs) to obtain oil and gas surrenders at both Walpole Island and Sarnia. Meighen implored Scott to make a "special effort" in the matter. He pointed out that the Dominion Sugar, Dominion Glass and Imperial Oil Companies were working together to prospect for oil and gas at Walpole Island.[21]

Scott took this advice to heart. He took the unusual step of using government officials outside the Department of Indian Affairs either to procure surrender or to legitimize his unilateral actions. In August, W.A. Orr, of the federal Lands and Timber Branch, under directions from Scott, failed to obtain a surrender from the Sarnia and Kettle Point First Nations for oil and gas on the Sarnia Reserve. Subsequently, Scott informed Charles McGrath, fuel controller for Canada, of the intransigence of the Walpole Island and Sarnia First Nations regarding the issue of surrender. Scott continued:

> The claim has been made by the companies—who are interested . . .—that the oil and gas are required in the prosecution of work connected with war activities. It may be that you will consider it essential at the present time to develop the fuel resources in that part of the country. If you can assure me of that fact, I will submit to the Hon. [Honourable] the Superintendent General, whether we should not, under the War Measures Act, permit prospecting and development of these reserves.[22]

This was a reprehensible attempt on the part of the state (as represented by Scott) and white-controlled business to use the war as an excuse to forcibly remove First Nation rights and control of the development of their minerals. The war was almost over. Although no one knew exactly when it would end, all knew Germany's days were numbered.[23]

Since at least the beginning of August 1918, Canada knew the war was winding down, yet D.C. Scott took it upon himself to prompt the fuel controller to agree to Scott's contention that a national scarcity of oil justified the Department in removing Aboriginal control over oil and gas. This was nothing more than a petty abuse of power, since prior to this oil had only been developed on the Sarnia Reserve and never amounted to more than $150 for the company concerned between 1906 and 1915. No oil had ever been developed on Walpole Island. It was not until 1918, when Imperial Oil and two other large concerns indicated interest in obtaining a lease for exploration, that "oil reserves" at Walpole Island and Sarnia suddenly became a matter of vital importance for the war effort. By 1890, Canada knew the "North was floating in oil." But technology was not advanced enough to remove it and even if it could have been removed there were no transportation systems in the area to move it south. The oil gush at Norman Wells in the Northwest Territories, which precipitated Treaty #11, did not occur until 1922[24] when the War was already over. Oil in southwestern Ontario was important.

On 6 September 1918, Scott received the letter he had previously instigated himself. The deputy fuel controller, Charles Peterson, detailed the necessity of oil and gas development in Eastern Canada due to "considerable scarcity of fuel oil owing to the increasing demands for allied shipping and war industries." This situation was allegedly aggravated by American restrictions on coal importation. Peterson said these conditions would continue for some time after the war and urged Meighen to proceed with the expropriation.[25]

Predictably, Scott brought this to the attention of Meighen, who in turn notified the governor general. On 19 September, the *War Measures Act* was invoked by order-in-council to allow the DIA to dispose of the oil and gas on the Walpole Island and Sarnia Reserves as they saw fit, without the consent of either First Nation.[26] This was in spite of the fact that between 12 and 14 September, the Germans retreated all along the western front. Whatever oil and gas was situated on the reserves could in no way be developed and processed before the *end* of the war. Between 4 and 23 October 1918, several requests for an armistice were made by the Germans and Austrians. By the latter date troops had been recalled to Germany.[27] Yet even after the war officially came to an end on 11 November, the *War Measures Act* was not revoked.

The Walpole Island First Nation immediately hired solicitor D.M. Grant to find out whether the Department leased oil and gas rights without their consent. The action was in violation of the Treaty of 1827,[28] which contained a solemn outside promise that the Walpole Island, Sarnia, Kettle Point and Stoney Point First Nations would never be disturbed in their lands again.[29]

Reverend Simpson Brigham wholeheartedly aided the Walpole Island First Nation in their struggle to reverse the expropriation decision. His prediction that something like this would occur, in the absence of Aboriginal consent, had come true. Again, Brigham had no choice but to take this stand since federal use of the *War Measures Act* not only violated the outside promise which was a term of the Treaty of 1827, but also impinged on the sovereignty of the Walpole Island First Nation, which had never been relinquished. As a runner, Brigham was obligated to protect the relationship established between his Nation and the whites under the treaties.

The Walpole Island First Nation sent an official statement of protest to the superintendent general and hired other lawyers to prepare petitions and inform the DIA of their opposition.[30] Both Brigham and Elijah Pennance [Pinnance] felt petitions were not enough. They decided to appeal to David Williams, the bishop of Huron, and Dr. Norman Tucker, president of the Social Services Council of Canada. Brigham wanted the matter put before this Council. Pennance and Brigham hoped to place a memorial before the governor general asking to have the federal government "reconsider" its recent expropriation of oil and gas rights under the *War Measures Act*. Brigham eventually did speak before the Council and called for their aid which was soon brought to bear on the Canadian government.[31]

Scott received a telegram from Williams and Tucker reiterating Aboriginal opposition to Department actions.[32] This was shortly followed by a long letter from Williams, outlining in great detail, the Aboriginal opposition. According to Williams, the Walpole Island First Nation viewed Department actions as illegal, and similar to the actions of Germany in Belgium. It was widely believed that oil development would ruin their farms. The First Nation also felt the DIA would authorize unsatisfactory terms, which they had done in the past in connection with timber resources. Williams implored the Department to act fairly and responsibly.

Williams also argued that Native people had surrendered large tracts to the Dominion and retained only small reserves. Thus, they should not be called upon to surrender even more. Williams continued to argue that the Walpole Island First Nation citizens strongly supported the war effort both at home and abroad, and that it would be a blot on Canadian honour to proceed with the expropriation. He concluded by noting that if Ottawa wanted to develop oil it should do so on neighbouring land owned by whites and that the federal argument regarding a war necessity was now no longer valid.[33]

Brigham's efforts with the Social Services Council were also paying off. That body agreed to accompany a Walpole Island delegation to see the governor general to have the expropriation reversed.[34] In addition, they also proposed to serve an injunction on the DIA until another petition was sent to Ottawa.[35] However, it is clear that the Walpole Island First Nation sought to utilize all avenues and resources available to it in terms of community support to impress upon the Department the unwarranted, unfair and unnecessary nature of its actions.

The DIA was no doubt embarrassed by Aboriginal hostility toward the proposed development. At the end of November, D.C. Scott sent Meighen a memo outlining how the present situation had come to pass. In this memo Scott assigned the "representations of the Fuel Controller" as the causative motive for the Department's actions.[36] What he failed to mention is very significant, namely that he was the one who prompted the fuel controller to make such "representations" in the first place.[37] Scott was no doubt trying to cover his back. Both he and Meighen knew Scott was responsible for the actions of the Department.

Scott remained unrepentant in replying to David Williams' letters. He regurgitated the fuel controller's letter as the basis of Department action and stated that in any case the deal would have been in the interest of the First Nations concerned. He said his Department had considered First Nation protest *after* the armistice was signed and denied any violation of law or treaty. Scott pragmatically observed that "the Indian and his property became subject to the abnormal conditions of the war." He argued that the *Indian Act*, under section 48, allowed the Department to appropriate First Nation property without their consent. Scott asserted that without such authority it would be difficult to conduct public business in relation to Indian Affairs.[38] In conclusion, Scott assured the bishop that no development would proceed on Walpole Island.

Tenders were solicited from 22 October to 20 November of 1918. Only one was received from A.I. McKinley, representing Imperial Oil, for Walpole Island. Vigorous protest emanated from the Walpole Island First Nation[39] and the issue was dropped. The matter of oil and gas development suddenly lost its former urgency. This was contrary to earlier arguments that an urgent need for oil would "prevail for a considerable time after the war." Scott's relentless bid to prompt the fuel controller to bring the absolute need for oil development on Walpole Island to the attention of the superintendent general and the governor general was nothing less than a gross abuse of Departmental power, federal emergency powers and an unnecessary imposition on the rights of Aboriginal people. There is no indication that the order-in-council authorizing the expropriation has ever been cancelled or rescinded.

In a last, almost pathetic, attempt to galvanize the Department into action, the Dominion Glass Company informed Scott that unless additional natural gas could be secured, Ontario would cut off supplies to various companies, including theirs. Dominion Glass wanted the DIA to "settle the question of leases with Walpole Island" because of its interest in sand and gas.[40] Canada was in very rough shape, indeed, when one of its leading concerns had no where else to turn but the unproven oil reserves of Walpole Island to stave off alleged industrial doom.

Aboriginal people at Walpole Island did not surrender mineral or other subsurface rights (among countless others) in any treaties with the Crown. Nevertheless, the settler government illegally took and sold their oil and gas lands in the Enniskillen Reserve in the mid-nineteenth century. Canada attempted to do so again during World War I. This latter action must be viewed as more than merely an example of increasing government intervention in the lives of Canadians during the War. Aboriginal property and rights had long been the subject of government appropriation in peace time. Colonial action at Enniskillen is a case in point. Pre-*Indian Act* and *Indian Act* legislation was incredibly intrusive into the lives, rights and property of First Nations. The expropriation of Aboriginal resources was not unprecedented, and it would happen again and again. The lengths to which the federal Department of Indian Affairs went to legitimize their actions certainly were equally intrusive and draconian.

This incident tells much about the nature of white and Aboriginal leadership. When the DIA and the federal government expropriated and then attempted to sell unsurrendered oil and gas rights they deliberately abused the powers of the Canadian nation-state for a Canadian, if not a British Imperial, cause. Aboriginal people at Walpole Island had good reason to be weary of Scott and his "narrow vision" as it applied to the development of their resources. Throughout most of the twentieth century little significant mineral development has occurred on reserves. Native people were disillusioned with both government and companies to a great extent. Thus, although Ontario experienced a mining boom in the 1920s, the Walpole Island First Nation, which had one of the most promising oil-bearing reserves, refused to develop its resources.

White-controlled companies, namely, Imperial Oil, Dominion Glass and Dominion Sugar, acted out of "graft"[41] and other base motives when they encouraged the DIA to facilitate their efforts to have access to oil and gas resources on the Walpole Island Reserve. White companies and their governments attempted to use the War as an excuse to dispossess the Walpole Island First Nation of valuable minerals. The Departmental attempt to claim and control oil and gas under this reserve, during and after World War I through the *War Measures Act*, failed miserably. That Ottawa wholeheartedly took up the cause of the companies regardless of the effects this would have on First Nations raises disturbing questions about who sets government agendas—government or industry.[42] Department actions were underhanded, secretive, overbearing and utterly in conflict with federal fiduciary obligations to First Nations. White actions fomented and ensured conflict with Native people.

The most complex set of reactions to the proposed surrender and then expropriation of oil and gas rights came from the Reverend Simpson Brigham of Bkejwanong. As a runner, it was Brigham's obligation to place himself between both worlds and attempt to promote harmony and understanding between the Nations. This is what he was initially doing when he actively, but unsuccessfully, attempted to encourage the surrender of oil and gas rights at the May 1918 vote. He seemed to be in favour of advancing Departmental plans because he feared what the government would do if Aboriginal consent was not obtained. His fears were not unfounded. Following the expropriation by order-in-council under the *War Measures Act*, Brigham vigorously aided chief and council in their efforts to stop government actions. Federal use of the *War Measures Act* violated the treaty relationship between the Walpole Island First Nation and the Crown. Brigham was bound to reaffirm this treaty promise in his responsibility as a runner. In the end, Brigham and the Walpole Island First Nation successfully resisted Canada's vision for their subsurface resources.

The people of Bkejwanong stood firmly against the expropriation of their Aboriginal Title and Rights to oil and gas. They moved quickly and decisively to counter government actions. Advice and support were obtained both within and outside their immediate community. They raised a vigorous protest campaign, including petitions, proposed deputations and injunctions and the use of sympathetic high profile members in the neighbouring white community. Through its own initiatives and acts of resistance, the First Nations successfully safeguarded their sub-surface oil and gas rights.

Notes

1 E. Brian Titley, *A Narrow Vision: Duncan Campbell Scott and the Administration of Indian Affairs in Canada* (Vancouver, BC: University of British Columbia Press, 1986).

2 Reference to Charles Robb's work is located in an unpublished manuscript by R.B. Harkness, Regional History Collection, Weldon Library, University of Western Ontario, Introduction, pp. 3-4; and to Petrolia, pp. 1-2. Robb's original paper: "On the Petroleum Springs of Western Canada," *The Canadian Journal*, new series, 34 (July 1861): 314-15. Similar information was printed in *The Daily Globe*, 12 September 1861, also referred to by Harkness.

3 "Petroleum Down the Centuries," *Imperial Oil Review* (March/April 1934): 17.

4 Brigadier General E.A. Cruikshank, LL.D, F.R.S.C., ed., *The Correspondence of Lieut. Governor John Graves Simcoe, with Allied Documents Relating to the Administration of the Government of Upper Canada* (Toronto: Ontario Historical Society, 1923), p. 290.

5 Personal communication, David McNab, 17 June 1994. For a discussion of Ojibwa clans and their responsibilities see Edward Benton-Banai, *The Mishomis Book: The Voice of the Ojibway* (St. Paul: Red School House, 1988), pp. 74-78 (particularly p. 76). The Miskokomons are citizens of the Walpole Island First Nation.

6 R.B. Harkness, "Ontario's Part in the Petroleum Industry," *Canadian Oil and Gas Industries* (February 1951), p. 32; and J.M.S. Careless, *Brown of the Globe: Statesman of Confederation, 1860-1880* (Toronto: Dundurn Press, 1898), vol. 2, p. 51. According to Harkness, provincial natural gas commissioner during the 1950s, the site of this particular seepage is now in the Bothwell oil field.

7 Michael O'Meara, *Oil Springs: The Birthplace of the Ontario Industry in North America* (Oil Springs, 1958), p. 45; and Earle Gray, *The Great Canadian Oil Patch* (Toronto: McLean Hunter, 1970), p. 34.

8 Edward Phelps, "Foundations of the Canadian Oil Industry, 1850-1866," in Edith G. Firth, ed., *Profiles of a Province: Studies in the History of Ontario* (Toronto: Ontario Historical Society, 1967), p. 157.

9 The guinea was equivalent to 20 shillings when it was first coined in 1663. After 1717 its value increased to 21 shillings, or at least $5. After 1813, it was no longer coined.

10 Elma E. Gray, *Wilderness Christians: The Moravian Mission to the Delaware Indians* (Toronto: Macmillan, 1956), p. 135.

11 Archivist Linda Smith of the Imperial Oil Company in Toronto states that no records have been placed in the archives dealing with Company attempts to obtain oil and gas rights on reserves—either in World War I or World War II.

12 Nin.Da.Waab.Jig. files, Simpson Brigham Papers, letter 20 November 1918, Brigham to "My Dear Ogemah." I am indebted to the Reverend Jim Miller for sharing these letters. ("Ogemah" means Chief, or Head Man.)

13 Little is known about Brigham before 1917.

14 Nin.Da.Waab.Jig. files, Simpson Brigham Papers, letter, 17 October 1918, Margaret Brigham (Simpson's white wife) to her mother. Following the expropriation, Margaret Brigham commented that "The Indians are kicking themselves now that they didn't take Jimmie's [that is, Rev. Simpson Brigham] advice, and lease the rights while the oil companies were falling all over each other to make concessions to them. Now they'll get just what the government pays, and I suppose that will be 'deposited to their credit.' . . . I'm awfully sorry they lose so much, but I'm glad they know that Jimmie was right in his advice. He was very discouraged and disappointed that more of the men couldn't see far enough ahead to know what would happen."

15 Personal communication on family history, Simpson Brigham (Reverend Simpson Brigham's son), 13 May 1994. See also Dean Jacobs, " 'We have but our hearts and the traditions of our old men': Understanding the Traditions and History of Bkejwanong," in David McNab and S. Dale Standen, eds., with an "Introduction," *Gin Das Winan: Documenting Aboriginal History in Ontario*, Occasional Papers of The Champlain Society, no. 2 (Toronto: The Champlain Society, 1996), pp. 1-13.

16 Personal communication on family history, Bernita Brigham (granddaughter of the Reverend Simpson Brigham), 13 May 1994. I am indebted to Bernita Brigham for sharing some of the history of her family with me. This information is not in the written record and sheds much light on the motives and actions of her grandfather as well as speaking to the importance of clan responsibility in general. Also Charles E. Cleland, *Rites of Conquest: The History and Culture of Michigan's Native Americans* (Ann Arbor: University of Michigan Press, 1992).

17 Personal communication, Bernita Brigham, 13 May 1994.

18 Nin.Da.Waab.Jig. files, Simpson Brigham Papers, letter, 17 October 1918, Margaret Brigham (Simpson's wife) to her mother.

19 Nin.Da.Waab.Jig. files, Simpson Brigham Papers, letter, 20 November 1918, Brigham to "My Dear Ogemah"; and RG 10, vol. 7645, F. 20040-1, pt. 0 (Walpole Island), letter of 13 November 1918, Kerr and McNevin, barristers and solicitors for Walpole Island First Nation, to the DIA.

20 See, for instance, the kinds of terms imposed by the Walpole Island First Nation in the leasing of their marshlands since the 1870s (David McNab, "The Walpole Island Indian Band and the Continuity of Indian Claims: An Historical Perspective," in Walpole Island: Nin.Da.Waab.Jig., Occasional Papers, 1985). See also RG 10, vol. 7645, F. 20040-1, pt. 0 (Walpole Island), letter, 22 November 1918, David Williams, bishop of Huron, to D.C. Scott.

21 RG 10, vol. 7643, F. 20029-1, pt. 0, "Sarnia Agency . . . ," memorandum dated 26 August 1918, private secretary's Office, minister of the Interior, to D.C. Scott. Note: Dominion Glass was interested in obtaining sand because

this was the mineral it used to make glass, but it was also interested in gas because this fuel was used in the production of glass. It had been taking sand without the permission of the First Nation from the reserve at least since the 1890s.

22 RG 10, vol. 7643, F. 20029-1, pt. 0, "Sarnia Agency...," letter, 30 August 1918, Scott to Charles McGrath.

23 At the beginning of August 1918 a final and vigorous offensive had been launched against the Germans, reclaiming almost all of the areas they held in France and Belgium. Their defeat at Amiens 8-12 August saw the virtual "collapse" of the German armies. Subsequently, the Kaiser abdicated and the Social Democrats took over, suing for peace. The war ended on 11 November. J.L. Granatstein et al., *Twentieth Century Canada* (Toronto: McGraw-Hill Ryerson, 1983), p. 135; R. Douglas Francis et al., *Destinies: Canadian History Since Confederation* (Toronto: Holt Rinehart and Winston of Canada, 1988), p. 195; and Robert H. Ferrell, general ed., *The Twentieth Century: An Almanac* (New York: World Almanac Publications, 1985), p. 121.

24 Rene Fumoleau, *As Long as this Land Shall Last: A History of Treaty 8 and Treaty 11, 1870-1939*, (Toronto: McClelland and Stewart, 1975), pp. 19 and 39.

25 RG 10, vol. 7643, F. 20029-1, pt. 0, "Sarnia Agency...," letter, 6 September 1918, deputy controller to D.C. Scott.

26 RG 10, vol. 7643, F. 20029-1, pt. 0, "Sarnia Agency...," the "Certified copy of a Report of the Commissioner of the Privy Council approved by His Excellency the Governor General on the 19 September 1918," Rodolphe Boudreau, clerk of the Privy Council, to the Hon., the superintendent general, Arthur Meighen. The sole basis for expropriation was Scott's letter. The legislative basis was the *War Measures Act*, but because this was done through order-in-council the expropriation was not discussed in the House of Commons or the Senate. Furthermore, this order-in-council was not published in the *Canada Gazette*.

27 Ferrell, *The Twentieth Century: An Almanac*, p. 125.

28 RG 10, vol. 7645, F. 20040-1, pt. 0 (Walpole Island), letter, 28 October 1918, D.M. Grant for First Nations at Walpole and Sarnia to the superintendent.

29 Enclosure File B-8260-174 (NS), vol. 1E, 13 August 1830, William Jones, assistant superintendent of Indian Affairs and Indian agent at Sarnia and Walpole Island, to Z. Mudge.

30 RG 10, vol. 7645, F. 20040-1, pt. 0 (Walpole Island), letter, 13 November 1918, Kerr and McNevin, barristers and solicitors for Walpole Island First Nation, to the DIA.

31 Nin.Da.Waab.Jig. files, Simpson Brigham Papers, letter, 20 November 1918, Brigham to "My Dear Ogemah," pp. 5 and 7-9.

32 RG 10, vol. 7645, F. 20040-1, pt. 0 (Walpole Island), telegram, 19 November 1918, David Williams, bishop of Huron, and Norman Tucker, president of the Social Services Council of Canada.

33 RG 10, vol. 7645, F. 20040-1, pt. 0 (Walpole Island), letter, 22 November 1918, David Williams, bishop of Huron, to D.C. Scott.

34 Nin.Da.Waab.Jig. files, Simpson Brigham Papers, letter, 20 November 1918, Brigham to "My Dear Ogemah," p. 9.

35 Nin.Da.Waab.Jig. files, Simpson Brigham Papers, letter, November 1918, Margaret Brigham to her mother, p. 5. It is unknown whether these measures were carried out.

36 RG 10, vol. 7645, F. 20040-1, pt. 0 (Walpole Island), memorandum, 26 November 1918, Scott to Meighen.

37 RG 10, vol. 7477, F. 20029-1A, pt. 1, "Sarnia Agency...," letter, 30 August 1918, Scott to Charles A. McGrath, fuel controller for Canada.

38 RG 10, vol. 7645, F. 20040-1, pt. 0 (Walpole Island), letter, 3 December 1918, Scott, deputy superintendent, to David Williams, bishop of Huron. In 1918, section 90 of that *Act* was amended to allow the DIA "to lease lands in the Indian Reserve without the consent of the Indians" (vol. 2641, F. 129690-3A, newspaper article: "Council of Ojibwas Ask for Recognition as a Nation," 7 May 1919). In December of 1919, under order-in-council no. 2523 the DIA amended section 48 of the *Act* so that the superintendent general could "without [a First Nation] surrender . . . issue leases for surface rights of Indian Reserves . . ." (ONAS, "Mining on Indian Lands, 1920-1929," ILF #363, copy of order-in-council in file).

39 RG 10, vol. 7645, F. 20040-1, pt. 0 (Walpole Island), memorandum, 22 November 1918, W.A. Orr, officer in charge, Lands and Timber Branch, to deputy minister.

40 RG 10, vol. 7645, F. 20040-1, pt. 0 (Walpole Island), letter, 17 February 1919, from Dominion Glass to Scott.

41 Nin.Da.Waab.Jig. files, Simpson Brigham Papers, letter, November 1918, Margaret Brigham to her mother, p. 3.

42 See, for example, Sally M. Weaver, *Making Canadian Indian Policy: The Hidden Agenda, 1968-1970* (Toronto: University of Toronto Press, 1981); and Marjane Ambler, *Breaking the Iron Bonds: Indian Control of Energy Development* (Lawrence: University Press of Kansas, 1990).

5

The Reverend Simpson Brigham (1875-1926): The Worlds of Henry Ford and Simpson Brigham Collide

Jim Miller

In 1918, Henry Ford of Detroit went to worship in the little Anglican Church on Walpole Island.[1] Seemingly, he was recognized by no one.[2] A year later he went to the church again and, on this occasion, was recognized by several of the parishioners. During this visit, he introduced himself to Reverend Simpson Brigham, rector of the church, and from this time until Brigham's death in 1926, he and the Native priest were friends. Later Ford gave the priest a car and presented the community with farm implements.[3] Who was this Native Anglican priest whom Ford befriended?

The Walpole Island Reserve includes waters and lands under the water of Lake St. Clair and the St. Clair River. The land portion comprises six islands at the mouth of the St. Clair River some thirty miles south of the city of Sarnia. These lands were inhabited for hundreds of years prior to the coming of the white European, and in all likelihood were used for summer fishing and for hunting in the fall.[4] Well before 1790, some Ojibwa settled on a piece of unsurrendered Indian land at

---

Notes to chapter 5 are on pp. 90-91.

Walpole Island that they had always used.[5] The Ojibwa were partners with the Ottawa and Potawatomi Nations,[6] and these three Nations comprised a political confederacy known as the Council of Three Fires.[7]

These three Nations belonged to the Algonquian linguistic family and they called themselves "Anishinabeg," which means "human beings," or "men par excellence."[8] The Algonquians lived in the Great Lakes region of present-day southern Ontario, and according to some commentators, "relied almost exclusively on hunting and fishing and planted very little."[9] However, other scholars have recently questioned the validity of this last statement.[10]

Permanent settlement led to the coming of the missionaries. The Methodist, Anglican and Roman Catholic missionaries were the most active in the Great Lakes region. One of the first missionaries active in this area was the Reverend Peter Jones, a Mississauga Indian and Methodist missionary.[11]

Jones attempted to establish the Methodist Church on Walpole Island. Peter and his Native helpers first arrived in the community in August of 1829 and met with Pazhekezhikquashkim, who was the spiritual and hereditary political leader of the Ojibwa and Ottawa living on the Island. He informed Jones that he and his people would not change their religion because they could not see where the white man's religion was any better than their own; in fact, he suggested that it was inferior. Jones made two more journeys to Walpole Island, but could not get the old chief to change his mind.[12]

Likewise, in 1844, Father du Ranquet and Brother Jennessaux of the Jesuit Order arrived on the Island. They remained for some five years, but were no more successful than the Methodists had been in establishing a church.[13]

During this early period, the Anglican Church had more success in establishing a church on Walpole Island. In 1842, Reverend James Coleman was working on the Island but he had limited success. In 1845, he was replaced by Reverend Andrew Jamieson, who remained until his death in 1885. Jamieson learned the Native language and was successful in establishing a church.[14] However, he had no success working among the Potawatomi. In 1858, the Methodist Missionary Society was successful in building a church and many persons within the Potawatomi community became Methodist.[15]

Simpson Brigham was born on 9 September 1875, some ten years prior to the death of Reverend Andrew Jamieson. Jamieson baptized Simpson's parents, Ziba and Elizabeth, as well as their six children.[16]

There can be little doubt that Jamieson influenced this family in many ways through his religious instruction. Simpson's brother Benjamin was ordained into the Episcopal priesthood in the United States in 1905.[17] Simpson's early education was similar to that of other Indian children. He attended residential schools—Shingwauk near Sault Ste. Marie and the Mohawk Institute near Brantford. Unlike most Native children, he attended Sarnia Collegiate; he was the first person from Walpole Island to attend Huron College in London, Ontario, where he studied theology.[18] He was ordained a deacon in 1899, the year he was assigned to St. John the Baptist Church on Walpole Island, and on 24 March 1901 at St. Paul's Cathedral in London, Ontario, he was ordained a priest by Bishop Baldwin.

Simpson followed Reverend John Jacobs (who had followed Andrew Jamieson) as the Anglican pastor on the reserve. Jacobs, who was raised on the Rama Reserve and was a protégé of E.F. Wilson, was the first Ojibwa man to be ordained in the Diocese of Huron.[19] Unfortunately, we know little of the relationship between Jacobs and Brigham. Brigham would have been away at residential school for the most of the years that Jacobs was on the reserve, and as a consequence, he probably had little or no contact with Jacobs.

We know little about Simpson's personal life between 1899 and 1917, the year he married Margaret Webb. In all likelihood he lived with his parents whom he would have assisted with the many household chores while carrying out his pastoral duties. Simpson met Margaret's father, Reverend Richard Webb, around the year 1905, when he came to Walpole Island with his wife and children for a holiday. Margaret, some twenty years younger than Simpson, married him on 12 September 1917. The letters that Margaret wrote to her mother until the time of Simpson's death in 1926 indicated a very happy marriage. Simpson showed great concern for his young wife, and when she was pregnant she went to live with her mother in Detroit. Both her children were born in the Henry Ford Hospital.

When Simpson returned to Walpole Island, he was in charge of the same church, St. John the Baptist, where he had been baptized. The church was built in 1872 and consecrated by Bishop Hellmuth in the same year. The first church on the Island, called St. George's, was built in 1845.[20] It was demolished when the present church was built. Simpson could be considered a rector and a pastor rather than a missionary, for the church and the parish were well established when he returned to the Island. On the church grounds was a second building, the parish

hall, which had been built during the ministry of John Jacobs. There was
no rectory. Andrew Jamieson had lived in Algonac, and John Jacobs
lived in Sarnia and commuted to his ministry on the Island. The church
grounds were spacious enough to host the annual agricultural fair. The
parish was debt free and remained so during his ministry.

One can only examine the success of Simpson's work in the church
by examining the Preacher's Books and the various parish registers.
However, it is difficult to make comparisons because there is no similar
source available for study prior to his coming to the Island. From 1899
until the beginning of World War I, attendance at the morning service
often exceeded 100 persons and attendance at the evening service, held
at five o'clock, often exceeded fifty persons. Most walked to church and
only a few came by horse and buggy. Attendance declined during the
Great War; this may have been because some sixty men from Walpole
Island enlisted in the Canadian Army. After the War and until his death
in 1926, the attendance at church services never reached the numbers
achieved in his early ministry.

Simpson Brigham trained persons to assist with the services. His
father became a licensed lay reader. Many of his sermons were in the
Native language and the Preacher's Books show notations when the ser-
mon was in English. During his term on the Island, he prepared almost
300 persons for confirmation and baptized many more. He was interested in the children of the community. He collected old clothes to give
to children in need. He held a special children's service at Christmas,
during which time the children received special food and gifts. He took
an interest in the schooling of the children and the teachers often visited
him at home.

The church was administered in the typical Anglican fashion of the
day. There were two wardens and a Board of Management. Vestry meetings occurred annually and delegates were sent to synod. The church
had a choir and a Sunday School. Most of the financial resources necessary for the parish, including Simpson's stipend, came from the diocese.
The church's most pressing problem during his tenure was building a
rectory. In writing to her mother in 1918, Margaret reported that Simpson's application for a location ticket was approved by the "Band council." Later she reported that the diocese had collected some $3,100 for a
rectory,[21] but that this sum was not sufficient. The rectory was finally
built in 1924 or 1925 and remains the church rectory until this day.
Where the funds came from to build it remains a mystery.

The most critical years in Simpson's ministry occurred after 1917 when he became involved in community affairs. Fortunately, we learn something about these years through the correspondence of his wife's letters to her mother and through Simpson's correspondence with the Ford Motor Company.

In 1918, the Indian Department of the Canadian government dismissed the Indian agent, Thomas McCallum,[22] for reasons that are not known. McCallum had also been the postmaster and, at the time of his dismissal, Simpson became acting postmaster. Shortly thereafter, he hired his father, Ziba, as postal clerk.[23]

The *War Measures Act* of World War I had an effect upon Walpole Island, and Simpson became further involved in the affairs of the community.[24] In writing to her mother on 17 October 1918, some twenty-five days before the signing of the armistice that would end the War, Margaret stated that "the government has commandeered all the oil and gas under the *War Measures Act*." Margaret went on to say that the First Nation citizens were disappointed in themselves for not following her husband's advice to lease the oil and gas rights to an oil company when the opportunity had presented itself. She also stated that Simpson was disappointed that the Council had not followed his advice.[25] If Simpson was discouraged, it did not show. Moreover, it did not prevent him from staying involved with this particular problem. One month after Margaret wrote her letter, Simpson wrote to his mother-in-law and described how he and Elijah Pinnance went to London and then on to Toronto to see Bishop Williams and to solicit his support on behalf of the Walpole Island people. This letter was written after the War was over.

Bishop Williams was attending a meeting of the church's social service council, and he permitted Simpson to speak to the assembly. Simpson told the council that Aboriginal men had enlisted in the army to help defeat the Kaiser. He reminded the council that the War was over and that the Natives held their lands by treaty, and that "surely we ought to be left in peaceful possession of our own remaining lands."[26] Simpson was well received by Bishop Williams and the members of the council, which sent a telegram to Ottawa telling the Department of Indian Affairs not to accept any tenders for oil and gas rights on Walpole Island until a delegation of church and Native peoples met with the government.[27] This incident showed the passion of Simpson and the support he received from the Anglican church in helping to resolve the problem in favour of the inhabitants of the Island. The government had given no reason for pushing this issue at a time when the War was almost over. This issue became still another reason not to trust the federal government.

It appears that Simpson was on the verge of getting involved at the national level when he was elected vice-president of the League of Indians of Canada at a meeting held in Alberta on 29 June 1922.[28] However, it is highly unlikely that he was in attendance at this meeting because the parish records show that he conducted services in the church on the Sundays preceding and following 29 June. As 29 June was a Thursday, it would have been impossible for him to be back to conduct Sunday services on 2 July. Also, Margaret made no mention in her letters about her husband's work at the national level.

It appears that Simpson's relationship with Henry Ford put him into conflict with many members of his community. As stated previously, he had first met Ford in 1918. When Ford went on vacation, he docked his private yacht at Walpole Island and thus he would renew his friendship with the Anglican rector at regular intervals. Perhaps out of kindness and interest, Ford decided to assist the citizens of Simpson's community with their farming activities. During the years 1921 and 1922, the Ford Motor Company donated three tractors, three two-furrow tractor plows, one double disc harrow, one thresher, one ditcher and two power balers. All of this equipment was put under the control of Simpson for use on the Island.[29]

Simpson sent three of his parishioners, William Fisher, Mitchell Pinnance, and his close friend Elijah Pinnance, to the tractor course at Ford's River Rouge Plant to learn how to operate the equipment. When the men returned to the Island, Simpson charged fifty cents an hour when thirty-five cents an hour was the going rate for the use of this equipment. Consequently, some of the Native people came to resent Simpson for the rates that he was charging.[30]

In 1921, Simpson complained about the service from the Ford dealer in Wallaceburg. This prompted the Ford Motor Company of Canada to send M.E. Pritchard to Walpole Island to prepare a report for G.M. McGregor, vice-president and treasurer of Ford Canada. The document was forwarded to Henry Ford's general secretary, E.G. Liebold. Simpson was absent when Pritchard visited the Island for three days in December of 1921. Pritchard reported that "Reverend Brigham is popular among the Indians with whom the writer came in contact." He also reported that some of the Indians thought that Mr. Ford wanted their land in return for his donation of the equipment, and because Ford had given Simpson a car, they believed that Simpson was implicated in some kind of deal with Ford.[31] There can be little doubt that some, if not many, of the Island people now looked upon Simpson with some suspicion. He had become acting postmaster; appointed his father as postal clerk; had accepted a new car from Ford; controlled the use of the farm machinery; hired his own parishioners to operate the machinery; and set the service charge for use of the machinery. In addition to all of this, he had married a white woman from Detroit, perhaps another of the reasons why church attendance declined after the end of the War. Although it had always been important, it was Simpson's contact with Henry Ford that advanced the cause of farming on the Island, and some seventy years later commercial agriculture on the Island remains an unqualified success.

Towards the final months of 1926, Simpson developed a series of health problems. Perhaps he always had a problem with his health. He was a patient at the Sarnia General Hospital from September to November of 1901 with typhoid fever.[32] During his career, he was absent from the parish on several occasions for periods ranging up to six months. We do not know if he was absent for health or for other reasons. Margaret wrote to her mother in October of 1926 to inform her that Simpson had undergone a series of medical tests and that the doctor saw no reason why his upcoming surgery should not be successful. In December, he entered Chatham General Hospital to have his appendix removed, but after surgery he developed peritonitis, which proved to be fatal on 22 December.[33] His funeral was conducted by Archbishop Williams on 24 December and was attended by six other clergy, including his brother-in-law, Reverend Charles Webb. He was buried in Highbanks Cemetery next to his brother, the Reverend Benjamin Brigham.[34]

Looking back on Simpson's life, the question that must be asked is whether or not the acculturation process he went through in his formative years caused him to misread the citizens of his community. He was acculturated at residential schools, at Sarnia Collegiate and at Huron College. He was terribly Anglican! He held memorial services for deceased British monarchs; he had Aboriginal people give money to Huron College; there was the annual collection for the Jews; and there were the mid-week Lenten services. His marriage to a woman from the dominant culture and his close relationship with members of her family furthered the acculturation process as part of his total life experience.

Some persons would claim that today's Aboriginal leaders reward their family members and friends when they assume positions of leadership. Of course, this practice is not unknown among white people. Simpson was not unlike many people in positions of power. When he was appointed acting postmaster, one of his first acts was to hire his father as postal clerk. His father also became a licensed lay reader in the church. In the dispute over oil and gas with the federal Department of Indian Affairs in 1918, it was clear that he was acting as a messenger as his forefathers had done.[35] When it was time to train tractor operators, he sent three prominent parishioners to Detroit for training, and for reasons that are not known, he charged more than the going rate to First Nation farmers wishing to have their fields ploughed. There is little doubt that he was a strong leader and a good organizer. He founded a Farmers Club and divided the Island into three sections; each section had a captain and a trained machine operator.

After his death, the farm machinery was not used and by 1932 it was in a deplorable state.[36] The problem of the ownership of this equipment remained in question for almost twenty years. Initially, Ford had loaned the implements to Walpole Island and placed them under the control of Brigham. In 1932, Margaret Brigham, who had by then married Archie Highfield, the Indian agent, wrote to Ford suggesting the equipment be put under the control of the Reverend Draper, the First Nation Council or the Indian agent, Archie Highfield. An official of the Ford Motor Company replied that they had no further interest in this matter. Perhaps Margaret (Brigham) Highfield wrote to Ford because she did not wish to see the work of her deceased husband disbanded.

Some ten years later, during World War II, Archie Highfield's replacement James W. Daley, wrote to Ford about the ownership of the same equipment and stated that the "machinery is practically of no value." The matter of ownership was, at least in part, resolved in 1942 when the Ford Motor Company informed R.A. Hoey, the director of the Indian Affairs Branch of the federal Department of Mines and Resources, that the First Nation Council may dispose of the farm machinery "in any manner they see fit."[37] Ironically, during World War II the federal Department of Indian Affairs ostensibly intended to confiscate the equipment by bastardizing the metal parts to assist with the Canadian war effort.

However, it was probably Brigham's agricultural policies that led him into conflict with the people. He was not the first Anglican pastor to assist with agriculture. Andrew Jamieson reported that there was very little cultivation when he arrived at Walpole in 1845 because people lived by hunting and fishing. He recorded in his journals that by 1882 the people grew wheat, oats, corn, beans, potatoes, apples and pears. He also recorded that the parish had held an agricultural fair for the past nine years.[38] However, it was likely that most of the First Nation's citizens still supported themselves mainly by hunting, fishing, horticulture and commercial agriculture. The latter was, as it is today, a significant, but nonetheless secondary, industry.

After centuries of contact with the white man, there can be little doubt that the Native people looked upon Ford's gifts of machinery with suspicion. Also, persons who preferred to live by hunting and fishing may well have thought that mechanized farming means would destroy their preferred method of livelihood. While Simpson may have believed that the future of the people lay in agriculture, such a belief was far from unanimous. Even today, the leaders in the community are careful to point out that agriculture does not interfere with the hunting and fishing activities desired by the people.[39]

Perhaps it was these perceptions by his fellow citizens that caused the average Sunday church attendance to decline from a high of 112 in 1903 to an average of seventy-five in 1925. Maybe he was spending too much time on community issues and ignoring his parish. Nevertheless, he remained loyal to Ford and was appreciative of his help. When his mother-in-law made a derogatory statement about Ford, he wrote to her and rebuked her for her remarks.[40] Simpson may have been seduced by the powers of his office of priest. This happens to some clergy regardless of their culture. When he married a white woman, when his children were born in Henry Ford Hospital and when he became a friend of Ford, he further distanced himself from his community.

Simpson came to the Island to be a pastor to his people with all the idealism of a young minister. He was kind and considerate in many ways. People were welcomed into his home; he helped his parents with the ploughing and the harvesting; when his wife was pregnant, he sent her to live with her mother; and he collected clothes for the needy and held a big Christmas party for the children. He died at the young age of fifty-one and what goals he may have had for the parish and the community had he lived longer, we will never know.

This paper is an exploration of the life of the Reverend Simpson Brigham. Much more research needs to be done. Although the issues are complicated and interwoven, a careful study of the life of Simpson Brigham would give people of both the Native and dominant cultures a better understanding of the problems faced by Native leaders today. He was faced with the problem of needing the help of the people from the dominant culture in order to better the material life of his people, and at the same time he had to give his community the perception that he had not gone over to the other side. Not surprisingly, this proved difficult for Simpson to do. Aboriginal leaders in Canada still face the same problem of perception that Simpson faced some seventy years ago.

Notes

1 I wish to thank the following persons who assisted me with this paper: Dean Jacobs, Director of the Heritage Centre on Walpole Island; Dr. Ed Danziger and Dr. David McNab, who made valuable comments; Diana Coates, who provided valuable materials from the Diocese of Huron Archives in London, Ontario; and to Helen Walton for permitting me to read a packet of personal letters that her mother, Margaret Brigham, wrote during the nine years she was married to Simpson. (Some years after the death of her husband, Simpson, Margaret married Archie Highfield who was the Indian agent on Walpole Island at the time of the marriage. Helen Walton was a daughter of this marriage.)

2 See also Dean Jacobs, "'We have but our hearts and the traditions of our old men': Understanding the Traditions and History of Bkejwanong," in David McNab and S. Dale Standen, eds., with an "Introduction," *Gin Das Winan: Documenting Aboriginal History in Ontario*, Occasional Papers of The Champlain Society, no. 2 (Toronto: The Champlain Society, 1996), pp. 9-10.

3 Henry Ford Museum Archives (hereafter HFMA), Greenfield Village, Michigan, correspondence pertaining to Walpole Island, 1921-42.

4 Nin.Da.Waab.Jig., *Walpole Island: The Soul of Indian Territory* (Walpole Island, ON, 1987), pp. 1-3.

5 Ibid., p. 7.

6 Robert F. Bauman, "The Migration of the Ottawa Indians from the Maumee Valley to Walpole Island," *Northwest Quarterly* (1949). The article is based on Bauman's MA thesis, University of Toledo, 1949, and is in the Nin.Da.Waab.Jig. files.

7 Nin.Da.Waab.Jig., *Walpole Island: The Soul of Indian Territory*, p. 7.

8 Donald B. Smith, *Sacred Feathers: The Reverend Peter Jones (Kakewaquonaby) and the Mississauga Indians* (Toronto: University of Toronto Press, 1987), p. 17.

9 Ibid.

10 And see Jacobs, "'We have but our hearts and the traditions of our old men': Understanding the Traditions and History of Bkejwanong," pp. 9-10.

11 Smith, *Sacred Feathers*, p. 97.

12 Ibid., pp. 108-10.

13 Nin.Da.Waab.Jig., *Walpole Island: The Soul of Indian Territory*, pp. 39-40.

14 Ibid., p. 40.

15 Ibid., p. 41.

16 St. John the Baptist Anglican Church, Walpole Island, "Parish Records."

17 Diocese of West Texas, "Journal of the General Convention, 1907."

18 *Chatham Daily News* (Chatham, Ontario), 22 December 1926.

19 David Nock, *A Victorian Missionary and Canadian Indian Policy: Cultural Synthesis vs Cultural Replacement*, Editions SR, vol. 9 (Waterloo, ON: Wilfrid Laurier University Press, 1988), p. 36.

20 St. John the Baptist Anglican Church, "Deed of Consecration."

21 Bishop David Williams to Rachel Haviland, 21 August 1923.

22 Nin.Da.Waab.Jig., *Walpole Island: The Soul of Indian Territory*, p. 123.

23 Margaret Brigham to her mother, Martha Webb, 23 April 1918.

24 For details of this issue see Rhonda Telford's " 'Under the Earth': The Expropriation and Attempted Sale of the Oil and Gas Rights of the Walpole Island First Nation during World War I" in this volume (pp. 65-79).

25 Simpson Brigham to Martha Webb, 17 October 1918.

26 Ibid., 20 November 1918.

27 Ibid.

28 Stan Cuthand, in J.R. Miller, ed., *Sweet Promises: A Reader on Indian-White Relations in Canada* (Toronto: University of Toronto Press, 1991), p. 382.

29 HFMA, M.E. Pritchard's Report on his visit to Walpole Island on 7-9 December 1921.

30 Ibid.

31 Ibid.

32 St. John the Baptist Anglican Church, "Preacher's Book, 1901," notation by Simpson Brigham.

33 *Wallaceburg News*, 30 December 1926.

34 "Preacher's Book, 1926" (Benjamin Brigham, 1878-1910).

35 See also Telford, " 'Under the Earth': The Expropriation and Attempted Sale of the Oil and Gas Rights of the Walpole Island First Nation during World War I" in this volume (pp. 65-79), for Brigham's role as a messenger.

36 HFMA, S.C. Hunking to J.J. Quinn, 2 July 1932.

37 Ibid.

38 Andrew Jamieson to R. Walpole Sealy Vidal, sometime after 19 October 1882 (a copy). Jamieson was the Anglican Rector on Walpole Island from 1845 until his death in 1885.

39 Sheila M. Van Wyck, "Harvests Yet to Reap: History, Identity, and Agriculture in a Canadian Indian Community" (unpublished PhD dissertation, University of Toronto, 1992), p. 337.

40 Simpson Brigham to Martha Webb, 16 March 1918.

Part III

Mi'kma'ki and the Mi'kmaq Nation

6

Mi'kmaq Fishing in the Maritimes: A Historical Overview

Janet E. Chute

Introduction

Riverine fishing has been pursued extensively in the
Atlantic provinces (which includes the present-day provinces of Newfoundland, Nova Scotia, Prince Edward
Island and New Brunswick) for over five thousand years. The most
labour-intensive equipment employed continues to be the stationary fish
weir, made of stone, or wood and brush.[1] Other fishing technologies,
spears, small wood fibre or hemp nets, hooks and gorges, demanded far
less investment in time and energy. Weirs set at tide-heads, or on the
upper reaches of rivers took smelt, gaspereau, salmon and sturgeon, as
well as catadromous eels. Estuarine weirs captured some pelagic as well
as anadromous species (Hoffman 1955: 151-67).

While riverine fishing did not predominate as *the* main economic
activity as it did among many Northwest Coast groups (Cohen 1986), it
occupied as central a place in the annual economic round as any other
major subsistence pursuit. It has been noted repeatedly however that the
Mi'kmaq failed to value fishing as highly as big game hunting; "their
attitude undoubtedly was that anybody could fish, but that only an
individual with power and skill could be a hunter (*ntooksooinoo*)"

Notes to chapter 6 are on pp. 105-106.

(Hoffman 1955: 151) Yet a taboo on roasting eels, and the adoption of a salmon symbol as a group identifier along the Restigouche River, suggest that certain fish species did warrant some symbolic and ceremonial recognition (Denys 1908: 430, 442; LeClercq 1910: 192-93). *Ntook-sooinoo*, moreover, relates to the Mi'kmaq word *netukulimk*, denoting the "natural bounty of the Creator for the self-support and well-being of the individual and community at large," and in no way restricts hunting to terrestrial species alone.[2]

An important item, involving ritual gift giving and barter, fish also developed commercial worth to the Mi'kmaq during the seventeenth century, when Isaac de Razilly set up a trade in salmon at La Have, Nova Scotia, and Nicolas Denys established similar operations in northeastern New Brunswick and Nova Scotia. Commercial incentives likely permeated Mi'kmaq fishing practices at a fairly early date. In the mid-eighteenth century, a Nova Scotian Liverpool merchant continued this trade by sending out a special vessel along the cost for the purpose (Dunfield 1985: 26-27, 49). Around the same time the lieutenant governors of Nova Scotia and Prince Edward Island, Michael Franklin and Samuel Perkins respectively, sought to encourage Native interest in both the riverine and cod fisheries by supplying bands with salt and barrels (CO 1768).

Mi'kmaq involvement in commercial enterprises other than the fur trade has virtually been ignored by ethnohistorians. Yet it should be noted that Native recognition of the benefits of the salmon trade proved sufficiently entrenched by 1786 that Mi'kmaq fears of losing rights to a commercial salmon fishery on the Restigouche River gave rise to a vocal campaign in support of local Native interests (PANB 1860-69).

Throughout the historic era, fishing provided the Mi'kmaq with a range of opportunities. Whether for subsistence or exchange, riverine fishing remained a pursuit that employed wholly Indigenous materials and did not depend for its continuation on articles obtained through European-controlled trade. Unlike hunting and trapping, it provided returns with little loss of autonomy.

Theoretical Consideration

The author realizes that, in emphasizing the importance of Mi'kmaq riverine fisheries, she may be regarded by some as "a voice crying the wilderness," since one riverine model, devised by F.G. Speck (Speck 1922; Speck and Eiseley 1939), has been roundly criticized

(Bourque 1989; Cooper 1946; Leacock 1954; Rogers 1963). Its denouncers hold that to suggest that distinctive riverine economies existed prior to the coming of the Europeans ignores changes wrought by the fur trade, which gradually constricted group activities to limited fur-trapping tracts along riverbanks. Yet the Mi'kmaq homeland is so riddled with rivers, streams, lakes and estuaries that to discern congruencies between ethnic boundaries and riverine topography at any time is truly a formidable and probably impossible task.

Despite involvement in the fur trade, Mi'kmaq organization suggested strong continued reliance on the fisheries. Historically, kinship exhibited a generational bias in the first descending generation, in which siblings and first cousins were treated as equivalents, both terminologically and behaviourally. Coupled with a proscription on first-cousin marriage (Denys 1908: 140; Lescarbot 1914: 165; LeClercq 1910: 237), this system would have heightened solidarity among closely related males when it came to task group activities such as building weirs (McGee 1977).

Although composite in nature, this system permitted the rise of leadership hierarchy. Since weir fishing sea mammal hunting fell to generational task groups, leaders could engage freely in diplomatic and trade activities with neighbouring bands, which increased their status and prestige. Yet one of their key roles, according to cultural ecologist Patricia K. Nietfeld, was to allocate people relative to resources (Nietfeld 1981: 490-92). By applying Nietfeld's leadership model to the riverine as well as to the terrestrial milieu, it seems reasonable to suggest that task groups were assigned to specific fishing locations by the chief, working in conjunction with a council of respected Elders. Nietfeld also stresses that, in return for access rights, chiefly retinues shared portions of their harvest with their leaders. While little definite evidence exists as to how Mi'kmaq leadership regulated relationships between persons and riverine resources, ties of reciprocal interest between leaders and followers likely served to endow chiefly decision making with a sense of stewardship.

Stationary fisheries were always vulnerable to overfishing, and one early French source notes that fish could be found rotting in Mi'kmaq weirs (Lescarbot 1914: 236-38). Yet such occurrences might be attributed far more to a disinclination to harvest and preserve large surpluses in an economy characterized by "steady state abundance" (Burley 1983: 162), than to any penchant for habitual overexploitation. It appears probable that Mi'kmaq social organization and leadership were admirably adapted to the riverine sector of their economy, for while it is difficult to determine how long such social systems existed in the Northeast, remains of large weir complexes dating back over 5,000 years—to the Archaic period—suggest that they were ancient indeed.

The Prehistoric Picture

The climate during the Archaic period, from approximately 5,500 to 2,500 years ago, was warmer than the present (Tuck 1978), and encouraged growth of a pine climax forest that would have produced little browse for big game.[3] Due to this lack of ungulates, seasonal exploitation of anadromous fish runs would have been almost mandatory, as the magnitude of three Archaic fish weir sites gives credence. Two of these—the 5,100-year-old Sebaskong Lake Fish weir in Maine, and the Atherley Narrows site on Lake Simcoe in Ontario, dating around 4500 B.P.—are located where a river descends into a lake (Wixen 1993; Johnson and Cassavory 1978). A third site—the 4,600-year-old Boylston Street Fish weir, discovered in the 1950s and covering many acres in the Boston back harbour area—is the only known example of a northeastern Archaic estuarine weir complex. That these constructions, formed of upright poles interlaced with daub and wattle, were evidently fairly ubiquitous and demanded considerable human labour to build, indicates the presence of very early complex social organizations in the Northeast. Grave goods distributions analyzed from late Archaic mortuary complexes nevertheless suggest that the societies associated with them were predominately egalitarian.[4]

Climatic cooling after 2500 B.P. marked the close of the Archaic period. Mixed woodlands and conifers, conducive to the growth of browse for big game, came to dominate the landscape. About this time several migrant peoples, with new ideas and technologies, arrived from the south and southwest (Allen 1981; Sanger 1987; Snow 1980). One such group, carriers of what has become known as the North Beach tool tradition,[5] may have brought the Algonquian language and the first notions of hierarchy to the Northeast (Denny 1989).

After 2400 B.P. multiple burials, characteristic of the late Archaic, disappeared from the archaeological record, and mound and pit burials, often housing the remains of one or two auspicious personages, appeared (Harper 1956; Hamilton 1867: 180). There is much to indicate that the cultures of these intrusive peoples also exhibited a strong riverine focus. For instance, an Adena-related Middlesex population near present-day Redbank, New Brunswick,[6] established base camps along the middle reaches of the Miramichi River, where salmon and sturgeon fishing would have been major subsistence pursuits (Stewart 1989). It seems that effective fishing strategies and technologies already in use among the late Archaic populations would have been readily adopted by these newcomers.

The warm altithermal around 2000 B.P. extended the range of clam flats—an important alternative food source. Cooling conditions followed, however, which restricted shellfish distribution and prompted greater mobility.[7] Recent views on the probable nature of the economic round by A.D. 1200 emphasize seasonal selection of resources from land and sea drawn from within a "mosaic" of slightly differing regional ecosystems (Burley 1983; Clermont 1986; Nash 1980; Nash and Miller 1987). The vicissitudes of deteriorating climate militated against year-round settlements either on the coast or inland. Semi-sedentary aggregations of dwellings—the "villages" of historic times—existed only for a few months of each year.

Trade nevertheless remained an important facet of proto-Mi'kmaq life.[8] Fish may have been an important local item of barter, in addition to "luxury" goods, such as copper, chert and *Busycon* shell beads (Bourque and Whitehead 1985). Three sites occupied for over 1,000 years, and considered to have been major trade centres, Redbank in New Brunswick, and Melanson and Indian Gardens in west central Nova Scotia, all lie along major fishing rivers (Erskine 1957: 5-7; Nash 1990). Distribution of these sites strongly suggests that trade, and religious and political ceremonies, may have been mainly spring and fall events, linked to anadromous fish runs. It is even possible that a reorientation of trade away from nearshore and inland centres to the coast only occurred after the coming of European trade.[9]

This is a contentious assertion however, since a view prevails that the proto-Mi'kmaq were primarily a coastal people and that the first incentives for penetrating the interior only accompanied the historic fur trade (Hoffman 1995; Snow 1980: 303). Yet prehistoric stone fish weirs on the upper Mersey and Tusket Rivers in southwestern Nova Scotia, and the middle Shubenacadie River system, attest that anadromous fishing occurred far above the tideheads long before the coming of Europeans (Erskine 1957; Ferguson 1986; Preston 1974). Such sites also indicate that large aggregations resided in the interior, and not just the small dispersed hunting groups of about twenty-five people associated with late historic times. As a peninsula, Nova Scotia has the unique character of being traversed by navigable rivers and streams. An interior centre such as Indian Gardens thus would have constituted not so much a distant retreat, but also a stopping place en route from one place to another. Evidently in many areas large groups stayed together at these inland base camps well into the fall, smoking and drying eels for the winter, before dispersing out onto winter hunting grounds when ice sealed the rivers and crusty snow facilitated tracking game.[10]

In keeping with prevailing models that emphasize regional resource diversity, it is stressed that not all bands followed a similar annual migration pattern. For instance, Mi'kmaq along the Northumberland Strait preserved eels for a midwinter departure to the Magdalenes to hunt sea mammals (Martijn 1989). Yet French missionaries and military personnel recognized the crucial nature of anadromous fish runs to Mi'kmaq subsistence everywhere, and tried not to interfere in this facet of the Aboriginal population's economy. Missions were always set up at traditional fishing sites and, during the early eighteenth century, campaigns against New England, which demanded Native assistance, were even timed so as not to clash with the fall fishing (Webster 1934: 69). The upper echelons of the Mi'kmaq hierarchy, by contrast, evidently had little to do with fishery matters during much of the early historic era, although this was to change with time. Bands periodically came together under a single headman, designated to speak on behalf of all. Later, and especially following the formal system of Native-French interrelationships instigated by the French at Louisbourg after 1720, a three-tiered rank order of chiefs emerged; band chiefs, often called "captains" in the historic literature, district chiefs—who represented a number of band chiefs at Grand Council gatherings—and, finally, a national leader of the Mi'kmaq nation, known as the grand chief (Hoffman 1955; Miller 1983). Concerns of the grand chief and Council focused on politics, war and diplomacy. By contrast, local bands and their leaders tended to follow their own economic practices, depending on the nature of the local environment in which they resided.

The Historic Era—Evidence from Field Work and Oral Tradition

It is possible to access some of the ancient weir sites, and legends still abound regarding these locales. During the summer of 1993 and the spring of 1994 I toured Native-constructed stone weirs, called "flume weirs," on the upper Tusket River and adjoining Quinan River in southwestern Nova Scotia. At least nine stone weirs protruded downstream in successive V-formations along the river course I examined. At first I speculated that each stone weir constituted a family-controlled site, similar to the individualized fur hunting territory on a much smaller scale. I was disabused of this idea, however, when I was shown the location of a historic Mi'kmaq base camp, known in Acadian parlance as the "cabano," lying back from the river. Presumably the local headman would have had a say in allocating the weir sites among weir-building groups. On speaking with a local Acadian biologist associated with St. Anne's College and a Mi'kmaq man whose ancestors used to fish in the area (Dr. Sylvestre Muise and Mr. Thomas Robinson, personal communication 1993), I determined that the weirs had not been fished by Mi'kmaq exclusively since the late eighteenth century. Oral traditions relate that pressures of colonial warfare and European coastal settlement made interior locations such as Quinan increasingly important as time progressed.[11] Local historians also hold that the Quinan weir sites became refuge areas for Acadians with Mi'kmaq kin, who were fleeing removal by the British in the mid-eighteenth century.

The Late Historic Era

While there may have been some limited competition between Acadians and Mi'kmaq over certain fishery sites (Nash 1990: 6), no outright confrontations of this nature have ever been recorded (Clark 1968: 67-70). Acadian settlements had not allocated exclusive rights to coastal and estuarine locations in the same manner as the British by 1758 (Calnek 1897: 175; 217-19; Knox 1914: 130). After the Acadians had been deported and British settlement had progressed apace, the seat of colonial government at Whitehall relinquished all ideas of reserving hunting and fishing tracts for the Native population's exclusive use. Instead, a concerted plan was laid to overwhelm the Mi'kmaq numerically by establishing British settlements near former French coastal trading sites and to bring the fur trade through a centralized truckhouse system. Between 1771 and 1783 a number of licences of occupation granted chiefs and their bands vague rights in specific areas to hunt and fish alongside white settlers, but none of these granted the Native people any protection should competition with whites arise on the fishing grounds (PANS 1771; PANS 1784-1830).

A telling indicator of the priority Native peoples have placed on maintaining access to riverine fisheries can be seen in the nature of their petitions sent to government by Native individuals during the late eighteenth and early nineteenth centuries. In recalling their reasons for petitioning for land along the Gold River in Nova Scotia, John Penall Agomartin and Penall's son-in-law, Thomas Hammond, stressed the abundance of salmon they had encountered there during one of their hunting trips (PANS, n.d.). Likewise, members of the Cape Sable Band claimed that Eel Creek in southwestern Nova Scotia retained special importance for them,[12] since it was major eel fishing station and lay near a traditional burying ground (PANS 1823).

White settlers frequently requested government to allow them to attain tracts, previously acquired by the Mi'kmaq by Crown grant or special orders-in-council. And the government often acquiesced, especially if such lands were used for fishing and hunting, but were not farmed. Twenty thousand acres granted the Mi'kmaq in 1783 along both sides of the Miramichi River in New Brunswick, containing sites along its course suitable for salmon, sturgeon and eel fishing, were reduced in this way to almost one seventh of its original size less than ten years later (PANB 1783-1805).

In the absence of government protection, pressures on chiefs to alienate lands along rivers must have been tremendous. For instance, land at Pugwash on the Northumberland Strait was sold to pay trader debts (PANS 1815; PANS 1820). Meanwhile, at East River, near Chester, Nova Scotia, the chief was induced while intoxicated to alienate his fishing grounds without his band's consent (PANS 1842). Chief Andrew of Richibucto wrote the lieutenant governor of New Brunswick, Thomas Carleton, that a man salmon poaching on Mi'kmaq land threatened "to shoot the first Indian that shall attempt to fish in the river" (PANB n.d.). Oral traditions gleaned from elderly residents of the Sambro and Prospect areas near Halifax told of similar clashes between Mi'kmaq and non-Native fishermen competing over good riverine salmon and gaspereau fishing locations (interviews at Prospect, Nova Scotia 1993).

By 1840 lumbering and mining interests seriously encroached on remaining traditional Native fisheries, especially at lower riverine locations. Unannounced log drives crashed through weirs and sunk nets (PANS 1853b). White fishers, furthermore, acquired exclusive rights to set fixed seines across river mouths, and fish populations upstream dropped radically.[13]

As long as these operations remained restricted to the lower courses of rivers, the Mi'kmaq pursued a new strategy—one that departed from earlier economic and social practices. In the past the interior had only been seasonally occupied; now it was expected to offer a tenuous year-round existence, when enhanced by limited crop growing. Small family groups in many areas began to push up towards the headwaters of river systems they already knew well and press for grants to small interior tracts where fishing could be supplemented by farming, guiding, logging and the manufacture of baskets and wooden items for sale. For instance, Joseph Penall, a son of John Penall Agomartin, requested land on Wallabuck Lake, near the headwaters of the Gold River, when the Native economy failed downstream (NAC 1857-74). The enterprising Penall band had formerly developed a Native-controlled angling outfit on the Gold River, but this had ended by the 1860s, owing to the activities of mining and logging interests. In response, the group had split into small nuclear family segments and moved to other locations.

Mi'kmaq who remained near the coast also faced problems. Between 1786 and the passage of the federal *Fishery Act* of 1878, which entirely outlawed spear fishing, various fishing regulations were implemented in the name of conservation, more to prevent abuses by whites than Natives, although the restrictions applied equally to both groups (Dunfield 1985: 62). Why "take even this little thing from us [?]" Peter Paul of Shubenacadie lamented (PANS 1853a). Not surprisingly, many Mi'kmaq felt like scapegoats in malaises they had done little, or nothing at all, to create (NAC 1875; 1876).

The historic era of traditional Native fishing appeared to have ended during World War I when many young Mi'kmaq men, who otherwise might have been seasonally engaged in the fishery, went overseas. In 1918 H.J. Bury, a timber inspector, visited reserves in Nova Scotia and found that many tracts were only occupied sporadically (Patterson 1985: 21). These, Bury maintained, might better be alienated to logging and sport fishing enterprises, or reserved as some sort of parkland, than retained for their owners, the Aboriginal inhabitants. Mi'kmaq from Nova Scotia and Prince Edward Island instead were to be encouraged to move to growth centres under an ambitious centralization policy. For the Native people involved, if the policy had been effectively implemented and enforced, this would have been a social and economic catastrophe.

In the end, it failed. However, in spite of the attempted implementation of the centralization scheme in the early 1940s, a history of 5,000 years of specialized Indigenous fishing practices, technologies and social organizational forms prevailed.[14] In 1923, when novelist Clara Dennis interviewed Jeremiah Bartlett Alexis, alias "Jerry Lone Cloud," the Mi'kmaq man from the Tusket River area not only could tell her of fishing camps, but also of an animated symbolic landscape replete with natural and spiritual entities. Yet, at the same time, his narrations were filled with reminiscence, for those from whom he had learned his stories had died, or had moved elsewhere (PANS 1923). Ironically, it was at this seeming nadir in Mi'kmaq history that the modern campaign for Mi'kmaq fishing rights gained its initial momentum.

A Brief Afterword

The modern struggle for Mi'kmaq Treaty fishing rights is guided and impelled by successive legal interpretations according to a 1752 Treaty of Peace and Friendship between the British and Mi'kmaq. As presently upheld by the Grand Council of Micmacs, the Union of Nova Scotia Indians and the Native Council of Nova Scotia, this treaty asserts that the Aboriginal inhabitants possess unextinguished rights to hunt and fish over most of the Maritimes, provided such activities are in keeping with special Mi'kmaq hunting and fishing guidelines.

One of the earliest tests for the existence of such rights occurred in 1927, when William Labrador of Bridgetown, Nova Scotia, pleaded not guilty, under the terms of the 1752 Treaty, to taking salmon out of season (Nova Scotia Museum 1927). Labrador lost his case, but successive court decisions, such as the Simon case, and one of the most recent pertaining exclusively to Mi'kmaq fisheries, *Denny v. Regina*, have proven the 1752 treaty terms to have considerable legal weight. In 1990 the now-famous *Sparrow* decision tended to restrict the scope of Aboriginal fishing rights to the spheres of subsistence and ceremonial use (D.L.R. 1990). Yet the historical participation of Maritime Native peoples in the commercial fishery is now under in-depth consideration, not only for its impact in legal terms, but also for its possible consequences for the development of uniquely Native-inspired conservation and management schemes. In an attempt to gain government acknowledgement of the responsible manner in which Mi'kmaq can conduct their own exclusively Mi'kmaq-managed fisheries, the Micmac Grand Council staged a special angling event in the Margaree River, Cape Breton, Nova Scotia, in conjunction with three bands, in defiance of joint provincial-federal fisheries regulations (*Micmac-Maliseet Nations News* 1993). This event, and others of the same nature, cannot be viewed as elaborations of one distinct sector of the Mi'kmaq traditional economy. Rather they continue as forays into the realm of Aboriginal rights, as defined by the Mi'kmaq Grand Council, other leading Mi'kmaq political organizations, and the outcomes of successive court decisions. In the final analysis, Canadian judges will have to make a major effort to understand the importance of traditional social organizational forms, values and technologies to the long-standing Aboriginal fisheries of the Maritime provinces. New and path-breaking strategies for modern Native fisheries management and development will then have a strong and sure foundation.

Notes

1 Large semicircular pole and brush weirs, with hinged doors which opened to admit fish but closed when the water level receded, were made by the Mi'kmaq who may have followed ancient prototypes (Dunfield 1985: 15-17; Rostlund 1952: 169-73; Wallis and Wallis 1955: 28). Weirs historically remained in use during the spring, summer and fall. Stone weirs often exhibited a V-shape across the stream, with the point of the V extending either upstream or downstream, depending on the direction of the seasonal migrations. A box-like bark trap or net nag set in a gap in the weir's fence captured the fish. In estuaries, regional variations in climate and fish availability affected the annual duration of weirs fishing, although in the Bay of Fundy region, during years of minimal ice conditions, weirs might have continued to take fish all year round. By contrast, riverine weirs located near spawning grounds were worked extensively only on a limited seasonal basis, mostly in the spring and fall.

2 "Mi'kmaq Interim Hunting Guidelines," in Patterson 1987: 14-15. It is also interesting that Abbé Pierre Maillard tells of a Mi'kmaq revitalization ceremony which apparently was held at the height of the first spring anadromous fish runs (Maillard 1863).

3 Warm climatic conditions also extended the range of swordfish farther north than at any other time in history. In response, a specialized sea mammal hunting complex arose along the northeastern Atlantic coast, which James A. Tuck considers diagnostic of the economy of a culture he terms the "Maritime Archaic" (Tuck 1978).

4 Distribution of grave goods in Archaic multiple burial sites, such as Port au Choix, Newfoundland, nevertheless suggest that northeastern Archaic society was egalitarian.

5 This tradition is characterized archaeologically by "Rossville-Lagoon" bipoints as diagnostic artifacts. Peoples of the North Beach tradition may have taught resident populations to exploit the quahogs and soft-shelled clams that grew abundant due to warm temperatures and the inundation of vast esturial clam flats as the sea level rose. In areas of the Gulf of Maine,

semi-sedentary village populations remained on the coast most of the year, where residents subsisted on shellfish during an era when lack of winter icing made access to clam beds possible all year long (Sanger 1987).

6 Around 2400 B.P., the Adena-related Middlesex mound builders undoubtedly retained a perspective on hierarchy similar to the Ohio Valley culture from which they sprang, and with whom they kept in regular trade contact (Allen 1981; Turnbull 1976).

7 In response, Maritimes populations began to favour the manufacture of bark containers over heavier pottery vessels, and adopted the snowshoe, toboggan and bark canoe for transportation.

8 Cherts from the North Mountain in Nova Scotia appear ubiquitously on late Woodland sites throughout the Maritimes and into Maine, which suggest frequent intertribal trade over wide areas.

9 The only coastal site of this nature excavated so far is the Delorey Island site, off northeastern Nova Scotia (Nash and Miller 1987; Stewart 1989). The rest are interior or near-shore sites. It is possible that leaders, well versed in trade tactics on behalf of their bands, arose before the coming of Europeans to their shores. With the onset of the European trade proper, use of specific coastal sites, known since prehistoric times, may have intensified, especially when Mi'kmaq and Malecite middlemen procured European shallops to extend the range of their coastal trade (McFeat 1989; Nietfeld 1981: 495; Bourque and Whitehead 1985).

10 The Gaspereau Lake and Kennetcook River regions—located near the ancient Melanson site—supported entire local band populations well into the eighteenth century and continued to be used as meeting places as readily as coastal sites (Hind 1889: 32; NAC 1783-97: 1069).

11 One effect of the fur trade on fishing may have been that, as beaver dams declined in numbers, the extent of unrestricted spawning grounds grew proportionately, and, in consequence, salmon numbers at upriver sites actually may have increased during the fur-trade era (Dunfield 1985: 19).

12 Bill Wicken has examined the Mi'kmaq land question in southwestern Nova Scotia in considerable depth (Wicken 1991: 113-22). Members of the Alexis family, who acted as spokespeople for the Cape Sable Band, tried repeatedly to attain, but ultimately failed to secure, land near Eel Creek.

13 Advancement in preserving fish, such as canning and, later, fast freezing, enabled a far greater export trade than heretofore in salmon, and hence encouraged overfishing in what had become an extremely profitable enterprise.

14 Centralization was essentially a failure. By the 1950s many Mi'kmaq, who in 1941 had been removed to two designated growth centres at Shubenacadie and Eskasoni, returned to their former communities or moved to cities.

References

Allen, Patricia
  1981   "The Oxbow Site: An Archaeological Framework for Northeastern New
    Brunswick." In D.M. Shimabuku, ed., *Proceedings of the 1980 Conference
    on the Future of Archaeology in the Maritime Provinces*, pp. 132-46.
    Occasional Papers in Anthropology, no. 8. Department of Anthropology,
    St. Mary's University, Halifax, NS.
Bourque, Bruce J.
  1989   "Ethnicity in the Maritime Peninsula, 1600-1759." *Ethnohistory*, 36,
    3: 257-84.
Bourque, Bruce J., and Ruth H. Whitehead
  1985   "Tarrentines and the Introduction of European Trade Goods in the
    Gulf of Maine." *Ethnohistory*, 32, 4: 327-41.
Burley, David
  1983   "Cultural Complexity and Evolution in the Development of Coastal
    Adaptations Among the Micmac and Coast Salish." In Ronald J. Nash, ed.,
    Evolution of Maritime Cultures on the Northeast and Northwest, pp. 157-
    72. Burnaby, BC: Department of Archaeology, Simon Fraser University.
Calnek, W.A.
  1897   *History of the County of Annapolis*. Toronto: Briggs.
Clark, Andrew Hill
  1968   *Acadia: The Geography of Early Nova Scotia to 1760*. Madison, WI:
    University of Wisconsin Press.
Clermont, Norman
  1986   "L'adaption maritime au pays des Micmacs." In Charles A. Martijn,
    ed., *Les Micmacs et la mer*, pp. 11-27. Montreal: Recherches amerin-
    diennes au Quebec.
CO (= Records of the British Colonial Office)
  1768   Michael Franklin to the Earl of Hillsborough, 20 July 1768, regarding
    a circular letter. CO 217/45/161-64.
  1808   George Monk to Sir George Prevost, 23 April 1808. CO 217/82/202-205.
    Microfilm copies of CO 217 are housed in the Public Archives of Nova
    Scotia, Halifax.
Cohen, Faye
  1986   *Treaties on Trial: The Continuing Controversy over Northwest Indian
    Fishing Rights*. Seattle and London: University of Washington Press.
Cooper, John M.
  1946   "The Culture of the Northeastern Indian Hunters." *Papers of the R.S.
    Peabody Foundation for Archaeology*, vol. 3, pp. 272-305.
Dennys, J. Peter
  1989   "Some Algonquian Connections to Salishan and Northeastern Archae-
    ology." In William Cowan, ed., *Actes du vingtième congrès des algon-
    quinistes*, pp. 86-107. Ottawa: Carleton University.

Denys, Nicolas
    1908   *The Description and Natural History of the Coasts of North America
          (Acadia).* 2 vols. Edited and translated by W.F. Ganong. Toronto: The
          Champlain Society.
D.L.R. (= Dominion Law Reports)
    1990   *Regina v. Sparrow,* 70 D.L.R. (4th) 385. Supreme Court of Canada,
          31 May 1990.
Dunfield, R.W.
    1985   *The Atlantic Salmon in the History of North America.* Ottawa: Depart-
          ment of Fisheries and Oceans.
Eales, J.G.
    1966   *A Survey of Eel Fishing in the Maritime Provinces.* Ottawa. Department
          of Fisheries, Industrial Development Service.
Erskine, John
    1957   "Micmac Notes: A Record of a Summer's Archaeological Survey and
          Sampling of Nine Prehistoric Camp-sites in Southwestern Nova Scotia."
          On file at the Nova Scotia Museum, Halifax.
Ferguson, Robert
    1986   "Archaeological Sites in Kejimkujik National Park, Nova Scotia."
          Manuscript on file, Parks Canada, Halifax.
Hamilton, Charles S.
    1867   "A History of King's County." Akin Historical Prize Essay, 1867.
          King's College Library, Halifax.
Harper, J. Russell
    1956   "Two Seventeenth Century Micmac 'Copper Kettle Burials.'" In the
          Appendix to *Portland Point: Crossroads of New Brunswick History.* His-
          torical Studies, no. 9. Saint John, NB: New Brunswick Museum.
Helin, Calvin
    1993   "Ontario Court Finds Right to Sell Aboriginally Caught Fish for Com-
          mercial Purposes." *Micmac-Maliseet Nations News* (December), p. 16.
Hind, Henry Youle
    1889   *An Early History of Windsor, Nova Scotia.* Printed by James J. Anslow
          at the *Hants Journal* office.
Hoffman, Bernard G.
    1955   "Historical Ethnography of the Micmac of the Sixteenth and Seven-
          teenth Centuries." Unpublished PhD dissertation, University of Califor-
          nia, Berkeley.
Interviews at Prospect, Nova Scotia
    1993   See "Acknowledgements."
Johnson, Frederick
    1942   "The Boylston Street Fishweir." *Papers of the R.S. Peabody Foundation
          for Archaeology,* vol. 2.
    _____ , ed.
    1949   "The Boylston Street Fishweir II." *Papers of the R.S. Peabody Founda-
          tion for Archaeology,* vol. 4, no. 1.

Johnston, Richard B., and Kenneth A. Cassavoy
  1978 "The fishweirs at Atherley Narrows, Ontario." *American Antiquity*, 43, 4: 697-709.
Knox, John
  1914 *The Journals of Captain John Knox*. Vol. 1. Edited by A.G. Doughty. Toronto: The Champlain Society.
Leacock, Eleanor
  1954 "The Montagnais 'Hunting Territory' and the Fur Trade." *American Anthropologist*, 56, 5, Memoir, no. 78.
LeClercq, Chretien
  1910 *New Relations of Gaspesia*. Edited by W.F. Ganong. Toronto: The Champlain Society,
Lescarbot, Marc
  1914 *History of New France*. Vol. 3, Book V. Translated by W.L. Grant. Toronto: The Champlain Society.
Lister, Kenneth R.
  1993 " 'A Most Abundant Weir': Fish Trap-Weirs, Adaptative Strategies, and the Hudson Bay Lowland." In William Cowan, ed., *Papers of the Twenty-Fourth Algonquian Conference*. Ottawa: Carleton University Press.
Maillard, Abbé Pierre
  1863 "Lettre à Madame de Drucourt." In H. Casgrain, ed., *Les Soirees Canadiennes*, pp. 291-426. Quebec: Brousseau Frères.
Martijn, Charles A.
  1989 "A Micmac Domain of Islands." In William Cowan, ed., *Actes du ving-tième congrès des algonquinistes*, pp. 208-31. Ottawa: Carleton University.
McFeat, Tom
  1989 "Rise and Fall of the Big Men of the Northeast: Maliseet Transforma-tions." In William Cowan, ed., *Actes du vingtième congrès des algon-quinistes*, pp. 232-49. Ottawa: Carleton University.
McGee, Harold F.
  1977 "The Case for Micmac Demes." In William Cowan, ed., *Actes du hui-tième congrès des algonquinistes*, pp. 107-14. Ottawa: Carleton University.
Micmac-Maliseet Nations News
  1993 "Mi'kmaq Conduct Atlantic Salmon Harvest." *Micmac-Maliseet Nations News* (November), pp. 12-13.
Miller, Virginia P.
  1976 "Aboriginal Micmac Population: A Review of the Evidence." *Ethnohis-tory*, 23, 2: 117-27.
  1982 "The Decline of the Nova Scotia Micmac Population, A.D. 1600-1850." *Culture*, 2, 3: 107-20.
  1983 "Social and Political Complexity on the East Coast: The Micmac Case." In Ronald J. Nash, ed., *Evolution of Maritime Cultures on the Northeast and Northwest*, pp. 41-55. Burnaby, BC: Department of Archaeology, Simon Fraser University.

Morris, Charles
    1905   "Description and State of the New England Settlements in Nova Scotia
        in 1761, by Charles Morris." In *Report of the Canadian Archives*, Ses-
        sional Paper, no. 18, pp. 291-92.
NAC (= National Archives of Canada)
    1783-97   George Monk's Letter Book, Indian Affairs. In Monk Papers, vol. 4,
        MG 23-G II, p. 1069. On microfilm.
    1849   See also NAC, RG 10, vol. 461, folder 2, doc. #9.
    1857-74   Accounts, petitions and returns. NAC, RG 10, vol. 459,
        package #3 (Lunenburg). See also NAC, RG 10, vol. 2130, file 25584.
    1875   John Mowat to the Honourable David Laird, 25 December 1875.
        NAC, RG 10, vol. 1978, file 5967/01.
    1876   John Barnaby and Alex Marshal to Lawrence Vankoughnet, 4 June
        1876. NAC, RG 10, vol. 1978, file 5967/01.
Nash, Ronald A.
    1980   "Research Strategies, Economic Patterns and Eastern Nova Scotia Pre-
        history." In D.M. Shimabuku, ed., *Proceedings of the 1980 Conference on
        the Future of Archaeology in the Maritime Provinces*, pp. 23-41. Occa-
        sional Papers in Anthropology, no. 8. Department of Anthropology, St.
        Mary's University, Halifax.
    1990   "Melanson: A Large Micmac Village in Kings County, Nova Scotia,"
        Curatorial Report, no. 67, Nova Scotia Museum, Halifax.
    _____, and Virginia P. Miller
    1987   "Model Building in the Case of the Micmac Economy." *Man in the
        Northeast*, 34: 41-56.
Nietfeld, Patricia K.
    1981   "Determinants of Aboriginal Micmac Political Structure." Unpublished
        PhD dissertation, University of New Mexico, Albuquerque.
Nova Scotia Museum
    1927   Rights of Indians. Letter from Ward Fisher to the Honourable W.L.
        Hall, Department of Marine and Fisheries, 10 February 1927. Typescript
        on file, Nova Scotia Museum, Halifax.
PANB (= Provincial Archives of New Brunswick)
    1783-1805   Regarding license of occupation on Miramichi River given by
        John Parr, captain general and governor-in-chief, to Chief John Julien
        concerning land on the Little Southwest River and the northwest branch
        of the Miramichi on 13 August 1783. PANB, RG 1, RS 345. Records of
        Lieutenant Governor Colebrooke, microfilm reel F-8872.
    1848   Report of Moses Perley to the House of Assembly, 3 April 1848.
        PANB, RG 1, RS 345, microfilm reel F-8872.
    1860-69   Documents relating to the Restigouche mission community. In
        William Spragge's correspondence, reports and enclosures, 1860-69.
        PANB, RG 10, RS 105, microfilm reel F-8875. Includes a copy of a
        report from the Restigouche New Mission by Nicholas Cox, lieutenant
        governor, and John Collins, deputy surveyor general, 29 June 1786.

N.d. (ca. 1784-85?) Letter from Chief Matthew Andrew of Richibucto to Lieutenant Governor Thomas Carleton, no date. PANB, RG 3, RS 557/A. Records of Indian Affairs, microfilm reel F-8874.

PANS (= Public Archives of Nova Scotia)

1771, 1783-84 License of Occupation to Francis Alexis, 22 June 1771. PANS, RG 1, vol. 128, p. 155. Licenses of Occupation to Mi'kmaq chiefs, 1783-84. PANS, RG 1, vol. 430, #23½.

1784-1830 Mi'kmaq land petitions for Nova Scotia lands are contained in PANS, RG 20, Series A. Two Cape Breton petitions are found in PANS, RG 20, Series B, vol. 3, documents #563 and #550.

1800 Copy of a letter from the Committee of His Majesty's Council House of Assembly to Edward Irish and Timothy W. Hierlicky, agents and distributors at Antigonish, Sydney County, Nova Scotia, 10 December 1800. PANS, RG 1, vol. 430, document #34.

1801 *Sketches of the Eastern and Northern Parts of the Province in the Years 1801 and 1802.* By Titus Smith. 3rd ed. Halifax, 1851, pp. 131-32. PANS, RG 1, vol. 380/A.

1815 Charles Morris to Henry Cogswell, 7 March 1815. PANS, RG 1, vol. 430, document #151.

1820 Minutes of Council, 22 December 1819 and 8 May 1820. PANS, RG 3, vol. 214½A, pp. 92, 136-39.

1823 Petition of John Baptiste Elexey to Sir James Kempt for land twenty miles from salt water up the Tusket River, 6 May 1823. PANS, RG 20, Series A, vol. 88, no. 61.

1842 Western Tour, 1842. In "Letters, Memoranda of Items of Importance, Plans and Descriptions of Indian Reserves etc., November 1841 to June 21, 1843." Joseph Howe, commissioner of Indian Affairs for Nova Scotia. PANS, RG 1, vol. 432.

1853a Petition of Peter Paul. PANS, RG 5, vol. 46, series P, document #202. On microfilm.

1853b A. Hendry to the Attorney-General, 9 October 1853. PANS, RG 1, vol. 431, document #65. W. Chearnley to Messrs. Webber and Co., 25 July 1853. PANS, RG 1, vol. 431, document #72.

1923 Clara Dennis Archives. Notebook IV. PANS, MG 1, vol. 2867.

N.d. The name "Hammond (Indians)." Cannon Harris Notes. PANS, MG 4, vol. 98, "G-H," #14.

Patterson, Lisa Lynne

1985 "Indian Affairs and the Nova Scotia Centralization Policy." Unpublished MA dissertation, Dalhousie University, Halifax.

————, ed.

1987 *The Mi'kmaq Treaty Handbook.* Sydney and Truro, NS: Grand Council of Micmacs, the Union of Nova Scotia Indians and the Native Council of Nova Scotia.

Preston, Brian

1974 *Excavations at a Complex of Prehistoric Sites along the Upper Reaches of the Shubenacadie River, 1971.* Curatorial Report, no. 19, Nova Scotia Museum, Halifax.

Rogers, Edward S.
  1963   "The Hunting Group-Hunting Territory Complex Among the Mis-
         tassini Indians." Anthropological Series 63, National Museum of Canada
         Bulletin 195. Ottawa.
Rostlund, Erhart
  1952   "Freshwater Fish and Fishing in Native North America." *University of
         California Publications in Geography*, vol. 9. Berkeley, CA.
Sanger, David
  1987   *The Carson Site and the Late Ceramic Period in Passamaquoddy Bay,
         New Brunswick*. National Museum of Man, Mercury Series. Archaeo-
         logical Survey of Canada Paper, no. 135. Ottawa: Canadian Museum of
         Civilization.
Scott, W.B., and M.G. Scott
  1988   *Atlantic Fishes of Canada*. Toronto: University of Toronto Press in co-
         operation with the Minister of Fisheries and Oceans and the Canadian
         Government Publishing Centre.
Snow, Dean R.
  1980   *The Archaeology of New England*. New York: Academic Press.
Speck, F.G.
  1922   *Beothuk and Micmac*. Indian Notes and Monographs, misc. series
         no. 22. New York: Museum of the American Indian, Heye Foundation.
  _____, and L.C. Eiseley
  1939   "Significance of Hunting Territory Systems of the Algonkian in Social
         Theory." *American Anthropologist*, 42: 260-80.
Stewart, Frances L.
  1989   "Seasonal Movements of Indians in Acadia as Evidenced by Historical
         Documents and Vertebrate Faunal Remains from Archaeological Sites."
         Man in the Northeast, 38: 55-77.
Tuck, James A.
  1978   "Regional Cultural Development, 3000 to 300 B.C." In Bruce Trigger,
         ed., *Handbook of North American Indians*, vol. 15. Washington, DC:
         Smithsonian Institution.
Turnbull, C.J.
  1976   "The Augustine Site: A Mound for the Maritimes." *Archaeology of
         Eastern North America*, 4: 50-63.
Webster, John C., ed.
  1934   *Acadia at the End of the Seventeenth Century: Letters, Journals and
         Memoirs of Joseph Robineau de Villebon, Commandant in Acadia,
         1690-1700*. Monograph Series, no. 1. St. John, NB: New Brunswick
         Museum.
Wicken, Bill
  1991   "Mi'kmaq Land in Southwestern Nova Scotia, 1771-1823." In
         Margaret Conrad, ed., *Making Adjustments, Change and Continuity in
         Planter Nova Scotia, 1759-1800*. Fredericton, NB: Acadiensis Press.

Wilson, D., and Ruth Sawtell Wallis
  1955 *The Micmac Indians of Eastern Canada.* Minneapolis: University of Minnesota Press.
Wintemberg, W.J., and H.I. Smith
  1929 "Some Shell-Heaps in Nova Scotia." Bulletin 47, Anthropological Series, no. 9. Ottawa: Department of Mines, National Museum of Canada.
Wixen, Jennifer
  1993 "Early Archaic Smarts." *Archaeology* (July/August), p. 21.

7

"We Cannot Work Without Food": Nova Scotia Indian Policy and Mi'kmaq Agriculture, 1783-1867

Theresa Redmond

While many Algonkian First Nations supplemented their economy by farming in the late nineteenth century, the Mi'kmaq of Nova Scotia had become a people who fished and made and sold crafts to residents and tourists. These activities supplemented their traditional economy obtained through hunting, fishing and gathering.[1] The literature on the Mi'kmaq has focused on these interactions with settlers, largely ignoring their other adaptations. Although many Mi'kmaq had expanded their use of gardens into European-style farms as Euramerican settlement increased after 1800, their agriculture had peaked by the mid-nineteenth century. Their disappearance from the land is matched by their disappearance from the historical records. This paper explores commercial agriculture as one facet of Mi'kmaq land use in the later nineteenth century. It does not examine the varieties of traditional horticultural activities of the Mi'kmaq Nation.

Notes to chapter 7 are on pp. 122-25.

Historians disagree sharply on the significance of commercial agriculture to the Mi'kmaq. Most commentators accept that they failed to adapt to agriculture for survival. L.F.S. Upton, among others, argued that the Mi'kmaq did not use agriculture to supplement their subsistence.[2] Others, including A.G. Bailey, claimed the Mi'kmaq had an agricultural tradition which was detrimentally affected by the arrival of the Europeans.[3] While Harold McGee and others acknowledged that the Mi'kmaq attempted to farm, they outlined various factors, including bureaucratic inefficiencies and lack of support, which contributed to their failure.[4] This paper argues that rather than failing at agriculture, the Mi'kmaq, when given sufficient support, successfully made the transition to agriculture.

The means by which the Mi'kmaq subsisted at the beginning of the nineteenth century can be determined through an examination of documents generated by and for the Mi'kmaq. These include responses to government questionnaires on the state of the Mi'kmaq as well as Mi'kmaq petitions for grants of land, for protection of the land they already used and for aid. While the Mi'kmaq had traditionally supplemented fishing with hunting and keeping gardens, they were increasingly choosing to farm to ensure a reliable source of food. The documents clearly demonstrate this adaptation to their changing environment.

The Mi'kmaq's increased tendency to farm evoked a number of responses from white people in the nineteenth century. For example, a Pictou farmer responded that "the greater part of the Indians who frequent this quarter have shown a disposition to settle."[5] Another respondent emphasized the importance of the Mi'kmaq choosing their own location. He suggested that the most effective means of selecting suitable land would be "to consult the Heads of their Respective familys with regard to their locations for if placed on land without they like the situation they will hardly be induced to settle."[6] These respondents were fully aware of the changes to the Mi'kmaq environment due to settlement and their resultant adaptation for subsistence.

The Mi'kmaq required more land to expand their use of farming in the first decades of the nineteenth century. Thus, they increasingly requested farm land in their petitions to government. Much of the best land was taken up by settlers, however, and these settlers denied the Mi'kmaq access to their traditional rights and means of subsistence.[7] Petitions to government reflected both the tension with Euramericans and the need for more land. Samuel, Francis and Gorham Paul asked for 200 acres near Shubenacadie for each family to farm since game was gone and settlers refused them access to the woods for fuel.[8] In 1813, Pierre Bernard requested a grant of land since he could no longer provide for his family by hunting and fishing.[9] In 1814, Thomas Paul wished to trade land held in the woods for 100 acres on the Shubenacadie River, where he could fish as well as farm.[10] The Mi'kmaq were being relentlessly pushed from the coast by settlers who also depleted the game. They requested farm land in suitable locations to replace their lost livelihood.

Even while under cultivation, Mi'kmaq land was not secure from encroachment. They attempted to defend their land and gardens from settlers, primarily through petitions to government. These petitions reveal that the Mi'kmaq's use of agriculture was well established. For example, in 1819, Joseph Luxey requested a grant on the Roseway River after having lived there for twenty-five years.[11] The Mi'kmaq of Whyco-comagh petitioned the government in 1821 to protect land that they had cultivated for forty years. Pictou Mi'kmaq petitioned in 1830 for a grant of land that they had traditionally occupied but which had been granted to Euramericans.[12] The Mi'kmaq required decisive government support since settlers did not respect their right of possession.

Thus, by the end of the early decades of the nineteenth century, the Mi'kmaq were adapting to farming and already facing challenges to this new means of survival. While they cleared and planted their farmland, keeping the land became increasingly difficult. Settlers squatted on their lands while the Mi'kmaq were away hunting or fishing. As noted earlier, many Mi'kmaq petitioned the government to protect their farms. When the government chose to take action on the petitions and ordered the squatters to leave, they often refused to go. Many Mi'kmaq families openly expressed their hesitancy to invest any more labour until they held title.[13] In the face of encroachment, others simply moved to areas where, in the words of Indian commissioner Joseph Howe, "the march of improvements is not so rapid."[14] Understandably, Indian commissioner Abraham Gesner held the view that, since they were being repeatedly driven from land they had cleared and cultivated, these actions were a "serious obstacle to their settlement."[15] Colonial officials recognized the ruinous effects white encroachments, such as squatters, were having on Mi'kmaq self-sufficiency, but failed to prevent it.

The Mi'kmaq of Nova Scotia chose to participate in agriculture, but in various ways. Some attempted to farm land which they had traditionally occupied but was not granted to them by the colonial government. Other groups formed communities on one of the land grants allotted for the Mi'kmaq.[16] Still others chose to request individual grants and farmed in the more independent, Euramerican style. Despite the different approaches, the fate of each group was similar.

The struggle of the Merigomish community reflects the obstacles the Mi'kmaq faced in becoming self-sufficient farmers on traditionally occupied land. The Mi'kmaq who lived on and around Merigomish Island near Pictou made a long and unsuccessful attempt to secure title to their land. In 1820, Surveyor General Charles Morris made the first of many requests on their behalf to obtain title for their land.[17] He suggested securing their land on Merigomish and nearby islands to ensure their subsistence. A series of petitions on their behalf failed to persuade the government to issue a deed.[18]

Despite the lack of title, the Merigomish Mi'kmaq made a concerted, if ill-fated, attempt to support themselves at least in part by agriculture. Besides fishing and making wooden crafts,[19] they planted potatoes, Indian corn and French beans on the rich land on Merigomish. The island's expanding population created new problems, however. The island contained no woods and the Mi'kmaq were denied access to firewood by non-Natives along the coast. Squatters' cattle destroyed their crops in 1843 and they ate their seed to survive.[20] The legislature refused their petition for a plough or funds to hire someone to plough their land.[21] In 1846, an outbreak of smallpox infected them, leaving many dead and many more in need of relief.[22] Despite their determination to farm, which corresponded with the objective of the colonial government, they were repeatedly denied much-needed relief.

In contrast to the neglect experienced by Mi'kmaq on traditional lands, several small Mi'kmaq settlements showed remarkable success. These communities were established on land granted for their use and they were given support similar to that provided to white settlers to allow the transition from traditional subsistence. With the help of Walter Bromley,[23] an English humanitarian, and of Judge Wiswall, the Mi'kmaq of Shubenacadie, Gold River and Bear River received extensive support in establishing farms. Bromley appealed to the English middle class, the New England Company and the British and colonial governments for aid. The Mi'kmaq used the resultant grants to established communities with a sawmill, roads, barns, cattle, farming implements and more.[24] As Bromley explained, he had "complete confidence that if given sufficient support, they would become self-sufficient and [would have] no further need of government assistance."[25] When Bromley returned to England in 1825,[26] Judge Wiswall continued his work, particularly in Bear River, and the communities continued to flourish.[27]

The prosperity of these communities was significant and long term. The community of Gold River was described by a Lunenburg County clerk in 1842 as "comfortably located there on land. . . . They dwell in houses, and follow agricultural pursuits and fishing."[28] In 1847, while many Euramerican communities were experiencing devastation, the Bear River Indians requested funds to build a barn to store their crops.[29] The Shubenacadie Mi'kmaq appear to have withstood the crisis equally well, for Gesner described the community in 1849 as a promising farming settlement with crops and livestock.[30] With the advantage of initial support, the Mi'kmaq showed they could consistently and successfully farm their communities.

In addition to these community efforts, some Mi'kmaq chose to farm more independently. The most notable example of this self-reliance was Charles Glode of Annapolis.[31] In 1822, Glode was a young married man with two small children. He and three others petitioned the government for a grant of land to replace hunting territory lost with the building of a road between Annapolis and Liverpool.[32] In 1823, surveyors laid off two hundred acres for each family by ticket of location. The four families farmed the land for the next two decades and, except for a petition for seed in 1835, did so without government help.[33] Having made extensive improvement to his land, Glode petitioned the government in 1840 for clear title so he could pass on his property to his children.[34] Glode was given title, but it was held in trust to prevent him selling the land.[35]

Charles Glode was an influential man by 1842. In a petition to government, he referred to himself as chief.[36] He had a large family, and his farm was prosperous, with twenty-five acres of cleared and fenced land, a hay meadow and roomy barn. He owned oxen, a plough and other farm equipment.[37] He supplemented farming with hunting and fishing.[38]

Glode was also an astute business man. Upon hearing that Howe planned to buy oxen for a nearby Mi'kmaq community, he asked a neighbour, Mr. Nichols, to approach Howe to buy a pair of his oxen.[39] To this request Howe responded, "Don't take Glode's Cattle unless you can get them as good and as cheap as elsewhere."[40] Howe may have mistrusted Glode, for he described him as "shrewd and intelligent."[41] In 1843, Glode asked to use the money normally allotted for seed to help with finishing a house for his family. Howe offered £4. Glode responded he would need £10 to complete the work.[42] Charles Glode was persistent and resourceful in his dealings with government.

By 1845, however, personal tragedy had destroyed Charles Glode's success. Glode had fathered seven children, the two oldest of whom were sons. All had since died, except his youngest daughter. His land being in trust, he could not sell and get the value from the improvement, so he petitioned for permission to sell his farm to enable him to buy a more modest one he could work alone.[43] The government approved the sale. The last petition from Glode, in 1856, sought a small grant to help construct a house on his new farm.[44]

The Mi'kmaq's increased reliance on agriculture without consistent government support left them vulnerable.[45] For three successive years after 1845, the blight that destroyed the potato crops in Europe also caused Nova Scotia's crops to fail, eliminating a major source of food for the Mi'kmaq. Many died. The flood of immigrants further prevented Mi'kmaq access to the fishery.[46] In 1847, too much rain ruined the hay crop, with a subsequent loss of cattle, and insects destroyed the wheat.[47] The Mi'kmaq were forced, in the words of H.W. Crawley, Indian commissioner for Cape Breton, "to desert their agricultural settlements, and disperse over the Country in search of sustenance."[48] Chief Louis Benjamin Pominout clearly articulated the Mi'kmaq dilemma when he addressed the Legislative Assembly in 1849:

> We have resolved to make farms, yet we cannot make farms without help. We will get our people to make farms, build houses and barns, raise grain, feed cattle and get knowledge. . . . They say make farms, this is very good, but will you help us till we cut away the trees, and raise the crops? We cannot work without food.[49]

The response of the Committee on Indian Affairs was limited to authorizing only enough relief to prevent starvation.[50]

As the agricultural crisis became more severe and many Mi'kmaq were in need of aid, the government began to shift responsibility for failure from its policies to the Mi'kmaq themselves. In January 1854, Indian commissioner Chearnley argued that "The complaints about wants is almost altogether the Indian's own fault."[51] By referring to successful Mi'kmaq communities such as Shubenacadie, Chearnley blamed those less successful for their want. Believing the Mi'kmaq were quickly becoming extinct, Chearnley suggested encroached lands should be "sold, or those residing on them placed under rent, and the monies payed into the treasury for the benefit of the Indians. . . . I think it would provide comfort for the few of the Micmac tribe left, and who are fast passing away."[52] In June 1854, Mr. Uniacke, commissioner of Crown lands, agreed with Chearnley that land should be sold to encroachers, suggesting they had settled on Indian land by accident.[53] Thus, the government of Nova Scotia abandoned its attempt to support the Mi'kmaq in farming.

In February 1859, Nova Scotia passed *An Act Concerning Indian Reserves*, which began the wholesale alienation of Mi'kmaq land. It provided for the sale or lease of Indian land with the money to be maintained in a fund for the Indians, less the "cost of surveys and other unavoidable expenses."[54] If the squatters refused to pay, they would be ejected and the land sold to others, with no mention of the lands reverting to the Indians. In 1861, Howe accelerated the alienation of reserve land by authorizing the sale of 1,000 acres in 100-acre lots to the highest bidder with the proceeds for the Indians. This land was apparently not under dispute with squatters. Thousands of acres of reserve land were sold between 1859 and 1867. However, the squatters showed the same defiance of authorities as they had when squatting, and delayed or refused paying for the land. In 1862, of the $1,301.00 owed by squatters in the Middle River Reserve, only $106.00 was collected.[55] By Confederation, the Indian fund totalled $1,790.77 and, according to Commissioner Fairbanks, no more was expected.[56]

During the first half of the nineteenth century, the Mi'kmaq of Nova Scotia expanded their agricultural land use so as to provide a reliable means of subsistence. Their most notable successes were at Shubenacadie, Gold River, Bear River and Annapolis. In these communities, they received ongoing support, similar to that provided to white settlers, which allowed their transition from hunting and fishing. Where possible they used means compatible with their traditional subsistence. For example, Howe found on his 1842 tour of the province that the Mi'kmaq cleared land and planted potatoes. However, these patches were often far in the woods to provide a food supply for their fall hunt.[57] Routinely, Indian commissioners found land planted and the Mi'kmaq away fishing or participating in other traditional activities. The most notable example, however, was Gorham Paul, who successfully farmed in Shubenacadie. "The labours of his farm," Howe noted, "seemed to be chiefly performed for him by his white neighbours" and were paid for with his coopered goods and the quill boxes and baskets his family produced.[58] The Mi'kmaq appeared to incorporate agriculture into their traditional ways as much as possible.

The fate of the various bands of Mi'kmaq throughout the colony of Nova Scotia was remarkably similar, despite the differences in their farming practices. Those who farmed traditional land soon found the land granted to or squatted on by settlers. Those who farmed independently or in reserve communities prospered until the crop failures of the 1840s and 1850s spurred the colonial government to revoke its policy to encourage farming and instead to sell Mi'kmaq land to provide relief. Without support or a secure land base, the prosperity of even the successful Mi'kmaq communities disappeared. While the Mi'kmaq still fished, made and sold crafts, and kept gardens where they could, their period of successful farming appears, from the written record, to have been forgotten by the late nineteenth century.

Notes

1 See Janet Chute's article on Mi'kmaq fishing in this volume (pp. 95-113).
2 Upton also stated the Mi'kmaq survived periods of famine more "by accident than design" (L.F.S. Upton, *Micmacs and Colonists: Indian White Relations in the Maritimes 1713-1867* [Vancouver, BC: University of British Columbia Press, 1979], p. 4). Janet Chute and Elizabeth Ann Hutton argued that the Mi'kmaq did not have a tradition of agriculture and failed to adapt to agriculture (Janet Chute, "A Clash of Management Cultures: The Interaction of Mi'kmaq and White Riverine Fishing in the Maritimes," paper presented at the Canadian Indian Native Studies Association, Carleton University, 12 June 1993, and Elizabeth Ann Hutton, "Micmacs of Nova Scotia" [unpublished MA thesis, Dalhousie University, 1961]). Wallis and Wallis stated that Lescarbot's reference to tobacco is the only evidence of pre-European cultivation (Wilson D. Wallis and Ruth Sawtell Wallis, *The Micmac Indians of Eastern Canada* [Minneapolis: University of Minnesota Press, 1955], p. 68). Bernard Hoffman maintained that Mi'kmaq traditions were consistent with Central Algonkian woodland peoples transplanted to an non-agricultural environment and that the lack of agriculture was more than compensated for by the "Micmac's extremely favourable location relative to the marine biome" (Bernard Hoffman, "Historical Ethnography of the Micmac of the Sixteenth and Seventeenth Centuries" [unpublished PhD dissertation in Anthropology, University of California, Berkeley, 1955]).
3 A.G. Bailey argued in his 1937 study that the Mi'kmaq abandoned the cultivation of corn due to cultural changes resulting from the fur trade (quoted in Phillip K. Bock [also as Back], *The Micmac Indians of Restigouche: History and Contemporary Description*, Anthropological Series, no. 77 [Ottawa, ON: National Museum of Man, 1966], p. 3). Bock also argued that maize was grown by the Mi'kmaq, but only to a limited degree because of the cool climate. The Reverend George Patterson claimed that, before the English came, the Mi'kmaq planted vegetables, particularly Indian corn and beans (George Patterson, D.D., *A History of the County of Pictou, Nova Scotia* [Belleville, ON: Mika Studio, 1972], p. 186; originally published in 1877 by Dawson Bros., Montreal).
4 Thirty years ago, Elizabeth Ann Hutton could assert that the prosperity in Nova Scotia after 1800 produced the means to provide "generous allot-

ments" of land by which the colonial government "effectively dealt" with the Indian problem (E.A. Hutton, "Indian Affairs in Nova Scotia, 1769-1834," in Nova Scotia Historical Society, *Collections* [1963], pp. 33-54). More recently, historians have argued that Nova Scotia's Indian policies were a failure, but disagreed over the causes. Judith Fingard asserted that this failure flowed from the pettiness of the colonial administration and a lack of co-operation from the Mi'kmaq (Judith Fingard, "English Humanitarianism and the Colonial Mind: Walter Bromley in Nova Scotia, 1813-1825," *Canadian Historical Review*, 54, 2 [June 1973]: 123-51). Harold McGee attributed the failures of the land and Indian policies to colonial sympathy for European immigrants over the interests of the Mi'kmaq (Harold Franklin McGee, Jr., "White Encroachment on Micmac Lands in Nova Scotia, 1830-1867," *Man in the Northeast*, 8 [1974]: 57-64). L.F.S. Upton argued that Indian and land policies were weak because of poorly defined surveys and a lack of strong laws against squatting (Upton, *Micmac and Colonists: Indian-White Relations in the Maritimes, 1713-1867*).

5 Edward Mortimer's 1801 response to government, quoted in Patterson, *A History of the County of Pictou, Nova Scotia*, p. 193.

6 George Oxley to Committee of Indian Affairs, 10 April 1801, PANS, MG 1, box 1889, file 2/5, #66.

7 Euramericans viewed Mi'kmaq rights to the fishery as more limited than their own and believed it was illegal for Mi'kmaq to fence or to cut and sell wood off Mi'kmaq land (Indian Commissioner Joseph Howe to Provincial Secretary, 29 April 1842, PANS, MG 1, box 1886, file 4, p. 38.

8 Petition of Goram Paul and others to the lieutenant governor, 1807, PANS, MG 1, box 1889, file 2/5, #140.

9 Petition of Pierre Bernard to the lieutenant governor, 1813, PANS, MG 100, vol. 86, #34, p. 3.

10 Surveyor General Charles Morris on behalf of Shubenacadie Mi'kmaq to the lieutenant governor, 18 May 1814, PANS, MG 1, box 1889, file 2/6, #150.

11 Petition of Joseph Luxey and others to the lieutenant governor, 1819, PANS, MG 100, vol. 86, #34, p. 7.

12 Petition of James Lulan to House of Assembly, 14 December 1830, PANS, RG 1, vol. 310, document 21-2, #105, and LP, *JLANS*, Minutes, 24 December 1830.

13 Some historians and contemporary colonial officials have stated that the Royal Proclamation of 1763 was not applicable to Nova Scotia. Similarly, the Peace and Friendship Treaties of the Maritimes have been seen by some commentators as military alliances and did not provide for extinguishing Indian title to the land since Britain believed it had acquired full title from the French (see W.E. Daugherty, *Maritime Indian Treaties in Historical Perspective* [Ottawa, ON: Research Branch Corporate Policy, INAC, 1981]). Between 1783 and the mid-1800s, government policy shifted several times, from allowing the Mi'kmaq to hold clear title to having title held in trust for them. By 1815, unless specifically authorized by the lieutenant governor, Mi'kmaq land was held in trust by the government (John Jeremy to Howe, LP, *JLANS*, 1844, App. 50, pp. 123-25).

14 Howe's "Report on Indian Affairs," 25 January 1843, PANS, MG 1, box 1886, file 4, p. 106b.

15 Abraham Gesner to Provincial Secretary, 7 June 1847, PANS, MG 15, vol. 4, #32.

16 The colonial government of Nova Scotia made several attempts to secure land for the Mi'kmaq, including outright grants in the late eighteenth century, a reserve system in 1819 and Joseph Howe's policies of family lots in the 1840s. None of the systems were backed with sufficient legal, administrative or financial support to ensure their success.

17 The Mi'kmaq had been granted the land earlier, but the deed had been lost before it could be registered. They needed a replacement deed (James Dawson to Howe, 25 June 1842, PANS, MG 1, box 1886, file 4, p. 96).

18 The latest in the series of petitions was by W.H. Keating to the lieutenant governor, 18 June 1863. The government agreed to look into the issue (PANS, RG 1, vol. 431, #137).

19 LP, JLANS, Minutes, 15 March 1842.

20 Dawson to Howe, 27 May 1843, PANS, MG 1, box 1886, file 4, p. 132.

21 Angus MacDonald to the lieutenant governor, 18 November 1844, PANS, MG 15, vol. 3, #80.

22 Secretary of Board of Health to provincial secretary, 27 June 1846, PANS, RG 1, vol. 431, #41.

23 Judith Fingard provides a detailed account of Bromley's contribution in "English Humanitarianism and the Colonial Mind," p. 145.

24 Petition of Walter Bromley to House of Assembly, 26 February 1819, PANS, RG 5, series P, vol. 80, #23.

25 Bromley to House of Assembly, 26 February 1819, PANS, RG 5, series P, vol. 80, #23.

26 Fingard, "English Humanitarianism and the Colonial Mind," p. 145.

27 Petition of Judge Wiswall to House of Assembly, 9 August 1831, PANS, RG 1, vol. 430, #180.

28 Return of Lunenburg County Clerk, 6 January 1842, PANS, MG 15, vol. 3, #67.

29 Gesner to provincial secretary, 20 August 1847, PANS, MG 15, vol. 4, #37.

30 Gesner's aid to Shubenacadie no doubt contributed to their prosperity (Upton, Micmac and Colonists: Indian-White Relations in the Maritimes, 1713-1867, p. 93). Gesner to Provincial Secretary, 4 June 1847, PANS, RG 1, vol. 431, #44.

31 Glode was originally Claude and was also spelled Gloade.

32 Petition by Glode and others to the lieutenant governor, 2 December 1822, PANS, MG 1, box 1889, file 2/7, #1.

33 Petition of Glode to lieutenant governor, 18 November 1835, PANS, RG 1, vol. 431, #17.

34 Ibid., 10 February 1840, PANS, RG 1, vol. 430, #188.

35 Ibid., 30 April 1841, #189.

36 Glode's brother disliked the duties of chief and chose Charles to replace him. However, the people did not support the appointment (Andrew Henderson to Howe, 27 May 1842, PANS, MG 1, box 1886, file 4, p. 83).

37 Howe journals, 1842, PANS, MG 1, box 1886, file 4, p. 74.

38 While Glode was away hunting, Howe was served herring at his farm (Howe to William Nichols, 2 November 1842, PANS, MG 1, box 1886, file 4, p. 77).

39 Nichols to Howe, 12 November 1842, PANS, MG 1, box 1886, file 4, p. 77.

40 Howe to Nichols, November 1842, PANS, MG 1, box 1886, file 4, p. 78.

41 Howe journals, 1842, PANS, MG 1, box 1886, file 4, p. 75.

42 Andrew Henderson to Howe, 21 June 1843, PANS, MG 1, box 1886, file 4, p. 145.

43 Petition of Charles Glode to the lieutenant governor, 1 March 1845, PANS, RG 20, series A, 1845, Glode, Charles.

44 "Return on Indian Grants," 1856, PANS, RG 1, vol. 431, #90.

45 By 1840, the government recommended a £1,000 annual grant to help remedy the problems white farmers were experiencing (LP, *JLANS*, App. 23, 1840).

46 Petition of Chief Benjamin Pominout to House of Assembly, 8 February 1849, PANS, RG 5, series P, vol. 45, #162.

47 Gesner to provincial secretary, 7 June 1847, PANS, MG 15, vol. 4, #32.

48 LP, *JLANS*, App. 36, 1848.

49 PANS, *The Acadian Recorder*, 24 February 1849.

50 LP, *JLANS*, App. 88, 1848.

51 Chearnley to provincial secretary, 19 January 1854, PANS, RG 1, vol. 431, #80.

52 The prevalent belief in the "vanishing Red-man" probably made this policy appear efficient to colonial officials (LP, *JLANS*, App. 26(2), 1854).

53 James B. Uniacke to provincial secretary, 9 June 1854, PANS, RG 1, vol. 431, #98½.

54 PANS, *Statutes of Nova Scotia*, Fourth Session of the Assembly, February 1859, p. 19.

55 Crown Lands Commissioner Fairbanks' Report, 21 February 1862, PANS, RG 1, vol. 431, #134.

56 NL, *JLANS*, App. 39, 26 April 1867.

57 Howe journals, 1842, PANS, MG 1, box 1886, file 4, p. 51.

58 Ibid., p. 44.

8

Glooscap Encounters Silas T. Rand: A Baptist Missionary on the Folkloric Fringe

Thomas S. Abler

Gordon Day (1976: 75) has noted that "in 1882 there began an efflorescence of Wabanaki [meaning the Mi'kmaq, Malicete-Passamaquoddy, Penobscot, and Abenaki] folklore and folklorists." Day feels that this is "a phenomenon which itself deserves study since it had parallels among the Iroquois and other tribes."[1] Hallowell (1960: 44-45) noted these publications were the first collections of Algonquian folklore since Schoolcraft's pioneering *Algic Researches* (1839). This paper, like that published by Thomas Parkhill (1992), deals with aspects of that "efflorescence" of folklore scholarship.

Considered here is the contribution of Silas T. Rand, a Baptist missionary to the Mi'kmaq, as a collector and aspiring publisher of Mi'kmaq myth. (On Rand's career see Blakeney 1974; Marshall 1975; Upton 1979: 167-70; Miller 1980; Fingard 1981; Mitcham 1985: 66-97; Abler 1992; Lovesey 1992.) Instead of examining the missionary activities of his career, the focus here is on Rand's discovery of the richness of Mi'kmaq and Malicete oral traditions, his relationship with other non-Indians collecting and publishing Wabanaki folklore, and his communication with the emerging professional world of ethnology and folklore situated south of the border in the United States.

Notes to chapter 8 are on pp. 136-37.

Rand was excited by the content of the oral traditions he heard from skilled Mi'kmaq and Malicete storytellers. He was anxious for these tales to reach a wide, non-Indian audience, through publication, at least partially because he felt their content supported his own views on the intellectual equality of "races."[2] This led him to be remarkably generous in sharing his transcriptions and translations of this oral literature with others who could get them into print. He did wish to publish actively himself and he found himself excited by the pioneering publications in folklore and ethnology of others. However, he was on the fringe of this growing number of ethnologists, both geographically and also intellectually. Hence he was disappointed in his attempts to be recognized as part of the ethnological community through publication of his works.

Rand claimed to have "discovered" Glooscap[3] (see Leland 1884: 223), which he did, at least in the same erroneous sense that Columbus "discovered" America. While Rand himself appreciated the entire range of myths, legends and tales embodied in Mi'kmaq folklore, the figure of Glooscap struck some chord with him and other non-Indian readers. Rand's Glooscap tales have been frequently recast for readers both young and old (Butler 1950; Hill 1963, 1970; Macmillan 1972; Partridge 1913). The Nova Scotia Tourist Bureau now attempts to lure tourist dollars down one of its highways by labelling it the "Glooscap Trail."

Current scholars praise, with a few reservations, Silas Rand's large collection of Mi'kmaq oral literature, including at least ten stories featuring Glooscap, recorded between 1847 and his death in 1889. The late Nova Scotian poet Alden Nowlan went so far as to claim "without Silas Rand, we might never have heard of Glooscap" (Nowlan 1983: 9). Ruth Holmes Whitehead of the Nova Scotia Museum wrote of "Rand's great body of tales, still the best source of Micmac stories" (Whitehead 1988: 218), and noted that "it is frightening to think how much would have been lost forever if Rand had not been able to speak Micmac" (Whitehead 1988: 219). While others with anthropological training have collected Mi'kmaq folklore since Rand (Speck 1915; Michelson 1925; Parsons 1925; Fauset 1925; Wallis and Wallis 1955; Brock 1966; see also Sark 1988; DuBlois 1990), the early-twentieth-century students of Mi'kmaq oral literature lacked Rand's command of the Mi'kmaq language. Whitehead, in her two recent elegant "retellings" of Mi'kmaq myths (1988, 1989), acknowledges that later variants flesh out Rand's record, but Rand's versions are the "basis" (Whitehead 1989: 8) or "core-stories" (Whitehead 1988: 222) of Whitehead's new volumes of Mi'kmaq myth.

Rand, born in 1810 in Cornwallis, Nova Scotia, was largely self-educated with both an aptitude for, and interest in, language. Ordained a Baptist minister in 1834, he was a preacher in Charlottetown, Prince Edward Island, in the 1840s. There he encountered both a study of Mi'kmaq grammar by the Irish Catholic Thomas Irwin in *The Prince Edward Island Register* (Irwin 1830; see Upton 1977) and Jo Brooks, a trilingual informant (Mi'kmaq-English-French), in the Charlottetown market. His encounter with the Mi'kmaq language proved a turning point in his life, for his enthusiasm for the language combined with his missionary inclinations to compel him to devote the remainder of his life to mission activity among the Mi'kmaq.

Rand was well on his way to mastering Mi'kmaq when he was introduced to Susan Barss, a relative of Jo Brook's first wife. From her, Rand discovered the oral tradition of the Mi'kmaq. Susan Barss was a learned and skilled storyteller. On the one hand, Rand found hearing Mi'kmaq myth invaluable to his self-appointed missionary task of biblical translation into Mi'kmaq. On the other hand, the first-hand experience of listening to Mi'kmaq oral performance both reinforced Rand's views of Mi'kmaq intellectual powers and convinced him of the intrinsic interest and value of the traditions themselves. It was from the humpbacked Susan Barss (also known as Susan Doctor) that Rand first heard of Glooscap in the summer of 1847 (Rand 1894: 71, 75). From that point (1847) to almost the end of his life, he sought out Mi'kmaq Elders who would be able and willing to relate to him oral traditions within their repertoire. All of these stories Rand heard in Mi'kmaq. He used his own knowledge of Mi'kmaq to record most of these in English. He then would check his translation with the performer and/or with a bilingual Mi'kmaq.

Over those forty years Rand recorded in translation a considerable body of Mi'kmaq myth. In his published collection (Rand 1894) of eighty-seven stories,[4] thirty-six lack attribution to a specific informant. Interestingly, of myths and legends or variants thereof, twenty-seven contributions were from males and twenty-eight were from females.[5] The majority of Rand's Glooscap stories emanate from male storytellers—at least six of them. Two were told by Benjamin Brooks, the others came from Josiah Jeremy, Stephen Hood, Thomas Boonis and Gabriel Thomas. Two of Rand's tellers of Glooscap tales were women, Susan Barss and Nancy Jeddore; the remaining two lack identification of their source.

The earliest reference in print to Glooscap comes from Rand—in his forty-page *A Short Statement of Facts Relating to the History, Manners, Customs, Language and Literature of the Micmac Tribe of Indians, in Nova-Scotia and P. E. Island* (1850a). This purported to be the "substance" of two lectures delivered by Rand in Halifax in November 1849, for the purpose of initiating a non-denominational Protestant mission to the Mi'kmaq. The final quarter of this work is related to the "darkness, superstition, and bigotry of Romanism" of the Catholic Mi'kmaq and to the prospects of bringing them Protestant enlightenment. This sales pitch for the Mi'kmaq mission was preceded by a sympathetic, even enthusiastic, exposition of other aspects of Mi'kmaq language and culture. Here Rand drew attention to Glooscap, "the most remarkable personage of their traditions" (Rand 1850: 28). Rand, however, did not in this publication present in detail any single text from the Glooscap cycle but rather the characteristics of the culture hero, his grandmother, and his younger brother-cum-helper, Marten. He presented a brief paragraph describing an encounter between Glooscap and Marten on the one hand and whites and a cannon on the other. Despite the inability of the cannon to destroy Marten, Glooscap chooses to leave the Mi'kmaq country because of white treachery (Rand 1850: 29). Rand's posthumously published volume of Mi'kmaq myth lacked this tale.

I am uncertain how wide an audience the *Short Statement* of Rand was able to reach. *The National Union Catalog Pre-1956 Imprints* lists only seven libraries in the United States and Canada holding the title (Library of Congress 1968-80, [480]: 573). Pilling (1891: 419) reported seeing it in the libraries of J.B. Dunbar of Bloomfield, NJ, Wilberforce Eames of Brooklyn, NJ, and Major J.W. Powell of the US Geological Survey and the Bureau of Ethnology, as well as possessing a personal copy himself.

Rand does seem to have achieved shortly after this publication a wide reputation as an expert on the Mi'kmaq. The fifth volume of Schoolcraft's *History*, appearing in 1855, contains a twelve-page Mi'kmaq vocabulary as well as numerals and the Lord's Prayer in Malicete, which Rand had communicated to Schoolcraft two years earlier (Schoolcraft 1851-57[5]: 578-90, 592, 690-91). Despite Schoolcraft's interest in Algonquian myth, however, he seemed to have been unaware of Rand's discovery of Glooscap. Glooscap failed to appear in Schoolcraft's massive, but completely unorganized, six-volume opus.

In 1855, however, Glooscap again reached the printed page. Campbell Hardy, a lieutenant in the Royal Artillery, was fond of roaming through the forests and barrens of Nova Scotia slaughtering caribou, moose and other wildlife. His first book describing these activities, *Sporting Adventures in the New World* (Hardy 1855), included two chapters on Mi'kmaq myth. Some of these Hardy claims to have heard and recorded himself. Others, though, came to Hardy from Silas T. Rand. Here Rand first demonstrated his willingness to share his intellectual discoveries (and property) with others.

Rand also provided translations of oral traditions he collected to William Elder. Elder incorporated these in his 1871 *North American Review* article on "The Aborigines on Nova Scotia." Elder's orthography reveals his debt to Rand. Indeed Elder's prose is a close paraphrase of that of Rand. It is instructive to compare Elder's (1871: 13-15) variant of the story of Marten and the cannon to that of Rand (1850: 29). Rand also provided legends for George Patterson's history of Pictou County, N.S. (1877: 31-37) and Sir John William Dawson's *Fossil Men and Their Modern Representatives* (1874; 3rd ed. 1888).

The most influential loan, and the most generous by far, that Rand made of the product of his labours was to Charles Leland. In February of 1884 Rand sent by post "a roll of manuscripts" to Leland (S.T. Rand to C.G. Leland 19-ii-1884, Pennell Collection—Charles G. Leland Papers—thanks to Thomas Parkhill for this reference). Apparently this was the 900-page manuscript, *Indian Legends*, which Leland acknowledges having received from Rand (Leland 1884: ix-x). Leland noted eighty-five tales in Rand's manuscript supplemented the "nearly a hundred among the Passamaquoddy and Penobscot Indians" which Leland claimed to have personally collected. Of the Glooscap stories in Leland's book, thirteen are of Mi'kmaq origin while twelve are attributed to the Passamoquoddy. Leland's cavalier approach to a folklore text, however, is such that almost all are composites assembled by Leland from tales he collected himself and the texts supplied him by others (notably Rand, but also Edward Jack, Miss Abby Alger and Mrs. W. Wallace Brown of Calais, Maine).

Rand's willingness to share his unpublished work should not be interpreted as a lack of desire to see his own words and his own name (as author or translator) in print. Initially, however, Rand's desire to publish his intellectual endeavours was met by a steady stream of publications of biblical translations and moralistic tracts in Mi'kmaq through the British and Foreign Bible Society. One should note, however, that Rand, both in public lectures and in print, presented impassioned support for issues of racial equality and for Mi'kmaq rights to lands, which have never been surrendered, in Nova Scotia and elsewhere in the Maritimes (Rand 1855).[6]

Rand's conviction of the equality of "races"[7] and of the intellectual ability of American Indians led him to the growing literature on Native North American languages and oral traditions. Despite his lack of formal schooling, Rand never shrunk from interacting with academics. His initial decision to pursue the Mi'kmaq mission was on the urging of a professor of geology at Acadia College in Wolfville, Nova Scotia. He suffered from isolation, though, for his Nova Scotia location was on the geographic periphery of North American academic life. Rand was, however, aware of, and enthusiastic about, the new discipline of ethnology. He noted with approval that *"Humanity* in all its diversified phases has become a subject of deep and intense interest" (Rand 1871d). He enthusiastically noted "the subjects of *Ethnology* and *Philology* are attracting a great deal of attention among the learned everywhere just now" (Rand 1875). He attempted to join the community of ethnologists, or at least achieve some recognition from them. He was sought out and visited by Albert S. Gatschet and Garrick Mallery, both of the Smithsonian's Bureau of Ethnology (later Bureau of American Ethnology), but his interaction with others, such as Sir Daniel Wilson, Daniel Brinton, James Pilling and John Wesley Powell was by limited correspondence only (see Rand Papers). He did have strong ties to Charles Leland, who was well connected in international folklore circles (Dorson 1970), but Leland permanently left North America in 1884 for residence in London and later Florence. The academic with whom Rand had the closest relationship was probably Sir John William Dawson of McGill University. Dawson shared with Rand the Baptist religion; Dawson has been styled by Bruce Trigger (1966) as "the faithful anthropologist," with the emphasis on faith rather than on anthropology.

In his later years Rand devoted an increasing amount of time, energy and postage in an attempt to get his two major works—a Mi'kmaq dictionary and his compendium of folklore—published. As a complete work, Rand seems to have given first priority to his Mi'kmaq dictionary. He was aware of and impressed by the Smithsonian's publication of Riggs' dictionary of Dakota Sioux (Riggs 1852). His failure to achieve publication with the Bureau of Ethnology in Washington may be related to problems in Rand's Mi'kmaq orthography. This is, in fact, possibly related both to Rand's limitations as a systematic linguist (his spelling of Glooscap demonstrates this) and his willingness to adapt uncritically phonetic systems he encountered enroute to his translation of the scriptures into Mi'kmaq. Clark, who edited the Mi'kmaq-English portion of the dictionary, complained, "it was found in a chaotic condition, written hurriedly, in three alphabets" (Clark 1902b:vii).

Eventually Rand was able to publish the English-Mi'kmaq portion of his Mi'kmaq dictionary. Both Mi'kmaq-English and the English-Mi'kmaq portions of the dictionary had been purchased by the government of Canada, but their initial decision was to publish only the latter. It has been suggested that the presence of Rand's maternal relative, Sir Charles Tupper, in the federal cabinet as minister of Finance, had an impact on the eventual decision of the Dominion government to purchase the manuscript and to publish the English-Mi'kmaq portion (Rand 1888). Rand himself viewed this as "the smallest and least important portion of the whole work" (Rand 1888: iii). The publication of the "larger and more important portion," to use Rand's (1888:iii) description of the Mi'kmaq-English dictionary, came only after Rand's death. Jeremiah S. Clark was funded by a Canadian government order-in-council of August 1900, which covered the expenses of editing and publishing the dictionary. It appeared in print two years later (Rand 1902). One must wonder, however, how the anti-racist Baptist minister, dead some twelve years, would have responded had he seen his editor's introductory paragraph in the preface to Rand's lifetime labour:

> Someone has said that the most difficult problem now facing civilizations is the proper treatment of the lower races. Let us assume, as we all do, without argument, that our forefathers were superior to the races they found in America a few hundred years ago, and that acknowledgment forces us, if we be true men, to obey the stentorian command of Kipling when he orders us to take up the White Man's Burden. (Clark 1902a: v)

Just as Rand's Mi'kmaq-English dictionary did not reach print in his lifetime, his manuscript on myths of the Mi'kmaq and Malicete was not published in full until after his death. However, Rand did publish some particular myths over his long career. I doubt that we can ever be certain we know all of the places he published variants of Mi'kmaq and Malicete tales. Rand had a penchant for enthusiastically proclaiming the merits of Indian oral literature (including a synopsis of a story or two) in the public press. It is doubtful that a bibliographer could discover all these newspaper articles. As early as 1848, when he had "obtained some half-dozen of these singular tales in the original; having written them down in Micmac from the mouth of an Indian," Rand published his lengthy text of the "Adventures of Usetabulaju and His Sister" (Tertius 1848a, 1848b).

He did in his lifetime initiate in journals two series providing texts of a portion of the myths he collected. In 1871, Rand published a number of tales in the *New Dominion Monthly* (not the *Dominion Monthly*, as cited by Leland [1884:x] and Webster [1894:vii], nor the *Old Dominion Monthly* as Leland elsewhere [1884: 74] named the periodical). The initial tale in this series (Rand 1871a), involving Glooscap and his four visitors, was later published as Legend 42 in Rand's published collection (Rand 1894: 253-58).[8] Rand had collected this story only on 14 October 1869 from Benjamin Brooks (Rand 1894: 257). This suggests that Rand was especially enthused by the story and sent it off to the publisher. This initial publication was followed quickly by a series, all with the title *The Legends of the Micmacs* (Rand 1871b, 1871c), which presented other examples of myth and legend. These included legends of the Kwedech wars (Rand 1871b) with two stories being of Malicete rather than Mi'kmaq origin (Rand 1871b: 333-34). Interestingly, if the initial article in this series features a tale recently collected by Rand, the final two present the first Mi'kmaq tales he recorded, coming from Susan Barss (Rand 1871c; see Rand 1894: 62-75, 81-93). This included the first Mi'kmaq myth he ever heard, which also included Glooscap, albeit as a supporting character (Rand 1871c: 89-93, 150-54).

The second set of myths submitted by Rand himself for publication appeared in the *American Antiquarian and Oriental Journal*. These were all more or less as later published in Rand's posthumous collection (Rand 1890b = Rand 1894: 225-27; Rand 1890c = Rand 1894: 185-89; Rand 1890d = Rand 1894: 232-37; Rand 1891a = Rand 1894: 183-84; Rand 1891b = Rand 1894: 321-25).

Rand died, however, before the myths solicited from him by Stephen D. Peet, editor of the *American Antiquarian and Oriental Journal,* reached print. Soon after Rand's death, Professor E.N. Horsford, for the library of American Linguistics at Wellesley College, purchased from his heirs a substantial portion of Rand's manuscripts, including *Legends,* but not his dictionary which was already owned by the Canadian government in Ottawa. The price was $500 (Webster 1894: vi; Clark 1902: vii). At Wellesley College the Department of Comparative Philology undertook the task of bringing the complete *Legends* manuscript to publication. Professor Horsford's contribution to the task ceased upon his death on 1 January 1893. Helen Webster carried the task to completion that year (Webster 1894: viii-ix).

In more than a geographic sense Rand was on the periphery of late-nineteenth-century folklore scholarship. He was convinced he found linguistic and folkloric evidence to tie Native North Americans to ancient civilizations of the Old World in general and the Mediterranean in particular (see Clark 1902b: xiii). Thus, he compares Mi'kmaq "kaloosit" as in "pretty woman" to the Greek "kalos" meaning pretty (Rand 1850: 20), the Mi'kmaq giant "kookwes" to the Greek "gigas" (Rand 1871c: 90; 1894: 62), the tale of Kitpooseagunow "looks marvellously as though it were made up out of the story of Moses" (Rand 1871c: 154) or having "some faint resemblance to the story of Moses" (Rand 1894: 75). Rand attributes some of the folkloric similarities to universal elements of the human mind (including universal elements of the relationship of humans to the divine), some to ancient ancestral links between North America and Europe, and some to recent interaction between Mi'kmaq-Malicete and French and British settlement of the region.

Mainstream folklorists of both Rand's day and today would reject the second of these assumptions. Rand, however, was ahead of his time in collecting and preserving tales clearly derived from recent Indian-non-Indian interaction. In his review in the *American Anthropologist*, James Mooney was extremely critical of the range of tales printed in Rand's *Legends*. Rand was guilty of "an utter inability to discriminate between the true and false, and a complete ignorance of the aboriginal range of thought." He noted that "we find the Arabian Nights and Grimm's Fairy Tales given as Micmac legends." Mooney writes: "As a contribution to aboriginal mythology [Rand's] book is a grievous disappointment. As a warning to ethnologists it is an unqualified success." His overall assessment is that the book "is of little scientific value except to the ethnologist already sufficiently familiar with the subject to be able to sift the material" (Mooney 1894). A.F. Chamberlain's review in the *Journal of American Folk-Lore* is more positive, but still notes "the discriminating faculty must be present to separate the later Old-World additions from the original Micmac data" (Chamberlain 1894: 164).

A quarter of a century later, Rand's work proved important as a source for Stith Thompson's (1919) monograph on European tales in North American Indian folklore. At least fourteen of Rand's tales are cited there. Indeed, when Thompson initiated his investigation of the topic, he began "with a small group of northeast Indians, the Micmac, Maliseet and Abanaki group" (quoted in Zumwalt 1988: 56). Interestingly enough, Mooney's study of Cherokee myth also contributed to Thompson's study (Thompson 1919: 446-49), although one might question "Tarbaby" and "briar patch" as "European" tales. Thompson had been trained not as an anthropologist but rather in English, as a student of folklorist George Lyman Kitterage at Harvard (Zumwalt 1988: 49, 55-56). In the course of his dissertation research, though, Thompson met and was influenced by anthropologists. He sought and received the blessing of Franz Boas to investigate European elements in American Indian tales (Zumwalt 1988: 118), and he later wrote Kroeber that his dissertation was "about equally in the fields of comparative literature and anthropology" (quoted in Zumwalt 1988: 119).

In his nearly half century of interaction with the Mi'kmaq, Silas T. Rand collected a large body of folklore. While aware of the growing interest in the folklore of Native North Americans, Rand, because of his geographic and intellectual isolation, failed to become part of the main-stream developments in ethnology and folklore as it emerged in the hands of amateurs, semi-professionals, and professionals in North Amer-ica. His Nova Scotia home was distant from the institutional centres of ethnology in North America. His ideas about links between North American peoples and the ancient civilizations of the Mediterranean were equally distant from the scholarly consensus on the past of Native North Americans. However, both his language skills, allowing him to record in translation tales he heard in Mi'kmaq and Malicete, and the catholic nature of his collection, including a large number tales diffused from Europe to Native peoples, have assured the value of Rand's nineteenth-century labours to modern scholarship.

Notes

1 Research which contributed to this paper was supported by grants 410-87-0244 and 410-89-1075 from the Social Science and Humanities Research Council of Canada. Staff at the libraries of Acadia University, Welles-ley College and the Public Archives of Nova Scotia were most helpful while I pursued archival research. My tentative forays into the nineteenth-century Mi'kmaq world have benefited from conversations with Harold McGee, Virginia Miller and Ruth Holmes Whitehead. Thomas Parkhill responded to my note to him with generous references and information from his own research on Charles Leland and Glooscap.

2 Rand argued that Indian legends demonstrated mental capacity. "Their legends indicate not only the cast of mind, the manners and customs of the Indians, their belief, &c., but they clearly indicate the mental calibre of the people, not only in the invention of the story, but also in retaining and relat-ing it. . . . [H]ere at Hantsport is an old almost blind Indian woman, Nomy Jeddore, who like many of her race can retell their legends I know not what extent. It is not . . . proof of *their* mental calibre? Are people possessed of such mental powers to be despised?" (Rand 1871d). Miller (1980: 246) justly lauds Rand, noting "he possessed none of the ethnocentrism common to the

social evolutionists" of his time, citing "his realization of the inherent value of Micmac culture and . . . his repeated favourable comparisons of the Micmac language with Indo-European languages."

3 Glooscap (Rand's usual spelling) has received a variety of spellings, most more sophisticated than that of Rand, in the literature. Rand's spelling (unsatisfactory as it is) will be used in this paper, except in direct quotations from other authors.

4 A few of the myths and legends are given additions. Hence the total number of named and unnamed sources is larger than the eighty-seven legends in Rand's volume.

5 Rand's experience can be contrasted with Wallis' observation: "In general, men appear to be superior to women as storytellers. This impression may be due in part to my limited acquaintance with Micmac women. But the impression is substantiated by the lack of reference by the Micmac to any woman as a gifted performer" (Wilson D. Wallis, in Wallis and Wallis 1955: 319). Nancy Jeddore told Rand eighteen of the stories published in his collection, and Rand records tales told by five other women. Eleven males are named by Rand as storytellers, the most prolific of whom, Ben Brooks, is the source of six stories.

6 Upton (1979: 135) notes Rand's supporting role in "[t]he most ambitious petition of them all" on Mi'kmaq land claims sent to Queen Victoria in 1853. In 1847 Rand lamented in print that the Mi'kmaq have been "driven . . . to the necessity often of begging permission to erect their frail habitations on the very land which, by every principle of justice and religion, is their own" (Tertius [Silas T. Rand] 1847e).

7 Rand wrote: "I can scarcely suppress a feeling of shame that I am a white man—since our colored brethren have been so unjustly and unmercifully treated by us, because, forsooth, like ourselves, they have the audacity to wear the skin which the great Creator gave them!" (Rand 1850b).

8 Leland published this (Leland 1884: 98-103), but removed one of the four visitors (the one who is turned by Glooscap into a gnarled cedar) since the same act by Glooscap occurs in another story. The other tale in which a visitor is transformed into a cedar (Leland 1884: 94-98) is also found, as Legend 35— "Glooscap, Kuhkw, and Coolpujot," in Rand (1894: 232-37).

References

Abler, Thomas S.
  1992 "Protestant Missionaries and Native Culture: Parallel Careers of Asher Wright and Silas T. Rand." *American Indian Quarterly*, 16: 25-37.
Blakeney, Sharon
  1974 "An Annotated Bibliography of the Works of Silas T. Rand." Typescript. Canadian Museum of Civilization, Ottawa. Copies in Public Archives of Nova Scotia and Acadia University Library.
Bock, Philip K.
  1966 "The Micmac of Restigouche: History and Contemporary Description." National Museum of Canada Bulletin 213.

Butler, Ethel H.
  1950   *Little Thunder's Wooing: A Legend of the Blomidon and Glooscap Country*. Port Royal, NS: Abanaki Press.
Chamberlain, A.F.
  1894   "[Review of] *The Legends of the Micmacs*. By the Rev. Silas Tertius Rand." *Journal of American Folklore*, 7: 163-64.
Clark, Jeremiah S.
  1902a   "Editor's Preface." In Silas T. Rand, *Micmac Dictionary from Phonographic Word-Lists*, pp. v-viii. Charlottetown: Patriot.
  1902b   "A Synoptical Grammar of the Micmac Language." In Silas T. Rand, *Micmac Dictionary from Phonographic Word-Lists*, pp. ix-xxxiii. Charlottetown: Patriot.
Dawson, Sir John William
  1888   *Fossil Men and Their Modern Representatives*. 3rd ed. London: Hodder and Stoughton.
Day, Gordon M.
  1976   "The Western Abenaki Transformer." *Journal of the Folklore Institute*, 13: 75-89.
DeBlois, Albert D.
  1990   *Micmac Texts*. Canadian Ethnology Service Paper 117. Canadian Museum of Civilization, Mercury Series.
Dorson, Richard M.
  1970   "America Folklorists in Britain." *Journal of the Folklore Institute*, 7: 187-219.
Elder, William
  1871   "The Aborigines of Nova Scotia." *North American Review*, 112: 1-30.
Fauset, Arthur Huff
  1925   "Folklore from the Half Breeds of Nova Scotia." *Journal of American Folklore*, 38: 300-15.
Fingard, Judith
  1982   "Rand, Silas Tertius." *Dictionary of Canadian Biography*, 11: 722-24.
Hallowell, A. Irving
  1960   "The Beginnings of Anthropology in America." In Frederica de Laguna, ed., *Selected Papers from the American Anthropologist*, pp. 1-104. Evanston: Row, Petersen.
Hardy, Campbell
  1855   *Sporting Adventures in the New World; or, Days and Nights of Moose-Hunting in the Pine Forests of Acadia*. 2 vols. London: Hurst and Blackett.
Hill, Kay
  1963   *Glooscap and His Magic: Legends of the Wabanaki Indians*. Toronto: McClelland and Stewart.
  1970   *More Glooscap Stories: Legends of the Wabanaki Indians*. Toronto: McClelland and Stewart.

Irwin, Thomas
  1830   *Sketches of the Manners, Customs, Language, etc. of the Micmac Indians.* Charlottetown: Prince Edward Island Register.
Leland, Charles G.
  1884   *The Algonquin Legends of the New England or Myths and Folklore of the Micmac, Passamaquoddy, and Penobscot Tribes.* Boston: Houghton, Mifflin.
Library of Congress
  1968-80 *The National Union Catalog Pre-1956 Imprints.* London: Mansell.
Lovesey, Dorothy May
  1992   *To Be a Pilgrim: A Biography of Silas Tertius Rand, 1810-1889: Nineteenth Century Protestant Missionary to the Micmac.* Hantsport, NS: Lancelot Press for Acadia Divinity College and the Baptist Historical Committee of the United Baptist Convention of the Atlantic Provinces.
Macmillan, Cyrus
  1962   *Glooskap's Country, and Other Indian Tales.* Toronto: Oxford University Press.
Marshall, M.V.
  1975   "Silas Tertius Rand and His Micmac Dictionary." *Nova Scotia Historical Quarterly*, 5: 391-410.
Michelson, Truman
  1925   "Micmac Tales" *Journal of American Folklore*, 38: 33-54.
Miller, Virginia P.
  1980   "Silas T. Rand: Nineteenth Century Anthropologist Among the Micmac." *Anthropologica*, n.s. 22: 235-49.
Mitcham, Allison
  1985   *Three Remarkable Maritimers.* Hantsport, NS: Lancelot.
Mooney, James
  1894   "[Review of] *Legends of the Micmacs.* By the Rev. Silas Tertius Rand." *American Anthropologist*, 7: 118-20.
Nowlan, Alden
  1983   *Nine Micmac Legends.* Hantsport, NS: Lancelot Press.
Parkhill, Thomas
  1992   "Of Glooskap's Birth, and of His Brother Malsum, the Wolf": The Story of Charles Godfrey Leland's 'Purely American Creation.'" *American Indian Culture and Research Journal*, 16: 45-69.
Parsons, Elsie Clews
  1925   "Micmac Folklore." *Journal of American Folklore*, 8: 55-133.
Partridge, Emelyn Newcomb
  1913   *Glooscap the Great Chief and Other Stories: Legends of the Micmacs.* New York: Sturgis & Walton.
Patterson, George
  1877   *A History of the County of Pictou, Nova Scotia.* Montreal: Dawson Brothers.

Pilling, James C.
　　1891　*Bibliography of the Algonquian Languages.* Bureau of American Ethnology Bulletin 13.

Rand, Silas T.
　　1850a　*A Short Statement of Facts Relating to the History, Manners, Customs, Language, and Literature of the Micmac Tribe of Indians in Nova Scotia.* Halifax: James Bowes and Son.
　　1850b.　"The Micmac Mission." *Christian Messenger,* n.s. 10: 326.
　　1855　"The Claims and Prospects of the Micmacs." *Christian Messenger,* 15: 81-82, 89, 97-98, 145.
　　1871a　"An Indian Legend." *New Dominion Monthly,* 1: 219-22.
　　1871b　"The Legends of the Micmacs." *New Dominion Monthly,* 1: 262-65, 331-34.
　　1871c　"The Legends of the Micmacs." *New Dominion Monthly,* 2: 89-93, 150-54, 211-16.
　　1871d　"Reply to the Rev. Mr. Sommerville." *Christian Messenger,* 35: 115-16.
　　1875　"The Micmac Mission." *Christian Messenger,* 39: 285.
　　1888　*Dictionary of the Language of the Micmac Indians.* Halifax: Nova Scotia Printing.
　　1890a　"The Legends of the Micmacs." *American Antiquarian and Oriental Journal,* 12: 3-14.
　　1890b　"The Coming of the White Man Revealed: Dream of the White Robe and Floating Island." *American Antiquarian and Oriental Journal,* 12: 155-56.
　　1890c　"The Beautiful Bride." *American Antiquarian and Oriental Journal,* 12: 156-59.
　　1890d　"Glooscap, Cuhkw, and Coolpurloz." *American Antiquarian and Oriental Journal,* 12: 283-86.
　　1891a　"A Giant Story—A Cookwes." *American Antiquarian and Oriental Journal,* 13: 41-42.
　　1891b　"The Story of the Moosewood Man." *American Antiquarian and Oriental Journal,* 13: 168-70.
　　1894　*Legends of the Micmac.* New York: Longman, Green.
　　1902　*Rand's Micmac Dictionary.* Charlottetown: Patriot Publishing.

Rand Papers
　　Atlantic Baptist Historical Collection. Acadia University, Wolfville, NS.

Riggs, S.R.
　　1852　*Grammar and Dictionary of the Dakota Language.* Smithsonian Contributions to Knowledge, vol. 4. Washington, DC: Smithsonian Institution Press.

Sark, John Joe
　　1988　*Micmac Legends of Prince Edward Island, Lennox Island.* Lennox Island, PE: Lennox Island Band Council and Ragweed Press.

Schoolcraft, Henry R.
　　1839　*Algic Researches.* New York: Harper & Row.

1851-57 *Historical and Statistical Information Respecting the History, Conditions, and Prospects of the Indian Tribes of the United States.* 6 vols. Philadelphia: Lippincott, Grambo.

Speck, Frank G.

1915 "Some Micmac Tales from Cape Breton Island." *Journal of American Folklore*, 28: 59-69.

Tertius [Silas T. Rand]

1847a "For the *Royal Gazette*: The Indians No. 1." *Royal Gazette* [Charlottetown, PE], 17, 889 (3 August): 1.

1847b "No. 2 for the *Royal Gazette*: The Indians—Their Language." *Royal Gazette*, [Charlottetown, PE], 17, 891 (10 August): 1.

1847c "No. 3 for the *Royal Gazette*: The Indians—Their Language." *Royal Gazette* [Charlottetown, PE], 17, 892 (17 August): 1.

1847d "No. 4 for the *Royal Gazette*: The Indians—Their Language." *Royal Gazette* [Charlottetown, PE], 17, 893 (31 August): 1.

1847e "No. 5 for the *Royal Gazette*: The Indians—Their Language." *Royal Gazette* [Charlottetown, PE], 17, 894 (7 September): 1.

1847f "No. 6 for the *Royal Gazette*: The Indians—Their Language." *Royal Gazette* [Charlottetown, PE], 17, 899 (12 October): 1.

1848a "For the *Royal Gazette*: The Indians—Their Legends." *Royal Gazette* [Charlottetown, PE], 18, 948 (12 September): 1.

1848b "For the *Royal Gazette*: A Tale of Indian Tradition: Adventures of *Ustabulaju* and His Sister." *Royal Gazette* [Charlottetown, PE], 18, 949 (19 September): 1.

Thompson, Stith

1919 *European Tales Among the North American Indians: A Study in the Migration of Folk-Tales.* Colorado College Publications (Language Series), 2, 34: 319-471. Colorado Springs: Board of Trustees, Colorado College.

Trigger, Bruce G.

1966 "Sir John William Dawson: A Faithful Anthropologist." *Anthropologica*, n.s. 8: 351-59.

Upton, L.F.S.

1977 "Thomas Irwin: Champion of the Micmacs." *The Island Magazine*, pp. 13-16.

1979 *Micmacs and Colonists: Indian-White Relations in the Maritimes.* Vancouver: University of British Columbia Press.

Wallis, Wilson D., and Ruth Sawtell Wallis

1985 *The Micmac Indians of Eastern Canada.* Minneapolis: University of Minnesota Press.

Whitehead, Ruth Holmes

1988 *Stories from the Six Worlds: Micmac Legends.* Halifax: Nimbus.

1989 *Six Micmac Stories.* Halifax: Nova Scotia Museum.

Zumwalt, Rosemary Levy

1988 *American Folklore Scholarship: A Dialogue of Dissent.* Bloomington: Indiana University Press.

Part IV

Ontario: History, Law and Sovereignty

9

Colonizing a People: Mennonite Settlement in Waterloo Township

---

E. Reginald Good

> As the white man advanced in his encroachments, the Indian retired farther back to make room for him. In this way the red men have gradually been stripped of their hunting-grounds and corn-fields, and been driven far from the land of comfort and plenty.[1]

The Myth of the Pioneers

Historians[2] have depicted the early European settlers of present-day Ontario as "noble pioneers" whose efforts to "transform the [hostile and threatening] wilderness of this province into smiling fields" were "as intense and romantic as the trials of any empire."[3] They "had to make a new start in a country where great virgin forests came everywhere down to the water's edge, defying the settler to find space to plant his seeds or even for his cabin."[4] This was "a problem of giant proportions. Before any grain could be planted the trees had to be cut down. The forest was inhabited by Indians and wild animals—a constant menace."[5] The pioneers tamed this savage wilderness and brought civilization to it. A romantic variation on this theme conceptualizes nature as friendly and hospitable. Visionary pioneers laid claim to the limitless resources of a bountiful environment by transforming them, through hard labour, for the benefit of humanity.

Notes to chapter 9 are on pp. 165-80.

Historians have repeated identical mythical phrases about the Mennonite settlers of Waterloo Township[6] in the upper Grand River Valley who established "the first inland settlement in the province" of Ontario at the turn of the nineteenth century.[7] The anonymous author of "The Early Settlement of Waterloo Township," for example, describes how "adventurous [Mennonite] pioneers . . . penetrated into this section of the country . . . then an unbroken wilderness . . . in search of land which should prove more suitable for farming purposes than that which their forefathers had hitherto occupied."[8] Waterloo Township was at that time "one of the most densely forested terrains in Canada,"[9] "given up to the Red men of the forest, bears, wolves, and other wild animals."[10] Mennonite pioneers were attracted to the area because they knew that this land, on which grew some of the province's "tallest [black walnut] trees, must be the best land." However, "no matter how excellent the land, it could not be of much value until it was cleared of trees," Indians and wild animals.[11] The pioneers' "stalwart character of mind and body" enabled them "to face and then subdue the hostile element of this, then continuous wilderness."[12]

The myth of the pioneers has been called "the most powerful myth in Ontario."[13] It treats history as the chronicle of progress that begins with the arrival of heroic European settlers. As W. Stewart Wallace wrote in 1930, "[t]he conquest of America by Europeans drew a red line across American history; and the civilization of America to-day owes very little to the Aboriginal inhabitants of the country. It has its roots, not in America, but in Europe."[14] The first edition of Wallace's book, published in 1928, referred to the Aboriginal peoples as "great thieves," "barbarians" and "savages of a very low order."[15] Major O.M. Martin, a Mohawk teacher at a Toronto school, took exception to these passages. A newspaper account of 1929 quoted him as saying:

> I am first of all a Canadian, but I am a Mohawk of the Six Nations. I am just as proud of my ancestry as most other people are of theirs, and naturally I am somewhat hurt and humiliated when I am obliged to teach my class that my ancestors were great thieves, dishonest, barbaric and essentially primitive. . . . There is nothing to prove that they were cruel, dishonest or primitive. As a rule, you will find that the records of the Indians were written by enemies, persons who had fought against them in the early wars.[16]

Martin succeeded only in persuading Wallace to camouflage these racist references. In the second edition of 1930, for example, the phrase "savages of a very low order" became "original occupants . . . of a somewhat primitive type."[17]

The myth of the pioneers provided an overriding interpretive paradigm that forced Wallace and other Canadian historians to negate or omit the role of Aboriginal protagonists in history.[18] This involved both the suppression of certain "facts" and the creation of alternate "facts" that were needed to construct the historical narrative. An analysis of the historiography of Aboriginal-newcomer relations in Waterloo Township provides a useful case study for fleshing out this process.

Historiography of Aboriginal-Newcomer Relations in Waterloo

At the time of first contact with Europeans, Aboriginal political relations in the St. Lawrence Valley and Great Lakes region were dominated by rivalry between the Huron and Iroquois Confederacies. The Huron Confederacy occupied the agricultural region on the southeast shore of Georgian Bay. The Iroquois Confederacy occupied the fertile Finger Lakes area southeast of Lake Ontario. Between them, "at the apex of a continental trade network," lay a buffer zone occupied by the Neutral Confederacy.[19] Neutral villages in the southern Ontario peninsula provided "neutral ports of trade [that] were essential to the intertribal flow of trade before the extensive proliferation of the fur trade with the Europeans."[20]

The Hurons were attacked and dispersed by the Iroquois in 1649-50. The Neutrals were destroyed by the Iroquois in 1652.[21] "This strategy aimed to provide the Seneca and the other western Iroquois tribes with a northern hinterland in which they could hunt and rob furs, as the Mohawk were already accustomed to do farther east."[22] Thereafter, the ports of trade "changed from a neutral area in an intermediate zone guaranteed by two strong powers (the Huron and the Iroquois) to Albany alone."[23]

By 1670 Ojibwa from Lake Superior had established themselves just north of evacuated Huron territory and were pushing south. "The revengeful Huron among them, the attraction of furs in the territory between Lakes Huron and Ontario, and the desire for cheap competitive trade goods with the English who were entering the market, and the shorter and safer canoe routes to the south were obvious reasons for their expansion into southern Ontario."[24] From the mid-1680s to 1700 the Ojibwa advanced into southern Ontario, destroying Iroquois "villages and fortifications as well as a considerable number of their warriors."[25] Finally, in 1701, treaties of peace and friendship were initiated at Montreal and Albany whereby the Western Confederacy and the Haudenosaunee agreed "to be united in ye Covenant Chain, our hunting places to be one, and to boile in one kettle, eat out of one dish, & with one spoon, and so be one."[26]

Britain continued to recognize southern Ontario as Iroquois territory until the conquest of New France in 1759-60. Thereafter it recognized the Ojibwa, or Mississaugas as they became known on the north shore of Lake Ontario, as the Aboriginal occupants of the area. When Loyalists fled north in the wake of the American Revolution, Britain obtained permission from the Mississaugas to settle them on Mississauga lands.[27] Indian allies, under the apparent leadership of the Upper Mohawks of the Six Nations Confederacy, also sought refuge on Mississauga lands. The Mississaugas granted them the use of a six-mile-wide strip of land on either side of the Grand River, from its mouth at Lake Erie to its source.[28] This grant was confirmed in 1784 by a proclamation of Frederick Haldimand, commander-in-chief of the Crown's forces in British North America and governor-in-chief of Quebec, and reconfirmed, in part, by the Simcoe Patent of 1793. Joseph Brant, acting as agent for the Six Nations, sold blocks of Grand River lands north of Dundas street to white speculators. They eventually resold them to settlers. Block Number Two (renamed Waterloo Township in 1816) was the first block to be settled, beginning with Pennsylvania Mennonites in 1799.

Historians typically confine the Mississauga and Six Nations presence in Waterloo Township to "prehistory."[29] Where Indians are mentioned at all in the historiography of Aboriginal-newcomer relations in Waterloo Township, they are reduced to allegorical roles in a narrative about the progress of European colonists. They are represented as nonexistent, extinct, a living impediment to agricultural progress, a commodity to be exploited, innocent prey of greedy whites, the white man's burden, and/or a hindrance to obtaining clear deeds. Often their national origin is ignored or misrepresented. They are denied their position as fellow humans.[30]

For James Nyce, the author of an MA thesis on Waterloo Mennonite settlement, Indians are non-existent. In "This Land that Was Desolate Is Become Like the Garden of Eden," Nyce claims that the Mennonite pioneers of Waterloo Township found a forest that "was completely empty. It had never been humanized."[31] The pioneers believed that "'the forest had to be removed . . . [because] there was nothing in the forest that would sustain human life.'"[32] They consequently "impose[d] a human design upon nature" by clearing the forest, building shelters and planting gardens.[33]

Barbara Sherk, in her reminiscences, takes a contrary view of nature but implicitly denies the existence of Indians as well. She maintains that the "Lord seemingly had directed [her Mennonite ancestors] to a land almost like Canaan of old, 'flowing with milk and honey.'" They found wild ducks, geese, fish "and wild pigeons by the million . . . [E]verything planted . . . in the rich virgin soil . . . then yielded largely."[34] She did not recall having heard anything about Indians.[35]

Other historians write as though Indians were extinct when the Mennonite settlers began moving into what became the Waterloo County area. Gottlieb Leibbrandt says that in ancient times "the forest and bush lands of Waterloo [Township] echoed Indian war cries."[36] The area was depopulated of its Neutral population through internecine warfare in 1652 and remained unoccupied thereafter.[37] However, Neutral trails remained long after the Aboriginal people had left and they facilitated Mennonite settlement of Waterloo Township.

According to James E. Kerr, a Neutral trail ran "from the middle Grand River to the head of lake navigation at Dundas."[38] Margaret Elliot wrote that the first Mennonite "settlers came through Dundas, over the old trail through Beverly Swamp on past Galt, to Blair."[39] From Blair, other trails radiated in several directions. Settlers homesteaded on them. Andrew Taylor describes how a string of old farm houses west of Blair "were located near an ancient Indian trail which ran from [Blair to] Doon to Roseville and thence on to Ayr. Old timers referred to it as the Oregon Trail."[40] Another string of farm houses, east of Blair, was laid out along the course of "the Indian Trail from Blair to Puslinch Lake." Ivan Groh recounts in an ode to that trail how his

> Grandma's Grandpa came that way
> And soon decided he would stay
> And build a cabin for his bride
> And clear a homestead there beside
> The Indian trail that wound about
> And turned and twisted in and out
> Among the maples, elm and pine—
> The only highway of that time.[41]

The anonymous author of an article written in 1869 on "The Early Settlement of Waterloo Township" records that Indians still occupied the area at the turn of the nineteenth century and that they were a living impediment to white agricultural progress. The author describes how "[t]he red man roamed in his native wilds, and looking upon the new-comers as intruders upon [his] rightful domains [was] at times disposed to be troublesome."[42] He or she tells an oft-repeated story of how, in 1804, a drunken Indian named "Old Jack" ordered the Mennonites off his hunting grounds at gunpoint; he shot at a party of them and shattered Abraham Stauffer's arm.[43] Peter Moyer editorialized in an 1866 account of this incident that "[i]t was certainly not a very pleasant predicament to be in, some 500 miles from home in an entire wilderness country to be shot by the wild savages of the forest."[44] "The settlers, however, were pre-eminently men of peace and by kindness gradually gained the good-will of the Indians, so that on the whole the relations between them became remarkably agreeable."[45]

Ezra Eby credits "Indian Sam" Eby with pacifying the Indians. Eby records that when "Indian Sam" settled in Waterloo Township in 1804 "there were but few white settlers in this beautiful community and the Indians were his next neighbours. He spent much of his time among the Indians and taught them many good things, in fact he was their law-giver, minister, interpreter and peace-maker."[46] After Indians were "domesticated" they came to realize that they had no proprietary rights in hunting grounds never subdued to the purposes of man through labour. They then compliantly retreated before the advance of the Mennonite settlers who would appropriate the wilderness to human use by committing it to commercial agricultural production according to God's plan.[47]

Frank H. Epp, in his *History of the Mennonites in Canada*, treats Indians as a friendly and hospitable commodity to be exploited by Mennonite pioneers.[48] They performed the valuable service of teaching the Mennonite settlers "the skills of survival in the woods" and introducing them "to the choicist lands, to the best hunting grounds and fishing waters."[49]

Ezra Eby describes how, "[f]or a small loaf of bread and a six-penny crock of thick milk the Indians would bring them the nicest quarter of venison or a large basket well filled with the finest of speckled trout."[50] "Often during cold nights when the inmates of the house had retired to their respective places of rest, their kitchen would be taken possession of by the Indians who would spend the night sleeping warm and comfortable around the large fire place."[51] This golden age of "cordiality and mutual helpfulness" did not last, however. The Indians got hold of the settlers' whiskey and degenerated.[52] Then they vanished from Mennonite history.

Mabel Dunham, in *Grand River*, portrays the Indians as "poor, deluded" people who "did not know the value of their possessions" and consequently were innocent prey for greedy whites.[53] The Mississaugas surrendered the Grand River Valley to the British Crown in 1784 for a pittance. The Crown then granted it to the Six Nations Indians the same year. Speculators turned "the gullibility of [the Six Nations' agent] Joseph Brant to their own advantage. . . . The white man's methods of finance may not have been entirely intelligible to Brant, but they were altogether alluring. Large dividends and no work was a consummation devoutly to be desired by his people. . . . Under the constant strain of the speculators' arguments Brant decided to convert at once into government annuities 352,707 acres of land."[54]

Dunham also portrayed the Six Nations as the white man's burden. She believes that it would never have occurred to the Six Nations "that life might hold for them a fuller, richer experience than their nomadic existence."[55] Consequently, settlers were obligated to share "the secrets of the universe" which God had "whispered to them." They were "to use the forests, the ore deposits, the waterpowers and the rich, virgin soil to make life easier and richer for men and for little children everywhere."[56] Unfortunately, that obligation was not fulfilled.[57]

Kenneth McLaughlin, in his histories of Kitchener (with John English), Cambridge, and Waterloo attempted to redeem the character of land speculators by blaming Joseph Brant for the fate of the Six Nations. McLaughlin maintained that "Brant was clearly selling land and giving title without authority . . . [and, in the case of Waterloo Township,] Beasley was trapped in the middle."[58] McLaughlin stated that "[b]etween the ultimate resolution of the ownership of these lands in 1805 and the original creation of an Indian Reserve in 1784 lies one of the most complex and fascinating accounts ever to unfold in the early years of Upper Canada."[59] He consequently devoted an introductory chapter in each book to repeating a variation of that story as told by Brigadier General E.A. Cruikshank in an article written in the *Waterloo Historical Society* annual report.

According to Cruikshank, "the wily Mohawk," Joseph Brant, purported to sell Six Nations lands to Beasley for personal aggrandizement.[60] British-Canadian officials initially "wished to avoid giving any offence to Brant, whose influence among the Indians was supposed to be much more powerful than it actually proved to be."[61] However, they finally came to blows with Brant in 1803 over whether Crown patents to individual lots could be released before Beasley had paid in full for

the township.[62] Mennonite farmers who already had purchased lots in
Waterloo Township with the expectation that they had obtained legal
title to them were caught in the middle of this conflict. These Mennonites appealed to their co-religionists in Pennsylvania "who [in 1805]
came equipped with a considerable fortune to extricate [Beasley] from
his embarrassment and, in so doing, laid the foundations for a large,
beautiful, and very rich German settlement in Waterloo."[63]

Indians do not count as a legitimate subject of historical inquiry in
their own right because they had failed to progress,[64] and information
about them cannot "be slotted in [to the master narrative] without damaging the plot." James W. St. G. Walker concluded that "[w]hat is necessary [to produce an accurate assessment of the Indian contribution] is
the abandonment of the old plot, the search for new significant epi-
sodes, and an entirely original school of historical interpretation."[65]

The abandonment of the old plot must begin with the recognition
that the land onto which Europeans moved was not vacant but already
occupied by dynamic and creative peoples.[66] Thus, Europeans "did not
settle a virgin land. They invaded and displaced a resident population."[67]
We must analyze the complex interactions between Aboriginal peoples
and European newcomers which ultimately forced Aboriginal peoples
off their lands. We must ask questions like: Who were the Aboriginal
people(s) that were here when Europeans arrived? How were European
newcomers received by them? Why did Europeans move on to their
lands? A historical reconstruction of the story of the Mennonite settlement of Waterloo Township, using these questions as a guide, will serve
as a useful case study for reconstructing the story of European agricultural settlement in Ontario.

Aboriginal People in the Upper
Grand River Valley ca. 1800

The Anishnaubeg (Ojibwa Nation), or Mississaugas, were an
Algonquian-speaking group who occupied the north shore of Lake
Ontario in the early nineteenth century.[68] Kahkewaquonaby (Sacred
Feathers), whose English name was Peter Jones, wrote in the 1830s that

[a]lthough the Ojebway nation of Indians is scattered over a vast section
of country there is no person among them recognized as king. . . . The
Indian country is allotted into districts, and each section is owned by a
separate tribe of Indians. These districts become so many independent

states, governed by their own chiefs, one of whom is styled the "head chief".... The chiefs of each tribe settle all the disputes which arise among the people, watch over their territories, regulate the order of their marches, and appoint the time for the general rendezvous. This generally takes place after sugar-making, or about the first of May, when they have their grand pow-wow dances and various games.[69]

Each tribe "manages its own affairs, within the limits of its territory, quite independently of other tribes of the same nation; but in matters which affect the whole nation, a general council is called, composed of all or a majority of the chiefs of the different tribes."[70]

The Mississaugas who lived in south-central Upper Canada were sometimes called the Credit River (or River Credit) Indians by the newcomers because they held the Credit River "in reverential estimation as the favourite resort of their ancestors" and annually gathered there en masse for the spring salmon runs.[71] Their territory commenced

at Long Point on Lake Erie, thence eastward along the shore of the lake to the Niagara River, then down the river to Lake Ontario, then northward along the shore of the lake to the River Rouge east of Toronto, then up that river to the dividing ridges between lakes Ontario and Simcoe, then along the dividing ridges to the head waters of the River Thames, then southwards to Long Point the point of beginning.[72]

The principal social and economic grouping for the Mississaugas was the extended family or village, which newcomers usually described as a "band."[73] But villages were not fixed geographical entities. Their size and location changed on a seasonal basis, as villagers sought food wherever it was seasonally most concentrated. When fish were spawning, many villages might gather at a single waterfall to create a dense temporary settlement; when it was time to hunt in the fall, the same villages might be found scattered over many miles of land. During the summer months the Mississaugas congregated on lakes or rivers for fishing and, on the river flats, for the planting of "Corn, Beans, or Potatoes."[74]

The Grand River Valley was a favoured location to establish summer villages[75] because annual flooding of the Grand River[76] cleared away the swamp grass from the river flats in preparation for spring planting. James Young, writing in 1880, stated that

the place where Galt now stands was one of their favourite camping-grounds. The locality abounded in [sturgeon] fish, game [especially red deer[77]], and fresh water. These were the chief objects of Indian pursuit, and they lingered long in places where they were plenty. . . . It was currently rumoured when the first settlers came in, that the Indians had, whilst fishing with torch lights on the river, either wilfully or negligently set fire to the woods near the mouth of Mill-creek.[78]

Other likely summer village sites were at the confluence of waterways, including present-day Blair, Doon, Freeport, Breslau, Bridgeport, Bloomingdale and Conestoga.[79]

Autumn saw the harvesting of corn, beans and potatoes, in addition to the gathering of acorns, chestnuts, groundnuts and other wild plants. It was a time of extensive festivals when people gathered in dense settlements and consumed much of their surplus food. Elizabeth Betzner Sherk (1811-94), who lived near the site of the present-day Waterloo Pioneers' Memorial Tower, recalled that Mississaugas from throughout the upper Grand River Valley met at the mouth of Schneider's Creek for feasting and celebration "every autumn."[80]

Once the harvest celebrations were over, Mississauga households stored the bulk of their plant food and moved to remote villages to conduct the fall hunt. Peter Jones wrote that "[e]ach tribe or body of Indians has its own range of country, and sometimes each family has its own hunting grounds, marked out by certain natural divisions, such as rivers, lakes, mountains, or ridges; and all the game within these bounds is considered their property as much as the cattle and fowl owned by a farmer on his own land. It is at the peril of an intruder to trespass on the hunting grounds of another."[81] The hunting grounds of Old Jack were "on the west side of the Grand River, in the township of Waterloo."[82] The hunting grounds of Joseph Brant, the famous Mohawk who had been adopted by the Mississaugas in 1798,[83] apparently were on the east side of the Grand River, in the township of Waterloo.[84] Other family hunting grounds were located in Waterloo as well.[85]

By late November, when the snows finally came, the Mississaugas would travel as a group into the interior to their hunting and trapping grounds. They would congregate in heavily wooded areas well protected from the weather, where fuel for campfires was easy to obtain.

In spring, called "seegwun" or sap season, the Mississaugas tapped the maple trees and made maple sugar. Waterloo Township's forest abounded with maple trees.[86] Thus, this would have been a desirable area to establish sugar camps. Kahgegagahbowh (Standing Firm), or George Copway as he was known in English, recounted that "one Indian family often have five thousand, six thousand, eight thousand, and ten thousand dishes to gather sap from the noble trees in the spring."[87]

After their sugar-making, "many of the families visited the trading post and then travelled to the Credit River for the spring salmon run."[88]

Here they reassembled in one large village. Around the beginning of May they held "grand pow-wow dances and various games."[89] Then they broke up into smaller summer villages.

Newcomers Are Received into Mississauga Domains

An aged Mississauga Indian, presumably Old Jack (or "Father Jackson," as he became known after his conversion to Methodism in 1826), recounted to Peter Jones in the 1820s that

> before the white man landed on our shores the red men of the forest were numerous, powerful, wise, and happy. In those days nothing but the weight of many winters bore them down to the grave. . . . [Then] a strange people landed, wise as the gods, powerful as the thunder, with faces white as the snow. Our fathers held out to them the hand of friendship. The strangers then asked for a small piece of land on which they might pitch their tents; the request was cheerfully granted. By and by they begged for more, and more was given them. In this way they have continued to ask, or have obtained by force or fraud, the fairest portions of our territory.[90]

The Mississaugas on the north shore of Lake Ontario numbered about one thousand people when settlers began moving into their domain in the early 1780s.[91] By 1787 their population had been reduced by almost half. Eleven years later, in 1798, only 330 persons and three unenumerated families remained.[92] The so-called settlement of Upper Canada was in part "a *re*settlement, a reoccupation of a land made waste by the diseases and demoralization introduced by the newcomers."[93] The British-Canadian state followed a policy of "negotiating with Indians for access to their traditional lands in advance of Euro-Canadian penetration,"[94] in accordance with the precepts of the Royal Proclamation of 1763. Initially both the Mississaugas and the British felt they had gained from the treaties. "The Mississaugas believed that they had made a series of useful and profitable rental agreements for the use of their land, in return for gifts and presents in perpetuity."[95] They also believed that they had reserved "the sole right of the fisheries . . . together with the flats or the low grounds . . . which we have heretofore cultivated and where we have our camps."[96] The British, in contrast, understood that they had extinguished the native title to the land and that the Crown had obtained full proprietary rights."[97]

These conflicting interpretations of the treaties led to friction in the 1790s. The Mississaugas understood that they had retained the right to "encamp and fish where we pleased"[98] throughout their territory and strictly reserved other specific lands, including rendezvous points and burial grounds, for their exclusive use. However, the Crown did little to protect the Mississaugas' land rights. In the winter of 1793 an eccentric white trader, David Ramsay, wrote down their grievances and presented them to Lieutenant Governor Simcoe. They complained that settlers intruded "on our hunting ground which is our farm." They also came to "our Creeks both fishing and hunting." But if Mississaugas "are found in any of there [sic] fields they take from us—what they think proper of ours untill we make them full satisfaction to their minds."[99]

The friction peaked in 1796 when a drunken soldier killed Wabakinine, the head chief of the Credit River Mississaugas. The Mississaugas attempted to organize a pan-Indian alliance to avenge Wabakinine's murder. However, the attack never occurred, "thanks largely to Joseph Brant of the Six Nations."[100] Brant had led almost 2,000 Six Nations Indians to Upper Canada (then part of the province of Quebec) in 1785 and established villages for them on lands in the lower Grand River Valley under the auspices of the British Crown. When the Mississaugas approached Brant to join them in attacking the British garrisons at York and Newark, the Mohawk cautioned them against such action. They reluctantly followed his advice.

By 1798 the Mississaugas were a demoralized people. They complained that fires set by settlers were "breaking around us & our Grounds becoming confined and not fit for hunting."[101] "Their children began to cry for food, their souls fainted for want, their clothes dropped from their shivering backs, the fatal smallpox and measles visited them."[102] Joseph Brant, land agent and attorney for the Six Nations, offered to help the Mississaugas by taking them under his "Protection" and sharing with them the annuities generated from Six Nations land sales to speculators. On 5 February 1798 the British Crown had sanctioned Brant's sale of lands in the Grand River Valley to which they, on this occasion, acknowledged the Six Nations had the right to sell.[103] However, the Mississaugas still occupied these lands. This probably explains why Brant offered to share the proceeds from resulting sales with the Mississaugas. On 13 April 1798 the Credit River Mississauga chiefs accepted Brant's terms because they desired Brant's patronage to retain title to their unsurrendered lands. The chiefs, accordingly, appointed Brant to succeed their deceased head chief, Wabakinine, "to do, transact, and negotiate all such matters as they may have occasion to do & transact with the white people."[104] "A tract of land four miles long by two miles wide on the Grand River" between present-day Galt (Cambridge) and

Blair (Cambridge), it was stated many years later, was to be reserved from Brant's sales for the exclusive use of the Mississaugas as a fishing station.[105]

The speculators to whom Brant sold Indian lands in the upper Grand River Valley hoped to meet their financial obligations by selling lots to white agricultural settlers. The Mississaugas facilitated these transactions. A.R. Sherk tells the story of how Jacob Bechtel, a Mennonite farmer from Pennsylvania, was guided to his homestead by a Mississauga guide:

> In the Spring of 1799 Mr. Jacob Bechtel came from Pennsylvania to the Niagara District along with a caravan of settlers that took up land in that District. . . . One fault [Bechtel found with the Niagara District] was the lack of spring creeks. . . . Bechtel looked up an Indian camp and told them what he wanted, a locality where there was good Spring water, as well as good land and good timber. The Indians knew of such a place, so Mr. Bechtel engaged one as a guide. . . . The Indian led them to a small creek known as Bechtel Creek and here remarked-Here is the best spring water in Canada and here is good land and fine timber, and here Mr. Bechtel located . . . [T]his small creek was . . . well know[n] to, and highly prized by . . . many of the Indians. Across the town[ship]line between Waterloo and Dumfries from the southwest corner of the Bechtel location [was a plain of] . . . light dry soil with a few pine trees on it making it an ideal place for a permanent Indian camp, which it no doubt had been.[106]

Possibly the plain referred to was part of the Mississauga reserve on the Grand River and the township line marked the northern boundary of that reserve. However, there were plains in other areas of Waterloo Township as well. An Indian trail, part of which is now called Plains Road, ran northwest from Bechtel Creek through the "Waterloo Plains"[107] into present-day Wilmot Township. The Speed River ran southwest into the Grand River through "the pleasant plains of Little Paradise" from present-day Puslinch Township.[108] The Mississaugas planted on these plains. Jacob Bechtel, on his prospecting tour in 1799, "found on the one hundred acres just to the east [of Bechtel Creek] a small patch of potatoes where someone [presumably a Mississauga] earlier in the Spring had cleared a small patch of ground and planted spuds and pumpkins and left again. Mr. Bechtel and his party here got new potatoes and roasted them in the hot ashes of their camp fire."[109]

The Mississaugas made important distinctions between sovereignty and ownership, between possession by communities and possession by individuals. Thus, it is likely that Jacob Bechtel had to rent a Mississauga family's rights to the lot on which his homestead was located, in addition to the legal title from the Crown.[110] Peter Jones tells the story of how

An Indian Chief on the Grand River was applied to, separately, by two white men, for a certain piece of land. One was an old honest Canadian Dutch farmer, well known to the chief. The other was a Yankee stranger, who came with many extravagant promises of what he would do for the Indian if he would only let him have the land, far outbidding his competitor. The chief gravely listened to these offers, and then coolly replied to the Dutch farmer: "My friend, I have known you these many years, and have never heard of your cheating an Indian, or sending him away from your house hungry." Then, pointing to the stranger, he said: "This man wants my land; his mouth is all sugar, and his words very sweet, but I do not know what is in his heart. I therefore turn away from his sweet words, and let you have my land."[111]

Individual transactions of this type were the only payment the Mississaugas ultimately received from Brant's sale of Indian lands in the upper Grand River Valley. The British-Canadian Indian Department managed the legal end of the transactions and used the interest generated from the land sales to pay for goods which were distributed annually among the Indians on condition of good behaviour. The Indian Department withheld even these goods from the Mississaugas until they severed their relationship with Brant. By 1801 the Indian Department had succeeded in its objective. The Six Nations complained: "[i]t is hard the Mesassgues [sic] should drop off . . . it is a material hurt to us that they have not come [to our council meeting]."[112] Later that year, the Mississagas replaced Brant with Kebonsence as their new head chief.[113] This compliance was rewarded with goods as treaty payments, which the Mississaugas regarded as perpetually renewed rent for the use of land surrendered in 1784. However, the Mississaugas complained about the amount received. They had been told by Colonel Butler "when he purchased our Lands from our deceased Chief Wabakanyne for our Great Father the King that in payment we should every fall receive presents to keep our women & children warm & that these presents never should cease, but now many of our women & children return naked[,] with tears in their eyes[,] from the smallness of our presents."[114]

The Mississaugas were becoming increasingly dependent on the caprice of Indian agents and handouts from white settlers for their survival. They jealously protected the tiny reserves throughout their former domain which they believed they had never surrendered. Thus, when Nathaniel Dodge constructed a primitive grist mill at present-day Galt (Cambridge) in 1802, they reacted swiftly and burned it down. Two years later when John Erb, another millwright, came with two companions to examine the site he was accosted by Old Jack. Old Jack threatened to shoot them unless they should "forthwith make themselves 'scarce' thereabout."[115] In the ensuing confrontation Old Jack fired a shot at the party and shattered the arm of one of Erb's companions.[116] Consequently, John Erb lost interest in Galt as a possible mill seat. Instead, he established a grist mill at present-day Preston (Cambridge) and his brother, Abraham Erb, established a grist mill at present-day Waterloo.

Mennonites and Mississaugas established a reciprocal relationship over the ensuing years. Mississaugas performed the valuable service of hunting wolves,[117] for which the Crown paid a bounty, and supplying the settlers with fish and game.[118] Mennonites permitted the Mississaugas to travel throughout Waterloo Township and to use land unoccupied by them for communal purposes. However, these benefits soon were offset by negative experiences.

Already in 1808 Mennonites complained that

> several of our Township inhabitors takes kegs and barrels full of spirits from the Distillers and trades with the Indians, which causes them to get drunk and lie about and not follow their hunting, and their young ones starving for hunger, going about begging and hallowing for victuals before our doors like beasts, and at the same time often the old ones coming along and being drunk, scaring ourselves and our families by their bad behaviour.

They prayed the "Honourable Assembly to take into consideration what is said, and prevent such trading by an Act."[119]

Twenty years later the Mississaugas took control of their own destiny by converting to Methodism and repudiating the use of liquor entirely. Kechejeemon (Man of the Stream), or John Thomas as he was known in English, "was once very poor here in Waterloo."[120] Then, in 1825, he wrote:

> I embraced this good religion. . . . When I heard preaching in my own language, I began to seek the Lord; but at first I felt very sick in my heart, and went mourning some time. When I put away whiskey, and all wickedness, and prayed with all my heart, then the Lord forgave all my sins, and I was very happy.[121]

Sobriety led John Thomas and his Mississauga kindred to "prosper in many things."[122]

When Old Jack died in 1829 the Methodist minister George Ryerson reported in his obituary that he "was the only survivor of those who, a few years ago, constituted a living nation, but who now survive in the mournful recollections of their converted children—a nation hurried into a premature grave, not by the desolating progress of war or pestilence; but by a much more efficient auxiliary of death, *intemperance*."[123] Of course, intemperance had its roots in social instability resulting from European settlement. As Leo Johnson has written, settlement "depleted or effectively closed" access to resources on which the Mississauga economy was based and "with this economic collapse, Mississauga morale and social life collapsed as well."[124] The Methodists' Indian temperance programme provided "an esoteric solution" to this "peculiar problem."[125] It promoted "thrift, punctuality, industry, and other Methodist ascetic values" as the means to "[r]espectability, middle-class status, [and] social mobility."[126] Thus, George Copway could conclude that as soon as the Credit River Mississaugas were converted "[t]hey began to work, which they had not previously done...; they gave up drinking, to which they had been greatly addicted, and became sober, industrious, and consistent Christians."[127]

The conversion of Mississaugas to model European middle-class values appeared complete. A continental German immigrant lawyer, Christian Klinckhardt, could report in 1833 that Mississauga travellers he met in the vicinity of Waterloo Township "are the most peaceable people, and a large number of them are Christians, of the Methodist sect." Mennonite settlers, on the other hand, were "to a large extent totally without education, and religious fanatics besides, among whom the devil plays almost as important a role as the worship of God."[128] Empirical evidence required that Klinckhardt flip the stereotypical cultural dichotomy between backward "tribal" societies and advanced "civilization" on the settlement frontier.

In 1837 William Peterson, a Methodist exhorter in Waterloo Township who edited *Canada Museum*, a local German-language newspaper, reported that "we hardly have anything to fear" from "a party of peaceful Indians [who recently] passed through Preston with wives and children" enroute to their "usual winter hunting grounds."[129] By 1840, however, his attitude had changed. In the intervening years over two thousand Potawatomi had moved into Upper Canada from Michigan and Wisconsin to escape removal by the American government to a new Indian reservation west of the Mississippi. Some moved temporarily to the upper Grand River Valley. They were "in a state of great poverty and degradation, and an annoyance to the white inhabitants" wherever they went.[130] One of them allegedly raped a European settler, Elizabeth Johnson, in Wilmot Township (which adjoined Waterloo Township to the west) on 26 October 1840. The Civil Secretary of Upper Canada, S.B. Harrison, reported to the chief superintendent of Indian Affairs in Upper Canada on the following 7 December that "the Indian has eluded the pursuit of Justice, and . . . still lurks in the neighbourhood of the place where the crime was committed, concealed and protected by the other Indians."[131] William Peterson now roused his neighbours to take matters into their own hands:

> All you men who have sisters, wives, or mothers, think of the grave, dreadful danger in which your loved ones find themselves, as long as such frightful Indians are near; as long as they sneak around your home, by day and night. You must be anxious and afraid when you leave home, that while you are gone, one of these two-legged wolves might enter your home, and snatch one of your lambs or sheep, and tear it to pieces! And Oh! How must the poor women feel, who live near these lawless Indians, and are often left alone at home! Therefore, we call you again, loudly and earnestly. . . . Do not rest, relax, or sleep, until you have apprehended the atrocious and cruel malefactor, and handed him over to the authorities . . . the others are scared away, and you may live in peace.[132]

Some settlers in the Township apparently followed Peterson's advice. About this time William Ellis, a local justice of the peace, is said to have chanced upon "an Indian tied to a tree with two white men whipping him . . . a little to the west of where Preston now stands." Ellis "routed the men and untied the Indian."[133] It is not known whether these men were Mennonites. However, Mennonites are known to have signed a petition circulated by Peterson which called upon the civil authorities to take "immediate and effectual means" to restore order among them.[134] The effect of these combined efforts was that the Mississaugas were forced out of Waterloo Township.[135] In 1840 Maungwudaus (Big Legging), or George Henry as he was known in English, "one of the [Methodists'] foremost Indian preachers" in Ontario, removed to Sarnia from Waterloo Township station where he had been serving Mississauga residents for the previous two years.[136] No one replaced him. Mississaugas virtually disappear from the Mennonites' historical record after 1840 and are no longer remembered by local historians even though their reserve is only about sixty miles away, near Hagersville.[137]

The Mississaugas, who numbered nearly 250 in 1841, soon found themselves confined to a 200-acre reserve on the Credit River because white farmers denied them access to former planting grounds and "hunting parks."[138] The Credit River reserve had been set aside in 1820, but until the early 1840s the Mississaugas had continued to exercise jurisdiction over a much broader territory.[139] In 1838, for example, the Methodist missionary Benjamin Slight reported that the Mississaugas had "820 acres of land in a state of cultivation" near the mouth of the Credit River.[140] Settlers gradually encroached on these lands. Kahkewaquonaby (Sacred Feathers), or Peter Jones as he was known in English, complained in 1845 that

> the Indian territories have been taken away till our possessions are now so small that you would almost require a magnifying glass to see them. We are surrounded on all sides by white settlers, still encroaching on us; and I am afraid that in a few years we will hardly have space enough left to lay down our bones upon, or ground enough to cover our bodies.[141]

Peter Schmalz observed that only "[a]nnuities from land sales and government assistance prevented mass starvation."[142]

In 1847 the Mississaugas decided to surrender their Credit River reserve and move to a fertile tract of 4,800 acres, in the southwestern corner of the Six Nations 55,000-acre reserve on the Grand River, near Hagersville.[143] The Mississaugas called this land base "New Credit."

Choosing Waterloo Township as a Settlement Site

Francis Jennings, in his study of Indian-European relations in colonial Pennsylvania, concluded that "the earliest white settlement was facilitated by *Indian* frontiersmen. The land cleared by Indians for their own farms and villages were the lands to which the white settlers invariably gravitated."[144] In 1707 Mennonites were the first white settlers to go over the low divide which separates the Delaware watershed from the Susquehanna. There they established the nucleus of what was to become the Lancaster Mennonite settlement on Shawnee planting grounds on Pequea Creek. Jennings speculated that "their coming may have caused the abandonment of Shawnee villages on Pequea Creek."[145]

Mennonites also settled on the fringe of European agricultural settlement in Upper Canada. The land the first settlers chose in the southern part of Waterloo Township was in an open and parklike forest that resembled the boundary area between forests and grasslands. This so-called edge effect had been created artificially by Mississaugas and their Aboriginal predecessors, through "prescribed burns,"[146] as an ideal habitat for a host of wildlife species. As William Cronon has written of New England, this "not merely attracted game but helped create much larger populations of it. . . . In short, Indians who hunted game animals were not just taking the 'unplanted bounties of nature'; in an important sense, they were harvesting a foodstuff which they had consciously been instrumental in creating."[147]

J. David Wood, in his study of Dumfries Township, notes that Indian hunting parks[148] were likely "one of the most influential determinants of the lines followed by the initial settlement in western Upper Canada, and a determinant which heretofore has remained unheralded." Thus, "it is obvious, perhaps as we should expect, that they were trying to get the best of both worlds—of the open land for farming activities, of the woodland for its critically necessary building and heating products."[149]

The trees that grew in Indian hunting parks were predominantly sprout hardwoods, trees such as oak and walnut which could regenerate themselves after forest fires by sprouting from their roots. Prescribed burns, which Indians repeated every year to rejuvenate the land, tended to destroy trees and shrubs which lacked this ability. Possibly, it was the association of walnut trees with hunting parks which gave rise to the myth that Mennonites preferred soil on which the black walnut tree grew.[150]

Waterloo Township was relatively accessible to European agricultural settlers because an Indian "Road leading to hunting grounds on the Grand River" ran there from Dundas.[151] A.R. Sherk, writing in 1937, noted that

> [m]uch has been written about the dogged perseverance and hardships of the early pioneers in making their way through the notorious Beverly Swamp. That simply is pure fiction. That the swamp existed is certainly true enough, but it was miles away from . . . the straight and direct route from Dundas to Preston. I satisfied myself on that point in my teen age, which none of the would-be historians or authors took the trouble of doing.[152]

If Mennonites had not settled in the southern part of Waterloo Township when they did, other Europeans would have moved there instead. The ecology of the area made it a desirable site for European agricultural settlement and the Indian road leading from Dundas to Preston provided a natural outlet for the expanding European population at the head of Lake Ontario. Mennonites undoubtedly speeded up the settlement process, however, by drawing attention to the area. It is said that Jacob Bechtel, the first Mennonite to scout out Waterloo Township in 1799, returned to the Niagara peninsula telling immigrants "where he had been and where he had located and how they could find the place by following the Indian trails."[153] That fall several non-Mennonite families followed Bechtel's directions. They camped on Bechtel's land until they chose locations of their own. The bulk of newcomers in the ensuing years, however, were Mennonites.

After lots in the southern part of Waterloo Township filled up, which occurred by about 1804, Mennonite settlers moved farther north.[154] They followed Indian trails, which served as the original avenues of penetration into the forest,[155] and generally located near meadows or river flats, which the Mississaugas used as planting grounds. These areas were ecologically similar to Indian hunting parks in that they provided settlers with desired access to both open land and woodland.

As more settlers moved into the Township the Indian trails were improved, abandoned or extended according to local needs. In particular, new roads were cut across the inherited network to tie remote areas to grist mills. This was beginning to happen as early as 1810. Surveyed roads came to predominate in the 1820s, when Mennonite immigration finally tapered off, and other newcomers then located along them.

Settlers in Waterloo Township claimed exclusive private property rights in Mississauga common-property resources (e.g., hunting parks, planting grounds and fishing stations). As these private property rights expanded, Mississaugas were effectively denied access to sufficient resources to sustain their mobile lifestyle which was "based on free access to a variety of common resources scattered over a wide territory."[156] In 1840-41 settlers banished Mississaugas from Waterloo Township because one Indian was accused of raping a local settler and all Indians were deemed to be accomplices in the crime. Mississaugas gradually adopted the European model of sedentary agriculture as an alternate means of subsistence and located in permanent villages for this purpose. The Mississaugas established their first permanent village at the Credit River, in the winter of 1826-27, on a 200-acre reserve set apart for them by the Indian Department for this purpose. This land base proved to be insufficient for Mississauga needs in the long term, however, as settlers denied them access to off-reserve resources. And then in the mid-nineteenth century, the government sold off the 200-acre reserve without making a treaty or taking a surrender of the reserve. Finally, in 1847 the Mississaugas accepted an invitation from the Six Nations to relocate to a fertile 4,800-acre tract, in the southwestern corner of the Six Nations 55,000-acre reserve, near Hagersville.

Conclusion

Mennonite settlement patterns in Waterloo Township followed Indian settlement patterns. The land that Mennonites found most desirable was not necessarily the most productive. Rather, it was the easiest to cultivate because it had already been cleared by Indian inhabitants and it was the most accessible because it lay on the route of Indian roads. In the early years of European settlement Mennonites and Indians appeared to benefit mutually from contact. However, in the long term, their interests came into conflict and eventually Indians were forced to leave the vicinity of European settlements and concentrate on reserves set apart by the Indian Department for their exclusive use.

The story of Mennonite settlement in Waterloo Township is the story of the colonization of the Mississauga people. Mennonites participated in depriving the Mississaugas of access to land and resources that would have allowed them a more autonomous existence. Mennonites participated in reducing the Mississaugas to poverty and dependence on the caprice of Indian agents and handouts from European settlers. Finally, Mennonites participated in forcing the Mississaugas out of their community and out of their history.

Notes

1 Peter Jones (Kahkewaquonaby), *History of the Ojebway Indians: With Especial Reference to Their Conversion to Christianity* (London: A.W. Bennett, [1861]), p. 27. This book was published posthumously.

2 I would like to thank Donald Smith, T.D. Regehr, David McNab and Dean Jacobs for their comments on an earlier draft of this paper. An earlier version of this paper was published as "Mississauga-Mennonite Relations in the Upper Grand River Valley," *Ontario History*, 87, 2 (June 1995): 155-72. My title is inspired by Francis Jennings, *The Invasion of America: Indians, Colonialism, and the Cant of Conquest* (1975; rpt. New York: W.W. Norton, 1976). Jennings writes that Europeans were "[i]ncapable of conquering true wilderness," although they were "highly competent in the skill of conquering other people." And "that is what they did. They did not settle a virgin land. They invaded and displaced a resident population" (ibid., p. 15). I basically concur with Jennings' thesis but prefer to use the term "colonization" rather than "conquest" to describe what happened in Waterloo Township, because I do not believe that the Aboriginal people there have ever been conquered.

3 David Boyle, quoted in an unidentified clipping dated June 1903, cited in Donald Macleod, "'Quaint Specimens of the Early Days': Priorities in Collecting the Ontario Archival Record, 1872-1935," *Archivaria*, 22 (Summer 1986): 12-39, at 36-37. Boyle was the first professional archaeologist in Ontario.

4 Gerald Craig, *Upper Canada, the Formative Years: 1784-1841* (Toronto: McClelland and Stewart, 1963), p. 7. This perspective is shared by R. Louis Gentilcore and David Wood, "A Military Colony in a Wilderness: The Upper Canadian Frontier," in R. Douglas Francis and Donald B. Smith, eds., *Readings in Canadian History: Pre-Confederation* (Toronto: University of Toronto Press, 1994), pp. 293-306. Robert Surtees adds that "because the arduous task of clearing forested land proceeded slowly, even the bands who had sold the shoreline continued to use portions of it [until after the War of 1812]" ("Land Cessions, 1763-1830," in Edward S. Rogers and Donald B. Smith, eds., *Aboriginal Ontario: Historical Perspectives on the First Nations* [Toronto: Dundurn Press, 1994], pp. 92-121, at p. 112). However, it is arguable that the First Nations never ceded the shoreline anywhere within the colony or later in the province and that, in fact, the shorelines were protected by the Gun Shot Treaty of 1792.

5 G. Elmore Reaman, *The Trail of the Black Walnut* (Toronto: McClelland and Stewart, 1957), p. xix. Robert Surtees concurs that Indians represented "a retarding influence and a nuisance" to European settlers, particularly prior to the development of an Indian reserve policy in the 1830s (R.J. Surtees, "The Development of an Indian Reserve Policy in Canada," *Ontario History*, 61 [1969]: 87-98, at 88).

6 Waterloo Township was known as Block Number Two from 1798 to 1816. It was dissolved in 1972.

7 Craig, *Upper Canada: The Formative Years*, p. 46.

8 Anonymous, "The Early Settlement of Waterloo Township" (1869); reprinted with annotations by Lorna Bergey in *Pennsylvania Mennonite Heritage*, 15, 2 (April 1992): 9-20.

9 Heinz Lehmann, *The German Canadians 1750-1937: Immigration, Settlement and Culture*, edited and translated by Gerhard P. Bassler (St. John's, NF: Jesperson Press, 1986), p. 68.

10 *Berlin Daily News*, 16 July 1879, p. 2.

11 Reaman, *Trail of the Black Walnut*, p. 143.

12 John S. Martin, "Unveiling of Memorial Tower Tribute to County Pioneers," *The Daily Record* (Kitchener, ON), 30 August 1926, p. 3.

13 Royce MacGillivray, "Local History as a Form of Popular Culture in Ontario," *New York History*, 65, 4 (October 1984): 367-76, at 371. In other parts of Canada different myths prevail. In the prairie provinces, for example, "the Northwest Mounted Police, the men who fought Riel at Duck Lake, were glorified as the truest examples of the Canadian historical epic" (Douglas Owram, "The Myth of Louis Riel," in Hartwell Bowsfield, ed., *Louis Riel: Selected Readings* (Toronto: Copp Clark Pitman, 1988), pp. 11-29, at p. 15.

14 W. Stewart Wallace, *The First Book of Canadian History* (Toronto: Macmillan, 1930), p. 10. I am grateful to Donald Smith for providing me with this reference.

15 W. Stewart Wallace, *The First Book of Canadian History* (Edmonton: Hurtig, 1928), pp. 3-4. I am grateful to Donald Smith for providing me with this reference.

16 "Indian Teacher Is Resentful," undated newspaper clipping in NAC, Elliott Moses Papers, MG 30, C 169, vol. 2, Scrapbook 1936-41, and "Professor Wallace to Revise," *Toronto Star*, 6 April 1929, in W. Stewart Wallace's file, A73-0020/493(28), University of Toronto Archives. I am grateful to Donald Smith for providing me with these references.

17 Wallace, *First Book of Canadian History* (1930), p. 3. In the 1944 printing of the 1930 edition, however, Wallace reverted to the phrase "savages of a primitive type" (ibid., pp. 7-8).

18 This myth has been framed in more recent histories as a contest between "indigenous nomads" and "sedentary agriculturalists" (J.R. Miller, ed., *Sweet Promises: A Reader on Indian-White Relations in Canada* [Toronto: University of Toronto Press, 1991], p. xii). Thus, the so-called conspiracy led by Pontiac in 1763 is explained as "only another angry response by hunter-gatherers to the encroachments of farmers" (J.R. Miller, *Skyscrapers Hide the Heavens: A History of Indian-White Relations in Canada* [Toronto: University of Toronto Press, 1989], p. 74). Similar violent confrontations did not take place in Upper Canada because the Crown removed Indians from the path of European settlement, following regulations established by the Royal Proclamation of 1763 in the wake of Pontiac's resistance, and assisted "the [displaced] Algonquians to adopt agriculture" as an alternate means of subsistence (Edward S. Rogers, "The Algonquian Farmers in Southern Ontario, 1830-1945," in Rogers and Smith, eds., *Aboriginal Ontario*, pp. 122-66, at p. 136. "[E]x-hunters" at the Credit River made "the best of a very difficult situation" (Olive Dickason, *Canada's First Nations: A History of Founding Peoples from Earliest Times* [Toronto: McClelland and Stewart, 1992], pp. 235, 237).

19 Abraham Rotstein, "The Mystery of the Neutral Indians," in Roger Hall et al., eds., *Patterns of the Past: Interpreting Ontario's History* (Toronto: Dundurn Press, 1988), pp. 11-36, at p. 25.

20 Ibid., p. 26.

21 A legendary spring in Homer Watson Memorial Park, Kitchener, was said to have gushed forth on the site where two lovers were killed during this war. See "Legendary Spring Gets a Fountain," *Kitchener-Waterloo Record*, 17 July 1967.

22 Bruce Trigger, *The Children of Aataentsic: A History of the Huron People to 1660*, 2 vols. (Montreal: McGill-Queen's University Press, 1990), vol. 2, pp. 838-39.

23 Rotstein, "The Mystery of the Neutral Indians," p. 27.

24 Peter S. Schmalz, *The Ojibwa of Southern Ontario* (Toronto: University of Toronto Press, 1991), p. 20.

25 Ibid., p. 28.

26 Propositions of the Five Nations to the Commissioners of Indian Affairs, 30 June 1700, in Edmund B. O'Callaghan and Berthold Fernow, eds., *Documents Relative to the Colonial History of the State of New York*, 15 vols. (Albany: Weed, Parsons, 1853-87), vol. 4, pp. 693-95. This treaty was subsequently renewed and on 21 January 1840 it would be renewed for the fifth time. On that occasion disagreement arose about the symbols on the wampum belts. Skanawiti, the official keeper of the wampum belts of the

Iroquois Confederacy, explained that the bowl "represented that the Ojebways and the Six Nations were all to eat out of one dish—that is to have all the game in common" (Minutes of a General Council held at the Credit River, 21 January 1840, NAC, RG 10, vol. 1011, p. 82). William Yellowhead, speaking for the "Ojebwas," countered that the dish meant "that the right of hunting on the north side of the Lake was secured to the Ojebways and that the Six Nations were not to hunt here only when they come to smoke the pipe of peace with their Ojebway brethren" (Minutes of a General Council held at the Credit River, 22 January 1840, NAC, RG 10, vol. 1011, p. 87).

27 At the point of initial contact with Europeans, Indians already possessed a land tenure system that amounted to an assertion of inalienable sovereignty over the land. Ian Johnson, in "The Early Mississauga Treaty Process 1781-1819 in Historical Perspective" (unpublished PhD dissertation, University of Toronto, 1986), documents that the so-called land surrender treaties concluded between the Mississaugas and the British-Canadian state between 1781 and 1788 were treaty alliances that included agreements to lease portions of their territory for limited uses. But government subsequently claimed absolute ownership of the leased land, failed to pay rent— or even acknowledge a responsibility to do so—and physically displaced the Mississaugas by facilitating the expansion of European settlement. The Mississaugas responded by developing new strategies, including the adoption of European land ownership rhetoric, to preserve political and economic control over national lands.

28 Jones, *History of the Ojebway Indians*, p. 211. The Mississaugas apparently conferred on the Six Nations the right to occupy the land jointly with them. The Mississaugas gave up none of their most important hunting, fishing and planting rights, and evidently intended to keep living on the land much as they had done before.

29 Elizabeth Bloomfield, for example, in her comprehensive bibliography of historical sources dealing with Waterloo County, entitles one thematic subchapter, "Prehistory, Aboriginal People and Archaeology," in *Waterloo County to 1972: An Annotated Bibliography of Regional History* (Kitchener, ON: Waterloo Regional Heritage Foundation, 1993), p. 21. She justifies this organization on the basis that these sources are "mainly before 1800" (ibid., p. xxiii).

30 Olive Dickason, *The Myth of the Savage and the Beginnings of French Colonialism in the Americas* (Edmonton, AB: University of Alberta Press, 1984), p. 82.

31 James M. Nyce, quoting the English author Graham Greene, in "This Land that Was Desolate Is Become Like the Garden of Eden: The Instance of the Pennsylvania Dutch" (unpublished MA thesis, McMaster University, 1977), p. 15.

32 E.W.B. Snider, "Waterloo County Forests and Primitive Economics," *Waterloo Historical Society*, 6 (1918): 14-17, at 14, quoted in "This Land that Was Desolate," p. 34. The quotation in the original is as follows: "There was nothing in the forest that would sustain human life *outside of fish and deer*" (emphasis added).

33 Ibid.

34 *The Berlin News Record*, 29 August 1900.

35 This omission would appear to have been deliberate because the obituary of Sherk's mother, Elizabeth Betzner Sherk, recounted how she had "often related to her grandchildren of the days when the Mohawk braves met and held their councils at a point on the opposite side of the river every autumn when on their hunting expeditions. She saw the incoming of the settlers, the clearing of the river farms, the construction of the Ferrie mill [at the mouth of Schneider's Creek], the disappearance of the red man and the crowning of the hill, at whose foot they used to gather, with a church, and the conversion of that district into fine farms with here [and] there a prosperous village." See "Death of (Rev.) Mrs. David Sherk," *The Daily Record* (Kitchener, ON), 27 August 1894, p. 1.

36 Gottlieb Leibbrandt, *Little Paradise* (Kitchener, ON: Allprint, 1980), p. 14.

37 James Coyne reported in "The Indian Occupation of Southern Ontario," *Waterloo Historical Society*, 4 (1916): 13-23, at 22, that "[a]fter the middle of the 17th century, the [former] Neutral country became a game preserve of the Iroquois who ranged the woods for deer, bear, wolves, lynxes, racoons [*sic*] and beaver. . . . When Dollier de Casson and Galinée passed through in 1669-1670, there were no human inhabitants."

38 James E. Kerr, "Early Days in Galt," *Waterloo Historical Society*, 8 (1920): 115-22, at 118.

39 Quoted in Andrew Taylor, *Our Todays and Yesterdays: A History of the Township of North Dumfries* (Preston, ON: Progress Printing, 1970), p. 269.

40 Ibid., pp. 270-71.

41 Ivan Groh, *The Pioneers of Clearview* (no publishing information), p. [iv].

42 Anonymous, "The Early Settlement of Waterloo Township," p. 2.

43 A Mennonite petition of 1808 reported that "a certain Abraham Stauffer, of our Township, was shot by a drunken Indian through his arm and other places, and was then in danger of losing his life" (Province of Upper Canada, *Journal of Legislative Assembly*, 18 February 1808). The attorney general, Thomas Scott, "stated that on the 22nd of this month about a quarter of a mile east side of Moss' Mills in the County of Haldimand, one John Ebb [*sic*] late of the County of Lancaster in the State of Pensylvania [*sic*], a purchase[r] of part of the lands sold by Mr. Beasley, was with a malicious intention shot at and wounded by a Mississagua [*sic*] Indian, known by the Name of Jack. The wound will not most probably prove mortal, but Mr. Ebb's [*sic*] arm is much shattered and he has received hurt on other parts of the Body—The Indian fired with a ball" (John Green to William Claus, 29 October 1804, NAC, RG 7, G 16, vol. 3, pp. 284-85). Presumably Scott confused John Erb with Abraham Stauffer.

44 Peter Moyer, "History of Waterloo," *Waterloo Chronicle*, 25 July 1866, reprinted in [Joseph Meyer Snyder], *Hannes Schneider and His Wife, Catharine Haus Schneider: Their Descendants and Times, 1534-1939* (Kitchener, ON: Miriam Helen Snyder, 1937 [this was clearly published much later]), p. 10.

45 Anonymous, "The Early Settlement of Waterloo Township," p. 2. Lorna Bergey adds that the Mennonite settlers of Waterloo Township "gained for themselves the respect of the Indians with whom they had friendly relations" ("Early Mennonite Migrations from Pennsylvania and Subsequent Settlements in Canada," *Pennsylvania Mennonite Heritage*, 9, 2 (April 1986): 2-12, at 7.

46 Ezra Eby, *A Biographical History of the Early Settlers and Their Descendants in Waterloo Township* (1895 and 1896; revised and expanded ed., Kitchener, ON: Eldon Weber, 1971), p. 144. Sam Eby held a somewhat different status in the memory of local Indians. Thomas McGee, a Mississauga Indian who lived in Waterloo Township, recalled that Sam Eby supplied local Mississaugas with whiskey. "I used to live here de Waterloo—All time get drunk—I go some times on dis road in the night, some times midnight—go up de river to Still house, after de whiskey. You know up to Sam Aby's Still-house. Me was very poor, me hungry, me naked, me know nothing about de Jesus. [Then,] [a]bout dree years ago, I go to River Credit, den me hear about Jesus. Me den very sick in my heart, I so poor, me cry, me pray to Great Spirit, den he hear me, and bless our de poor hearts. Now me no more get drunk, me no more ask for de whiskey; but sometimes when me get hungry, me go white man's house me ask for some bread me eat; dis is good, whiskey, no good" (*Christian Guardian*, 26 December 1829).

47 A Mennonite preacher visiting Ontario from Pennsylvania reflected in his travel diary that "God blessed the settlers of this land, the labours of their mind and hand. [As] [t]he population increased, bears, wolves and Indians decreased" (Samuel Godshalk, "Journal of a Journey to Ontario in the Year 1869" [typescript], Mennonite Archives of Ontario, Hist. Mss. 17.1). Similar sentiments were shared by non-Mennonite settlers in the upper Grand River Valley. A.D. Ferrier, a Scottish settler near Fergus, reckoned that "it seems to be the will of Providence that they [the Indians] should gradually disappear as the white man gets possession of the country" (*Reminiscences of Canada and the Early Days of Fergus* [Guelph, ON: Mercury Book and Job Office, 1866], p. 45).

48 Frank H. Epp, *Mennonites in Canada* (Toronto: Macmillan, 1974), p. 69. Ted Regehr, in his comments on a draft of Epp's manuscript in 1973, notes that Epp's interpretation "obviously could use some documentation. Nonetheless it is an important point and your description is good. Often in cases where you have more evidence your style gets bogged down with the narrative and consequently makes your point much less effectively" (Readers' Committee Reports, Mennonite History Project, Conrad Grebel College Archives).

49 Epp, *Mennonites in Canada*, p. 78.

50 Eby, *A Biographical History of the Early Settlers* p. 10.

51 Ibid.

52 Epp, *Mennonites in Canada*, p. 78.

53 Mabel Dunham, *Grand River* (Toronto: McClelland and Stewart, 1945), p. 21.

54 Ibid., pp. 74-75.

55 Ibid., p. 15.

56 Ibid., p. 16.

57 Ibid., pp. 185-86.

58 Quoted in an interview in the *Kitchener-Waterloo Record*, 11 May 1990, p. B2.

59 Kenneth McLaughlin, *Waterloo: An Illustrated History* (Burlington, ON: Windsor Publications, 1990), p. 13.

60 E.A. Cruikshank, "The Reserve of the Six Nations on the Grand River and the Mennonite Purchase of Block No. 2," *Waterloo Historical Society*, 15 (1927): 303-50, at 322.

61 Ibid., p. 309.

62 The deputy superintendent general of Indian Affairs, William Claus, argued that "by subdividing the land the good and bad might be separated, the good kept by the purchaser and the bad thrown back on the Indians" (ibid., p. 326).

63 Eduard Klinckhardt, "Einige Bemerkungen ueber die Provinz Ober Canada, besonders in Bezug auf die Deutsche Einwanderung," *Canada Museum*, 23 February 1837, p. 2. The *Canada Museum* was a German-language newspaper published in Berlin, Waterloo Township, 1835-40.

64 "A whole new discipline of anthropology was established to study the static, primitive, and soon to be extinct native peoples who had lived in North America prior to the coming of the White Man" (Bruce Trigger, "Indians and Ontario's History," *Ontario History*, 74, 4 [1982]: 246-57, at 247).

65 James W. St. G. Walker, "The Indian in Canadian Historical Writing, 1972-1982," in Ian A.L. Getty and Antoine S. Lussier, eds., *As Long as the Sun Shines and Water Flows: A Reader in Canadian Native Studies* (Vancouver, BC: University of British Columbia Press, 1983), pp. 340-61, at pp. 350-51.

66 Olive Dickason describes the complex Aboriginal societies that Europeans first encountered in her seminal study *Canada's First Nations*.

67 Jennings, *The Invasion of America*, p. 15.

68 Donald B. Smith, in "Who Are the Mississauga?" *Ontario History*, 67, 4 (December 1975): 211-22, rejects the view that the Mississaugas constitute a distinct Aboriginal Nation. Nevertheless, the Mississaugas are referred to as a Nation in early-nineteenth-century council meetings and treaties. In Treaty #22, for example, three tracts of land at the Twelve and Sixteen Mile Creeks and the Credit River were surrendered upon the trust that the Crown would "make provision for the maintenance and religious instruction of the people of the Mississauga Nation and their posterity" (Treaty #22, 28 February 1820, NAC, RG 10, vol. 1842).

69 Jones, *History of the Ojebway Indians*, pp. 107-109.

70 Ibid., p. 39.

71 William Claus to Lieutenant Governor Maitland, 1 May 1819, NAC, MG 11, CO 42, vol. 362, p. 203. A full historical account of the Credit River Mississaugas from the 1780s to the 1860s is contained in Donald B. Smith, *Sacred Feathers: The Reverend Peter Jones (Kakewaquonaby) and the Mississauga Indians* (Toronto: University of Toronto Press, 1987).

72 Peter Jones to the Indian Department, Brantford, 13 February 1855, in
    Mississaugas of the Credit (Toronto: Warwick Brothers and Rutter, 1895),
    p. 38, in NAC, RG 10, vol. 2357, f. 72,563.

73 Lord Selkirk wrote of the Mississaugas in the early nineteenth century that
    "50 or 60 individuals is considered as a large band" (Patrick C.T. White,
    ed., *Lord Selkirk's Diary 1803-1804: A Journal of His Travels in British
    North America and in the Northeastern United States* (1958; rpt. New
    York: Greenwood, 1969), p. 162. This statement was not accurate, how-
    ever, because over two hundred Mississaugas gathered as a "band" at the
    Credit River for the spring and fall salmon runs. Thus, the bands to which
    Lord Selkirk referred were small, not large.

74 William Claus to Lieutenant Governor Maitland, 1 May 1819, NAC,
    MG 11, CO 42, vol. 362, p. 203. The Mississaugas traditionally have been
    characterized as "nomadic peoples" who "relied almost exclusively on
    hunting and fishing" (Donald Smith, "The Dispossession of the Mississauga
    Indians: A Missing Chapter in the Early History of Upper Canada,"
    Ontario History, 73, 2 [1981]: 67-87, at 68). During the autumn and win-
    ter, it was said, they could be found "wandering around the shores of Lake
    Ontario" (Smith, *Sacred Feathers*, p. 63). I would concur with Francis Jen-
    nings that "[t]he basic difference between Indian and English subsistence
    economies was not farming but herding" (*The Invasion of America*, p. 63).
    Indians did not fully domesticate their animal herds. Consequently, they
    lacked dairy products, woollen textiles and fences because they did not
    have animals to milk, shear, or "draw logs to inclose [enclose] our corn-
    fields" (Mississauga council meeting at Fort George, 12-13 January 1798,
    Prideaux Selby's "Record of Councils and Speeches, to and from, the
    Indian Nations in the Province of Upper Canada" [hereafter cited as
    Prideaux Selby's Copybook], New York Historical Society Library, New
    York City).

75 Deputy superintendent general of Indian Affairs, William Claus, reported
    that in August of 1806 many of the Mississauga Indians "are in the River
    Thames and others in the head waters of the Grand River" William Claus
    to Alexander Grant, 1 August 1806, NAC, RG 10, vol. 1, pp. 423-35.

76 The Mississaugas called it Pesshinneguning, "the one that washes the tim-
    ber down and drives away the grass weeds" (Augustus Jones, "Names of
    the Rivers, and Creeks, as they are called by the Mississaugas...," 4 July
    1796, Provincial Archives of Ontario, Surveyor's Letters).

77 The Mississaugas hunted "red Deer" in "the head waters of the Grand
    River" (William Claus to Alexander Grant, 1 August 1806 and 24 July
    1806, NAC, RG 10, vol. 1, pp. 423-25 and 408-10).

78 James Young, *Reminiscences of the Early History of Galt* (Toronto: Hunter
    and Rose, 1880), pp. 11 and 24.

79 "[D]uring the early 1800's small patches of 'wild corn' were found growing
    [along the Grand River] but the settlers paid little attention to it and actu-
    ally destroyed the plants believing them to be an inferior corn which would
    cross-pollinate with their domestic variety and cause crop failure" (Pat
    Mestern, *Looking Back: The Story of Fergus through the Years* [Fergus, ON:
    The Author, 1983], p. 7).

80 "Death of (Rev.) Mrs. David Sherk," p. 1.

81 Jones, *History of the Ojebway Indians*, p. 71.

82 Ibid., p. 254.

83 "Inclosure: [Speech of Wabenip, the Head Chief of the Mississaugas, to Joseph Brant, 2 May 1798]" in E.A. Cruikshank, ed., *The Correspondence of the Honourable Peter Russell with Allied Documents Relating to His Administration of the Government of Upper Canada* (Toronto: Ontario Historical Society, 1935), vol. 2, pp. 186-87.

84 One of Joseph Brant's former slaves, Sophia Pooley, recalled that "Brant lived part of the time at Mohawk [present-day Brantford], part at Ancaster [i.e., Burlington], part at Preston, then called the Lower Block" (Benjamin Drew, ed., *The Refugee: Or the Narratives of Fugitive Slaves in Canada Related by Themselves* (Boston: John P. Jewett, 1856), p. 192.

85 Peter Jones tells the story of how Peter Wompegoosh, a Mississauga "residing in the township of Waterloo, on the Grand River, came on a visit to the Credit for the purpose of hearing the words of the Great Spirit. Being much interested, he tarried longer than he expected. On his return home, he found his family out of provisions and very hungry. P[eter] Wompegoosh rose up very early in the morning in search of deer; he travelled till the middle of the afternoon without seeing a sign of one. He now began to despair; in this emergency he made known his wants to the Christian's God, and began to call aloud on him. To his first prayer he received no answer. He then travelled on some distance, again praying aloud as before that God would give him deer for his family. On rising from his knees, he looked and saw three deer standing not far from him; taking his rifle he shot one on the spot; when he discovered he had killed it, he again fell upon his knees and returned thanks to God. As he rose from his thanksgiving behold he saw another standing within gunshot; as soon as he could load, he shot the second and again gave thanks. After this he went in search of the third, and soon killed him. He was thus provided with an abundant supply for his family. Surely 'God is a prayer-hearing, and a prayer-answering God, a very present help in time of trouble'" (Jones, *History of the Ojebway Indians*, pp. 228-29). Catherine Wompegoosh, "wife of Peter Wompegoosh," was one of twenty-seven Credit River Mississaugas and Saugeen Ojibway who were baptized in Waterloo Township on 26 December 1830 by the Reverend John Ryerson (*Christian Guardian*, 22 January 1831). Two names, presumably including that of Peter Wompegoosh, are obliterated from the printed list of those baptized on that occasion.

86 The surveyor's notes for Waterloo Township are not extant, hence this information must be extrapolated from other sources. According to W.H. Smith, 62,513 pounds of maple sugar was produced in Waterloo Township in 1845 (*Canada: Past, Present and Future*, 2 vols. [Toronto: Thomas Maclear, 1851], p. 121). This was a greater quantity than that produced in any other Ontario township at that time. M.B. Shantz, writing ca. 1930, noted that in the first half of the nineteenth century "every good farmer [in Waterloo Township] gave considerable attention to his Maple trees. J.Y. Shantz had the largest Maple Grove in that vicinity, tapping over four hundred trees. The work of making maple sugar generally lasted from early

March to the middle of April. The sugar was used mostly for domestic purposes instead of white granulated sugar, which at that time was a luxury. The beginning of the maple sugar season was the ending of the school season for many of the farmer boys of that day" ("Adventures in Colonization," unpublished manuscript at the Kitchener Public Library, ca. 1930).

87 George Copway, *The Ojibway Conquest* (New York: George P. Putnam), note 18. The text of *The Ojibway Conquest* was said to have actually been written by Julius Taylor Clark, a former Indian agent. All that Copway "added to Clark's manuscript was an altered introduction; a short poem of his own to his wife, Elizabeth; and revised end notes" (Donald B. Smith, "The Life of George Copway or Kah-ge-ga-gah-bowh [1818-1869]—And a Review of His Writings," *Journal of Canadian Studies*, 23, 3 (Fall 1988): 5-38, at 21. This quotation is from an endnote, so it presumably was written by Copway.

88 Smith, *Sacred Feathers*, p. 7.

89 Jones, *History of the Ojebway Indians*, p. 160.

90 Ibid., pp. 26-27. The speaker presumably was Old Jack, whom Peter Jones referred to as "Father Jackson" in 1829 (*Life and Journals of Kah-ke-wa-quo-na-by (Rev. Peter Jones), Wesleyan Missionary* [Toronto: Anson Green, 1860], p. 266). He was "the only *aged* man amongst the Credit River Indians" (George Ryerson, "To the Senior Editor of the Christian Guardian," *Christian Guardian*, 12 December 1829). I am grateful to Donald Smith for providing me with these references to Old Jack.

91 Smith, *Sacred Feathers*, p. 24.

92 Ibid., p. 30.

93 Jennings, *The Invasion of America*, p. 30.

94 Miller, *Skyscrapers Hide the Heavens*, p. 274.

95 Smith, *Sacred Feathers*, p. 26.

96 "Provisional Surrender," dated 2 August 1805, NAC, RG 10, vol. 1842, Treaty #13a.

97 Smith, *Sacred Feathers*, p. 26.

98 Quinipeno quoted at a meeting with the Mississaugas at the Credit River, 2 August 1805, NAC, RG 10, vol. 1, p. 299.

99 "The Memoreal [Memorial] of Differant [Different] Famley [Family] of the Massesagoe Indeans [Mississauga Indians] to His Excellancy [Excellency] John Graves Simco [Simcoe], North Side of Lake Onteareo [Ontario] the Winter 1793," PAO, Simcoe Papers, Canada, Loose Documents, 1793, Envelope 17.

100 Smith, *Sacred Feathers*, p. 28.

101 Mississauga council meeting at the Credit River, 25 October 1800, Prideaux Selby's Copybook.

102 Jones, *History of the Ojebway Indians*, p. 27.

103 For more information on this transaction, see E. Reginald Good, "Crown-Directed Colonization of Six Nations and Métis Land Reserves in Canada" (unpublished PhD dissertation, University of Saskatchewan, 1994), chap. 4.

104 Speech of Wabakinine, 2 May 1798. William Dummer Powell advised John Askin on 7 May 1798 that "the Missasague's who own the Territory between York and the western population of the Province have adopted

him [Brant] in place of their great chief Wabkenine who was murdered as is
supposed by some rangers" (Milo M. Quaife, ed., *The John Askin Papers*,
2 vols. [Detroit: Detroit Public Library, 1931], vol. 2, pp. 139-40). The
Indian Department never recognized Brant's appointment and on 14 October 1801 the Mississaugas presented Kebonsence as Wabenip's successor"
(Mississauga council meeting at the Grand River, 14 October 1801,
Prideaux Selby's Copybook).

105 Memorial to the Duke of Newcastle, 17 September 1860, NAC, CO 42,
vol. 624, pp. 458-59. At a General Council held at the Credit River on
22 January 1840, "Joseph Sawyer enquired of the chiefs of the Six Nations
if they knew anything about a small reserve of land lying near Galt, which
was claimed by one of our chiefs, Pahdequong" (NAC, RG 10, vol. 1011,
p. 87). The chief referred to is probably Pahtahquahong (Coming Thunder), or Henry P. Chase, as he was known in English, a resident of Muncey-
town. See Donald B. Smith, "Henry Pahtahquahong Chase," in *Dictionary
of Canadian Biography*, vol. 12: *(1891-1900)*, pp. 186-87, and Jones, *Life
and Journals of Kah-ke-wa-quo-na-by*, p. 59. John Tecumseh Henry, "Interpreter to the Chippewas of the Thames," followed up the memorial to the
Duke of Newcastle with letters to the Department of Secretary of State and
the Indian Department in 1867, 1869 and 1876 concerning "the alleged
claim of the Chippewa Indians to a piece of land near the Town of Galt"
(NAC, RG 10, vol. 528, p. 375, and vol. 1979, f. #6007.

106 [Snyder], *Hannes Schneider and His Wife, Catharine Haus Schneider*,
p. 298.

107 Gottlieb Bettschen, *Genealogical, Biographical and Pictorial History of the
Bettschen Family and Its Connections* (N.p.: The Author, 1910), pp. ii, 69,
72, 75.

108 Leslie Witmer Fonds, "Fifty Years of Married Life and How It Came
About" (1946), Mennonite Archives of Ontario, Hist. Mss. 1.14.5,

109 A.R. Sherk to J.M. Snyder, n.d. Algonquian-speaking Indians in the Great
Lakes Region, including the Mississaugas, cultivated "corn, beans, and
squashes" (Helen Hornbeck Tanner, ed., *Atlas of Great Lakes Indian
History* [Norman, OK: University of Oklahoma Press, 1987], p. 18). Frank
Little, writing about Algonquian-speaking Indians in Michigan, wrote that
"they cultivated, in a rude fashion, small patches of sugar corn, beans,
squashes and melons" ("Early Recollections of the Indians about Gull
Prairie," *Historical Collections, Michigan Pioneer and Historical Society*, 26
[1897]: 330-38, at 334).

110 As Francis Jennings writes, "the main implications of the . . . [Aboriginal]
land tenure system were not so strange and baffling as they are sometimes
characterized. Once the misleading term 'purchase' is put out of the way,
payment for land use is not so terribly different from rent. . . . Government
looked forward to a perpetual income from [taxes] . . . even as the [Abo-
riginal Nations] . . . looked forward to perpetually renewed presents"
("Miquon's Passing: Indian-European Relations in Colonial Pennsylvania,
1674 to 1755" [unpublished PhD dissertation, University of Pennsylvania,
1965], p. 62).

111 Jones, *History of the Ojebway Indians*, pp. 218-19. A revealing statement here is that the Mississaugas respected those who did not send them away hungry. As Peter Jones wrote in another context, the Mississaugas were willing to walk with their good "white brethren in one path, eat out of one dish, and to love as brethren" (*Christian Guardian*, 14 December 1831). Jones typically referred to Pennsylvania Mennonites as "Dutch." See his description of public worship services conducted in Mennonite Abraham Erb's "Dutch school house" in Waterloo Township: "When I got through speaking to my Indian brethren, I spoke in English to the Dutch people present, who listened with the greatest attention. . . . The Dutch people who crowded the house, looked on the Indian speaker with astonishment." Jones criticized them as "nominal christians [*sic*]" who were "ignorant . . . of the operations and power of the Spirit of God upon the human heart" (ibid., 28 December 1829).

112 Six Nations council meeting, 29 July 1801, Prideaux Selby's Copybook.

113 Mississauga council meeting at the Grand River, 14 October 1801, Prideaux Selby's Copybook.

114 Ibid., 13 October 1801.

115 *Illustrated Atlas of the County of Waterloo* (1881; rpt. Port Elgin, ON: Ross Cumming, 1972), p. 6. This is the same incident referred to above, as described in Anonymous, "The Early Settlement of Waterloo Township."

116 See note 43. Another account of this incident says that Erb and his companions "lost the trail . . . just south of the present site of the town of Galt . . . and in their aimless wandering they reached an Indian hut, from which ran out several squaws, who motioned them to flee. The white men did not understand their motions, and approached until suddenly a drunken Indian rushed out, and, levelling his gun, fired at the party, hitting Abraham Stauffer in the arm" (*Berlin News Record*, 24 August 1904).

117 Captain William Ellis, Waterloo Township's first magistrate, "was employed by the government to pay the Indians the wolf-pelt bounty" (Mabel Dunham, "The Ellis Family," *Waterloo Historical Society*, 35 [1948]: 29-32, at 30). As late as 1845, "Henry Wite (an Indian) produced . . . *Seven* Wolf Scalps with the ears on the same" to George Wilson, a magistrate in Waterloo Township (receipt of Henry Wite, Wellington County Museum-Archives, A980.14, series 1, file 12). However, the Mississaugas did not attempt to exterminate the wolf population. In the winter of 1841 or 1842 A.D. Ferrier "asked one of their hunters one day why he did not kill more wolves, as the bounty was so high. His answer was, 'Indians no care to kill wolves; they hunters as well as Indian'" (*Reminiscences of Canada and the Early Days of Fergus*, p. 45).

118 Harry Kinzie (b. 1888) recalled hearing from his grandmother that "[w]hen the white people were friendly to the Indians they never forgot. They would share the best they had. . . . The Indians used to sleep in their kitchen on the floor when the weather was below zero. . . . A few days later they would come back with a nice quarter of venison or a nice mess of speckled trout. . . . They would even give furs to make garments for children . . ." (Harry Kinzie, "Historic Events," in South Waterloo District Women's Institute, "South Waterloo District and Its 15 Branches: 50 Years

of Achievement, 1903-1953," unpublished manuscript, Doris Lewis Rare Book Room, University of Waterloo).

119 Province of Upper Canada, *Journal of Legislative Assembly*, 18 February 1808.

120 *Christian Guardian*, 22 January 1831.

121 Ibid., 31 July 1833. In 1828 John Thomas and Thomas McGee, both residents in Waterloo Township, travelled one hundred miles to bring the Methodists' message to the Saugeen Ojibway (ibid., 29 February 1832). The first Saugeen converts subsequently were baptized on 26 December 1830 in Waterloo Township by the Reverend John Ryerson (ibid., 22 January 1831).

122 Peter Jones, quoted in F. Laurie Barron, "Alcoholism, Indians and the Anti-Drink Cause in the Protestant Missions of Upper Canada, 1822-1850," in Ian A.L. Getty and Antoine S. Lussier, eds., *As Long as the Sun Shines and Water Flows: A Reader in Canadian Native Studies* (Vancouver, BC: University of British Columbia Press, 1983), pp. 191-202, at p. 199.

123 George Ryerson, "To the Senior Editor of the *Christian Guardian*," *Christian Guardian*, 12 December 1829.

124 Leo Johnson, "The Mississauga-Lake Ontario Land Surrender of 1805," *Ontario History*, 83, 3 (September 1990): 233-53, at 249.

125 Barron, "Alcoholism, Indians and the Anti-Drink Cause," p. 195.

126 Ibid., p. 199.

127 The Report of the Bagot Commission of 1844 on the Indians in the Canadas, quoted with approval by George Copway in *The Traditional History and Characteristic Sketches of the Ojibway Nation* (London: Charles Gilpin, 1850), p. 186. For a critique of Copway's *Traditional History*, see Smith, "The Life of George Copway," pp. 22-23.

128 Christian Gottlieb Klinckhardt, *C.G. Klinckhardt's Reise nach Nord=Amerika und dessen erste Ansiedelung daselbst, aus Briefen von demselben gezogen und herausgegeben von C.G. Temper, Pastor in Ruppertsgrün* (Leipzig: Carl Andra, 1833), p. 60.

129 *Canada Museum*, 21 November 1837.

130 Jones, *History of the Ojebway Indians*, p. 245. A.D. Ferrier contrasted the Mississaugas with the Potawatomies. He reported that "[i]n the winter of 1841 or 1842, a large encampment of Indians was made in my woodland [near Fergus], and of course I went up to see them. They were very respectable people from the river Credit, and Wesleyan Methodists. We used to hear them in the evenings singing hymns, and they had testaments in their wigwams, and many of them could read. They were well behaved and honest, and the squaws made quantities of baskets and sold them in the village.... A winter or two afterwards, another lot of them [i.e., Potawatomies] camped near the village, but of a very different character, being drunken, thieving fellows, and the people in the village were in constant fear of them and heartily glad when they took themselves off" (Ferrier, *Reminiscences of Canada and the Early Days of Fergus*, p. 45).

131 Report of the Civil Secretary, S.B. Harrison, 7 December 1840, NAC, RG 1, E 1, vol. 86A, pp. 302-304. Harrison noted that the Indian was supposed to belong to the Chippewa (i.e., Ojibway) "tribe."

132 *Canada Museum,* 18 December 1840.

133 Dunham, "The Ellis Family," p. 30.

134 Petition to Sir George Arthur, 14 November 1840, NAC, RG 1, E 1, vol. 86A, pp. 305-308.

135 Prior to 1840 there are references to Mississauga villages in Waterloo Township. Isaac B. Shantz, for example, remembered "the tribes of Indians which used to have their wigwams in the nearby forests" in the 1830s. "At that time they were quite peaceable and were on friendly terms with the few farmers of the neighbourhood" ([Snyder], *Hannes Schneider and His Wife, Catharine Haus Schneider,* p. 120C). After 1840 the Mississauga villages disappear. There are only occasional references to Indians engaging in Christmas and New Year's festivities in Waterloo Township for the next few years. Then, after the Mississaugas relocated from the Credit River Reserve in present-day Mississauga to the New Credit Reserve near present-day Hagersville in 1847, there are virtually no primary references to Indians in Waterloo Township.

136 Smith, *Sacred Feathers,* p. 188. George Henry (b. 1811) had been raised in Waterloo Township but relocated to the Credit River about 1828. About 1838 Henry "returned to Waterloo and was there perhaps two years and then he went to Sarnia where he has resided ever since" (Joseph Sawyer to S.P. Jarvis, 1843, NAC, RG 10, vol. 1011, p. 92). I am grateful to Donald Smith for providing me with this reference. Henry left Waterloo before the publication of Peterson's racist editorial but presumably his departure was influenced by settlers' racist sentiments.

137 When a beaded belt, obviously made by a Mississauga artisan, turned up in a museum display in 1991 the curators did not know what to make of it. They described it as an "unusual beaded band made for Christian Erb [the son of miller John Erb of Preston] before 1849, a unique personal object that documents perhaps more strongly than any other artifact in the exhibition the Mennonite's [*sic*] remarkable sense of time and place" (Susan M. Burke and Matthew H. Hill, eds., *From Pennsylvania to Waterloo: Pennsylvania-German Folk Culture in Transition* [Kitchener, ON: Friends of the Joseph Schneider Haus, 1991], p. 14). Possibly this belt was a wampum belt. Michael Sherk wrote that "[i]t was quite common for an Indian chief to bestow a belt of wampum upon a white man for favours received. This belt, if hung in an exposed place, served as a protection to the settler's house" ([Michael Sherk], *Pen Pictures of Early Pioneer Life in Upper Canada* [Toronto: William Briggs, 1905], pp. 36-37).

138 Indian hunting grounds are usually referred to as "parks" in ethnohistorical studies (Jennings, *The Invasion of America,* p. 13). The term is occasionally found in primary sources as well. In 1882, for example, an anonymous writer described a portage route that had once led up from the Whitby shore "through a famous deer park ... [and on to] the bass fishing on Lakes Scugog and Simcoe" (G.M. Grant, ed., *Picturesque Canada: The Land as It Was and Is,* 2 vols. [Toronto: Beldon Brothers, 1882], vol. 1, p. 624.

139 The Mississaugas understood that in 1820 they had surrendered their territory to the trusteeship of the Crown, believing that the Crown would pro-

tect their land and "keep it for our children for ever" (Joseph Sawyer and John Jones to Sir John Colborne, 3 April 1829, NAC, RG 10, vol. 5, p. 47). They recalled that William Claus, deputy superintendent general of Indian affairs, had told them at the time (1820): "The white people are getting thick around you and we are afraid they, or the yankees will cheat you out of your land, you had better put it into the hands of your very Great father the king to keep for you till you want to settle, and he will appropriate it for your good and he will take good care of it; and will take you under his wing, and keep you under his arm, & give you schools, and build houses for you when you want to settle" (ibid).

140 *Methodist Missionary Notices*, 5 April 1838, quoted in Elizabeth Graham, "Strategies and Souls" (unpublished PhD dissertation, University of Toronto, 1973), p. 107.

141 Newsclipping of 15 August 1845, quoted in Smith, *Sacred Feathers*, p. 223.

142 Schmalz, *The Ojibwa of Southern Ontario*, p. 151.

143 The Mississaugas had recognized that their Credit River reserve was insufficient for their needs as early as 1832. In that year a Mississauga council meeting was held at the Credit River "[t]o petition for a township to be assigned them, as a resort for surplus population. If it should be agreeable to the Sah-keeng Indians, they may wish it near them" (William Case to John Benham, 8 February 1832, in John Carroll, *Case and His Contemporaries*, 5 vols. [Toronto: Methodist Conference Office, 1867-77], vol. 3, p. 325).

144 Jennings, "Miquon's Passing," p. 6. Jennings makes the same point less forcefully in *The Invasion of America*, p. 65, observing that "the colonists of the early contact period avoided the heavy labor of clearing woods whenever possible, bending their chief efforts instead to acquiring the lands already cleared by Indians."

145 Jennings, *The Invasion of America*, p. 164.

146 This is the preferred term used by the First Nations in Ontario for fires that they set in the spring and fall to regulate plant growth (personal communication with Dean Jacobs, Executive Director of Nin.Da.Waab.Jig., Walpole Island Heritage Centre, December 1994). The term is occasionally found in ethnohistorical studies as well: S. Little and E.B. Moore, "The Ecological Role of Prescribed Burns in the Pine-Oak Forests of Southern New Jersey," *Ecology*, 30 (1949): 223-33.

147 William Cronon, *Changes in the Land: Indians, Colonists, and the Ecology of New England* (New York: Hill and Wang, 1983), p. 51. Gordon M. Day makes a similar point in "The Indian as an Ecological Factor in the Northeastern Forest," *Ecology*, 34 (1953): 329-46.

148 Wood does not use this term. At the time of his writing he noted that "[t]he explanation for these openings has not been resolved, but the most promising line of research would seem to be into the attempts of the Indians to clear land through repeated burnings" (J. David Wood, "The Woodland-Oak Plains Transition Zone," *The Canadian Geographer*, 5, 1 [Spring 1961]: 43-47, at 45).

149 J. David Wood, "The Stage is Set: Dumfries Township, 1816," *Waterloo Historical Society*, 48 (1961): 40-50. Wood did not consider that settlers

also sought the advantages of game animals within Indian hunting parks, as well as the fish at Indian fishing stations and horticultural products from Indian planting and gathering grounds.

150 This myth is the source of the title of G. Elmore Reaman's *Trail of the Black Walnut*.

151 "Map of His Excellency Lieutenant Governor Simcoe's Route to Detroit from Niagara, February 1793," reproduced as plate 7.23 in Goldwin French et al., eds., *Ontario's History in Maps* (Toronto: University of Toronto Press, 1983), p. 228.

152 [Snyder], *Hannes Schneider and His Wife, Catharine Haus Schneider*, p. 298.

153 Ibid.

154 A surge in immigration after 1804 coincided with a bulk purchase of 60,000 acres in the northern part of Waterloo Township by Pennsylvania Mennonite investors. For a history of this purchase see E. Reginald Good, *Frontier Community to Urban Congregation: First Mennonite Church, Kitchener, 1813-1988* (Kitchener, ON: First Mennonite Church, 1988), chap. 2.

155 A "Township Report" prepared for Waterloo in 1817 noted that pine, oak, sugar maple, beech, cherry and cypress trees predominated (Robert Gourlay, *Statistical Account of Upper Canada*, edited by S.R. Mealing [1822; rev. ed., Toronto: McClelland and Stewart, 1974], p. 193). Large, even-aged pine stands grew on abandoned cornfields which formerly had been cultivated by Neutral Indians. David Boyle observed one such pine stand in proximity to a Neutral "village site" at the source of Schneider's Creek in the heart of present-day Kitchener. He noted that "[t]his land is covered with a dense growth of pine, many of the trees . . . being from a hundred and fifty to two hundred feet high. . . . In the neighbourhood, wild fruit was abundant, including plums, cherries and huckleberries, and butter-nuts, beech-nuts and hazel nuts grew in profusion" (David Boyle, *Archaeological Report, 1894-95, Appendix to the Report of the Minister of Education Ontario* [Toronto: Warwick Bros. & Rutter, 1896], pp. 34-35).

156 Irene Spry, "The Tragedy of the Loss of the Commons in Western Canada," in Ian A.L. Getty and Antoine S. Lussier, eds., *As Long as the Sun Shines and Water Flows: A Reader in Canadian Native Studies* (Vancouver, BC: University of British Columbia Press, 1983), pp. 203-28, at p. 216.

10

The Six Nations Confederacy, Aboriginal Sovereignty and Ontario Aboriginal Law: 1790-1860

Sidney L. Harring

> But savage as those distant tribes are, they have their
> treaties, their peace and war agreements, constantly in
> their minds; they would insist upon their presents estab-
> lished by long custom, and if not complied with on rep-
> resentation, they would do themselves justice to their
> own satisfaction, and we should soon find them most
> formidable enemies.[1]

It is a foundational myth in Canadian history that the frontier, including Indian/white relations there, was legally structured, with a rule of law creating a peaceful and orderly settlement process. Canadian law has been clear from the early nineteenth century: Native people had full access to Canada's civil and criminal courts, both as plaintiffs and defendants.[2] The corollary of this position was a refusal of British law to recognize Indian customary law. This denial of recognition of customary law was derivative both of a racist, colonial belief in the "myth of the savage," which denied the existence of any Native

Notes to chapter 10 are on pp. 214-29.

capacity for law or anything "civilized," and from a strong British nationalist position, following the American Revolution, to make Canadian institutions British. The various pronouncements on this could not have been clearer, yet there was an aura of unreality to the simple statement of juridical equality. This statement of legal ideal emanated from colonial authorities, who often remained ignorant of frontier conditions. Native people still held to their customary laws, the early *Indian Act* did not directly interfere with customary law, and frontier officials often deferred to customary law. If anything, the assertion that British law fully applied throughout Canada was a policy intended to control the excesses of frontier whites who had, throughout British North America, violated the Royal Proclamation of 1763 and destabilized the frontier.

The remedy for this evil, seen as one of the causes of the American Revolution, was a British colonial policy of an orderly frontier, regulated by the rule of law and extending "the privilege of British justice" to all of Upper Canada's inhabitants.[3] Sir Peregrine Maitland put this policy simply: "the speedy settlement of the Colony, however desirable, is a secondary object compared to its settlement in such a manner as shall best secure its attachment to British Laws and Government."[4]

Yet, there was a failure on this policy front as well: more than any other single issue, the failure of colonial government to deal effectively, or even honestly, with the squatter problem reveals the enormous gap between the juridical ideal and the reality of colonial law. Similarly, the Indian Nations vigorously asserted their own views of their legal rights and continued to do so irrespective of views that British and Canadian judges took on Native rights. This was another great gap between judicial ideal and the legal reality.

The Development of Indian Law in Upper Canada

Upper Canada, later Ontario, produced more nineteenth-century cases in Native law than any other Canadian jurisdiction, and more than any comparable American jurisdiction.[5] While the meaning of this is complex, at the outset it means that disputes involving either Indian people or Indian rights did regularly reach the Ontario courts. While these cases can only be understood in their political, economic and social context, they also have a jurisprudential logic of their own, reflecting the opinions of a colonial judiciary trained in the British common-law tradition. This rich legal tradition carries within it a good deal of its own methodology, a jurisprudence, that takes strange meanings in a colonial context. For example, at its simplest level, how could reliance on British precedent help judges in cases involving Indians or Indian rights in colonial society?[6]

A search of the indexes to Ontario's seven major reporting systems reveals fifty-two reported nineteenth-century cases concerning Indian rights in some form, four of which were appealed to a higher Ontario court leading to a second reported opinion in the same case.[7] Three of these cases were appealed to the Supreme Court of Canada, and two of these were further appealed to the Privy Council. Two more cases, between the Province of Ontario and the Dominion of Canada were original cases in the Supreme Court of Canada. Thus, a total of sixty-three Ontario cases involved Indians and Indian rights were reported in the nineteenth century. Reporting systems were commercial enterprises, published for sale to the legal profession. The selection of cases for inclusion was not random, but based on the commercial importance of the case to the profession. There can be no question that important Indian rights cases were omitted from the reporters because two of the most important nineteenth-century Ontario Indian cases were not reported. *Attorney General of Ontario v. Francis et al.* was the first major case calling for an application of the *St. Catharine's Milling* decision. It was unreported until published nearly a hundred years later in *Canadian Native Law Cases* from notes found in the files of a lawyer.[8] *Caldwell v. Fraser* further applied *St. Catharine's Milling* in a "learned and elaborate" judgment that has been quoted from and discussed in a legal treatise, but it has never been reported.[9] There is no simple way of determining how many equally important cases went unreported: such cases lie in obscure records, among the hundreds of bench books in the provincial archives.[10] Courts were held in dozens of rural locations. Judges, lawyers and clerks travelled long distances to bring British justice to the farthest corners of Upper Canada.[11] Their records were kept in bench books, fifty-pound volumes in which notations of each case before the court were made. Judges, even in capital criminal cases, often kept their own notes on the evidence. These sixty-five cases (including *Francis* and *Caldwell*) represent the best record existing of the legal status of Native people in nineteenth-century Ontario. Analysis of these cases reveals a great deal about the role of the law in structuring the place of Native people in English-speaking Canada. This is true because of the historical importance of Ontario as the political centre of English-speaking Canada even if we acknowledge that largely independent legal histories exist for British Columbia and the Maritime Provinces.[12] Quebec had its own legal tradition, as well as its own legal history of Native rights, but this tradition was largely irrelevant in English Canada.[13]

Litigation in Upper Canada involving Indians and Indian lands was concentrated on the Six Nations Reserve at Grand River, especially before the decade of the 1860s. Twenty-nine of sixty-four reported cases arose from either controversies involving Grand River Indians or Grand River lands. The reasons for this concentration of litigation are straightforward: First, the Six Nations Indians were well organized and prepared to use whatever means necessary to defend their political sovereignty and their lands. Second, the value of those lands made it worthwhile for white litigants to spend fortunes on lawsuits, hiring the best lawyers in the province, including, at one time or another, most of the men who became the judges who authored the legal opinions now foundational to Canadian Indian law. Land was the economic foundation of early-nineteenth-century Ontario society and the value of white claims on Indian lands was enormous.[14] Finally, the position of Chief Justice John Beverley Robinson, the leading legal mind in Upper Canada and an important political leader, in these cases adds to their preeminence: Robinson personally authored thirteen published opinions on Indian legal issues during his thirty years on the bench, more than any other judge in North America at that time.[15] In many of these cases no Indians were even parties, their title having been alienated to competing white interests. As far as nineteenth-century Ontario's 28,000 Indians came to know Canadian law, it was either as the legal foundation of white claims to Indian lands or being locked in a jail cell for violation of some petty crime under Canadian law, most often an offense unknown to Native tradition.[16] This should not be surprising because the avaricious designs of colonial whites on Indian lands was the basis of the original colonial Indian policy, the extension of British law to the frontiers of the colonies in the Royal Proclamation of 1763 that was a part of the reason for the American Revolution.[17] Among other provisions, the Proclamation forbade the alienation of Indian lands except by the Crown. The courts, however, while officially pronouncing the illegality of the squatter's actions, came to extend the law of equity to recognize squatter's rights to lands they occupied completely in violation of the law. The court's refusal to protect the Six Nations land base ultimately led to the alienation of most of the Six Nations lands.

In theory a system of orderly procedures in place to purchase and distribute Indian lands should have led to a relatively stable process of white acquisition. Nearly twenty reported cases, however, indicate that the process was systematically abused. If we assume that these cases are representative of the range of problems that arose, the land alienation process was fraught with confusion and corruption. Given the difficulty of access to the courts and the large proportion of unreported cases, there must have been many such cases. While these cases commonly raise issues of "Indian title," they do not involve Native people, but rather settle competing white claims for land that was formerly held by Indians. The Haudenosaunee, also known as the Six Nations Confederacy, however, were not passive victims of a colonial legal order. Rather, the Confederacy very early used Canadian law in an effort to protect their sovereignty and their lands.

The Legal Position of the Haudenosaunee

Like other Loyalists, the Six Nations received a grant of a large tract of land extending for six miles on either side of the Grand River, from its mouth to its source, including that river.[18] This land, like most of the land granted to Loyalists, had been surrendered in 1784 by the Mississauga to the British in one of the first of their treaties with the Indians of Upper Canada.[19] Thus, while the lands of all of the other Indians in Upper Canada were subject to the common law of Aboriginal title, the lands of the Iroquois had been purchased by the British and, argued the Six Nations, granted them in fee simple for services rendered as allies in the war, on the same basis as all other Loyalist lands.[20]

This original grant, from Lieutenant Governor Frederick Haldimand authorized the Six Nations to "take Possession of, & Settle upon the Banks of the River called Ours or Grand River, running into Lake Erie, allotting to them for that Purpose Six Miles deep from each side . . . which them & their posterity are to enjoy for ever."[21]

Joseph Brant and about 2,000 Six Nations—Seneca, Mohawk, Cayuga, Oneida, Tuscarora, Onondaga—accepted this grant as a deed to these lands and moved onto a large tract of valuable agricultural land in what would become the centre of Ontario, an area of dense population concentration near Brantford and Hamilton, forty-five miles southeast of Toronto.[22] For a number of reasons, the Six Nations immediately began to grant, lease and sell parts of their lands to whites. While these reasons are complex, including charges of personal egotism or even corruption, the result was that Canadian authorities blamed the squatter problem on the Indians.[23]

But the extent and isolation of the Indian lands in Upper Canada, the impossibility of exercising a surveillance over those vast tracts, and still more, the uncontrollable force of those natural laws of society to which even governments must bend, have prevented the efficient protection of the Indian reserves, any more than the Crown and clergy lands under similar circumstances.

These reserves contained some of the finest and most valuable land in the province. Hence they have attracted the attention of the indigent emigrant, and the fraudulent speculator, who, either in ignorance or with a view to future gains, have settled upon portions of them, sometimes without leave or observation, but more frequently under colour of titles obtained from individual Indians.[24]

For the Six Nations, the right to alienate these lands was a measure of their sovereignty, a recognition of their status as "allies" of the Crown, and of the equality of the rights of Indians with those of whites.[25] The land policy of the Six Nations changed over the period from 1783 to 1800. It seems clear that the Indians wanted to hold a huge tract of land, sufficient to maintain their traditional way of life. Even recognizing that they would live in a country with a large agricultural white population, this large tract of land would allow the Six Nations to structure the frontier on favourable terms. Individual Indians who wanted to acculturate to white ways could live on the edges of the reserve, as Brant himself did. White farmers, living among the Six Nations people but on Six Nations terms, might serve a number of economic and social functions useful in the accommodative process.[26]

The huge size of the tract, the perception of the chiefs that the Nations needed money, and perhaps a desire to put white allies of the Six Nations on the borderlands of Indian settlements, led the chiefs to agree to sell some of the land to individual whites as early as 1787.[27] By 1798 large-scale sales of lands labelled blocks 1 through 6, intended to provide a substantial income to the Six Nations, were the source of a number of legal problems. They were illegal under British law and also were poorly documented.[28] In these later sales it seems the tribes realized that the continuation of a traditional economy was impossible, therefore a large proportion of their lands could be alienated as surplus: the tribes had far more land than they could use.[29] It has also been argued that Brant recognized that the tribes needed both money and white neighbours to become acculturated and gain the appropriate skills needed for modern agriculture, both measures advanced by selling some of their lands.[30] Peter Russell, a senior member of the Executive Council, was unprepared for this struggle with Brant over the legal status of the Six Nations lands. After repeatedly burying him in procedural formalities and delays, he exhausted Brant's patience: Brant made a formal statement accusing the administration of "trifling so often with the Indians that they lost all confidence in it."[31]

Brant insisted that Lieutenant Governor John Graves Simcoe had promised the Aboriginal Nations deeds to their lands. Simcoe had issued a patent of the Grand River lands to the Six Nations in 1793, but it did not help resolve the title dispute; it clouded it instead. Like the Haldimand grant, the Simcoe patent used the language of a deed to convey lands to the Six Nations:

> To them the Chiefs Warriors Women and people of the Six Nations and to and for the sole use and behooves of them and their heirs for ever freely and clearly of and from all and all manner of Rents, fines, and services whatever to be rendered by them or any of them to Us or Our Successors. . . . Giving and Granting and by these presents confirming to the said Chiefs Warriors Women and people of the Six Nations and their heirs the full and entire possession use benefit and advantage of the said District . . . securing to them the free and undisturbed possession and enjoyment of the same.[32]

The patent went on to restrict the rights of the Indians to alienate those lands to anyone except the Crown.

The purpose of the Simcoe patent was to "confirm" the Haldimand grant. Both documents have the appearance of deeds, and were clearly understood as deeds by the Six Nations. It is unclear precisely what Haldimand and Simcoe meant, but it seems likely that they had a duplicitous intent: on one hand they wanted to satisfy their Indian allies with a substantial land grant, at a time when many land grants in fee simple were being made to white loyalists.[33] At the same time, both deliberately hedged by using legally ambiguous language that sounded like the language of a deed, but held back key language appropriate to a fee simple deed. The language still, on balance, is the language of a deed, a large land grant understood to be "forever," that could be passed on to heirs, and sold, albeit only to the Crown.[34] There is a substantial modern body of law on the interpretation of early agreements with Native people that requires interpreting them "large and liberal" in the sense that they would be naturally understood by Native people, and not according to the narrow technical meaning of legal terms, resolving all ambiguities in favour of the Aboriginal Nations.[35]

By this time, however, it seems clear that the real issue underlying this dispute was the sovereignty of the Six Nations and not the law of real property: Brant insisted on the Six Nations' right to sell the land because tribal ownership was inherent in their conception of their independence and political status as "allies of the Crown." Moreover, Brant insisted that tribal law governed the disposition of such lands, another assertion of the political sovereignty of the Six Nations. As one element of this assertion of the supremacy of tribal law, Brant insisted that under Iroquois law the women had to agree to land cessions.[36] Brant not only hired attorneys to ensure that Six Nations land sales had the form of law, but secured a personal "power of attorney" from Six Nations chiefs empowering him to sell tribal lands.[37]

Peter Russell, a weak administrator of a weak colony, was afraid of an Indian war and ultimately, in a series of negotiations, the government confirmed his land sales in spite of the explicit prohibition of those sales in the Simcoe patent.[38] This action reinforced the Aboriginal view that these lands were Six Nations lands, to be disposed of at their will. Their position here seems simple: the Iroquois chiefs could not understand why the title they held to their lands was any different than the titles of the white loyalists to adjacent lands.[39] This was a tenable legal position, which followed the simple logic of English law. Any different position depended on an Iroquois understanding of a unique legal status, of an "Indian law," and on a corresponding recognition of their own inferior legal status, either of which was unknown in late-eighteenth-century Canada. Even British authorities had not settled their own views of the legal status of Indian lands.[40] Indeed, it is clear that Brant hired the services of a lawyer to arrange the Six Nations land sales, as well as to assist white purchasers in the proper procedural requirements of their land transactions.[41]

The fact that the British authorities confirmed the Six Nations land sales, convinced the Six Nations that they did, indeed, own those lands in fee simple. William Dummer Powell, a leading Upper Canada jurist, noted this legal impact:

> The pretension of a part of the Six Nations, under the direction of Joseph Brant, to a right of alienation, without Control, of the tract purchased for their use by General Haldimand, underwent much discussion last year, and from various circumstances, sufficiently untoward, the President and Council were induced to accede to those pretensions in part, a condescension lost on those people, who consider it as the result of fear, and who consequently will not only persist themselves in the exercise of their presumed right, but instill the same notions into the other neighbouring Indians.[42]

The study of legal history includes a consideration of choices to use, or not use, formal legal mechanisms, the study of very formal legal arrangements and the study of legal relationships that degenerate into chaos. The legal structuring of land rights on the Six Nations Reserve involves both the consideration of a formal system of land rights for whites that was imperfectly enforced, coupled with a system for the legal control of Indian lands that was still in the making, its parameters not understood yet by any of the responsible colonial authorities.

One important illustration of this confusion in the making of Indian law involves the early application of British criminal law to the Six Nations Indians. In 1795, Isaac Brant, son of Joseph, shot and killed Lowell, a white man, in an early killing of a white by an Indian in Upper Canada. The case never went before a magistrate, but the government prepared to initiate legal proceedings. At the same time, it was not clear that the Mohawks would give up Isaac Brant. Joseph Brant apparently equivocated on the issue, both leading the Canadian authorities to believe he would defer to Canadian law, and, at the same time, rallying their support in refusing to do so. There was an exchange of letters within the government in contemplation of what actions to take, but the government was unwilling to challenge Brant.[43] Judge William Dummer Powell was sent to see Brant, who took the position that British law did not reach into the Six Nations territory, although he hoped that young men would follow it. To this astute and perhaps duplicitous political position, he added that it would take the militia to enforce white laws in Indian territory and that he doubted that the militia would act against him. Powell was of the opinion that the Indian tribes were "entirely independent in their villages," a legal position never taken again in Upper Canada, but one that must have some weight given his later position as chief justice. Finally, Powell characterized the murder victim as a "white vagabond," denying that the case was worth further trouble. British authorities were not willing to challenge the Six Nations, and did not proceed with the case.[44]

This murder case unhappily turned into another: Joseph Brant himself killed Isaac Brant, evidently in self-defense as the young man attacked his father in a drunken rage. No charges were brought against Joseph, evidently for the same reasons no charges had been brought against Isaac. Rather, he turned himself over to the tribal council for their determination of justice in the case. The council found Brant acted in self-defense, proving that tribal law was functioning at the Grand River in murder cases at the time.[45] Two other clansmen of Brant

murdered a white man at Grand River in 1791. There was a jurisdictional struggle with the British insisting that the two be turned over to
Crown authorities for trial and the Iroquois refusing. Colonel Andrew
Gordon cut off delivery of presents and provisions for a time to force
the Indians to turn over the accused, but authorities in Quebec finally
resumed the practice.[46]

Nor was the "clear" position of Indians in civil law any less ambiguous in actual practice. According to Upper Canadian courts, British
law, rather than tribal law, applied to Indian lands. *The King v. Epaphrus
Lord Phelps*, the first reported Grand River case, pitted the Mohawk
Nation against the Crown in an early dispute over which law governed
Mohawk lands, Canadian or tribal.[47] Joseph Brant leased a Grand River
tract of one thousand acres to Phelps for 999 years. Phelps put the lands
in trust for the support of his Mohawk wife and children.[48]

Later, guilty of treason against Great Britain in the War of 1812,
Phelps fled to the United States. Britain's treason statute provided for
the forfeiture of property and the Crown proceeded against Phelps' tract
of land. The Six Nations hired a lawyer to defend the wife's lands, making the tribe, not Phelps, the real defendant in the case and the real issue
in the case the Six Nations right to determine questions of the legal
ownership of tribal lands. The Six Nations lawyer, William Warren
Baldwin, a judge, politician and treasurer of the Law Society of Upper
Canada, argued that the Mohawks were allies, not subjects of the
Crown, and that their lands were theirs to dispose of under tribal law,
and therefore could not be taken by the Crown in a legal action under
British law.[49] The solicitor general, arguing the Crown's case, took the
position that "the supposition that the Indians are not subject to the
laws of Canada is absurd," analogizing Indians with French settlers. The
Court upheld this view, and the Crown took the lands.[50] In the first case
in which Canada's Indians appeared in court with their own hired
lawyer to defend their lands and sovereignty, they lost completely, their
argument dismissed as "absurd." This set the tone for nineteenth-
century litigation. Tragically, in most cases involving Indian rights, the
Indian Nations were not even represented by counsel, but the Six
Nations, determined to defend their lands and sovereignty, generally
retained good lawyers.

While Native people had full legal access to the courts, the reality
was that justice was so often denied that a report of the Aborigines Protection Society, a major Native rights organization in London, England,

confused the reality with the law. Concerned about the "neglect of a means of securing justice to Indians in courts of law. . . ." the group charged (in an 1839 report) that the Indians were "disabled by the colonial laws to appear in courts of justice either singly or as tribes. . . ." The object of the Society was clear: the full extension of law to Indians was necessary to assimilate them into the mainstream of Canadian life. "It is not easy to conceive how a barbarous people can accommodate themselves to the usages of a civilized country when they are studiously excluded from sharing its laws." A lack of provision for Indian land rights was of special concern.[51]

White Squatters on the Grand River Reserve: A Legal History

The squatter issue received extensive attention in two government reports—1840 and 1844 on Indians in Upper Canada.[52] The term "squatter" loosely applied to anyone who moved onto lands without a legal title; thus it was understood by all at the time to be a legal category. While now the term has a pejorative meaning, it is not clear that this was as true in the nineteenth century.[53] Government reports put squatters into two categories, deserving and undeserving, and, in the context of the land shortage of the time, a huge proportion of early nineteenth-century Ontario farmers started off as squatters. Nineteenth-century Ontario was an agricultural settlement that gained nearly one million white settlers in the fifty years between 1800 and 1851.[54] The legal regulation of this huge influx of settlers would have been a difficult matter under any conditions, even with the best of intentions to protect Indian land rights. The most extensive of the government reports, done in 1844, expressly deferred to the facts of an 1840 report on the squatter question, and reached the same conclusion: that the Crown could not possibly protect Indian lands from squatters. This conclusion was false, but it served the purpose of forcing Indian land surrenders:

> That complete protection of such (Indian) property can only be looked for as the result of that charge which shall assimilate the Indians with people accustomed from infancy to the idea of separate and individually appropriated property, where each is, under the Law, the protector of his own possessions; but they are also of the same conviction.[55]

The conclusion is a striking policy statement: Canadian law could not protect the Indians from squatters. Rather, the tribes could only protect their own property after their reserves had been broken up into individual allocations of small parcels.

Not surprisingly, this conclusion belies both logic and reality, and the Grand River Iroquois pointed it out at the time. No "crime" is more easy to detect than squatting, which, by definition, was open and prolonged. The Grand River Reserve alone in 1840 had, by one count, 400 white families, including about 2,000 individuals, occupying 45,000 acres out of a total of 160,000 acres.[56] Surely, these squatters, numbering roughly equal to the Indian population (about 2,200), and occupying 20 percent of the land, could not have been difficult to find and punish.

Moreover, the government had formed a clear policy regarding squatters as early as 1794. The Executive Council found that squatters lived in every township in Upper Canada. When squatters became troublesome to land surveyors, the Council set out simple measures to deal with them. Deputy surveyors were to report suspected "trespassers" to the surveyor-general who, "if the trespassing was proved, was to issue a notice requiring them to vacate immediately." If this warning was not obeyed, he was to report the measure to the Council, so that the attorney general could take legal action. All squatters who refused to vacate would never be allowed any grant of Crown lands.[57] Since Upper Canada had a complete legal system in the hands of the government, these legal procedures should have been pro forma. Similarly, as a frontier colony potentially in danger of attack from the United States, at least through the 1840s, Britain had to allocate whatever military or police resources were necessary to defend the colony.

The Iroquois complained. A lengthy resolution of the Six Nations Council on 1 March 1809 details a number of specific encroachments by name, requesting Canadian authorities to take action:

> There is a part of our lands that Mr. Mallory pretends to claim a little distance above the place our mill stood; this we disallow of, as we knew nothing about it. . . .
>
> The next place we come to, is that of John Nelles, we were not generally acquainted with the quantity of the manner in which it was granted by our late Chief; but we imagine that he has caused the survey to pass the limits and he has behaved very improper to some of our people, therefore we leave it to the consideration of our Superintendent General if he shall be removed or if he shall be constrained to reform. Mr. Anderson agreed to keep a mill in order when 200 acres of land was granted him, but he has extended his limits, left the Mill, which seldom does any . . . and rents it to people that in general are not agreeable to us—we also lay this before him. . . . A piece of land that was given to a John Huff for the good of his

family who are of a Delaware mother—we find he is selling off—therefore as we have forbid these sales it is our request that all those who have attempted to purchase be expelled and his family left in peaceable possession. . . . We had forgot to mention 4800 acres marked out for Mr. Augustus Jones near the Delaware village—as we have never agreed to this we forbid his getting it—there are others below there who we wish to get off.[58]

The same council meeting listed other tracts that they recognized as being in the hands of white owners under a valid Indian title, distinguishing between the two groups of settlers. For example, a grant to John Dochester had been divided, with Dochester selling a piece that exceeded his grant to a Mr. Canby. Since the tribe expected Canby to make payments to Dochester's family they did not oppose the transaction, but when Canby did not make payments, the council asked that "justice be done them."[59]

Sir Isaac Brock, administrator of Upper Canada, issued a proclamation on the Indian lands that acknowledged the law. The proclamation admitted that "many white persons are settled on the Indian land in the County of Haldimand (including Grand River) without due authority or License." It went on to state that "by law all white persons are forbidden to establish themselves or reside in any Indian Village or Country without such license, under a penalty for the first offense of ten pounds, and for the second and every other subsequent offense of twenty pounds." Finally, Brock announced that by issuing the proclamation he was making it clear that settlers could not "pretend ignorance of the law." All those claiming to reside on Indian lands under some valid license were required to report themselves to William Claus, deputy superintendent general of Indian Affairs.[60]

A number of squatters did report under this proclamation, although, given the confused state of the land titles and absence of written records this could not have resolved title problems. Ezra Hawley, for example, reported purchasing a hundred and seventy-five acres of land granted to William Crum, a volunteer under Joseph Brant in the Revolutionary War, together with fifty acres granted to Benjamin Fairchild, another associate of Brant, together with another farm, a part of a 999-year lease, that he purchased for nine hundred dollars from Stephen Carpenter. Thus, Hawley's farm, of average size, involved two separate grants and one long-term lease, all unrecorded.[61] The policy was not enforced: no major removals of white squatters followed from the Brock proclamation. Rather, it spoke loudly in its ineffectiveness. It established that the Canadian government had a policy of ignoring squatters and of non-enforcement of the laws regulating squatters from the beginning of the nineteenth century.

It was a political reluctance to either punish squatters or protect Indian lands that was at the heart of Canadian policy. Government reports equivocated on the squatter problem. On one hand they did describe the extent of the depredations of squatters who often, for example, clear-cut thousands of acres of valuable oak forest and moved on, engaged in liquor traffic or illicit and corrupt trade with the Indians, and were white men of the "lowest sort." Judge John Beverley Robinson probably represented the views of the aristocracy in his viewpoint on the problem:

> I have no sympathy with the genus squatter.... If I were like Louis Napoleon legislating for a country I would allow no preemption right to be [given those] who have gone upon land to which they well knew they had no ... claim ... but would give them plainly to understand that so far from the impudent act of trespass giving them a claim they might be satisfied that whatever others persons might get a grant of land, they simply never should on any terms.
>
>   I think the favor that has always been shown to squatters has a democratizing tendency.[62]

In spite of these strong views, and Robinson's reputation as a conservative, as chief justice of Upper Canada his opinions were generally careful to acknowledge the rights of squatters to their lands.[63] This inconsistency cannot be understood from the standpoint of legal doctrine: rather it was a political compromise.

Objections more rooted in policy than morality were raised by A.J. Russell, assistant commissioner of Crown lands:

> Squatting is injurious to the future character of the settlement. The land is taken up by a poorer and inferior class of settlers. The best lands are picked out by them before the survey takes place, to the exclusion of settlers with more means who cannot be expected to join in the squatting or settle on the inferior lots afterwards.[64]

Yet, in direct contradiction, the reports also made clear that many of the squatters were honest and hard-working farmers who had secured their lands either by mistake or by an honest reliance on a sale or lease from an Indian:[65]

> The interests of the Indians, and a humane consideration for the numerous families of white settlers, who are not in a state of doubt and uncertainty, alike require that measures should be speedily taken for the

adjustment of difficulties; continued applications have been made by the settlers to know the determination of the Government, and many have expressed a desire to take leases. . . . [66]

The reports are so contradictory as to be disbelieved on this issue:

It was on this occasion, clearly ascertained, that an indiscriminate removal of the white settlers would be most prejudicial to, and was not at all desired by the Indians; while by a judicious arrangement, that estate might be managed to their great and manifest advantage.

Within the same report, separated by one page:

Repeated remonstrances had been made by the Indians against the encroachments of the whites, and the injury their property was daily sustaining from the plunder carried on by the intruders; and the faith of the Government was as often pledged, that steps should be taken to redress the grievance.[67]

These steps can only refer to legal measures to remove and punish squatters. This view that white squatters were innocent people, deserving the consideration of the Crown, rather than removal and punishment, is repeatedly expressed, but is disingenuous. It is impossible, in the Upper Canada of the 1840s, to believe that any white person did not know how land was legally obtained: only by a written patent from the Crown.[68] Brock's 1812 Proclamation was specifically intended to remove any defense of ignorance of land laws from the squatters' claims. Simcoe's 1793 patent deed to the Grand River lands referred to the problem of squatters resident there, providing that no land transfers from the tribe to outsiders were valid, and providing that no white person should live there under pretence of any such land title. Such existing persons were to be dispossessed and evicted.[69] Indeed, one of the salient central themes (and a myth when the legal history of Indian lands is considered) of Ontario history is the centrality of an orderly land policy in provincial development.[70] Similarly, every white person must also have known that it was illegal under British and Canadian law to secure land in a private transaction with an Indian.[71] The Crown commissioners failed to give effect to the government's elaborate legal policy governing the white settlement of either Crown or Indian lands, making these policies very close to a dead letter on the Indian reserves. The white squatters, in fact, were relying on the unwillingness of the Canadian government to remove them and believed that ultimately they would get legal title to their lands. This created a de facto land law based on the law of equity at odds with the statutory land law: frontier whites relied on the de facto law recognizing an equitable right to Indian or Crown lands and simply ignored the statutory law.

A prolonged dispute between Thomas Clark and Nelson Cozens illustrates the rough state of Upper Canadian land law. In 1806 Clark attempted to purchase lands in Block 4, originally sold by Joseph Brant.[72] Cozens objected to the purchase, claiming that his father, Joshua Cozens, had purchased the lands—an entire township of 92,160 acres—in 1796 from Brant personally, although the deed was never recorded and had, through a series of accidents, been lost.[73] Cozens claimed that the transaction was so well known that it should be given legal effect.[74] In the meantime, the legal history of the deed came to include "a lost deed, the theft of legal papers, fraudulent practices upon the person of an old man, an old trunk containing valuable papers left in a garret, and other details."[75] While at one point the Legislative Assembly passed a resolution supporting Cozens' claim, he ultimately lost in the Executive Council and finally, in 1836, in an appeal to the Colonial Secretary.[76] Chief Justice Robinson was fully aware of the case, commenting on its general hopelessness in a private letter.[77] He had kept his claim alive for thirty years, through all of the legal processes of Canada, and probably at substantial legal expense, with no documentary proof whatever.[78] This was not entirely Cozens' fault but was inherent in the nature of land sales that were illegal under British law.[79]

A similar tract of land, Block 1 of the original Brant grants, 94,035 acres, had an equally complex legal history, also marked by forgery and fraud. The original purchaser, Philip Stedman, a land speculator, had wound up in an American debtors' prison, but had allegedly assigned his interest in the land others with three different parties, all American land speculators, coming forward. Daniel Penfield, the most aggressive of these purchasers paid huge sums of money to the Iroquois representing amounts owed by Stedman under the terms of the grant.[80] In the strongly anti-American climate which followed the War of 1812, Canadian authorities decided that Penfield's deed was nothing but a "clumsy forgery," but not without considerable legal activity, leading to a judgment in favour of William Dickson, who took title under a deed from Stedman's widow.[81] Dickson's lawyer in this matter was none less than John Beverley Robinson, then attorney general of Upper Canada. His legal fee of £699 underscores the complexity of the case and belies the "clumsy forgery," which, presumably, would have been easily detected.[82]

This level of uncertainty of Grand River land tenure at the highest legal and political levels set a stage for the squatter controversies which followed (and belies the myth of the orderly land policy of Upper Canada): the Cozens and Penfield cases tied up over 187,000 acres of prime land—almost three hundred square miles—for forty and twenty years respectively, during a period of rapid agricultural settlement. Some measure of the extent of the aggressiveness of squatters, and their success in using these methods to gain control of land, can be seen in the report's reference to the squatter presence in two townships, Dunn and Cayuga, which were surrendered by the Six Nations in 1831 and 1834, at least in part to secure some income from these lands.[83] The "intruders exceed calculations" reported Commissioner (and Superintendent of Indian Affairs) Samuel Peters Jarvis. The townships held "one hundred settlers, who had possession of the lands for five or six years without paying anything, occupying 10,000 acres. During that period, all the most valuable timber had been cut down and sold," depriving the tribe of the revenue of these lands.[84] It is important to note here that the Canadian government is admitting that it completely failed to exercise any control over two townships of very valuable land that it had induced the Six Nations to sell to the Crown for their benefit, the money being invested for them. This land was in the centre of the area of rapidly expanding Upper Canadian agricultural settlement in the late 1830s, not at all remote, and there can be no justification for the Crown's failure to protect either their own settlement policy or the Six Nations' annuities. Rather it was based in a government policy that officially discouraged squatting, but unofficially supported it as necessary to provide land for white settlement and economic development, and also to force the Indians onto small reserves.

Although the 1840 report had recommended a strengthened law against squatters, the government, intent on fully occupying Upper Canada with white farmers, was unwilling to even pretend to enforce it.[85] The existing *Act* for the protection of Indian reserves permitted the appointment of special commissioners to investigate and try cases; even making Indian agents special commissioners. The 1844 report went far beyond this, urging the appointment of Indian "rangers" to enforce the laws against squatters and extending the *Act* to Indians who sold or leased their lands to whites, as well as to whites who took advantage of those illegal land transactions.[86] The final appendix of the 1844 report, extensively cited the laws of the Cherokee Nation, focusing on the creating of the Cherokee Rangers to enforce similar laws.[87] While the Six Nations did use rangers to protect their remaining lands later in the nineteenth century, this suggestion in 1844 shifts responsibility for the loss of Indian lands to the Indian Nations, denying the reality that Indians could not have carried out law enforcement activity against whites in early-nineteenth-century Canada.

The Wilkes case follows a logic made clear in the commissioner's 1840 report: there were two classes of squatters. While both were technically illegal, one set was to be protected by the law, the other distinguished and either not protected or punished. The juridical problem with this reality must be clear: it is difficult for a legal system to administer two distinct types of illegality:

> As to the course to be adopted with respect to Squatters upon Indian lands. These may be divided into two classes—First, of those who have taken illegal possession of the Land, either under some pretended license from individual Indians, or without even such a colour of title, for the purpose of farming alone, and have cleared and cultivated, and built upon the land.
>
> Secondly. Such whose illegal possession is accompanies by circumstances of a still more objectionable nature—such as cutting and plundering the valuable Timber—keeping houses for the sale of spirituous liquors, and otherwise disseminating the vices into which the Indians, so easily fall. . . .
>
> The first class by the valuable improvements upon and attached to the lands, have given a sort of security for their ultimately making to the Indians full compensation for their temporary usurpation and their cases may for the present be postponed, and taken into consideration in connection with the scheme above alluded to (essentially providing credit in the purchase of their lands upon surrender).
>
> The second class of squatters, your Committee conceive to be entitled to no consideration . . . but that the Commissioners appointed under the Act for the protection of Indian Reserves, ought to be instructed promptly to enforce the law against them.[88]

This analysis, in a government report, is revealing. It shows that legality had nothing at all to do with the difference between "deserving" whites, like Wilkes, who deserved every consideration from the government, and those deserving no consideration. Those who got their lands from Indians in some kind of agreement with the Indians were grouped with those who took their land from the Indians under no representation at all other than pure theft and trespass. The only critical issue was whether they were productively farming the land—and Wilkes, who got full consideration for his industry and improvements, was not even doing that. Many, like Wilkes, were falsely claiming improvements, or put up "instant" improvements, shabby buildings and cheap fences, to mask their depredations on the land. Moreover, this idealistic distinction between law violators who were farming productively (whether under the pretension of an Indian sale or lease, or not even bothering with the formality of an illegal lease) and those who were raping the land, does not fit the reality of the wholesale carnage to Indian lands described in the same reports: the two valuable townships of Dunn and Cayuga, surrendered by the Six Nations in the middle 1830s, and occupied by one hundred settlers farming 10,000 acres, had been stripped of all its timber, the value of which belonged to the Six Nations.

Six Nations Reserve Lands and the Courts of Upper Canada and Ontario

A number of these squatter cases reached the courts or Legislative Assembly and illustrate the duplicitous quality of Canadian law on matters of Indian lands.[89] At the core of Canadian legal and political culture was a Tory support of the Crown, hence a broad defense of the Crown's authority over Indian lands is set out in consistently in case after case.

The consistency of the reported cases in holding that whites could not alienate Indian lands except through the Crown reveals a great deal about the short reach of nineteenth-century Upper Canadian, and then Ontario, law. These reported cases, fewer than twenty in number, represent no more than a minute fraction of the thousands of white attempts to alienate Indian lands. The complexity of white schemes can be seen in the above cases, and must represent the range of devices employed in gaining control of Indian lands. *Bown v. West* (1846) brought out the best legal minds in Ontario, again denying a white claim on Indian lands, but clearly troubled by the magnitude of the problem.[90] Isaac Davids, a Mohawk from the Grand River Reserve, had assigned to a white man whatever interest he had in several buildings and improvements on thirty-four acres of cleared land that he "owned" according to the customary law of the Six Nations. Bown, who later entered into a contract to buy this interest in the land and the tavern located on it, got into a dispute over the value of the property after finding parts of David's ownership of the lands in dispute under tribal customary law and rescinded the contract.[91] While the court's holding was simple—no contract for exchange of Indian lands was valid—the complexity of the land-holding arrangements in effect at Grand River at mid-century was plainly almost beyond the capacity of the law to adjudicate. Chief Justice John Beverley Robinson, for example, pointed out that the Crown, while recognizing that Indian title could not be acquired by whites, often protected white property rights to improvements built upon Indian lands under traditional doctrines of equity. Robinson further recognized that some interests of white squatters were so substantial that a court of equity could hardly refuse to acknowledge them.[92] Yet, he did not recognize any equitable right on the part of Bown, and no reported case ever granted a squatter an equitable right in Indian lands. Squatters, however, did occasionally get equitable rights recognized against the Crown. Such rights, however, were more often recognized by political authorities who granted a great deal of land to squatters who had improved it. This recognition came so frequently that false claims of "improvements" became a common scam.

At the same time, Robinson described Indian interests in a completely different way: "The government, we know, always made it their care to protect the Indians, so far as they could, in the enjoyment of their property, and to guard them against being imposed upon and dispossessed by the white inhabitants."[93]

This is the language of dependency and paternalism. The jurisprudential logic of positioning white property rights against a policy of Native paternalism and dependence creates a much stronger legal position for white interests than it does for Native interests. Nevertheless, property rights did not attach until a person acquired a legally recognized property interest. Robinson, long a colonial official, solidly stood behind the Crown prerogative over the alienation of Indian lands. Since only the Crown could take land title from an Indian tribe, no settler with a land claim not traceable to the Crown could prevail in Robinson's court.

This result is consistent with another case that recognized substantial rights of squatters, and illustrated the chaotic state of land tenure along the Grand River. *Westbrooke v. the Attorney General* involved squatters in the village of Cayuga who lived on lands along the Grand River canal. The Grand River Navigation Company was empowered to take through an arbitration process any lands it needed for the canal it was building.[94] In 1847 it submitted to the arbitration process two tracts of land owned by the Haudenosaunee. The Six Nations was awarded £159 5s for the lands. Although the money was paid, the company never took possession of the lands, which continued to be occupied by white squatters.[95]

In 1864 assignees of the company applied for a title to the land, alleging falsely that the company had taken full possession of the land under the award. The squatters argued that they had no idea of the arbitration process and had never received any notice of the sale of their lands. The lawyers representing the purchasers of the lands from the Grand River Navigation Company argued that squatters had no right of any kind to file this action because they had no legal status at all in relation to the lands they squatted on. Vice chancellor, later premier of Ontario, Oliver Mowat sided with the squatters, finding that the Grand River Navigation Company had not needed the land, hence did not take lawful title under the statute empowering them to take lands for canal building purposes.[96] While technically this might be true, it begs the opposite question: how did the squatters get any legal right to defend their "titles" when the Crown clearly held title to the land in 1847? While this court recognized an equitable interest in the land on the part of white squatters, it was not an equitable interest exercise against Indian lands. The Crown had purchased these lands in the early 1830s.

The same issue had arisen ten years before in a much simpler case, *Doe D. Wilkes v. Babcock*.[97] Wilkes had, about eight years previous, purchased land from Dalton along the Grand River. The land was taken for the canal by the Grand River Navigation Company in 1849 and Wilkes had been awarded £8 15s. However, Wilkes argued that he owned another parcel on the west part of the canal. The defendant denied that Wilkes had any valid title to the land at all. The lands in question were part of the Grand River Reserve and had never been sold by the Indians or the Crown to anyone. Wilkes was simply a squatter. Justice James Macaulay upheld the common-law doctrine that possession was prima facie evidence of title that if Wilkes had entered peaceably under colour of claiming a right he could assert his possessory right as a defense against ejectment.[98] Such a doctrine may have made sense in settled England, but this application of the common-law rule against the Crown was a gross injustice: any squatter could claim some kind of claim of right. Again, as in *Westbrooke,* although these were originally Indian lands, the Crown had acquired them in the early 1830s, so these squatters took title from the Crown and did not gain possession of Indian lands through these common-law doctrines. The question of the legal right of Joseph Brant to sell Grand River lands, like the larger question of Indian land title, was generally avoided by the Upper Canadian courts. Cases involving Indian lands were decided on a wide range of technicalities and common-law doctrines that avoided the question of

Indian land title: laws that forbade whites from alienating lands from Indians had nothing to do with the legal issue of Indian title. The Grand River lands issue was taken up in 1852 by Chief Justice John Beverley Robinson in *Doe d. Sheldon v. Ramsay et al.*[99] Like many of the other land tenure cases, the simple legal issues belie the chaos of land title in Upper Canada. Two groups of landowners disputed title of a large tract of Grand River lands. The plaintiff, Sheldon, claiming title under an 1820 sale from the commissioner of forfeited estates, who had seized the lands through legal process from Bonajah Mallory, who had a 999-year lease from Joseph Brant, brought an action for ejectment of squatters inhabiting those lands. Mallory had legally forfeited his lands through his treason in fighting for the United States in 1813.[100] Defendants argued that Mallory had not forfeited his lands because he could not acquire a legal title from Brant; therefore Sheldon had no title.

The largest part of the opinion is spent on a wholly unrelated issue: the land was so poorly described in the forfeiture sale that it was not clear what lands were being conveyed: the parcel was variously described as sixty acres and as 420 acres; was delineated by a hut and a marked tree that no longer existed; and described by a surveyor's description that was factually impossible: all indicative of the chaos in land tenure on the Grand River Reserve at that time.[101] Based on this conflicting testimony, believed "unreasonable and inadmissible" by Chief Justice Robinson, a jury had awarded Sheldon the large parcel of land he claimed, almost three miles along the south bank of the Grand River.[102] Robinson went on to remark that it was "not easy to understand" how the jury could come to such an unjust result. In the context of Upper Canadian politics of the time, it is not unlikely that the jury was simply sympathetic to Sheldon, the landowner, construing his title against the Crown as extensively as possible.

Robinson, clearly intending to use his judicial authority to put an end to the legal claims of the Six Nations, then turned to the question of Brant's land tenure as the legal key to defeating Sheldon's title. Citing *Doe Ex. Dem. Jackson v. Wilkes*, an 1835 case, which held that a land grant from the Crown must be of record under seal, Robinson held that Brant could not lease or sell tribal lands to Mallory because the Six Nations did not own those lands.[103] This defect was not inherent in Brant's title, in Robinson's view, rather it traced back all the way to General Haldimand's original grant of the land to the Six Nations. Haldimand himself, in Robinson's disingenuous analysis, did not own the land and had no legal right to give it to the Six Nations.[104] Even though this holding would permanently put an end to Six Nations land litigation, Robinson continued with an entirely different, equally dishonest analysis. Even if he had such right, the grant was defective for "want of a grantee or grantees. It grants nothing to any person or persons by name, and in their natural capacity."[105] The Six Nations were not legal entities under British law, entitled to hold land. Haldimand has no authority to "incorporate" them as a collective legal entity, and British law did not recognize "tribes" or Indian Nations.[106] Finally, Robinson argued that Brant had no legal authority to sell lands occupied by the Six Nations because they did not own those lands in fee simple:

> We cannot recognize any peculiar law of real property applying to the Indians—the common law is not part savage and part civilized. The Indians, like other inhabitants of the country, can only convey such lands as they legally hold, and they must convey such lands as they legally hold, and they must convey by deed executed by themselves, or by some person holding proper authority.[107]

It followed then that "no legal estate in any land was created by Captain Brant's lease" and that Mallory had no interest which could be forfeited to the Crown.[108] The core of this holding, however, had nothing to do with the nature of Indian title: rather it turned on legal defects in Haldimand's land grant, a technical problem deriving from the common law of property, and from the precise nature of Haldimand's authority as a British military governor. To the extent that it directly affected Indian title the opinion was simply ludicrous: evidently, not being either an individual, a partnership, or a corporation, an Indian nation could not own anything at all, therefore there could never be any discussion of Indian title in any Canadian court.

Judge Robert Easton Burns wrote a concurring opinion that, while it does not go beyond Robinson's in his views on the land dispute, denies, in dicta, the political sovereignty of the Six Nations:

> It can never be pretended that these Indians while situated within the limits of this province, as a British province at least, were recognized as a separate and independent nation, governed by laws of their own, distinct from the general law of the land, having a right to deal with the soil as they pleased; but they were considered as a distinct race of people, consisting of tribes associated together distinct from the general mass of inhabitants, it is true, but yet as British subjects, and under the control of and subject to the general law of England. . . .
>
> Whether the Indian tribes of this continent acknowledge such absolute authority [of a chief to sell land], and whether it would require to be

delegated by a council, I do not know; but whatever may be the Indian laws or customs in this respect, I take it to be clear that the property in the lands which were confessedly at one time in the crown, must be dealt with and disposed of according to the general law of the country. . . . [109]

Illustrating the centrality of land litigation in Upper Canadian law, Justice William Henry Draper, having taken part in the case while a member of the bar, gave no judgment. He had represented Wilkes in *Doe ex dem. Jackson v. Wilkes* and had, in that case, argued for the legal recognition of the Six Nations title through the Haldimand grant.[110] He apparently only took that view as an advocate: as a judge he never supported any view that the Six Nations had either political sovereignty or a title to their lands. Chief Justice Robinson had also represented parties in disputes over Grand River lands but, presumably because he had never represented a party in this particular case, he did not disqualify himself. In 1819 he had represented William Dickson in a case disputing ownership of 94,000 acres of Grand River lands.[111] Dickson prevailed and Robinson earned a fee of £699.[112] Overall, squatters' interests fared very well in the courts of Upper Canada.

The common element of all these cases is that they involve whites claiming recognition of land rights somehow derived from Indian title. Most of these cases did not directly involve Indians as parties and Indian rights, while clearly lost or diminished in these cases, were not directly decided, but were dismissed in dicta. The courts, in each case, defended Indian lands against the alienation of individual whites, although several white squatters, for equitable reasons, were allowed to prevail against the Crown over lands that had recently been in Indian hands. With the exception of one case decided on highly technical grounds, the opinions were not overly technical, relying instead on broad statements of Crown Indian and lands policy.

In *The Queen v. James Hagar* (1857) the court held narrowly for the Crown, restricting the repeated designs of one Grand River settler on Indian lands.[113] Mary Martin, an Iroquois woman, lived alone on a cultivated lot on the reserve. She was very poor, living on the proceeds of a few vegetables and a government payment of £6 a year from Indian funds. Desiring to make her lot more profitable, she thought it would be better to have her lot worked by whites rather than by Indians and asked James Hagar, a white man, to work the land on shares. They made an oral agreement that he would farm the land for five years, giving her one-third of the proceeds.

Upon hearing of the agreement, Onondaga chiefs persuaded the woman to break it off. They had been involved in an ongoing land dispute with Hagar, a squatter, dating back to 1832 when he settled on land that he had illegally "bought" from an individual Onondaga, but which the Onondaga Nation had opposed because it contained a sacred site, used in the white dog ceremony. Unable to legally remove Hagar because they lacked recourse to Canadian authorities, the Onondaga took the law into their own hands. They attacked Hagar, striking him in the head with an axe and leaving him for dead. He lived and went to court against both his assailants, and the tribe, later getting his illegal title confirmed.[114] Mary Martin, deferring to the will of her tribe, agreed to terminate the lease and informed Hagar of her decision. As he had done twenty years before, he defied the tribe and insisted that she honour the agreement. He planted wheat on the disputed land. Convicted of making a lease for Indian lands without the consent of the Crown, Hagar appealed, arguing that the statute referred only to "legal leases" and not informal ones. The Court of Common Pleas construed the statute broadly, citing its language prohibiting such leases "in any manner or form, or upon any terms whatsoever."[115] The courts had moved beyond narrow formalism in these cases, deciding them in clear defense of the government's Indian policy.

In fact, the *Hagar* court addressed the policy behind these statutes in response to Hagar's argument that his agreement was a benefit to Ms. Martin. To give effect to such an agreement, stated the court, would be to legislate instead of administer the law. Characterizing the statute as "designed to protect the Indians from all contracts made by them in respect to lands set aside for their use, in consequence of their own improvidence," the court denied any interest in the substance of the bargain, limiting its inquiry to the question of whether the Crown had given consent.[116] Indians were, as a matter of law, improvident, even when they made a good bargain for land they did not want. Of course, the same Indians were not improvident when they made agreements to sell these same lands to the Crown.

Hagar defied the Six Nations for twenty years. He appears to have been very aggressive in his pursuit of Onondaga land, dealing with individual Indians, under circumstances that we cannot know. The Six Nations always resisted him but could not remove him from their lands. Hagar became an established and prosperous farmer, living in the middle of Indian lands and evidently using whatever ingenious chicanery he could to gain access to additional land. Like other local whites he may have been quite hostile to Indians—a hostility fuelled by repeated land disputes.

This same kind of squatter aggressiveness emerges in another case, *The Queen v. Strong*, an 1850 action for trespass against another white squatter on the Grand River Reserve.[117] Strong was among many squatters at Grand River whose ejectment was sought by the tribe. Strong mounted a substantial defense, grounded in procedural issues and formalities of land title. Losing before the two commissioners, he appealed. Among his arguments was that there was insufficient evidence to prove that the lands in question were Indian lands, an issue grounded in the fact that there was no adequate system of land registration on the frontier. Strong was charged with trespass on Indian lands because, like most white squatters, he made no effort to purchase the land. Therefore, the court could not evade deciding that the lands in question were Indian lands within the meaning of the statute. The Court of Chancery rejected Strong's argument, holding specifically that the parole testimony of one Indian witness was sufficient to establish that the lands in question were occupied by Indians, although ceded to the province.[118] The Indians in *Strong* had requested the assistance of the Crown in removing trespassers from their lands with Peter Smith, an Indian leader and interpreter, providing the evidence.[119] The fact that Strong, in 1850, went to chancery court on a simple question of geographical fact illustrates the tenacity of squatters to seize legal title to the lands they occupied. At the bottom of the whole case was the legal issue of whether an Indian could testify whether lands were "Indian lands."

This judicial attitude toward the land rights of the Six Nations was a continuation of the Upper Canadian policy that had initially forced the general surrender of Six Nations lands in 1841. The law was unable to protect Native lands from the squatters' depredations. There was to have been a solution: if the Indians would surrender their lands and just keep a few acres each for their own use, the depredations would cease and the Six Nations would have a recognized sovereign position within the framework of Upper Canada. That is precisely what Samuel Peters Jarvis proposed in 1841:

> The Lieutenant-Governor has directed me to inform the deputation of Chiefs from the Grand River that he has considered their speech to him (protesting white occupation and depredations on their lands). [He] is of the opinion that very great difficulty will be found in any medium course between the expulsion of all the intruders or non-interference as experience has shown that with all the anxiety to do justice, and with all the care

exercised to prevent injury to the Indian interests, the interference of the Indians themselves, continually, has created new difficulties, to which there seems to be no end. . . .

[He] is of the opinion that there can be no remedy formed for the continuance of the unsatisfactory and embarrassing state of affairs, while the lands remain the general property under circumstances which it is no reproach to the Indians to say that they cannot manage the estate for general interests of the tribes.

The Lieutenant-Governor therefore, considers that it would be very much for the benefit of the interest of the Indians if they surrendered into the hands of the Government the whole tract, with the exception of such part of it which they may choose to occupy as a concentrated body . . . and the Lieutenant-Governor strongly recommends that this course be adopted by them. . . . [120]

The reaction of the Six Nations chiefs to this document was one of incredulity: it was a transparent ruse for a land grab: withdrawing legal protection from the Indians in order to force them to sell their lands. There was great dissatisfaction at Grand River, prompting Jarvis to send another letter on 15 January.[121] This letter was far more blunt in a number of ways. First, he was clear that the squatting problem was their own fault:

From a careful inquiry into the nature of the claims of the white man, to the lands in their occupation, it is but too plainly apparent that they have been invited by the great majority of the Indians and that the latter have received large sums of money which they are wholly incapable of ever refunding. So far, indeed from the repeated remonstrances and calls upon them for protection, they find every measure proposed thwarted by the conduct of the Indians themselves, by the repeated pretended sales of their public property, and that, too, not only within the last year, but if I am correctly informed, within the last fortnight by some of the Chiefs and Indians who have been the most urgent in their remonstrances.[122]

This accusation is dishonest. Whites were not living on the Grand River Reserve because they chose to pay high prices for Indian lands. Mrs. Hill and her children had not become rich from their 999-year lease to Mr. Wilkes. The charge that Six Nations chiefs were, at the same time, selling their land and protesting the sale of Indian land to the government, is without documentation. Indeed, even Jarvis appears to qualify his citation to an unnamed informant. The Iroquois council had brought the issue of the removal of squatters to the attention of the government since at least the turn of the century: witness their remonstrance of 1809 in which they had carefully listed, by name, a number of squatters and demanded their removal.[123] The real issue, however, is in the next sentences:

> Under such circumstances it cannot be expected, nor would it in any man-
> ner tend to the interests of the Indians, but upward of 2,000 white per-
> sons nearly equal in number to the Indians upon the Grand River, should
> be utterly removed from their homes, for which in some instances they
> have paid so dearly to individual Indians; neither justice nor policy, or a
> due regard to the Indians interests, requires, or will permit of such a mea-
> sure nor can any such be expected or approved of by me or recommended
> to the government.

Jarvis was not about to evict 2,000 white squatters. Finally, Jarvis interjected himself into tribal politics:

> The above plan proposed meets with the approbation of the most intelli-
> gent of industrious and worthy of the Indians. . . . Those who are opposed
> to it must therefore reflect that any private division in the Council from
> whatever cause proceeding, cannot prevent the Government from interfer-
> ing in seconding the wishes of the Industrious and from promoting the
> wealth of the Nations as a body.
>
> In case any further division should take place in Council and by
> declining amicably to meet their views of Government, the Indians should
> continue to thwart the measures devised as most conducive to their inter-
> ests, I am apprehensive that the Government will be compelled, however,
> reluctantly, to take into their own hands the exclusive management of
> their affairs, and as Chief Superintendent it will be my duty immediately
> upon by return, to recommend such a course, to prevent the public prop-
> erty of the Six Nations from being sacrificed to the avarice and rapacity of
> individuals.

Jarvis' reference to the "avarice and rapacity" of individuals is unclear. Did he mean the white squatters? A year later the Executive Council awarded a good part of their reserve to Wilkes, who was avaricious and rapacious. Similarly, Jarvis' determination to protect the "public property" of the Six Nations can only be taken as a political statement. Jarvis was later removed as Indian commissioner in disgrace, having stolen thousands of dollars of money he managed for the Six Nations and others.[124]

As in any political message, those to whom it was intended clearly understood its meaning. On 18 January, three days after Jarvis' letter, a few of the chiefs and other factional leaders assembled and surrendered their lands, keeping only the 20,000 acres Jarvis suggested, approxi- mately 100 acres per person, plus the improved lands individual members of the tribe actually occupied, totalling about 55,000 acres.[125] We know little about the actual deliberations that led to this process but the outlines are clear. The tribe was divided into at least two factions, one led by elected chiefs and one by traditional chiefs, and had been since at least the time of Brant's original land sales. "The Indians of the Six Nations have been long divided into parties, one of which was in the interest of the Brants, and another supported by the chiefs opposed to them."[126] Jarvis threw his support behind one faction, threatening the other. It is not difficult to explain the viewpoints of the Iroquois chiefs who wanted to hold on to their lands: this ideology of not selling lands went deep in Iroquois culture. Those who wanted to sell may have been motivated by individual gain from land sales, as well as from a feeling that the annuity money would benefit the tribe, the same kind of ideology that may have moved Brant in his land sales.[127] But the forced land sales that followed were not according to Six Nations law.

This land surrender did not stop squatters, although obviously there were fewer squatters on much less land, with a much denser concentration of Indians. Their claims for Indian lands were still going to Ontario courts when an 1858 report on Indian affairs was published.[128] For the most part, the government was now determined to defend the remaining reserve lands from squatters as one key element of the permanent Canadian resolution of the problem of Indian land rights, but legal process ground on slowly.[129] A special act provided for trials of squatters by land commissioners with an appeal to the Court of Chancery. The chancery court repeatedly held against the squatters.[130] However, the government still treated them as entitled to some measure of special consideration for all the labours they had expended to develop the country: £8,000 in Six Nations annuity monies were paid individual squatters for their "improvements" on the 55,000 acres retained by the Indians.[131]

John Beverley Robinson, Upper Canadian Legal Culture and Native Rights

British Imperial and Upper Canadian authorities, who did have authority to eject whites from Six Nations lands, did not do so. At first, they deferred to Iroquois claims of sovereignty, but by the early 1800s, they were refusing to honour the requests of Iroquois chiefs that certain white squatters be removed. By the 1820s, it seems clear that the Upper Canadian authorities were permitting illegal white occupation of the reserve as one element of a strategy to force the Iroquois to cede their lands to the Crown. Frontier whites became masters of legal strategies to maintain their precarious legal status, inventing all sorts of documents to provide some colourable claim of right. Ironically, in the legal chaos that followed, even a colourable claim of right became irrelevant with mere occupation of the land sufficient to accord a substantial legal claim. Canadian judges have not adequately addressed the issue of Native rights, deferring to legislative power in "legal" issues concerning Native people. Virtually all commentators on nineteenth-century Ontario (and Canadian) law agree that it was dominated by "judicial conservatism," a judicial reluctance to depart from narrow interpretations of existing precedent and judicially shape a substantive law more responsive to the needs of a changing and expanding nineteenth-century society.[132]

Legal formalism, the construction of elaborate opinions carefully following precedent, is one manifestation of judicial conservatism. Risk, a careful observer of late-nineteenth-century Ontario law, succinctly states the impact of this formalism on the courts' decision-making process:

> In Ontario the courts seemed to assume that the common law was composed of rules firmly settled by authority, primarily English authority. It was almost never expressly justified, beyond the justification implicit in its mere existence and the internal authority of courts in a hierarchy. . . . The process of making decisions seemed usually to be simply finding facts and applying rules. If the law was obscure or uncertain, the court simply had to look harder to find it.[133]

Moreover, this judicial conservatism occurred in a context where the highest appeal was to the Privy Council, making British law, an unusually formalistic body of law, the law of Canada. Obviously, the implications of such conservatism in the law of Indian rights are clear: there was no legal precedent, leaving the courts to narrowly follow legislative policy, itself weakly developed until after the 1876 consolidation of the *Indian Acts*.[134] Judicial conservatism, in itself, does not explain the course of Indian law in Ontario, for this decision-making process was the product of a very narrow circle of judges. The highest levels of nineteenth-century legal policy making in Ontario were occupied by only a few people who exercised great, often unchallenged influence, for long periods of time. For reasons both political and personal, none of these men had the slightest concern for questions of Native rights and were, in fact, active in seeing that Native rights were suppressed. John Beverley Robinson was chief justice of Upper Canada from 1829 to

1862, capping a public legal career as solicitor general and attorney general of Ontario, a career that began with his appointment as acting attorney general in 1812 at the age of twenty-one.[135] There is not a single piece of evidence to suggest that Robinson, whose legal mind dominated Ontario jurisprudence in the first half of the nineteenth century, had any consciousness at all of any legal issues presented by the presence of Ontario's 25,000 Indian people, a far more substantial portion of the population of Ontario early in the century than at the end.[136] Robinson was a loyalist, son of a Virginia planter, who had fought the revolutionary forces in the United States and moved to Kingston, Upper Canada, to create a loyalist colony there after their loss in the Revolutionary War. Ontario was their creation, the political and legal embodiment of colonial loyalism. At the centre of this jurisprudence was more than legal conservatism: it was loyalty to the Crown, and a strong legal defense of the Crown's prerogatives.[137] This political and legal conservatism was consistent with prevailing models of legal education and legal reasoning. Robinson was educated at Lincoln's Inn, one of the London Inns of Court that controlled entry into the British legal profession. This education consisted of dull recitations at formal dinners, exercises in simply finding the proper rule of law to apply to each case presented. The leading text of the time, Blackstone's *Commentaries*, sought to record eight hundred years of English common law, making it easy for any lawyer to "find" the law.[138] Colonial lawyers had access to few legal treatises. The modern case reporting systems did not exist; hence a lawyer could not readily do his own legal research. The problem with importing this system of formal law and legal reasoning to the colonies should be obvious: nowhere do Indians or Indian rights appear in Blackstone. Thus, Robinson, and Upper Canadian lawyers generally, simply brought British law to Canada and applied it to Indians. Six Nations or Aboriginal sovereignty and land rights was not to be found in this law.

Not surprisingly the legal issue as Robinson saw it in *Regina v. Baby* was that the lands involved—"Indian lands"—were simply "Crown lands" and therefore could not be alienated without the consent of the Crown.[139] Robinson actually had to express some view on Native people two years later in *Totten v. Watson,* a case involving the white alienation of land granted to an Indian chief in fee simple.[140] His opinion again turned on his view of Crown prerogatives, only this time cast in racial terms:

While, in general, the legislature might *possibly* have intended to protect the Indians . . . for they are a helpless race, much exposed, from their want of education and acquaintance with business and the intemperate habits of many of them this policy conflicted with the action of the Crown in granting this particular plot of land to leading persons among the Indians, who . . . had been treated by the Crown as officers in their service, and who, it might be assumed, had sufficient intelligence to take care of their property.[141]

Thus, Robinson would not even judicially recognize what everyone knew about the policy behind legislation to protect Indian lands from alienation. He inferred a distinct status to the Indian land at issue because the Crown's land grant must carry with it the Crown's judgment that the Indians in question were distinct from the majority of the Indians in Upper Canada and intelligent enough to manage their own affairs. Similarly, in *Sheldon ex rel. Doe v. Ramsay*, it mattered to Robinson that the Six Nations tribe not appear in law as either a person or a corporation. As a result, they could not hold title to land either under British or Upper Canadian or Canadian law.

Thus, a framework of judicial conservatism, of carefully framing every legal question in the form of rigid adherence to legal precedent, in Indian cases, created a context where no juridical concept of Indian rights could find any recognition. It neither previously existed in British law, nor could it be easily derived by analogy from related legal principles. Whenever an Indian came into an Upper Canadian (and then Ontario) court, the court took jurisdiction over her or him because it took jurisdiction over all persons. It then treated their cases as any other case under Ontario law, with only a slight deference to the Dominion policy of paternalism, embodied in statutory law.

Conclusion: The Six Nations in the Legal History of Canada

Events since the 1860s make it clear that the doctrinal paradigms set forth by William Dummer Powell and John Beverley Robinson have no place in the legal traditions of the Six Nations. The Six Nations has a long history of a struggle for sovereignty against Canada, and one that is continuing. The courts of Upper Canada, literally as soon as they were created, became one of the arenas of that struggle. The early structuring of legal relations between the Six Nations and

Ontario became, in the late nineteenth century, the Indian law of Canada. The Six Nations cases provided much of the doctrinal foundation for the *St. Catharine's Milling* case. Yet, as we have seen, the reported cases leave out Iroquois sovereignty, a sovereignty that was at the heart of each of the Grand River cases. The British law applied in Canada was not capable, doctrinally or politically, of recognizing that sovereignty. But that sovereignty must have a legal place in modern Canadian law. This legal tradition, while it has British and colonial roots, recognizes the rights and legal traditions of all Canadian people.

Sir Francis Bond Head, not ordinarily known as a legal scholar, recognized that the common-law jurisprudence of Canadian Indian law was filled with legal contradictions dangerous to Indian rights:

> moral considerations and elastic adaptations which are totally incompatible with the straight Railroad habits of a Public Accountant . . . [and] . . . if the Two parties are brought into Contact, either the Accountant must abandon his Principles or the poor Indian must be made the Victim of the Four Rules of Arithmetic. The Migration of these simple People from Equity to Law would be productive of the most serious Evils to them as well as to the government.[142]

Head's intent was clear: he favoured a paternalistic policy of government protection of Indians that is completely inconsistent with the formal recognition of any Indian legal rights, rights of an inferior level that might exist under equity, but not under the common law. This policy of "equity" would, in Head's view, have been defeated by the formal requirements of the common law. The problem with this analysis is that once Indian rights are viewed as of an inferior legal status, the law of "equity" balanced the moral rights of Indians with those of whites, as measured in the cultural worldview of Ontario judges. Indians and Indian nations did not get "equity" from Canadian law: their rights were not recognized, their lands were alienated extra-legally by white squatters acting under the implicit sanction of Canadian law. Could the Six Nations, under tribal law, expel squatters from their sacred lands? They tried to expel James Hagar and now he has a village, Hagersville, on the original Six Nations tract, named after him.

There always, however, has been another legal position, another system of laws, another jurisprudence: that of the Aboriginal Nations. The distribution of "presents" and treaty "annuities" are a unique feature of British Indian relations in Canada that have continued to have legal, political and symbolic dimensions. In elaborate annual ceremonies, Indian agents personally distributed goods to Indians representing the

Covenant Chain of Silver linking the Crown with the Aboriginal Nations. These trade goods were useful and valuable in frontier commerce, including cloth, blankets, knives and cooking implements. The ceremony involved the gathering of an entire Nation for a number of days of feasting, speeches and meetings, celebrations which, with the use of alcohol, became increasingly wild. British authorities, from the 1830s, were determined to end the distribution of presents, both because of their discomfort with the annual events, but also because they highlighted the tribes' unique political status in Canada and encouraged dependency.[143]

Not surprisingly, the tribes, including the Six Nations, saw the issue differently:

> Father, these "presents" (since we are taught to call them by that name), are not in fact presents. They are a sacred debt contracted by the Government, under the promise made by the Kings of France to our forefathers, to indemnify them for the lands they had given up, confirmed by the Kings of England since the cession of the country, and, up to this time, punctually paid and acquitted.[144]

Both the annual event of the distribution of presents and the value of the goods themselves had a powerful symbolic meaning to the Indian tribes. It represented a British deference to their sovereignty and nationhood, an annual payment by the British for valuable services rendered by the tribes, for the loss of tribal lands, and an acknowledgment of their sovereignty and distinct legal and political status in Canada. The Six Nations position on the legal status of those presents was a legal position, arrived at through their own legal imagination and creativity. It represents their continuing use of the law as one arena of the Haudenosaunee's continuing struggle for sovereignty. In so doing, it reaffirmed the Covenant Chain of Silver with the British Crown.

Notes

1 Despatch, Lord Dalhousie to Mr. Secretary Huskisson, Quebec, 22 November 1827, in *British Parliamentary Papers: Correspondence and Other Papers Relating to Aboriginal Tribes in British Possessions*, vol. 3: *Anthropology: Aborigines*, Irish University Press Series of British Parliamentary Papers (Shannon: Irish University Press, 1834), p. 5.
2 Sidney L. Harring, "The Liberal Treatment of Indians: Native People in Nineteenth Century Ontario Law," *Saskatchewan Law Review*, 56 (1993): 297.

3 Great Britain, Parliament, House of Commons, Subcommittee Appointed to make a Comprehensive Inquiry into the State of the Aborigines of British North America, *Report on the Indians of Upper Canada* (1839), p. 29.

4 Maitland to Bathurst, 18 January 1826, Colonial Office Papers, 42/377, p. 10, quoted in Gerald M. Craig, *Upper Canada: The Formative Years* (Toronto: McClelland and Stewart, 1963), pp. 124-25.

5 Quebec, the only other province with a sizable number of cases, produced eighteen cases during this period. Joseph Duquette, arrested for selling liquor to Indians on Dickenson's Island in Lake St. Francis, defended himself in an Ontario court by arguing that his offense had been committed in Quebec. The court held Dickenson's Island a part of Ontario (*Regina v. Duquette*, [1881], 9 P.R., p. 29). Indian law in the United States develops primarily at the state level until the 1880s and 1890s when hundreds of cases are brought into federal courts (Sidney L. Harring, *Crow Dog's Case: American Indian Sovereignty, Tribal Law, and United States Law in the Nineteenth Century* [New York: Cambridge University Press, 1994]).

6 "British precedent dominated legal reasoning in Upper Canada, but Robinson relied on precedent only when it served his purposes" (Patrick Brode, *Sir John Beverley Robinson: Bone and Sinew of the Compact* [Toronto: University of Toronto Press, 1984], p. 104). Obviously, the selective use of precedent leads to the same problems for Native people under British law as the use of precedent: Native rights were never litigated in England; hence there was no precedent. Ironically this might have operated in favour of Indian customary law and national sovereignty if British courts had relied on international law in approaching Native cases. Lord Mansfield approached slavery, another issue for which there was no precedent in the British common law, by holding it unlawful because there was no common-law precedent. Thus, British and colonial courts selectively used precedent in colonial law.

7 The reports searched were the *Upper Canada Reporter* (*U.C.R.*), *Upper Canada Common Pleas Reports* (*U.C.C.P.*), *Ontario Weekly Reports* (*O.W.R.*), *Ontario Practice Reports* (*O.P.R.*), *Ontario Appeals Reports* (*O.A.R.*), *Ontario Reports* (*O.R.*), and *Grant's Chancery Reports* (*Gr.*). Brian Slattery, *Canadian Native Law Cases* (*C.N.L.C.*) (Saskatoon: Native Law Centre, University of Saskatchewan, 1980), vols. 1-3, reprints most of these cases, but not all of them. This number represents the total number of reported opinions delivered by Ontario courts; thus, several cases are counted twice, having produced reported opinions by both a trial and appellate court.

8 Slattery, *C.N.L.C.*, vol. 2, p. 6. The case was found in the Aemilius Irving Papers, Ontario Provincial Archives, box 42, file 42, item 9. Irving, a prominent Ontario lawyer, represented the province in the case.

9 Delivered 31 January 1898 by Judge Rose, of the Ontario Court of Queen's Bench, discussed in William David McPherson and John Murray Clark, *The Law of Mines in Canada* (Toronto: Carswell, 1898), pp. 15-16.

10 The Ontario Provincial Archives is still collecting original court records from nineteenth-century Ontario, records that have been inaccessible to modern scholars, often for a century or more.

11 There is a voluminous traditional legal history of the early judges of Upper
    Canada: Patrick Brode, *Sir John Beverley Robinson* (Toronto: University of
    Toronto Press for the Osgoode Society, 1984); William Renwick Riddell,
    *The Life of William Dummer Powell: First Judge at Detroit and Fifth Chief
    Justice of Upper Canada* (Lansing, MI: Michigan Historical Commission,
    1924); David B. Read, *The Lives of the Judges of Upper Canada and
    Ontario from 1791 to the Present Time* (Toronto: Rowsell and Hutchinson,
    1888); and Robert Fraser, *Provincial Justice: Upper Canadian Legal Por-
    traits* (Toronto: University of Toronto Press, 1992).

12 British Columbia, a colony with little relationship to Canada before Con-
    federation, has a unique Native history that is well documented, including
    legal history: *Papers Connected with the Indian Land Question, 1850-1875*
    (1875; Victoria: Queen's Printer, 1987); Paul Tennant, *Aboriginal Peoples
    and Politics: The Indian Land Question in British Columbia, 1849-1989*
    (Vancouver, BC: University of British Columbia Press, 1990); Robin Fisher,
    *Contact and Conflict: Indian-European Relations in British Columbia,
    1774-1890* (Vancouver, BC: University of British Columbia Press, 1977);
    Douglas Cole and Ira Chaikin, *Iron Hand Upon the People: The Law
    Against the Potlatch on the Northwest Coast* (Seattle, WA: University of
    Washington Press, 1990); David Williams, *The Man for a New Country: Sir
    Matthew Baillie Begbie* (Don Mills, ON: Fitzhenry & Whiteside, 1980);
    and Barry M. Gough, *Gunboat Frontier* (Vancouver, BC: University of
    British Columbia Press, 1984). For the Maritimes, see L.F.S. Upton, *Micmacs
    and Colonists: Indian-White Relations in the Maritimes, 1713-1867* (Van-
    couver, BC: University of British Columbia Press, 1979); Judith Fingard,
    "The New England Company and the New Brunswick Indians, 1786-1826:
    A Comment on the Colonial Perversion of British Benevolence," *Acadien-
    sis*, 1 (1972): 29-42; and Daniel N. Paul, *We Were Not the Savages: A Mic-
    mac Perspective on the Collision of European and Aboriginal Civilizations*
    (Halifax, NS: Nimbus Publishing, 1993).

13 Native people in Quebec and French Canada have a legal history that is dis-
    tinct and is not considered further here (Cornelius J. Jaenen, "French
    Sovereignty and Native Nationhood During the French Regime," *Native
    Studies Review*, 2, 1 [1986]: 83-113). English Canadians refused to live
    under French law, forcing changes in Quebec law after 1783. William
    Dummer Powell, later chief justice of Upper Canada, and fluent in French,
    practised commercial law in Montreal in the 1780s without regard for
    French civil law; the English-speaking community simply ignored it
    (Riddell, *The Life of William Dummer Powell*, pp. 41-47).

14 About half of the reported cases concerns some kind of land issue. Most
    unreported cases were criminal cases.

15 *Doe Ex. Dem. Jackson v. Wilkes* (1835) U.C.K.B. (O.S.) 142; *Little et al. v.
    Keating* (1842) 6 .U.C.Q.B. (O.S.), 265; *Bown v. West* (1846) 2 U.C. Jur.
    675; *Byrnes v. Bown* (1850) U.C.Q.B. 181; *Doe d. Dickson et ux. v. Gross*
    (1852) 9, U.C.Q.B. 580; *Doe d. Sheldon v. Ramsay et al.* (1852),
    9 U.C.Q.B. 105; *Young and Young v. Scobie* (1853) 10 U.C.Q.B. 372; *Jones
    v. Bain* (1854) 12 U.C.Q.B. 550; *Regina v. Baby* (1854) U.C.Q.B. 346;
    Totten v. Watson (1858) 15 U.C.Q.B. 392; *Regina v. McCormick* (1859)

18 U.C.Q.B. 131; *Vanvleck et al. v. Stewart et al* (1860) 19 U.C.Q.B. 489; *Regina v. The Great Western Railway Company* (1862) 21 U.C.Q.B. 555. By contrast, Chief Justice John Marshall, in a thirty-six year term on the bench, authored only five opinions.

16 The 1844 *Report on the Affairs of the Indians in Canada* gave the whole Indian population of Ontario and Quebec at 43,000, with 28,000 living in Ontario (*Journals of the Legislative Assembly of Canada*, App. EEE [1844-45], unpaginated). Completely inconsistent is a report of 13,107 Indians in Ontario at Confederation (1867). The same report lists a 1924 Indian population of 26,706 (*Indians of Ontario* [Ottawa: Department of Citizenship and Immigration, Indian Affairs Branch, 1962], p. 42).

17 Kenneth M. Narvey, "The Royal Proclamation of 7 October 1763, the Common Law, and Native Rights to Land Within the Territory Granted to the Hudson's Bay Company," *Saskatchewan Law Review*, 123 (1973-74): 38; Robert Clinton, "The Proclamation of 1763: Colonial Prelude to Two Centuries of Federal-State Conflict Over the Management of Indian Affairs," *Boston University Law Review*, 329 (1989): 69; Brian Slattery, "The Land Rights of Indigenous Canadian Peoples, as Affected by the Crown's Acquisition of Their Territories" (PhD dissertation, University of Oxford, 1979); J. Stagg, *Anglo-Indian Relations in North America to 1763 and an Analysis of the Royal Proclamation of 7 October 1763* (Ottawa: Department of Indian Affairs and Northern Development, 1981). The full text of the Proclamation is reprinted in Ian A.L. Getty and Antoine S. Lussier, eds., *As Long as the Sun Shines and Water Flows: A Reader in Canadian Native Studies* (Vancouver, BC: University of British Columbia Press, 1983), pp. 29-37.

18 Charles M. Johnston, "Joseph Brant, The Grand River Lands and the Northwest Crisis," *Ontario History*, 55 (1963): 267-82, and William L. Stone, *Life of Joseph Brant* (Albany, NY: J. Munsell, 1864), chaps. 12-16. Maps of these lands, totalling 570,000 acres, are found in R. Louis Gentilcore and C. Grant Head, *Ontario's History in Maps* (Toronto: University of Toronto Press, 1984), pp. 84-85. Charles M. Johnston, *The Valley of the Six Nations*, (Toronto: The Champlain Society, 1964), is an extensive collection of primary documents on the legal history of the Six Nations. Isabel Thompson Kelsay, *Joseph Brant, 1743-1807: Man of Two Worlds* (Syracuse, NY: Syracuse University Press, 1984), is the best biography of Brant, including a detailed analysis of his land dealings at the Six Nations Reserve. Andrea E. Green, "Land, Leadership, and Conflict: The Six Nations' Early Years on the Grand River" (unpublished MA thesis, University of Western Ontario, 1984), is an excellent study of early land issues, but Green uncritically accepts the British legal position that the Six Nations were not sovereign. The grant was made before the lands had been surveyed, leaving Governor Haldimand ignorant of the source of the Grand River—therefore of the extent of the grant. The Haudenosaunee, having traditionally hunted and fished in the region, knew the true extent of the lands.

19 Treaty #3, 22 May 1784, in Canada, *Indian Treaties and Surrenders* (Ottawa: Queen's Printer, 1891; rpt. Saskatoon: Fifth House Publishers, 1992), vol. 1, pp. 5-7. See also Donald Smith, "The Dispossession of the

Mississauga Indians: A Missing Chapter in the Early History of Upper Canada," *Ontario History*, 73 (1981): 67-87, at 72; Robert J. Surtees, "Indian Land Cessions in Ontario, 1763-1862: The Evolution of a System" (unpublished PhD dissertation, Carleton University, 1983), chaps. 1-3, provides a detailed history of the early land cessions.

20 This issue was not legally settled by a court of law until *Logan v. Attorney General of Canada* (1959) O.W.N. 316, although the colonial government of Upper Canada consistently took the position that the Six Nations Iroquois were subject to the same laws governing land tenure as all other Indians in Canada. The Six Nations do not accept that judgment. See Malcolm Montgomery, "The Legal Status of the Six Nations Indians in Canada," *Ontario History*, 55 (1963): 93-105; Darlene Johnston, "The Quest of the Six Nations Confederacy for Self-Determination," *University of Toronto Faculty of Law Review*, 44 (Spring 1986): 1-32; and Donald J. Bourgeois, "The Six Nations: A Neglected Aspect of Canadian Legal History," *Canadian Journal of Native Studies*, 6, 2 (1986): 253-70. Charles M. Johnston, *The Valley of the Six Nations* (Toronto: The Champlain Society, 1964), reprints the documents underlying the Six Nations lands in "A Disputed Title," chap. C, pp. 70-119. Political issues of self-government, although not land issues, were at the heart of another major Six Nations case: *Isaac v. Davey* (1974) 51 D.L.R. (3d), 170; (1973) 38 D.L.R. (3d) 23; and (1977) D.L.R. (3d) 481. See also Peter Maxwell Jacobsen, "Who Rules the Valley of the Six Nations? A Discussion of *Isaac v. Davey*," *McGill Law Journal*, 22, 1 (1976): 130-47. At the trial-court level in *Isaac v. Davey*, an Ontario judge held that the Six Nations Iroquois had been granted their land in fee simple. This was overturned on appeal.

21 "Haldimand's Proclamation of October 25, 1784," NAC, Haldimand Papers, B222, 1061, reprinted in Johnston, *The Valley of the Six Nations*, pp. 50-51.

22 Mabel Dunham, *Grand River* (Toronto: McClelland and Stewart, 1945), presents a popular history of the settlement of the Grand River Valley by both Indians and whites. The *Report on the Affairs of Indians in Canada* (in *Journals of the Legislative Assembly* [1847], vol. 6, Appendix T, unpaginated) gives the Six Nations population at 2,223, the largest Indian population in Upper Canada. The total Indian population of Upper Canada is given as 8,862. Hereafter, these reports are cited as *Report*, then identified by the year of publication.

23 Joseph Brant, never a chief, has been the subject of numerous books and articles, giving rise to a kind of "great chief" view of Indian history. While not intending to deny the importance of Brant in the history of the Grand River Iroquois, I believe these exaggerate his personal role in the development of the Grand River land problem (Stone, *Life of Joseph Brant*; Harvey Chalmers, *Joseph Brant: Mohawk* [East Lansing, MI: Michigan State University Press, 1955]; and Isabel Thompson Kelsay, *Joseph Brant, 1743-1807: Man of Two Worlds* [Syracuse, NY: Syracuse University Press, 1984]). His most controversial contributions to the ongoing land conflict at Grand River are two: first, he claimed a special status for the Six Nations, based on their role as "allies of the Crown," a position almost certainly

shared with all of the Iroquois chiefs. Second, and more complex, he was closely allied with a number of whites and invited them to move to Grand River with the tribe, either giving them grants of land outright or selling them land. This latter action is more controversial, especially in that it personally enriched Brant.

24 *Report*, 1844 (1847), Section III" (unpaginated).

25 Stone, *Life of Joseph Brant*, pp. 399-403, contains extracts from a speech by Joseph Brant clearly setting out his views on the nature of his agreement with the British on the Six Nations lands. The entire speech is reprinted in Johnston, *The Valley of the Six Nations*, pp. 81-84. Thirty-five Iroquois chiefs had given Brant a signed power of attorney to sell their lands in a lengthy document stating the history of their understanding of the land agreement they had with the British (ibid., pp. 79-81). Harvey Chalmers (*Joseph Brant: Mohawk*, pp. 284-95) presents a more colourful description of this disagreement.

26 It is important here to be clear that admitting limited white settlers to Six Nations lands on Six Nations terms does not compromise national sovereignty. Tribes throughout eastern North America did so in the late eighteenth and early nineteenth centuries in an effort to strike a reasonable accommodation to the new reality of white settlement of the frontier. This process has been most extensively documented for the Cherokee (William McLoughlin, *Cherokee Renascence, 1789-1833* [Princeton, NJ: Princeton University Press, 1986]).

27 Gilbert C. Patterson, "Land Settlement in Upper Canada, 1783-1840," in *Sixteenth Report* (1920), Department of Archives, Province of Ontario, pp. 222-23.

28 Kelsay, *Joseph Brant, 1743-1807*, pp. 561-63.

29 Ibid. See also Stone, *Life of Joseph Brant*, pp. 397-98.

30 Ibid., pp. 396-98.

31 Patterson, "Land Settlement in Upper Canada, 1783-1840," p. 223.

32 "Simcoe's Patent of the Grand River Lands to the Six Nations," 14 January 1793, Public Archives of Canada, Q. 329, p. 91, reprinted in Johnston, *The Valley of the Six Nations*, pp. 73-74.

33 There can be no question that both Simcoe and Haldimand intended to satisfy the Indians that they were being granted lands, that is, given their lands to own. If they did not actually intend to convey such title, then they appear to have intended to perpetrate a fraud upon the Six Nations.

34 An exhaustive analysis might be made of these deeds from the standpoint of British law of property, but land grants in Upper Canada simply did not conform to the precise legal requirements of England. Even the restriction allowing land to be sold only to the Crown had parallels in restrictive covenants and in the law of primogeniture.

35 Jack Woodward, *Native Law* (Toronto: Carswell, 1989), p. 405; William Pentney, "The Rights of the Aboriginal Peoples of Canada and the Constitution Act, 1982," *University of British Columbia Law Review*, 22 (1988): 21-59, at pp. 38-49. There is a substantial body of Canadian case law on treaty interpretation. See *R. v. Taylor* (1981), 34 O.R. (2d) 360 (C.A.), and *Nowagijick v. R.*, [1983] 1 S.C.R. 29 (Fed.).

36 Lieutenant Governor Russell to Prescott, *Russell Correspondence*, vol. 2, pp. 85-90, reprinted in Johnston, *The Valley of the Six Nations*, p. 98.

37 "Brant's Power of Attorney to Sell Indian Lands, Nov. 2, 1796," P.R.O., C.O. 42, vol. 321, pp. 35-36, reprinted in ibid., pp. 79-80.

38 Stone, *Life of Joseph Brant*, p. 401. The government appointed three commissioners to administer these sales and hold the money in trust for the Six Nations. These three commissioners did not competently administer the lands, and numerous title problems followed (Kelsay, "This Land is Ours," in *Joseph Brant, 1743-1807*, chap. 25, pp. 553-78).

39 Joseph Brant, in fact, had himself put on an official list of United Empire Loyalists (Kelsay, *Joseph Brant, 1743-1807*, p. 646).

40 This issue on Indian title under British law was not seriously addressed until 1885 in the *St. Catharine's Milling Company* case, Canada's leading Indian title case. In this particular context, Lieutenant Governor John Simcoe and Joseph Brant openly disagreed on the question of the Six Nations title, and Simcoe referred the issue to Lord Dorchester, governor of British possessions in America (ibid., pp. 561-67).

41 Alexander Stewart, a Toronto lawyer married to the daughter of Brant Johnson, a half-breed son of Sir William Johnson, regularly served as Brant's lawyer, evidently at a high fee (ibid., pp. 530, 571, 589, 592).

42 "Memoir of William Dummer Powell, 1797," in Johnston, *The Valley of the Six Nations*, pp. 89-90. Powell, a loyalist lawyer originally from Massachusetts, had practised in Montreal since 1779. In 1789 he was appointed judge in the District of Hesse, the frontier of southwestern Ontario, but then including Detroit and much of what is now Michigan. In 1794 he was appointed a judge of King's Bench at Newark, now Niagara-on-the-Lake, holding that position there, and later at York, until appointed chief justice of Upper Canada in 1816, serving until 1825. He was therefore in an official position to handle issues of the legal status of Indians for his entire thirty-six-year period as a judge (S.R. Mealing, "William Dummer Powell," in *Dictionary of Canadian Biography*, vol. 6, pp. 605-13).

43 Brendan O'Brien, *Speedy Justice: The Last Voyage of His Majesty's Vessel*
• *Speedy* (Toronto: University of Toronto Press, 1992), p. 38, and Kelsay, *Joseph Brant, 1743-1807*, p. 529.

44 Riddell, *The Life of William Dummer Powell*, p. 90. This result may appear inconsistent with Powell having already tried Mishinaway, and having indicted Chabouquoy and Cawquochish, all on murder charges, but Powell's logic focuses on the political sovereignty of Indians "in their villages," which is consistent with United States Indian law. The three Indians at Detroit (although this is not completely clear) were apparently functioning in white society, outside of their traditional villages. Powell and Brant already knew each other: they had dinner together in June of 1789 at Niagara when Powell passed through on his way to Detroit to assume his first judicial post (ibid., p. 66). Two days later, on the American side of the Niagara River, Powell had witnessed a meeting of the Six Nations Council, consisting of upwards of two hundred chiefs (ibid., p. 69). During his term as Canadian judge at Detroit (he actually sat across the St. Clair River at L'Assomption), Powell gained considerable experience in dealing with fron-

tier legal matters, including many cases involving Indians. While Powell believed that British law fully applied to Indians as a general proposition of law, he also believed that Indian customary law might be recognized by treaty (Mealing, "William Dummer Powell," p. 611). Powell's view that existing legal rights were recognized by treaty is consistent with Indian treaties as international treaties.

45 Kelsay, *Joseph Brant, 1743-1807*, pp. 563-65.

46 Ibid., pp. 529-30. It is apparent that even this opinion from the Colonial Office and execution did not fully resolve this issue for it received attention in two of the *Reports on Indian Affairs* commissioned in 1839 and 1844. Judge James Buchanan Macaulay, in his 1839 *Report* to Governor George Arthur, devoted several paragraphs to the legal status of Indians in Upper Canada. While making it clear that the "resident Tribes are peculiarly situated," he went on to point out that "it would be difficult to point out any tenable ground on which a claim to an exempt or distinctive character could be rested. The Six Nations have, I believe, asserted the highest pretensions to separate nationality, but in the Courts of Justice they have been always held amenable to, and entitled to the protection of the Laws of the land" (Mr. Justice Macaulay to Governor Sir George Arthur, 1839; reprinted in *Report*, 1844 [1847], Appendix 99).

Macaulay went on to report that Indians had been tried on criminal charges for homicides committed against both whites and each other in different parts of the province. He personally recalled a trial before him of a Six Nations Indian at Niagara on charges of stealing one or two blankets from an Indian woman. The woman had sworn out a complaint with a justice of the peace. The defendant's lawyer argued that the Court lacked jurisdiction because the "matter was only cognizable among the Indians themselves, according to their own usages and customs: but I had to refuse the plea, not being able to point out any legal authority by which the protection of the Criminal Law could be refused to the Indians inhabiting the county of Haldimand . . . and I observed, that however important it was that a sound distinction should be exercised by local magistrates in cases not of an aggravated character, I could not but admit that, in my opinion, the Indians were responsible for crime." Macaulay went on to remark that he had also convicted a Delaware Indian of a larceny committed in a house owned by the Earl of Egremont, in Caradoc Township (Macaulay to Governor Arthur, *Report*, 1839).

This did not fully resolve the issue for a year later the superintendent of Indian Affairs asked C.R. Ogden, attorney general of Canada, for an opinion on the legal status of Indians. Ogden's response was simple: "The Indians have legal capacity, either as plaintiffs or defendants" (Memorandum of C.R. Ogden, Montreal, 9 May 1840, reprinted in *Report*, 1844 [1847], Appendix 99).

47 *The King v. Epaphrus Lord Phelps* (1823) 1 Taylor 47. The case is discussed in detail in William Renwick Riddell, "The Sad Tale of an Indian Wife," *Journal of the American Academy of Criminal Law and Criminology*, 13 (1922): 82-89. This issue was not settled by *Phelps* and went through the Ontario courts to the Supreme Court of Canada in the 1970s in *Isaac v.*

Davey (1973), 38 D.L.R. (3d) 23 Ont. H.C.; (1974), 51 D.L.R. (3d) 170 (Ont.C.A.); and *Davey v. Isaac* (1977), 77 D.L.R. (3d) 481 (S.C.C.). To the Iroquois these issues are still unresolved.

48 On the early history of Indian and white settlement of the Grand River Valley, see Charles M. Johnston, "An Outline of the Early Settlement in the Grand River Valley," *Ontario History*, 54 (1962): 43-67.

49 Robert Fraser, "William Warren Baldwin," in *Dictionary of Canadian Biography*, vol. 7, pp. 35-44. Baldwin, son of an Irish gentleman farmer, had a lucrative commercial law practice and was appointed judge of the Surrogate Court in 1816. He was a land speculator and held large landholdings, with his wild (uncultivated) lands alone yielding an income of £1,400 a year, twice that of his law practice, although it is not clear that any of these lands were Grand River lands. In politics, Baldwin was a Whig, opposed to the elite "family compact" that governed Upper Canada. Obviously, the legal position that Baldwin argued was favourable to both the Six Nations and to the white speculators who held land titles deriving from the Six Nations.

50 Ibid., pp. 88-89.

51 Aborigines Protection Society, *Report* (London: Aborigines Protection Society, 1839).

52 The politics of the reports is discussed in Anthony Hall, "The Red Man's Burden: Land, Man, and the Law in the Indian Affairs of Upper Canada, 1761-1851" (unpublished PhD dissertation, University of Toronto, 1984), pp. 303-306. The 1840 *Report* was not published until it was included as an appendix of the 1844 *Report* (*Journals of the Legislative Assembly of the Province of Canada* [1847], vol. 6, Appendix T). The 1844 *Report* was published in two parts. The preceding citation is to the second part. The first part was published in *Journals of the Legislative Assembly of Canada* (1844-45), Appendix EEE.

53 Still, even in the 1840s the term "squatter" was not without negative connotations. The underlying pejorative context of the term is evident in that some of the histories of Ontario land settlement do not use the term, while others use it extensively. For example, Gilbert C. Patterson ("Land Settlement in Upper Canada, 1783-1840") does not use the term at all. Lillian F. Gates, *Land Policies of Upper Canada* (Toronto: University of Toronto Press, 1968), uses it hundreds of times. It also had general use in Australia, usually in the same way that it was used in Upper Canada in the 1840s (Brian H. Fletcher, *Landed Enterprise and Penal Society: A History of Farming and Grazing in New South Wales before 1821* [(Sydney: Sydney University Press, 1876]).

54 Gates, *Land Policies of Upper Canada.*

55 *Report*, 1844 (1847), unpaginated, quoting "Report of Committee No. 4, on Indian Department," 1 February 1840, also reprinted in *Journals of the Legislative Assembly of the Province of Canada* (1847), Appendix T. This quotation can be found within the *Report* on the fourth page of Appendix 1 attached to Appendix T.

56 "Report of Samuel P. Jarvis, Superintendent of Indian Affairs," 17 April 1841, in *Journals of the Legislative Assembly of the Province of Canada* (1847), Part III, Appendix 16, unpaginated.

57 Patterson, "Land Settlement in Upper Canada, 1783-1840," pp. 50-51.

58 "Resolutions of a Six Nations Council at the Onondaga Village, March 1, 1809," in Johnston, *The Valley of the Six Nations*, pp. 110-12.

59 Ibid., p. 111.

60 "Proclamation on the Indian Lands," 1 February 1812, in Johnston, *The Valley of the Six Nations*, pp. 113-14.

61 "Leases of Isaac Whiting and Ezra Hawley," in Johnston, *The Valley of the Six Nations*, pp. 114-15.

62 Robinson to Macaulay, 20 July 1852, Macaulay Family Papers, Public Archives of Ontario, quoted in Gates, *Land Policies of Upper Canada*, p. 295.

63 Robinson's opinions on squatters land rights are discussed below on pp. 200-203.

64 *Journal of the Legislative Assembly* (1854-55), vol. 13, Appendix MM.

65 "Report of Samuel P. Jarvis, Superintendent of Indian Affairs," 17 April 1841, in *Journals of the Legislative Assembly of the Province of Canada* (1847), Part III, Appendix 16, unpaginated.

66 Ibid.

67 Ibid.

68 Gates, *Land Policies of Upper Canada*, p. 7 and passim. Gilbert C. Patterson takes the view that many of the squatters were innocent purchasers, ignorant of the legal status of their lands ("Land Settlement in Upper Canada, 1783-1840," pp. 233-34). The most difficult cases doubtlessly involved hard-working farmers who were remote purchasers of lands initially alienated illegally by speculators, perhaps thirty or forty years before, land that might have changed hands five or six times or more. But the chaotic legal status of the Six Nations Reserve was common knowledge: it was an issue in local elections, for example.

69 "Simcoe's Patent of the Grand River Lands to the Six Nations," 14 January 1793, Public Archives of Canada, Q. 329, p. 91, reprinted in Johnston, *The Valley of the Six Nations*, pp. 73-74, at p. 74.

70 Ibid. See also Leo A. Johnson, "The Settlement of the Western District," in F.H. Armstrong et al., eds., *Aspects of Nineteenth Century Ontario* (Toronto: University of Toronto Press, 1974), pp. 19-35. J. David Wood, ed., *Perspectives on Landscape and Settlement in Nineteenth Century Ontario* (Toronto: McClelland and Stewart, 1975), includes several important essays on Ontario land policy, including his own ("Introduction: A Context for Upper Canada and its Settlement," pp. xvii-xxviii) and Alan G. Brunger's ("Early Settlement in Contrasting Areas of Peterborough County Ontario," pp. 117-40). This process is described and displayed in map form in Gentilcore and Head, *Ontario's History in Maps*, pp. 25-110. Comparable with the rapid development of the American northwest at the same time, Ontario's white population grew from 10,000 in 1790 to 951,000 in 1851, essentially an agrarian population inhabiting a narrow strip of land along the north side of Lake Ontario, then expanding across the peninsula between Lake Erie and Lake Huron.

71 The Royal Proclamation of 1763, a major statement of Indian policy and the source of most British law on Indian policy, expressly forbade the tribes

to sell their lands to whites, and expressly forbade whites to make direct land purchases from Indians. Joseph Brant deliberately ignored this law, but William Claus both expressly restated this law as the basis of Canadian land policy in a speech at the Six Nations Council, on 17 August 1803. At the same time he sent a runner to the chief justice of Upper Canada at Fort Erie ("Speeches by Brant and Claus at Six Nations' Council, Fort George," 17 August 1803, Upper Canada State Papers, Public Archives of Canada, vol. 7, pp. 33-49, reprinted in Johnston, *The Valley of the Six Nations*, pp. 133-36, at 136). Obviously, the fact that Claus felt the need to send a messenger to remind the chief justice of the existence of this law means there was some confusion about it on the Niagara frontier in 1803. It is clear that Joseph Brant had both ignored and flaunted the law, arguing that the Six Nations were sovereign and could dispose of their lands as they saw fit. Canadian authorities were caught off-guard by these actions and equiv-ocated in their response. Thus, Claus is taking this measure to make certain that all branches of the government are being consistent on the legal status of Six Nations lands (see ibid.).

72 Clark was a Queenston land speculator. Brant had been trying to sell these lands since 1795, but had not been able to get buyers with the money to pay the prices they agreed. Since Block 4 was one of the blocks originally put up for sale in 1795, it seems highly likely that some agreement on its sale had been reached at that time. However, it was not recorded, and apparently, like many of the other Blocks sold at that time, the speculators involved had defaulted on their payments. This would support the view that Joshua Cozens had bought the land at that time, but had not been able to pay for it (Kelsay, *Joseph Brant, 1743-1807*, p. 643.

73 Cozens' claim is quite specific on the details of the deed. He claimed that Joshua Cozens, on 8 October 1796, paid £500 to Brant in front of Judge Robert Kerr, of the Surrogate Court for the Home District, and Angus McDonnell, barrister, who both served as witnesses. Further, in June 1797 Cozens paid Brant another £500 for a receipt acknowledging the payment of the money. Upon receipt of a title from the government, Cozens was to pay Brant a further £1,000. Cozens was allegedly in the secret service of Lieutenant Governor Simcoe, who was to receipt two sevenths of the value of the land. The remainder of the land was to be used to resettle Loyalists from New York, although Simcoe recommended selling the lands in Europe at great profit ("Report on Petition of N. Cozens" and "Affidavit of N. Cozens, July 1, 1834," in Upper Canada House of Assembly, *Journals* [1836], Appendix 37, pp. 5-6, reprinted in Johnston, *The Valley of the Six Nations*, pp. 164-67). Obviously the details of this affidavit are completely self-serving, but they were believable to many, and illustrate the chaos of the land transactions of the time.

74 Isabel Thompson Kelsay (*Joseph Brant, 1743-1807*, pp. 562, 570, 588, 595, 616, 621, 630) recognizes that Joshua Cozens probably made some kind of land purchase from Brant in 1795 or 1796. The sale has a complex legal history: it originated as an "illegal" sale, made personally by Brant without the approval of British authorities, but it was later recognized. Brant, however, either did not keep, or lost, his records of the sale. On top

of this, almost all of the purchasers of these lands defaulted on their payments, and many of the lands were resold.

75 Patterson, "Land Settlement in Upper Canada, 1783-1840," pp. 228-29. Many of these details are set out by Nelson Cozens himself in "Report on Petition of N. Cozens" and "Affidavit of N. Cozens, July 1, 1834," reprinted in Johnston, *The Valley of the Six Nations*, pp. 164-67.

76 Patterson, "Land Settlement in Upper Canada, 1783-1840," pp. 228-29, and "Report on Petition of N. Cozens." See also *Report*, 1844 (1847), Appendix 16.

77 Robinson to John Macaulay, 7 July 1834, Macaulay Family Papers, Public Archives of Ontario.

78 No records exist that would show exactly how Nelson Cozens financed his claim. Considering the value of a township of land in land-hungry Upper Canada—92,160 acres of rich agricultural land immediately north of Brantford—it was obviously worth a great deal to Cozens to keep his claim alive.

79 Kelsay, *Joseph Brant, 1743-1807*, pp. 562, 570, 588, 595, 616, 621, 630.

80 Daniel Penfield to Brant, 27 April 1807, Records and Correspondence of the Deputy Superintendent General, Public Archives of Canada, Indian Affairs, vol. 27, p. lvi, reprinted in Johnston, *The Valley of the Six Nations*, pp. 149-50.

81 Ibid., p. lvii, and William Dickson to Claus," 1817, NAC, Upper Canada Sundries, vol. 34, reprinted in ibid., pp. 152-53. The case, *William Dickson v. Daniel Penfield* (Hilary Term, 1818) is unreported (J.B. Robinson Docket Book, 1817-21).

82 Brode, *Sir John Beverley Robinson*, p. 103.

83 The Cayugas surrendered 20,671 acres in 1831. In 1834, 50,212 acres in the township of Dunn was surrendered by several Six Nations tribes (Dunham, *Grand River*, pp. 182-83).

84 *Report*, 1844 (1847), Appendix 16.

85 Ibid., Appendix 1.

86 "Protection of Indian Reserves," in ibid.

87 Ibid., Appendix 100.

88 Ibid., Appendix l.

89 The Legislative Assembly had quasi-judicial power throughout most of the early nineteenth century. Not only did the chief justice sit on the Assembly, but the Assembly heard appeals in some matters from the courts.

90 *Bown v. West* (1846) 1 U.C. Jur. 639; appealed to the Upper Canada Executive Council, (1846) E & A 117. It is important to note that this case occurred after the general surrender of Six Nations lands in 1841 that was supposed to solve the land tenure problem.

91 *Bown v. West* (1846) 1 U.C. Jur. 639, at 642-50.

92 *Bown v. West* appealed to the Upper Canada Executive Council, (1846) E & A 117, at 121.

93 Ibid., p. 118.

94 The Grand River Navigation Company was chartered by Upper Canada to make the Grand River navigable from Lake Erie to Brantford. Without the knowledge of the Six Nations, their annuity monies were invested in the Company which, without their approval, took Six Nations lands to build

the canal. The Company never made a profit and the annuity monies were lost. Claims against the Crown for the loss of these lands continue (Donald Bourgeois, *Research Report on the Six Nations Indian Land Claim to the "Tow Paths" Along the Grand River* [Toronto: Office of Indian Resource Policy, Ontario Ministry of Natural Resources, 1982], and *Research Report on the Six Nations Indian Land Claim to the Bed of the Grand River* [Toronto: Office of Indian Resource Policy, Ontario Ministry of Natural Resources, 1981]).

95 *Westbrooke v. the Attorney General* (1865), 11 Gr. 330.

96 Ibid., pp. 335-37.

97 *Doe D. Wilkes v. Babcock* (1852), 1 U.C.C.P 388.

98 Ibid., pp. 389-90.

99 *Doe d. Sheldon v. Ramsay et al.* (1852), 9 U.C.Q.B. 105.

100 Sheldon, seeming to cover his bases, complicated matters by sending an agent to Mallory in the United States and getting William Mallory, an agent of Bonajah, to assign him Mallory's interest in the lands. It must reveal something of Sheldon's lack of faith in the Canadian legal process that he backed up his forfeiture deed, issued by the Crown, with an assignment of the legal rights of a convicted traitor.

101 Ibid., pp. 106-27, contains a history of Mallory's tenure on this parcel of land. A map is included at p. 114. This chaotic history, like that of Cozens, must be typical of many of the tracts that Brant granted or "leased" to whites.

102 Ibid., p. 119.

103 *Doe Ex. Dem. Jackson v. Wilkes* (1835), 4 U.C.K.B. (O.S.) 142. This case involved a lot in Brampton. Jackson held title through letters patent from the Crown. Wilkes held title through a deed from Joseph Brant and Haldimand's grant to the Six Nations.

104 *Doe d. Sheldon v. Ramsay et al.* (1852), 9 U.C.Q.B. 105, at 122.

105 Ibid.

106 The effect of this dictum is to deny any distinct legal or political status to the "tribe" or "Indian nation" (Bruce Clark, *Native Liberty, Crown Sovereignty* [Montreal: McGill/Queen's University Press, 1992], p. 19). Robinson's legal analysis here is wrong on every level, even within the context of the common law at that time. The Crown had long recognized Indian nations and tribes as both political and legal entities, with a history of this recognition going back perhaps two hundred years. The Privy Council, the highest legal authority in England, had decided the *Mohegan* land claim against the Colony of Connecticut in 1773, eighty years before Robinson's opinion, recognizing both the Mohegan nation's right to hold land under British law and also their right to use British courts to enforce their land rights (Joseph Henry Smith, "The Mohegan Indians v. Connecticut," in *Appeals to the Privy Council from the American Plantations* [New York: Columbia University Press, 1965], pp. 422-42).

107 *Doe d. Sheldon v. Ramsay et al.* (1852), 9 U.C.Q.B. 105, at 123.

108 Ibid., p. 125.

109 Ibid., pp. 133, 135.

110 Ibid., p. 136. See *Doe ex dem. Jackson v. Wilkes* (1835), 4 U.C.K.B. (O.S.) 142, at 261.

111 *William Dickson v. Daniel Penfield* (Hilary Term, 1818), in J.B. Robinson Docket Book, 1817-21.

112 Brode, *Sir John Beverley Robinson*, p. 103. This case was over title to Block 1 of the original Brant grants, discussed above at p. 196. The fee of £699 was an enormous amount of money at the time.

113 *The Queen v. James Hagar* (1857), 7 U.C.C.P. 380. This is the same James Hagar who had intruded on Onondaga lands in 1832 and was instrumental in forcing the Onondaga to sell (Dunham, *Grand River*, p. 182).

114 Ibid., p. 182.

115 Ibid., pp. 381-82.

116 Ibid., p. 382.

117 *The Queen v. Strong* (1850), 1 Gr. 392. On the designs of white squatters on the Grand River see Johnston, "An Outline of the Early Settlement in the Grand River Valley."

118 Ibid., p. 405.

119 Ibid., p. 393.

120 "Report of Samuel P. Jarvis, Superintendent of Indian Affairs," 5 January 1841, in *Journals of the Legislative Assembly of the Province of Canada* (1847), Part III, Appendix 16, unpaginated.

121 A. Leon Hatzan, *The True Story of Hiawatha, and History of the Six Nations Indians* (Toronto: McClelland & Stewart, 1925), pp. 123-25.

122 "Report of Samuel P. Jarvis, Superintendent of Indian Affairs," 15 January 1841, in *Journals of the Legislative Assembly of the Province of Canada* (1847), Part III, Appendix 16, unpaginated.

123 "Resolutions of a Six Nations' Council at the Onondaga Village, March 1, 1809," in Johnston, *The Valley of the Six Nations*, pp. 110-12. The refusal of the Crown to remove squatters from Six Nations lands is still the subject of outstanding Six Nations land claims.

124 Douglas Leighton, "The Compact Tory as Bureaucrat: Samuel Peters Jarvis and the Indian Department, 1837-1845," *Ontario History*, 73, 1 (1981): 40-53.

125 *Report*, 1844 (1847), Appendix 16. See also Hatzan, *The True Story of Hiawatha*, pp. 125-31, for the same account.

126 Sir John Colborne, Lieutenant Governor of Upper Canada to Goderich, 30 November 1832, Great Britain, Colonial Office, *Aboriginal Tribes, Parliamentary Paper* (1834), no. 617, p. 142, cited in Johnston, *The Valley of the Six Nations*, p. 297.

127 Every treatment of Joseph Brant and Six Nations history has an explanation of his land transactions and these various explanations are discussed herein. It seems impossible to say precisely why Brant made his land sales, but some combinations of the reasons scholars commonly put forth are adequate as explanations. Most troublesome to historians has been some kind of balancing his personal pecuniary interests, which were substantial, with his assessment that the Six Nations needed both white neighbours to aid in acculturation, as well as the income from the sale of lands to continue functioning as a nation. These issues divided the Six Nations.

128 "Report of the Royal Commission of Enquiry into Indian Affairs (Pennefather Commission)," *Journals of the Legislative Assembly* (1858), vol. 16,

Appendix 6, Appendix no. 21—hereafter cited as *Report* (1858)—unpaginated.

129 Robert Surtees, "Indian Land Surrenders in Ontario, 1763-1867," Treaties and Historical Research Centre, Department of Indian and Northern Affairs, Ottawa. Once almost all Indian land had been surrendered and the Indians were confined to small reserves, the entire nature of the land surrender system changed. Obviously, there was no reason for frontier whites to sense this change: squatting had always been illegal and the laws had always been ignored. Frontier whites probably anticipated that the reserves would be available for settlement in a few years.

130 *Report* (1858), Act 2, Vic. c. 15.

131 Ibid.

132 Jennifer Nedelsky, "Judicial Conservatism in an Age of Innovation: Comparative Perspectives on Canadian Nuisance Law 1880-1930," and R.C.B. Risk, "The Law and the Economy in Mid-Nineteenth Century Ontario: A Perspective," both in David Flaherty, ed., *Essays in the History of Canadian Law* (Toronto: University of Toronto Press for the Osgoode Society, 1981), pp. 281-322 and 88-131, respectively. See also James Forbes Newman, "Reaction and Change: A Study of the Ontario Bar, 1880-1920," *University of Toronto Faculty of Law Review*, 32 (1974): 51-74.

133 R.C.B. Risk, "'This Nuisance of Litigation': The Origins of Workers' Compensation in Ontario," in Flaherty, ed., *Essays in the History of Canadian Law*, pp. 418-91, at p. 449.

134 All of Canada's Indian laws were consolidated in 1876—nine years after Confederation—into a single *Indian Act* (Robert Moore, "The Historical Development of the *Indian Act*," Treaties and Historical Research Centre, Department of Indian and Northern Affairs, Ottawa, pp. 60-70).

135 Brode, *Sir John Beverley Robinson*, and Terry Cook, "John Beverley Robinson and the Conservative Blueprint for the Upper Canadian Community," *Ontario History*, 64 (1972): 79-94.

136 This would have represented about 10 percent of Ontario's 1840 population of about 250,000. By 1900, Ontario, typical of the growth of the white population of all of North America, had a population of 1,200,000, reducing the Indian proportion to about 2 percent. The term "Indians" appears twice in Robinson's biography, both times referring to his service with Indian allies in the Detroit area in the War of 1812 (Brode, *Sir John Beverley Robinson*, pp. 14, 16).

137 David Howes, "Property, God and Nature in the Thought of Sir John Beverley Robinson," *McGill Law Journal*, 30 (1985): 365.

138 Sir William Blackstone's *Commentaries* were originally published in London in four volumes, beginning in 1758. These volumes were continuously reissued in popular editions and were the basis of legal study through the nineteenth century throughout the common-law world.

139 *Regina v. Baby* (1854), 12 U.C.Q.B. 346, at 353.

140 *Totten v. Watson* (1856), 15 U.C.Q.B. 392, at 395-96.

141 Ibid. Robinson also referred to both Native rights and government policy in *Bown v. West*, discussed above on pp. 199-200.

142 Head to Lord Glenelg, Secretary of State for Colonies, 4 April 1837, Public Archives of Canada, Manuscript Group 11, Q Series, vol. 396, part 4, quoted in James Clifton, *A Place of Refuge for All Time: Migration of the American Potawatomi into Upper Canada, 1830-1850*, National Museum of Man, Canadian Ethnology Service Paper, no. 26 (Ottawa: National Museum of Man, 1975), p. 55.

143 *Report*, 1844 (1844-45), Part I, contains a lengthy discussion of the issue of presents, including a consideration of the possibility of discontinuing them. The payment of presents was discontinued by the British Imperial government in 1856.

144 "Memorial of the Seven Nations to the Governor of Lower Canada," 17 June 1839, *Parliamentary Papers*, no. 323, p. 62, quoted in *Report*, 1844 (1844-45). The reference to the "Seven Nations" includes the Delaware, many of whom had accompanied the Six Nations to Canada and settled with them on their reserves. While the term "Six Nations" was used by both the Iroquois and British, the Six Nations themselves never included the Delaware as full members of their Confederacy.

11

The Uses and Abuses of Power in Two Ontario Residential Schools: The Mohawk Institute and Mount Elgin

Elizabeth Graham

This paper examines the uses and abuses of power and the techniques of control used by the school administrations over the students of two Ontario residential schools.[1] The Mohawk Institute at Brantford was founded as a Mechanics Institute in 1831 by the New England Company and became a residential school in 1834. Mount Elgin at Muncey was founded by Peter Jones and the Methodist Church and opened in 1850.

Residential schools removed children from their homes and placed them in a community where they can be educated and moulded into shape. An institution of this kind for Native children provided almost experimental conditions for would-be civilizers bent on total culture change. The history of these schools also reflects the wider society's changing images of what has been referred to throughout the nineteenth and twentieth centuries as the "Indian Problem." As perceptions of the "Indian Problem" changed, so did solutions, and although the schools were always part of the solution their roles changed over the decades.

Notes to chapter 11 are on pp. 243-44.

The schools were founded to solve the Indian Problem through "civilization."[2] The founders of the schools, who equated civilization and salvation, had benevolent intentions. They envisaged a plan of self-help for Native communities in which Native students would acquire education, manual labour, agricultural and domestic skills, become teachers and ministers and become the agents of civilization in their communities. With the *Indian Act* and relegation of Indians to government wards, dependency was fostered and the role of the schools changed to the training of domestic servants and farmhands. The legacy of the reserve system, which marginalized Indians and kept them in poverty, was the image of Indians as a true "problem," with no direct relevance for Canadian society. After the World War I the schools became shelters for poor, orphaned or "problem" children who had no place in their society.

In May 1920 the principal of Mount Elgin wrote:

> we were under no illusion what ever as to the difficulties of the task awaiting us—the business management of a thousand acre farm, the purchase and sale of all the live stock connected therewith, the judicious expenditure of approximately $25,000 per annum for wages, food, clothing, fuel, light and many other things incidental to the life of the school. Add to these the final responsibility for the health, happiness and discipline of at least 120 boys and girls always in residence, the selection of suitable officers and teachers, and the blending of all these varied interests into something like a happy and suitable community life, and we have a job quite big enough to tax the energies of any one man.[3]

The principals appointed to do this job were usually ministers of religion, who could not cope with *all* the jobs—almost none of which had anything to do with being a minister.

The financial situation at both schools was difficult from the very beginning. Most improvement schemes were wrecked on financial rocks. At both schools it became expedient to make the farm carry the school and necessary to make the children do the work to make the farm pay.

As both schools moved away from the original purpose of providing an education and manual training for the students, as a result of a shortage of funds and burgeoning bureaucracy, the students started working for the school, the girls making all the clothes, cooking and cleaning, and the boys doing the farm work. Running the institution profitably became the major purpose of the institution. Having "created the monster," survival of the institution, with total power over its inmates, became the goal.

The first task in achieving total power was separating children from their parents. This is what residential schools do, but at Indian residential schools the goal of eradicating "Indianness" was added to the process by removing the children from their homes, restricting their holidays, and not allowing them to communicate with their parents or with each other in their Native languages. Communication between brothers and sisters was severely restricted. Parents were often described as interfering. Letters were censored. Principals even saw themselves as *protecting* the children from their parents, who were considered a bad influence, or immoral, with dirty, unhealthy houses. This exclusion not only kept parents out, but kept students in. The schools came to resemble prisons with prison cells in the school, fire escapes locked and truancy as the major crime and primary problem.

Michel Foucault has described the resemblance between prisons and factories, schools, barracks and hospitals. The aim for total power on the part of the authorities, and the techniques used to achieve it, are similar in these institutions. To achieve total power the right of the authorities to hold it must be accepted by everyone in the system. Foucault asks: "how were people made to accept the power to punish, or quite simply, when punished, tolerate being so?"[4] Foucault pointed to Jeremy Bentham's model of the Panopticon as the ideal prison—a central tower from which every aspect of the institution was visible. The inmate saw this tower too and believed that someone might be observing him at any moment, and he had to monitor his own behaviour constantly so as not to be caught unawares. This "Big Brother is watching you" fear of surveillance had the permanent effect that the inmate took over from the watchers the responsibility for his behaviour and "he becomes the principle of his own subjection."[5]

Through surveillance and discipline schoolchildren, as well as prisoners, can be controlled with the economical use of power, the institutions using similar techniques—timetables, uniforms, training and discipline. The schools depended on rigid timetables. Bells marked the course of the day, telling the children where they should be and what they should be doing at each moment, ensuring that they were under surveillance for most of the day:

> You had five minutes when the first bell would ring, to get up and put your clothes on, to run two flights of stairs and be downstairs and stand in line. Five minutes to wash your hands and face, brush your teeth, comb your hair and stand in line again. They'd be standing at the bottom of the stairs to make sure you were down there when the second bell rang, or up you would go to get the strap. (Dorothy)

Uniforms, which, while removing the identity of individuals so that they could be controlled more effectively, gave them an outward identity as members of the school—another technique designed to engineer the internal acceptance of the rules. Similarly, numbers were used to identify the children.

The compulsory use of English also removed the children's Indian identity and gave them a school identity. Language surveillance was extended to include the parents when they intruded into the school sphere and were forced to communicate with their children in English.

At both schools the rules of conduct were comprehensive and strict—another technique which left little room for individuality. Students had to line up and march to the dining room, the classroom, to work, to go to chapel, to take baths, and even to get a beating, which trained the children to "keep in line" literally. At any particular time each student was supposed to be in a particular place. Certain areas were designated as "in bounds." Boys were not allowed on the girls' side and vice versa. In many places silence was mandatory in the dining room:

> Chester and I were sitting together in the dining room and we couldn't speak a word of English. We were talking back and forth and laughing, and suddenly this woman, Miss Barnett, hit us BANG! BANG! with a ruler right on the head. It wasn't really our language that they were after, it was to be quiet. You couldn't talk in the dining room when you were eating. . . . Everybody had to stand up and our seats went back together. Everybody stood up, and faced the way they were going to go, and they marched out. (Manson)

Students were expected to work hard and be polite. Any appropriation of school property such as food or clothing was regarded as theft—even windfall apples—but the students became quite expert at taking food and not getting caught. "It wasn't really stealing, it was survival" (Frank). Although it might seem that all individuality is lost in this kind of system, Foucault argues that one function of discipline and punishment was to give individuals a separating identity within the carceral, rather than allowing them to form a homogeneous mass, which would have a potential for gaining power. Children at the residential schools were differentiated by the discipline system—in particular by the military-type hierarchy with squads and monitors—that was set up at the Mohawk Institute in the 1870s. Punishment records kept at the Mohawk Institute (1914) show how children were differentiated by the number of punishments they received, but also illustrate the extent of surveillance on all aspects of behaviour, with details of every child's misbehaviour recorded.

Any system requiring total power needs rules and the consequence of breaking the rules is punishment. Forms of punishment included corporal punishment, solitary confinement, cutting off hair, removal of privileges, walking around the playground, extra work, scrubbing the floor, being sent to bed, standing out in the hall, cancelling visiting privileges of parents or siblings, etc.

Offenses for which students can remember getting the strap included throwing yarn across the sewing room instead of getting up and handing it, throwing a rotten potato in the storeroom, running in the hall, being in the wrong place, sassing a teacher, talking to a sibling, speaking their Native language, stealing apples and other food, running away and numerous others.

Corporal punishment is a flagrant invasion of personal dignity; the intent is to cause humiliation as well as pain. Another form of surveillance, humiliation, destroys dignity and subsequently identity. However, in the playroom subculture of the Mohawk Institute the children did not cry if they received the strap, but had to "tough-it-out":

> I was up in the dorm where I wasn't supposed to be and I was helping the other kids make beds and I got caught, so this supervisor gave me the strap. There was about seven of us girls and she gave the strap to my wrist, and I didn't cry. I vowed to myself I wasn't going to cry. So she said "Get to the end of the line." So she strapped two and she got to me, and she strapped me up to the elbow, and I still didn't cry. "I'll get to you later." So she strapped all the rest of them and it was just me up there and she strapped me up to my shoulder, and it was really red, and it was just all swollen, just a dreadful sight. And I got downstairs determined I wasn't going to cry, and my sister saw it and she started to cry. That's when I started to cry. (Karen)

This refusal to cry and be broken, which is mentioned time and again by the former students, allowed them to retain their dignity and identity, but sometimes at great cost in terms of physical punishment.

Many of the students did accept the right of the administration to make and enforce the rules, making observations such as: "When I was bad I deserved what I got" (Erna), "You made it yourself what you wanted to be—you could be bad, you could be good" (Walter), "If I was punished it was my own fault" (Ina), "You got a licking if you needed it" (Jo-Bear). However, there were individuals who refused to accept punishment:

Miss Hardy said, "Put your hands up." "Nope." She said, "I said put your hands up." "Nope." Saturdays our parents could come and take us out, but this day, when my mother and Dad got there, Miss Hardy told my mother I couldn't go out, and my mother turned to the principal and says, "What has she done?" So the principal told her and said, "She won't take a licking." My mother says, "Have you got the strap handy?" She laid me across her lap, pulled my skirt up and she walloped my butt with the strap. (Martha)

So the principal took the strap out of the desk, and I went to the opposite side of the room. I thought, "Boy, you're going to have to catch me before you do it." So he says, "Come over here and hold your hands out." I says, "If you can catch me you'll strap me ... !!!" I'd wait till he came close and then I'd just jump on the desk and on to the other one. He chased me for a good half hour until he got so tired. (Dorothy)

Others had parents who confronted the principal:

One time my uncle came with this car and took us for a ride to my grand-mother's. When we got back Strapp was standing there and he pulls out his strap. He was going to start on me but Uncle Don said, "Don't you ever touch that kid." (Ronald)

My Dad caught Strapp hitting my sister. We just happened to come in the front door and he said, "Where's your sister?" I said, "That's her holler-ing in there." He went in there and pushed him down. He said, "Don't ever touch my kids again." That's why nothing happened to us after we run away. (Emma)

Truancy was a frequent and significant crime. Of the former students interviewed thirty-four out of sixty-six ran away, and of these five never went back. Others from Mount Elgin used to sneak home or out to dances or the store. Ironically, but predictably, there was more truancy during periods when strict discipline prevailed and there was more of a need for the inmates to challenge the total power of the school administration.

Both prisons and schools have areas where overt surveillance by the officials is lacking. However, it is taken over by the inmates, who have absorbed the principles by which they accept subjection and use them on their weaker fellow inmates. Students from the 1950s at the Mohawk Institute actually complain of a lack of surveillance by officials, which allowed the older children to bully the younger ones with fighting, torture and beatings, taking their food, and making them steal for them. This was a very efficient extension of surveillance, with the authorities not needing to use power directly. It had the effect of maintaining the hierarchy which differentiated the children, preventing them from uniting against the administration. One principal used this technique overtly, by getting the students to punish their peers by putting them "through the mill" in the playroom after they had run away:

> The kids would run away because they didn't like being confined—they were lonely for their parents. They didn't get any love in the school, and they didn't get enough to eat—so no matter how poor their home they wanted to get back home for food and love. (Kenneth)

Food was another arena in the struggle for power in which the administration was not always able to gain total control over the students. Food held a value for the children which expressed their feelings about home life, which could not be taken away from them, and which became a symbol of resistance. Many of the complaints from parents were about the food and the children's state of health. Parents who were powerless to speak on academic and vocational matters could intrude their parental role into the school world only by complaining on these grounds on which they still held value.[6]

However, children who went to residential school in the 1930s came from poor homes—because of the Depression their parents could not afford to keep them at home. Grateful for three meals a day and clothes, they accepted the discipline: "It was good for us—it was discipline" (Edward), and found it stood them in good stead for the rest of their lives. After welfare came in and improved financial conditions somewhat on the reserve, children coming from broken homes, and orphans, did not like the food and did not accept the discipline.

Abuse of Power

The term "abuse"—"to make a bad or wrong use of," "to mistreat"—is widely used these days, and the definition of what actually is abusive has changed considerably since the founding of the schools. The most drastic change of view is in the judgment of the whole premise on which the schools were founded, changing a culture. Although the policy of civilization was implemented with good intentions, it had disastrous results. This destructive, racist policy is viewed by many today as "cultural genocide." The definition of abuse has also expanded to include not only deliberately cruel or abusive actions, but the consequences of actions, and failure to act or care. The whole socio-political situation that led not only to the existence of residential schools, but to their continuation for a hundred years after losing sight of the original purpose of the schools, could with hindsight be thought of as the major form of abuse. Within the schools there were various manifestations of abuse.

Punishment

Physical abuse as punishment was used freely in most periods. Children were usually strapped on the hands, sometimes in front of the whole school. Sometimes students were tied down and beaten on their bare buttocks, with a strap or a whip:

> I only just got there, and Ashton was going to give my brother a strapping. He done it right in the schoolroom. And when he strapped them, he strapped them right down to the bare butt with the cat-o'-nine-tails. He had to lay on the bench and I'm sitting there and every time he brought the strap down I cried all the harder because he was whipping my brother. (Martha)

There is no doubt that corporal punishment was administered abusively, even by the social standards of bygone eras. These standards were not always so different from our own. Ashton, the principal of the Mohawk Institute mentioned above, was convicted by a court in 1913 for overly harsh treatment when he ordered a young girl to be whipped. The deputy superintendent general of Indian Affairs from 1913-32, Duncan Campbell Scott, said then, "I do not believe in striking Indian children from any consideration whatever."[7] From both schools there are many first-hand accounts of vindictive punishment which often consisted of more than the regulation four strokes on the hand—children were left with arms cut, swollen and purple up to their elbows or shoulders. Many former students experienced or witnessed principals and other staff members lashing out with the strap, hitting at random, strapping them until they cried or apparently enjoying administering punishment. Only thirteen of the sixty-six people interviewed never got the strap:

> I think the real terrible thing that happened for me was: there was this young woman and she went up into the dormitory during the day when you weren't supposed to be up there. She went there for privacy because she was having her period, and the nurse caught her and reported her to the principal. The principal came down and he strapped her until she had an epileptic seizure. The kids tried to protect her but we couldn't, because he was starting to strap her and lick her and he just kept on, and the girls were standing around and one of the girls pulled the strap from his hand

from behind and kicked it, and all the girls tried to kick it away, and he shoved everybody aside, knocking girls down. So everybody ran out of the lavatory and into the playroom, and that's when he got the strap and came after everybody and started strapping everybody wherever he could swing the strap. And then he got to her, because the kids backed away—nobody wanted to get hit—and she was left alone, and he strapped her and strapped her until she had this seizure. And the next time at line-up, the principal's wife came down and told the girls not to talk about what had happened. She said if we talk about it one to another, or if we talk about it to anybody, and if they find out, we would get worse. (Lorna)

Emotional Abuse

Even more destructive to the identity of the children than the strap was the emotional abuse suffered—extreme loneliness, the lack of caring, the lack of love. Emotional abuse runs the gamut from subtle cruelty through rigid rules, to a lack of sensitivity and awareness that small children might have feelings. The fear that many lived in constantly—not only of the staff, but of the bigger children—had a devastating effect on them. Loneliness was compounded by the fact that many of the children were too young to understand the reason why they were separated from their parents and placed in the school: "When I first went there I cried and I cried and I cried, but it didn't help any. One day you're a baby, the next day you're a man—you look after yourself. I often say, 'I have no heart'" (Harry). Brothers and sisters were virtually separated from the only family they had: "I couldn't even go and talk to my sister. They'd want to know what you were talking about. 'We were just talking.' They'd say, 'Go to the Principal,' and I'd get the strap just for talking to my sister" (Emmert).

Two students recall horrendous experiences of being sick or injured:

We used to play hide and go seek, and I jumped over the pile of leaves we used to hide in under the porch, and I hit my head on the brick. I had this big cut in my head, and I bled and bled and bled and I passed out. When they finally found me they saw I was laying in my blood, and they carried me to the lavatory and they used my towel to wash out my hair. We couldn't get the blood out of the towel, and there was a high fence there and I hid my towel over there, because I didn't want to report that I had gotten hurt. I was afraid of the strap so I threw my towel over there. I got the strap for losing my towel. (Lorna)

I remember getting the flu and getting sick and almost delirious from the fever, and throwing up, but still being forced to get up out of my bed and clean up the mess I made, and got strapped for making a mess.

I had fallen and probably had a concussion after bumping my head. I remember crawling into a great big cupboard that was in the girls' play-room, and I lost a day and I got punished for not being accounted for, and I got the strap. (Vera)

Lorna tells how they had to line up by their numbers at Christmas and were given new pyjamas or a nightgown. These would then be col-lected again at the end of the day and given to the "poor children," using Christmas gifts to send the message to the children that they were expected to be grateful to the school, that they were better off than the poor children. Calvin tells of being given a toy at a Christmas party in Brantford and having it taken from him when he got back to the school because "he did not need it." Karen won first prize at the fair for a cake she baked—the staff ate the cake: "We never got a pat on the back even for anything that we did. Nobody said: 'That's a nice job you're doing—gee that was great'" (Edward).

Cultural Abuse

Many former students feel strongly that the worst thing about the school was that it took away their language and culture. This was a devastating, irreparable loss to several generations.

After 1872 the Mohawk Institute children were not allowed to speak in their Native language, even amongst themselves. Eight out of thirty-six of the former students interviewed could speak their Native language when they went there. Only one can speak it now with any flu-ency. All were punished if they spoke Indian, with punishments ranging from being strapped to being thrown in the clothes press.

Seven out of thirty of the interviewed Mount Elgin students who spoke their Native language managed to keep their language by speaking it among themselves when staff members were not around (five of these were from Oneida with homes just across the river and a close-knit group of friends to talk to): "I got the strap a lot of times for speaking my language" (Susie).

Sexual Abuse

None of the former students interviewed directly experienced sexual abuse. However there are witnesses of a minister abusing boys at the Mohawk Institute in the 1960s:[8]

> I can remember laying in bed wondering when it was my turn at night. One of the housefathers was gonna come around, and I was wondering when it was my turn to take me down that aisle and back. My turn came but I never went. I wouldn't get out of that bed, and I kicked and screamed and cried, and the guy just left. (Kelly)

There is also a certain amount of speculation about certain principals being involved in abuse, at both schools. One principal at the Mohawk Institute was shocked by finding homosexual abuse among the boys in the dormitory in the 1940s, and three or four of the former boys confirm that this went on though it did not happen to them personally.

However, the majority of people interviewed state categorically that they never heard of any sexual abuse at the school.

Physical Living Conditions

The attention paid to decent living conditions can be described as barometers of caring, expressing the attitudes of the wider society to the status of the Native children. Lack of attention to proper health care and providing a good diet can also be abusive. Certainly they were perceived as such by hungry children who spent their days caring for cows, pigs and chickens, or preparing meals, and never got eggs or cream, or meat that they remember:

> The food was bad. We had mush every morning with worms—we only ate down to the bugs! We never had any eggs though they had thousands of chickens. We did have a bun every Sunday, but when I first went there I never got my bun, because I had traded it away and always owed it to someone. We had whole milk once a year and we never got any meat. The officers ate good though. The girls would cook a roast for the officers and we'd steal it. Christmas was the only time we got meat—then we got chicken. We became good peach and pear pickers at night. (Ronald)

Low status was also reflected by the sanitary conditions which frequently showed no concern for individual privacy and dignity. This is another form of surveillance. At Mount Elgin, as late as the 1940s, they literally put the boys into the shit to clean out the cesspit. There were many other instances of neglect and humiliation:

> If you were sick you had to sleep in your vomit until the next time they changed the beds. (Ronald)

> If you peed your bed you had to take your sheets and everything to the laundry room, and walk by in front of everybody so they'd all know you peed the bed. (Lisa)

> When I was younger if you peed the bed you had to sleep in it all night—they wouldn't change it—even if it got dried out, the next day they wouldn't change it either. (Erna)

Many students complain that they did not have warm clothes or adequate footwear for winter. They did not have warm bedclothes.

There is a process in the life of an institution where the building itself, rather than its occupants, can come to represent the institution. Like churches,[9] the school buildings can be seen as monuments to their purpose. The outward magnificence symbolized the munificence of church or government, while the condition in which the buildings were maintained represented the value society put on their use at various times. At both schools there was steady expansion and additions through until the 1890s, and both were rebuilt around the turn of the century, the Mohawk Institute sporting a cupola, and Mount Elgin a tower. Thereafter, there were periods of maintenance, but generally the buildings became run-down; Mount Elgin was eventually demolished. In the 1940s at Mount Elgin, although the girls were forever cleaning, they could not stay ahead of the physical condition of the crumbling, dilapidated buildings, and the filthy, unsanitary bathroom facilities, kitchens "literally alive with cockroaches." At the same time the farm buildings were described as being in A1 condition. This reflects attitudes to children who were orphans or from troubled or poor homes. Throughout the literature there are reports of depressing conditions, depressed children. Buildings were burned down in times of dissatisfaction.

The failure to prevent truancy is concrete demonstration that the schools failed to achieve total surveillance and power. Burning down the school was another drastic measure denying total power. Many incidents of resistance similar to the ones quoted in this paper are to be found. Where students did accept the right of the administration to make and enforce the rules, they frequently broke them and often got away with it.

The techniques used for achieving total power may appear to have been overwhelming for individuals who lacked any power on three major counts—they were poor, Indian and children—and the dimensions of the struggle to maintain an independence of spirit were so enormous that we must pay tribute to the survivors that their submission was not total. The resilience and ability to keep a sense of humour displayed by the people who went to these residential schools is very impressive. In fact the reactions to their experiences are as varied as the people themselves. Many former students hated their school, ran away frequently and suffered much from the physical punishment and the sense of abandonment and confinement, attributing their troubles in life, such as alcoholism, imprisonment, lack of parenting skills and family breakdown and the inability to love or be loved, to the trauma of the residential school.

This paper has a negative emphasis that many former students would take exception to because they liked their school and believe that they were given opportunities in life that their economic circumstances would have denied them otherwise. Many appreciate the discipline and domestic skills they learned. Others formed friendships that lasted them through their lives and gave them a "family." Others found a home better than the abusive foster home or family they came from. Others accepted that this was the only home they had and made the best of it. There were good days and bad days.

Notes

1 All the material in this paper is taken from a work in progress by Elizabeth Graham, *The Mush Hole: A History of the Mohawk Institute and Mount Elgin Residential Schools*. This paper comprises part of Part I: Voice-over. Quotations from former students are taken from Part III: Voice of Experience, containing transcripts of interviews with thirty former students of Mount Elgin and thirty-six former students of the Mohawk Institute.

2 "Civilization" is (still) defined in the Oxford English Dictionary as "to bring out of a barbarous or primitive stage of society to a more developed one." For a description of the process of "civilization" in southern Ontario, see Elizabeth Graham, "Strategies and Souls" (unpublished PhD dissertation, University of Toronto, 1973), and Elizabeth Graham, *Medicine Man to Missionary* (Toronto: Peter Martin, 1975).

3 "Mount Elgin Residential School: The Story of Seventy Years of Progress," *Missionary Bulletin*, 16, 2 (1920): 162.

4 Michel Foucault, *Discipline and Punish* (New York: Vintage Books, 1979), p. 303.

5 Ibid., p. 203

6 For first-hand accounts of experiences at some Ontario residential schools, see also Shirley Cheechoo's *Path With No Moccasins* (West Bay, ON: The Author,

1993), Basil Johnston's *Indian Schooldays* (Toronto: Key Porter Books, 1988), Enos Montour's *Brown Tom's Schooldays*, edited by Elizabeth Graham (Waterloo, ON: The Author, 1985), Vicki White's "Breaking the Spirit" (*Brantford Expositor*, 6 July 1991) and Elizabeth Graham's *The Mush Hole*. "Mush Hole" is the soubriquet used by students of both schools to refer to the school, so-called because of all the porridge they had to eat.

7 Scott to Roche, 28 October 1913, National Archives of Canada, RG 10, vol. 2771, file 154,845, part 1.

8 See also White, "Breaking the Spirit."

9 Thanks to Jean Manore ("A Vision of Trust: Chief Shingwaukonse, E.F. Wilson and the Founding of Shingwauk Hall," paper presented at the Annual Meeting of the Canadian Historical Association, 1992, p. 17) for bringing up the concept of churches built to show the power and glory of God on earth.

12

The Crown Domain and the Self-Governing Presence in Northern Ontario

Bruce W. Hodgins

Increasingly, Northern Ontario[1] First Nations—Anishnabai and Nishnawbe—and Métis have been successfully challeng-ing the fiefdom-like rule of the Ontario Ministry of Natural Resources (OMNR) over the vast Crown domain.[2] The First Nations continual presence on the unprotected lands of Northern Ontario for the purpose of hunting, fishing, gathering, travel and recreation, among other activities, was clearly asserted, or at least implied, in all of the treaties. Thus, a large part of traditional Aboriginal title and rights were converted into treaty rights, both of which are now guaranteed by the 1982 Constitution. They would continue to harvest resources with care for their own and their communities' use, and, in at least the cases of trapping and the harvesting of wild rice and fishing, probably for com-mercial sale as well. For the few communities not covered by treaty, such Aboriginal rights obviously still prevail unimpeded. First Nations people have a presence on the land and its waterways and make use of all of their resources. The harvesting of country food remains important, though often statistically lost inside their informal economy.[3] Although there was a recent but very significant decline in wild fur trapping, as a result of depressed world markets and world prices, Aboriginal presence

Notes to chapter 12 are on pp. 257-60.

on and use of the lands are generally increasing, over and beyond the clearly inadequate official Indian reserves. Furthermore, Aboriginal political and legal authority has also been increasing.

Each First Nation community or group of communities now has one or more governments recognized as such by the Ontario government. These governments might, or might not be, the same as the band councils recognized by the Canadian government. That remains a serious problem. With relations with Aboriginal communities on a "government-to-government" basis[4] and with the Aboriginal and treaty rights of the Aboriginal peoples of Canada (Indian, Inuit and Métis) reaffirmed and protected under the Trudeau-led constitutional arrangements of 1982, the situation on the ground has changed drastically. The abortive Charlottetown Accord of August 1992 did not come into effect. But if the Aboriginal part of it, or something close to that part does (as this author believes it eventually will), then First Nation governments will become entrenched as a genuine third order of Canada's federalism. Meanwhile, that is the pragmatic approach of the Ontario government and the Chrétien federal government. Aboriginal governments and their very broad but as yet not carefully defined powers are seen as "inherent." These are rights which exist in law both before and after contact with Europeans, through the Confederation of 1867 and down to the present day. First Nations have a form of domestic sovereignty. The Aboriginal and/or treaty rights have been exercised, beyond even the pre-emptive harvesting of wildlife, in a stewardship manner on the unpatented, that is, the public lands and waterways, including parks, of their former living and hunting territories. Moreover, these rights have been vastly broadened by a recent series of Supreme Court of Canada decisions and sometimes by the wise political action of provincial governments.

Until relatively recently, unpatented land was regarded by Ontario officials as Crown domain in the untrammelled right of Ontario. This right was first seriously challenged by the Anishnabai of Temagami. Furthermore, beginning in the N'Daki Menan (the "Deep Water" country of the Teme-Augama Anishnabai), Aboriginal-Ontarian co-management and stewardship of the natural resources, especially the forests, was (until the 1995 election of the Mike Harris government) territorially expanding both as a philosophical concept and an administrative system. Cree participation in, and veto over, new hydroelectric generation in Northern Ontario's James Bay watershed appears to be underway. For the Cree, there will not be an Ontario James Bay crisis at all similar to the Quebec Crees first one, in the 1970s, and their second one in the early 1990s. Despite a perceptible and probably growing backlash from people in precarious single-industry, northern-residence towns, from certain sports fishing and hunting groups and even from some of the most radical, urban-based wilderness buffs, the initiatives of Aboriginal communities seem still to command widespread public support.

In the past, Ontario has tried, with considerable success, to reduce Aboriginal presence, use, practices, and for a time, even rights. Now, especially since the 1989 Sparrow decision and the increased provincial governments' firm recognition both of First Nations rights to broad (and not yet defined) self-determination and internal sovereignty and also to government-to-government relations with Ontario, that presence has been further recognized as legitimate and just. Non-status local interests and provincial organizations such as the Ontario Federation of Anglers and Hunters have often objected and the local MNR managerial and forest authorities are often very unco-operative. Progress is slow, faltering and frustrating. But the direction is clear.

Let us glance backwards. After the 1920s, the treaty-making era seemed to be at an end. Yet, most socio-economic traumas which befell Aboriginal communities during the 1930s related only in a minor way to treaty or land changes. Rather, they concerned the growing conflict of values, as contact with Euro-Canadians increased, the presence of missionaries, the spirit-destroying Indian Affairs paternalism, alcohol abuse and residential schools. The Indians stayed on the land. They trapped in winter. They fished in the spring and hunted in the autumn. Country food remained significant. Around Temagami and other areas readily accessible from the south, seasonal employment, such as guiding for recreationists and wilderness lodges, increased. Many families were, however, callously flooded out by power dams. Many had their hunting territories taken from them by other users, or for town sites and other developments. They learned to keep clear of winter logging—and a few found employment. They were interviewed and documented by anthropologists like F.G. Speck, and they were romanticized by Grey Owl.[5] During World War II, even more than in World War I, they enlisted in the Canadian Army. A few became heroes; a few became officers.[6]

Around 1939 Ontario began to regulate fur harvesting, often ignoring hereditary hunting and trapping territories in the issuing of exclusive trapline licences—to non-Indians and Indians alike. Ontario even curtailed and controlled wood cutting for fuel. Game wardens tried sporadically to enforce upon Indians general hunting regulations and open seasons and to curtail Indians' commercial activity on the land.[7] After the War, federal authorities at Indian Affairs began to enforce school attendance, usually on the damaging off-summer school calendar, so that the family year and its life-cycle patterns were broken; bush skills were weakened.[8] Those families that somehow escaped these rules would have their family allowances and other developing social services cut off. Some of the schools were on reserves. Many children were, however, sent far away to boarding schools run by the churches, where, we know, they suffered, until the mid-1960s, attempts at forced assimilation (but segregation), along with psychological, physical, hygienic and sexual abuses. In Northern Ontario, the Aboriginal dark decades were not during the nineteenth century but during the mid-years of the twentieth— during this author's lifetime.

But somehow they stayed on the land or at least more than half of it—lightly but extensively. Throughout most of the bush country, they were at any one time clearly in the majority. Most of the northland was bush. They did all this while remaining, with exceptions, relatively quiescent politically. Travel outside one's community and territory was restricted, apartheid-like pass laws, though only sporadically enforced, existed,[9] and funding and other activities related to land claims were forbidden.

Something serious had happened earlier in the perceptions of the urban-based culture of Ontario. Apart from the Ottawa Valley and Glengarry, southern Ontario had not, at least in the nineteenth century, participated significantly in the fur trade or in the heroic age of the voyageurs. With exceptions, social and cultural leaders had long had little contact with Indians, especially bush ones. But such leaders were building a regionally based national Anglo-Canadian culture. They believed in what became Harold Innis' staples theory of economic development (from fish and fur to wheat and lumber); yet they ignored the Indians' role in especially the fur trade.

They saw the rugged bush, rock and lakes of the Canadian Shield, just to their north—which they were beginning to call wilderness (in a positive sense)—as empty, at least before they themselves appeared to have found it. This was true even if they used Indian guides at first to travel through it. The southern reaches of this Shield, the Near North, became the symbol of the Canadian national landscape. They claimed that it had been effectively empty! Further north, the Indian would be able to "roam" the inhospitable James Bay lowlands, which was then still beyond the Euro-Canadian imagination.

This emptiness in the Near North at least seemed to be the message of Tom Thomson and the Group of Seven painters, as they focused on the Laurentian landscape of eastern Georgian Bay, Algoma and Algonquin Park.[10] Admittedly, their art still speaks emotionally to this author. Similarly, to D.C. Scott, the poet (and Indian Affairs administrator), the Indian was now pathetic, merely a remnant of a dying "race" whose only faint hope was in individual total assimilation; the same was true with so many (but not all) other authors.[11] Ernest Thompson Seton was different; he wanted young men (and hopefully women as well) to mould their lives on the integrity, outdoor skill and strength of character of "Indian braves," but his stylized Indians seemed to be those of the American southwest, not Algonkians. Later and more recently, as the urban-based movement for parks and wilderness preservation grew,[12] a movement of which this author was and is a part, Indians even became a real threat to its most uncompromising, deep ecology advocates. For them, even today, the "Indians" are not supposed to be there, but they are there.[13] Happily, perceptions are changing in many sophisticated circles.

Meanwhile, the Ontario Department of Lands and Forests, and after 1972, the newly reorganized MNR, increasingly acted as if the Crown domain was their huge private fiefdom. They controlled these public lands with little public input, usually without public scrutiny, much less with any meaningful consultation with First Nation communities or citizens. Their aim, even stated bluntly, was to increase the yield and revenue from the sale of timber rights and the collection of stumpage fees. Profits came before people. Increasingly, the white pine forests were severely overharvested until the northern pine tree line (roughly the divide) was reached, leaving only remote back-country pockets of old-growth forest around and west of Temagami and inland from Georgian Bay and the Ottawa. At times conservationist pressures increased, but then economic, political or unemployment upheavals would again remove these pressures. To a lesser degree, the same thing was happening, more slowly and with only slightly less devastating effect, to the more accessible pulpwood spruce tracts.[14] It is little comfort that practices with regard to pine were even worse in neighbouring northern Michigan and Wisconsin and unprotected areas of Minnesota. The second purpose of the MNR resource management seemed to be to conserve the moose and deer herds for sports hunting and fishing.

For Ontario, in all this lands and resources activity, the Indians— who were after all constitutionally a federal responsibility—hardly seemed to exist, or if they did, they seemed but a nuisance. Yet they remained on the land.

In the mid-1970s it all began to change and unravel. In 1973, following the collapse of the 1969 assimilationist Trudeau-Chrétien White Paper, the traditional aim of absorbing the Indian remnant was at least officially abandoned. Boarding schools were closed. Financial support for Indian cultural, legal and political activities increased drastically. Indian young people appeared at universities and colleges. Young men and women secured election as chiefs and councillors, with the backing of their Elders. Aboriginal rights and Indian land claims became serious, even popular, issues; southern support groups grew. The OMNR came under severe attack from both environmental and recreationalist groups for its allowing of unsound cutting practices and generally for its undemocratic approach to land management. In 1973 young Chief Gary Potts secured land cautions on the unpatented lands in 110 geographic townships of the N'Daki Menan, one which basically existed until the summer of 1996; only lumbering, road building and recreational travel continued on these so-called public lands. Individuals and companies could not purchase or obtain Crown land. As with the Robinson treaties, private land (and existing mineral leases) were unaffected.

Further north, Treaty #9 Indians, now styled the Nishnawbe Aski Nation, organized and researched their treaty and other issues. Previously "hidden" Cree communities loudly surfaced. Known ones demanded restoration of their land base, fraudulently reduced over the years or never adequate in the first place. Gradually, as provincial power in the Canadian federation grew dramatically over federal power, the provinces assumed with federal funding the major governmental role in the social, educational and health services to Indians—despite the terms of the *BNA Act*.[15] Soon there was talk that Indians, with Ontario provincial help, would fully take control of their own schools and social services.

So, as matters began to improve, the Indians, or at least a large minority of them, were still extensively on their ancestral lands. The further north one went, the more persistent was this situation—even if so many Indians remained very poor and were receiving welfare. The Cree-led political explosions in Northern Quebec over the first James Bay power development project inspired their political cousins in Northern Ontario to more self-assertion, even though they did not face the same challenge. Throughout, Indians formed sophisticated lobby groupings. Often they worked out modern boundary agreements with neighbouring

Aboriginal communities, concerning their historic homelands and hunting territories.

In the 1982 Trudeau-led constitutional restructuring, the existing rights of the Aboriginal peoples of Canada were reaffirmed and entrenched, almost in spite of Trudeau, the doctrinaire liberal. The Aboriginal part of the Royal Proclamation of 1763 was effectively made part of the Constitution. But in the Constitutional conferences thereafter, all attempts to define Aboriginal self-government and land rights proved elusive, though in the mid-1980s, passage of Bill C31, involving the reinstatement of Aboriginal women and their children who had lost their status, led almost to the doubling of the number of status Indians. Furthermore, the four Canadian Aboriginal organizations, with their broad-based assemblies, were operating effectively with strong, capable, dynamic leadership.

For Northern Ontario, political matters came to a head in 1988-90, as the Ontario Liberal government of David Peterson (1985-90) moved quickly toward self-destruction. Environmental and Aboriginal protests multiplied. Temagami was merely the most spectacular and intense.[16] There were extensive roadblocks and other direct actions. In the autumn of 1989, dozens of Anishnabai and hundreds of their supporters (many being university-based) were arrested or detained. Quebec in 1990 had its "Summer of Oka." In 1991, in upstate New York, Quebec's second James Bay project, seemingly proceeding against Cree objections, was the chief political issue on campus. Most political activists and environmentalists were changing their views concerning the Indian presence on the land. Such people studied and were struck by the Aboriginal peoples' historic and contemporary stewardship role. Though Ontario's MNR was slowly reforming, its stewardship role over the lands of more than half of the province was being examined and found wanting. Surely the Indians would at least do better. Even the UN's Bruntland Report, *Our Common Future* (1987), said that they had indeed done better and that today they should be heard, heeded and involved—in Canada, Brazil and elsewhere. On Earth Day, in April 1990, the Peterson government did change some policies, but it was too little, after the Temagami blockades, and far too late. The political damage to the Peterson Liberal government had already been done. The Meech Lake accord was brought down by Elijah Harper. And the Liberals were going to lose the 1990 provincial election right in the middle of the Oka crisis.

Furthermore, in the northern areas, there were many explosive issues—such as those at Longlac. Elsewhere, there were Manitoulin challenges, Saugeen challenges. More than fifty land claims were being pressed throughout Ontario. Even the Moose River Crees were organizing sufficiently to challenge Ontario Hydro's plans for its junior James Bay River Development projects. Hydro was the province's second greatest fiefdom, second in territory but huge in power (politically and electrically).

Linked, but proceeding independently of all this, came great (though still inadequate) judicial changes emanating from the Supreme Court of Canada. The *Guerin* or *Musqueam* case (BC, 1985) clearly entrenched the validity of the Royal Proclamation of 1763 on the Pacific Coast, where few Indian treaties yet exist; it also expanded the concept of the undifferentiated Crown's fiduciary and legal obligations to protect Aboriginal interests and to require governments to compensate communities generously for unfairly selling off or giving away Indian lands and resources. *Sioui* (Quebec, 1990) reaffirmed, as a formal treaty fully guaranteed under constitutional law, Governor Murray's 1760 Treaty of Montreal to protect local forests for use by the Huron remnant (from the 1648-49 disasters) near Quebec City. *Sparrow*[17] (1990), the most important, emphasized Aboriginal communities' prior claims to continuing, permanent use of at least their traditional resources, in this case the coastal fishery, using the latest technology, fettered only by conservation imperatives. Sports fishing and non-Aboriginal fishing had to come second. Sparrow effectively spelled out in constitutional terms the old provisions of the Robinson Treaty, as well as other treaties, concerning continual use of resources on their hereditary lands.

In September 1990, Bob Rae became the first NDP premier of Ontario, as Peterson lost both the environmental and the pro-Aboriginal vote. Rae had been arrested (and released without a charge) on the first day of the Temagami environmentalists' blockade. He thought that he was primarily defending Aboriginal stewardship rights in attempting to prevent MNR from extending a major bush road (the Red Squirrel Road extension) to continue its old style clear cutting of the last remnants of the area's old-growth forest. Other prominent NDP members were arrested and convicted; one leading MPP was both fined and sent to jail. Now his first statements as premier were to accept the inherent right of self-government, in its Constitutional context, and place it as the chief priority of the new regime. Henceforth, it was declared and later, on 6 August 1991, signed with representative chiefs gathered near Thunder Bay on First Nation land, that all Ontario dealings with Aboriginal communities would be on a government-to-government basis.[18] The land base of the Aboriginal people would be expanded, as would their self-determination and their role in resource management beyond their reserves.

Bud Wildman, part Indian himself and a member from Sault Ste. Marie in Northern Ontario, became both minister of Natural Resources and minister responsible for Native Affairs. Wildman, however, was soon in for a rough ride as the populist backlash against Aboriginal land rights grew in precarious northern resource communities, such as Blind River, and among some of the hunting and fishing lobbies.

With respect to Temagami, the former Liberal government had signed a memorandum of understanding in April of 1990, pledging negotiation toward a treaty of coexistence; the province initiated various aspects of co-management of the land, the curtailment of pine cutting, and effectively the abandonment, at least temporarily, of the controversial road extensions. In May 1991, the Rae-Wildman regime and the Teme-Augama Anishnabai added an addendum, concerning actual negotiations toward such a treaty; they also set up the Wendahban Stewardship Authority of twelve members, six appointed by the Teme-Augama Anishnabai and six by Ontario (including this author), to steward and manage the resources on the four geographic central townships to the controversy (around northern Obabika, Wakimika and southern Diamond Lakes). The addendum also gave the Teme-Augama Anishnabai a very significant stewardship role in advising MNR on forest management decisions throughout N'Daki Menan.[19]

But that August, the Supreme Court of Canada, after an unprecedented four days of hearings, did not present the Teme-Augama Anishnabai with the victory which their historical record and research gave them reason to expect.[20] Full Aboriginal ownership over the entire N'Daki Menan (except the private property which was not claimed) was too much for the Court to handle, evolving as it has from the British Imperial tradition of Crown supremacy.[21] Instead it confirmed the Teme-Augama Anishnabai's version of most of their history (which the lower courts had rejected), that they once had Aboriginal title to the entire homeland and had not signed the Robinson Huron Treaty. But it declared that by accepting the $4 annuity and by having the federal government buy in 1943 one square mile of Bear Island from the province for them and having it declared an Indian reserve in 1971, that they had somehow "adhered" to the treaty and were thus now under its provisions and not under original Aboriginal title. It was almost as if they would have been better off to have resisted forcibly any earlier inclusion. But the Court did say that the "Crown" (undifferentiated) had failed in its fiduciary responsibility to the Teme-Augama Anishnabai through the Robinson Huron Treaty of 1850 and that this was being and should be negotiated through the political process. Their land and resource base had been found inadequate. So certainly the scope of earlier Supreme Court decisions had been somewhat enlarged.

Negotiations then proceeded sometimes intensely, sometimes very slowly. Wildman and Ontario bought only partly into Gary Potts' and the Teme-Augama Anishnabai's vision relating to the integrity of the entire N'Daki Menan bio-region.[22] Stewardship over the land was never to be divided into three categories, one part Teme-Augama Anishnabai (far beyond any enlarged "reserve"), one part Ontario, and one part joint authority or co-management. Input from each government was to be expected in that portion administered by the other. The old regime appeared to be passing.

In December of 1993 a draft agreement-in-principle (AIP) was finally agreed upon by Ontario and the Teme-Augama Anishnabai. The AIP was intended to secure the trifold division of the land, financial compensation from Ontario (and hopefully more from Ottawa), and a joint stewardship body, with one-third (not 50 percent as requested by the TAA), Aboriginal membership over a very wide area around Lake Temagami and northwestward to the Lady Evelyn Smoothwater Wilderness Park. The TAA secured involvement in all resource and development decisions outside the municipalities; they secured the monies of their own timber lease for some land outside of their own lands and a say in the management of the Park. Their lands, as Chief Potts wished, would be lands under unalienable freehold title under the laws of Ontario (though conversion to reserve status for some of these lands would be possible with a TAA request later). These lands were over 110 square miles in extent, but the development on them was subject to the principles of the joint stewardship body and presumably plans had to secure that body's approval.

So far, alas, the AIP has remained unratified. At the last minute, Ontario demanded that the AIP also secure the approval of the federally recognized, status-only Temagami First Nation (formerly styled the Temagami or Bear Island Band). That smaller body had not been corporately part of the negotiations, certainly not part of the painful concessions process. Allowing the vote only for adult status Indians who were resident on N'Daki Menan (that is, Bear Island and Temagami), the ratification failed. Twice it secured large majority support from the TAA, including majority support from status registered Indians.[23] Ontario held firm and the negotiations collapsed like a flimsy house of cards. All funding from the TAA and the WSA was suspended or not renewed by the NDP government. Meanwhile, some members of a small group of traditional families, the Ma-Kominising Anishinabeg, attempted to secede and to claim a separate identity with lands they assert were not covered by the Supreme Court decision. A very advanced complex agreement became tragically unstuck. This occurred largely as a result of the complete ineptness of provincial officials, especially the Ontario Native Affairs Secretariat.

In 1995 a new, militantly right-wing Conservative government, under Mike Harris, was elected. It promptly moved to continue to lift the 1973 cautions through the courts and no new negotiations were contemplated. Today, in 1998, the Temagami land claim is a low-grade political issue for the provincial government which has adopted a practice of shooting at, as at Ipperwash, rather than negotiating with, Aboriginal people. But, on 28 June 1996 that government at least put the land portion (offering some alternative lands as well) back on the table for two years. On 27 August 1996 it was probably persons linked to the Ma-Kominising who blew up part of a bridge on a major logging road north of River Valley.[24]

Elsewhere in Northern Ontario other Aboriginal communities are receiving or negotiating for an increase in their land base. Longlac was about to receive a major addition to its reserve territory.[25] Six other very remote Nishnawbe-Aski Nation communities, with a total population of over 1,000 people, groups who were left out, created or recognized since Treaty #9, are about to obtain very significant amounts of reserve land.[26] Several other small groups in Robinson-Superior territory, such as Longlac, are in a similar position.

A great breakthrough came on Manitoulin Island, situated between Georgian Bay and Lake Huron, the largest freshwater island in the world. It had been the centre of two old Aboriginal-colonial controversies, the one in 1836 when Lieutenant Governor Sir Francis Bond Head set aside Manitoulin as a "permanent" reserve. This was from Bond Head's perspective, to be a haven for Indians. The other occurred in 1862 when the Sandfield Macdonald cabinet settled a very tense, explosive situation with a flawed, special treaty (called the McDougall Treaty). In the summer of 1990 this land settlement agreement, with five of the First Nation communities as represented by the United Chiefs and Councils of Manitoulin, was signed, involving $9 million in land and financial compensation, relating to 32,800 hectares (80,000 acres) of mainly unsold reserve land under the 1862 Treaty.[27] However, the agreement addressed only one outstanding aspect of the 1862 Treaty and only the province, not the federal government, signed the agreement.

Furthermore, the Ontario government and the entire Nishnawbe-Aski Nation signed an "Interim Agreement on Lands and Resources," on 28 November 1990. NAN represented forty-six communities in the Treaty #9 area. It provided for major Aboriginal involvement—not quite co-management—through a tripartite body (Ontario, Canada and NAN) to advise on and consider all land resource development projects, including timber extraction, that even indirectly affected any NAN communities and their livelihood, during extended self-government negotiations.[28]

In early 1991, Wildman announced, following logically from the *Sparrow* decision and from plans to undertake serious land claim negotiations, that Golden Lake Algonquins could hunt for food, with rifles and using snowmobiles, in Algonquin Park—a great blow to the purists and the wildlife preservationists. Later, an interim enforcement policy was accepted bilaterally.[29] Challenges are now before the courts to determine (in the Atlantic provinces) whether this prior and continuing Aboriginal right extends to commercial harvesting of traditional resources. Much more is in prospect—especially relative to strong Aboriginal rights, influence and co-management beyond reserve land.

Meanwhile the Ojibways of Mississauga, near Blind River, accepted an agreement for a major land restoration, one which even places 100 cottage properties within Anishnabai authority in 1995.[30] Although the backlash against all this has been strong, sometimes ugly, the opposition Liberals did not denounce the process or the NDP-led trend. Overall, at least until the Harris Tories came to power later in 1995, provincial public opinion seems to be on side.

The crucial point is not just that the size of Indian reserve land is growing substantially, which it is. The major changes relate also to the new government-to-government relationships, to the place of Aboriginal communities in Canadian-Ontarian federalism (for which in meetings leading to the abortive Charlottetown Accord, the four Canada-wide Aboriginal leaders, including the Grand Chief of the Assembly of First Nations, were at the table), and to the growing presence, power and influence of Aboriginal people on the land of Northern Ontario. Of great importance were the new initiatives in co-management and co-stewardship of that land and the fact that First Nations were increasingly involved in decisions on such matters as power dams, diversions and anti-pollution protocols. Under Cree pressure, Ontario Hydro has postponed any plans for new power dams or diversions in the lower Moose River watershed, and discussions on co-management are underway.[31] When the Rae-Wildman regime appointed a major Old Growth Policy Advisory Committee, to examine the state of and policy toward old-growth forests, the chair was a woman (Brennain Lloyd) who had been very active in the Temagami environmental protests and blockades. In addition, a key member of the committee was the Aboriginal woman (Mary Laronde) who headed the Teme-Augama Anishnabai stewardship committee and was on their negotiating team—and with the Wendahban Authority. This would all have been unthinkable more than fifteen years ago.

For up to a century after treaty (or missed treaty), Aboriginal people survived on the Northern Ontario land and its waterways as individuals and as unequals, for a time merely as wards of the federal state, even within their own so-called reserves. Now that presence and their collective power are being felt and accepted by a majority of their fellow Canadians. This is true even if it means that Aboriginal people will become more than equal, indeed special, in a constitutional sense.[32] Aboriginal people in Northern Ontario are still relatively unequal economically and socially. Thousands of them are moving into the cities, at various socio-economic levels. They are, however, becoming, through their more than equal self-governing presence on the land and their diverse co-stewardship of it, a powerful force in Ontario affairs, far beyond the weight of their fast growing numbers. Many Ontarians, including this author, are applauding. So, too, I believe, is the living land.

Notes

1 Sometimes "Northern Ontario" is considered to be the area above the Mattawa River-Lake Nipissing-French River line. That would exclude the southern part of the District of Nipissing and the District of Parry Sound. The Ontario far north is often called "Ontario North of 50" and has an overwhelmingly Aboriginal majority. An earlier version of this paper was presented to the Conference of the Association for Canadian Studies in Australia and New Zealand, Victoria University of Wellington in New Zealand, 14 December 1992.

2 For Ontario, Aboriginal numbers must include status Indians, non-status Indians and Métis. Legal definitions of the latter two categories do not yet exist. The Ontario Native Affairs Secretariat asserts an overall Ontario total of 177,000. The 1986 census reports 55,560 single-origin Aboriginal people plus 111,815 "multiple"-origin ones for a total of 167,375. A majority of

the latter would not call or define themselves as Métis. In the late 1980s, the number of status Indians was almost doubled, subsequent to "Bill C31" (1986) which allowed women and their children, who had lost status by marrying "outside," to reacquire or acquire status on request.

3 Plate 43 of the ORCNE (Ontario Royal Commission on the Northern Environment) *Atlas of Far Northern Ontario* claims and notes 600 to 800 registered traplines (nearly all Aboriginal), and asserts that between 1,500 and 2,000 people were involved in trapping for a 1977 value of $1.6 million or 15 percent of the provincial total. The bulk but not all of the remaining fur harvesting would take place in the other portion of Northern Ontario. Plates 19 and 20 deal with animals, hunting and, indirectly, the obtaining of country food. While big game (moose, deer, etc.) is very valuable nutritionally for Aboriginal people, the economic non-market meat value of the furs on the market is also of significance. Plate 44 deals with wild rice and fishing; the former is restricted to the southwest corner and is more important in the Treaty #3 area.

Study 5 for the ORCNE, *The Kayahna Region Land Utilization and Occupancy Study* (1985) is particularly valuable concerning far northern land use for fur markets and for country food.

Note also the work by Judith Harris, especially her as-yet-unpublished paper, "In Search of 'Good Planning' in Northern Ontario: The Case of Resource Management in the Temagami Area" (March 1992), and also Edward J. Hedican, *The Ogoki River Guides: Emergent Leadership Among the Northern Ojibwa* (Waterloo, ON: Wilfrid Laurier University Press, 1986).

Also note Kerry Abel and Jean Friesen, eds., *Aboriginal Resource Use in Canada: Historical and Legal Aspects* (Winnipeg, MB: University of Manitoba Press, 1991), and Fikret Berkes, Peter George and Richard J. Preston, "Co-management: The Evolution in Theory and Practice of the Joint Administration of Living Resources," *Alternatives*, 18, 2 (September-October 1991).

4 "Introduction" and Wallis Smith, "Ontario's Approach to Aboriginal Self-Government," both in Bruce W. Hodgins, Shawn Heard and John S. Milloy, eds., *Co-Existence? Studies in Ontario-First Nations Relations* (Peterborough, ON: Trent Frost Centre for Canadian Heritage and Development Studies, 1992), pp. 1-5 and 50-57, respectively (hereafter cited as *Co-Existence?*).

5 Donald B. Smith, *From the Land of Shadows: The Making of Grey Owl* (Saskatoon, SK: Western Producer Prairie Books, 1990).

6 Janet Davison, "We Shall Remember: Canadian Indians and World War II" (unpublished MA thesis, Trent University, 1992).

7 Fiona Sampson, "An Historical Consideration of Ontario Aboriginal Policy," in *Co-Existence?*, pp. 11-26, and her "Ontario Aboriginal Policy with an Emphasis on the Teme-Augama Anishnabai" (unpublished MA thesis, Trent University, 1990).

8 Ibid.; Jean Barman, Yvonne Hebert and Don McCaskill, eds., *Indian Education in Canada*, 2 vols. (Vancouver, BC: University of British Columbia Press, 1986); and Geoffrey York, *The Dispossessed: Life and Death in Native Canada* (London: Vintage, 1990).

9 F.L. Barron, "The Indian Pass System in the Canadian West, 1882-1935," *Prairie Forum*, 21, 1 (1988): 25-42, and Sarah A. Carter, "Controlling Indian Movement: The Pass System," *NeWest Review* (May 1985), pp. 8-9.

10 Bruce W. Hodgins and Jonathan Bordo, "Wilderness, Aboriginal Presence and the Land Claim," in *Co-existence?*, pp. 67-80.

11 Brian E. Titley, *A Narrow Vision: Duncan Campbell Scott and the Administration of Indian Affairs in Canada* (Vancouver, BC: University of British Columbia Press, 1986).

12 Lori Labatt and Bruce Littlejohn, *Islands of Hope: Ontario's Parks and Wilderness* (Willowdale, ON: Firefly Books for the Wilderness League, 1992). Note also Bruce W. Hodgins and Kerry Cannon, "The Aboriginal Presence in Ontario Parks and Other Protected Places," paper presented to Changing Parks: A Conference on the History, Future and Cultural Context of Parks and Heritage Landscapes," 22-24 April 1994, Peterborough (to be published).

13 Hodgins and Bordo, "Wilderness, Aboriginal Presence and the Land Claim."

14 See, for example, the Ontario sections of Peter R. Gillis and Thomas R. Roach, *Lost Initiatives: Canada's Forest Industries Forest Policy and Forest Conservation* (New York: Greenwood, 1986); H.V. Nelles, *The Politics of Development: Forests, Mines and Hydro-Electric Power in Ontario. 1849-1941* (Hamden, CT: Archon Books of Shoe String Books, 1974); and Bruce W. Hodgins, "The Temagami Dispute: A Northern Ontario Struggle Toward Co-Management," in *White Pine Symposium Proceedings* (Duluth: University of Minnesota Press, 1992).

15 Fiona Sampson, "An Historical Consideration of Ontario Aboriginal Policy," pp. 11-26. Also note David T. McNab, "Aboriginal Land Claims in Ontario," in Ken Coates, ed., *Aboriginal Land Claims in Canada: A Regional Perspective* (Toronto: Copp Clark, 1992).

16 Ibid., and Matt Bray and Ashley Thompson, *Temagami: A Debate on Wilderness* (Toronto: Dundurn Press, 1990).

17 See Michael Asch and Patrick Macklem, "Aboriginal Rights and Canadian Sovereignty: An Essay on *R. v. Sparrow*," *Alberta Law Review*, 29, 2 (1991): 498-517, and Peter J. Usher, "Some Implications of the *Sparrow* Judgement for Resource Conservation and Management," *Alternatives*, 18, 2 (1991).

18 "Statement of Political Relationship," in "Remarks of Bob Rae to Assembly of First Nations Banquet," ONAS Release, 2 October 1990, and "Ontario and the Chiefs of First Nations in Ontario," ONAS Press Release, 6 August 1991.

19 Teme-Augama Anishnabai Media Releases and their *Masinahigan*, Bear Island and Temagami, 1989-92, and Wendahban Stewardship Authority, Papers and Documents 1990-92, Temagami.

20 Bear Island et al., *The Attorney General for the Province of Ontario, Reasons for Judgement*, 15 August 1991.

21 Patricia Bowles, "Cultural Renewal: First Nations and the Challenge to State Superiority," in *Co-Existence?*, pp. 132-50.

22 Gary Potts, "Teme-Augama Anishnabai Last-Ditch Defence of a Priceless Homeland," in Boyce Richardson, ed., *Drumbeat: Anger and Renewal in Indian Country* (Toronto: Summerhill, 1989), and Gary Potts, "The Teme-Augama Anishnabai and the Land," in *Co-Existence?*, pp. 128-31.

23 ONAS/TAA, *Agreement-in-Principle* (draft), December 1993; TAA Reports and Press Releases, 1993-94; ONAS Bulletins, 1993-94; and Temagami First Nation, Reports and Releases, 1993-94.

24 OMNR, 28 June 1996, "Fact Sheets" and "News Release" concerning Temagami Comprehensive Planning Area and the *North Bay Nugget*, 28-29 August 1996.

25 ONAS News Release, 2 November 1990. Note also Tony Hall, "Blockades at Long Lac 58," in Anne-Marie Mawhiney, ed., *Rebirth: Political, Economic, and Social Development in First Nations* (Toronto: Dundurn Press, 1993), pp. 66-89.

26 ONAS New Release, 22 October 1990.

27 ONAS News Release, 5 December 1990. Canada has not yet signed on; this would be necessary to have it entrenched. A sixth community (South Bay West) has not yet joined, and Wikwemikong is a large First Nation community on unceded Indian land which is not covered by the 1862 or any other treaty.

28 ONAS News Release, 28 November 1990.

29 *Toronto Star*, 1, 9 and 11 March 1991, and "Interim Enforcement Policy," ONAS News Release, 20 May 1991.

30 *Bulletin: Proposal for Land Claim*, 28 August 1992 (ONAS, MNR and Mississauga First Nation).

31 Andrea Hodgins, "Co-Management and Hydro-Electric Development of Ontario's Northern Rivers: A Case Study of the Moose River Basin" (unpublished ERS Honours BA thesis, Trent University, 1992).

32 As P.E. Trudeau feared. See "Trudeau says No," *Toronto Star*, 2 October 1992.

Part V

The North, Gender and Aboriginal Governance

13

Some Comments upon the Marked
Differences in the Representations
of Chipewyan Women in Samuel
Hearne's Field Notes and His
Published Journal

Heather Rollason

Between 1769 and 1772 the explorer Samuel Hearne recorded his observations of the Canadian western subarctic
and the Chipewyan peoples; the journal was published in
1795.[1] This journal became incorporated into the ever-expanding mass
of knowledge concerning the geography and people of the "New
World." Academics and other commentators with a scholarly interest in
the Chipewyan used documents, like Hearne's account, as primary
sources for writing the history of that period. The beliefs and observations of Hearne and other explorers would become part of the history,
the truth, the myth, the fiction and the discourse surrounding our
knowledge of the Chipewyan.

Samuel Hearne's journal, *A Journey from Prince of Wales's Fort in
Hudson's Bay to the Northern Ocean, 1769, 1770, 1771, 1772,* has
been published in a number of editions since 1795.[2] The published jour-

Notes to chapter 13 are on pp. 272-74.

nal contains the account of Hearne's three attempts to complete his
tasks. Hearne was employed by the Hudson's Bay Company to find the
copper mines and the Northwest Passage, and to persuade the Chipewyan
people to become involved in the fur trade. Hearne attempted unsuccessfully to reach the Coppermine River twice before he acquired the
guiding services of the Chipewyan leader Matonabbee. Only the field
notes[3] for Hearne's third attempt to reach his goal are known to have
survived. They are extant because they were copied for the Marquis of
Buckingham in 1791 and were later discovered in his library, apparently
bound together with the notes from someone else's divorce.[4]

It will be demonstrated that there are a number of significant differences between the field notes and the published journal in how Chipewyan
women were represented. This is an important observation because it
suggests that the representations in the published journal, which have
been used by scholars as evidence about Chipewyan society in the past,
do not reflect Hearne's original observations, much less the position of
women in their society.

There are a number of reasons to question the validity of Hearne's
representations of the Chipewyan in the published journal, even without
using the field notes as a comparison. The historical evidence reveals
that Hearne's journal underwent considerable editing. Hearne stated
that he revised much of the journal to prepare it for publication. This
was not unusual; nor is it different today. He wrote that

> I have taken the liberty to expunge some passages which were inserted in
> the original copy, as being no ways interesting to the Public, and several
> others have undergone great alterations; so that, in fact, the whole may be
> said to be new-modelled, by being blended with a variety of Remarks and
> Notes that were not inserted in the original copy, but which my long resi-
> dence in the country has enabled me to add.[5]

Richard Glover, editor of the 1958 edition of Hearne's journal, included
in his introduction a letter dated 1792 from Hearne to his publisher
Andrew Strahan. It stipulated that

> anything in reason shall be allowed to the person that prepares the Work
> for the Press. . . . I wish nothing more than it shall specify that the Book
> shall be sent into the World in a style that will do credit both to you, and
> myself.[6]

This observation suggests that the journal was, at least in part, "ghost-
written" by someone else, and moreover that Hearne realized and
expected changes to be made to the journal. As can be deduced from the

difference between the publication date and the time of Hearne's expedition, there was a period of twenty-three years for Hearne to work on rewriting his journal. He realized that relying on his memory to accurately convey impressions from so long ago was a problem:

> Being well assured that several learned and curious gentlemen are in possession of manuscript copies of, or extracts from, my Journals, as well as copies of the Charts, I have been induced to make this copy as correct as possible, and to publish it; especially as I observe that scarcely any two of the publications that contain extracts from my Journals, agree in the dates when I arrived at, or departed from, particular places. To rectify those disagreements I applied to the Governor and Committee of the Hudson's Bay Company, for leave to peruse my original Journals. . . . With this assistance I have been enabled to rectify some inaccuracies that had, by trusting too much to memory, crept into this copy.[7]

While it is clear that revisions to Hearne's journal were made, it is the nature of these revisions that is interesting. By using the field notes as a comparison, it is possible to see the additions, deletions and alterations in wording in the published journal.

Due to the amount of imagery on the Chipewyan in Hearne's journal, a decision was made to focus on those images dealing with Chipewyan women. If the journal is examined from patriarchal and ethnocentric perspectives, it is the images of the Chipewyan women that are the most disturbing. Other scholars have noted this bias. Referring to Hearne's journal, Sylvia Van Kirk wrote that "Particularly abhorrent was the Chipewyan custom of wrestling for wives."[8] James Parker used the journal as a reference for the following statement: "Plundering women and wives was another trait of Chipewyan culture. . . . It appears that the treatment of women was a reason why most traders regarded the Chipewyans as a lowly tribe."[9] Robert Bone, when considering the status of Chipewyan women within their own society, up until the 1920s, felt that "women were, indeed, proverbially subordinate and subject to distressing ill use."[10] Many of these statements by commentators on Hearne's journal have involved the projection of personal feelings and biases in Hearne's account.

In this brief paper, the purpose is not to decide whose version of reality is the most accurate, but rather to examine how a particular version of the truth has been created and been infused into Hearne's discourse in his field notes and journal about Chipewyan women. However, if it can be shown that there is good reason to be suspicious of Hearne's representations of the Chipewyan, then the accepted descriptions of

Hearne's perspectives on Chipewyan culture can be challenged. For this reason this paper will refrain from trying to describe Chipewyan culture and society. The focus will be upon suggesting why scholars need to be highly critical of how Hearne's journal, and sources based upon his journal, are used to represent the Chipewyan.

One must keep in mind that, from what can be discerned from the text, Hearne was witness to the public life of the group of Chipewyan with whom he was travelling. One does not know how much access, if any, he had to the private discussions between husbands and wives, or amongst women themselves. As a result, one must continue to question the source of the information behind these images. One must always ask whether these women were really as lifeless and voiceless as Hearne portrays them in his journal.

A consistent theme throughout the published journal is the treatment of Chipewyan women as material objects or commodities. They are things to be used, they are property, they are owned. They may be bought, sold, traded and returned, as the following passages will demonstrate. When Hearne was modifying his journal for presentation to his Hudson's Bay Company employers, he was writing to tell them things he felt would be helpful in running their business. He justified the practice of polygamy by saying that it would be useful to the fur trade to encourage this way of living because the women were "accustomed to carrying heavy loads."[11] It would make sense to try and justify this statement by referring to the usefulness of women in this sense periodically throughout his text.

In an excerpt from a lengthy speech in the published journal, dated 18 April 1771, Hearne commented that though women's beauty is compromised by the hard labour they do, "This, however, does not render them less dear and valuable to their owners."[12] It was noted on this same day that Matonabbee had purchased another wife.[13] In one of the two occurrences of this pattern in the field notes, this image varies a little in that the marriage partner was not purchased but that Matonabbee traded something for her.[14] On 29 May 1771, a man spoke of trading goods for one of Matonabbee's wives. This same man had sold Matonabbee this woman a while back.[15] A similar description is found for this day in the field notes.[16] Matonabbee's mother was a slave woman bought by Mr. Richard Norton, governor of Prince of Wales' Fort during the period of Hearne's journeys.[17] In the beginning of June 1771, women are listed as one of a series of incumbrances that their husbands wished to be rid of, along with the heavy baggage.[18]

When Hearne and Matonabbee met in October 1770, in the published journal Matonabbee stated, according to Hearne, that "Women . . . though they do every thing, are maintained at a trifling expense; for as they always stand cook [sic], the very licking of their fingers in scarce times, is sufficient for their subsistence.[19] Here one is given the impression that women formed the ideal source of labour; once one owned a woman, there was little one had to do to maintain the working capacity of this object. He noted on 23 June 1771 that men with numerous wives could generally count on the women to be "humble and faithful servants."[20]

When husbands and wives had to be apart, there were usually some men left with them to watch over them. On 22 January 1771, the group with whom Hearne travelled encountered an Indian man who "had one of Matonabbee's wives under his care."[21] Women, particularly wives, were things that had to be watched over, protected, guarded. Young girls were guarded and watched "with such an unremitting attention as cannot be exceeded by the most rigid discipline of an English boarding-school." This was to prevent them from spending time with boys.[22] The reason for this could be interpreted, considering the tone of the text, as being that the parents wished to preserve the potential value of their daughters for their future husbands.

In striking contrast to the published journal, a description of the composition of Matonabbee's family in the field notes stated that there were "three young lads who are as servants to his wives."[23] That these young men were to help or work for the women in Matonabbee's family contradicted the web of imagery woven to portray Chipewyan women as subservient things. Seeing as this phrase was stricken from the journal, so as not to appear in the published text, one must see this as evidence of deliberate editing designed to bias our perceptions of male-female relations toward a male-dominant hierarchy in England. The idea of men being employed to work for women was at odds with the general message of the published journal because it places women in positions of authority and control.

The ultimate sign of one's ownership, is the possessor's socially tolerated ability to kill the object at his or her discretion. It was written in the published journal that the Chipewyan disapprove of the murdering of one of their people. "A murderer is shunned and detested by all the tribe."[24] Yet the attitude in the journal changed when it was a woman who was murdered by her husband, "The women, it is true, sometimes receive an unlucky blow from their husbands for misbehaviour, which occasions their death; but this is thought nothing of."[25] Indeed on 11 January 1772, Matonabbee murdered one of his wives for speaking out against bringing another wife into the family. No punishment was noted in Hearne's journal for his action. This is consistent with the attitude noted above regarding the murdering of wives by husbands. Hearne, who in the journal is often given to judging the actions of the Chipewyan, made no comment on Matonabbee's actions.[26]

The omission of surprise, horror or any emotion whatsoever, in the journal reveals more about the rationale of the creator(s) of the journal than it says about the Chipewyan people. If Hearne's commentary to this situation is compared with the passage about the Inuit girl who was killed by Chipewyan men, Hearne's silence regarding the murder of Matonabbee's wife seems all the more strange. When he witnessed the Inuit girl's death, Hearne wrote that

> My situation and the terror of my mind at beholding this butchery, cannot easily be conceived, much less described; though I summed up all the fortitude I was master of on the occasion, it was with great difficulty that I could refrain from tears; and I am confident that my features must have feelingly expressed how sincerely I was affected at the barbarous scene I then witnessed; even at this hour I cannot reflect on the transactions of that horrid day without shedding tears.[27]

In both cases women were killed in Hearne's presence, yet only in one case does he record that he was emotionally upset. What is different is not the Chipewyan men's actions but how these deeds were recorded and interpreted in the published journal.[28]

Another pattern of representation in Hearne's journal is that of Chipewyan women as "beasts of burden." There are many references to women carrying things in the published text. There is nothing innately female in these actions nor is there anything degrading about this work. It is a clear division of labour. It is the manner in which these passages and phrases surrounding the images are worded that suggest otherwise, rather than the actions themselves. The phrase "beasts of burden" is never directly used in reference to women. Actually, the only use of this phrase occurs in reference to a man carrying Hearne's luggage: "we were lucky enough at the time to meet with a poor forlorn fellow, who was fond of the office, having never been in a much better state than that of a beast of burthen."[29]

The following excerpts demonstrate that it has been Hearne scholars who have labelled this pattern of representation as belonging solely to the realm of the women. In a brief passage about the Chipewyan, J.D.

Leechman stated that "They were noted for the harsh way in which they treated their women, making them but little better than slaves and beasts of burden."[30] In his introduction to Hearne's journal, Richard Glover describes Chipewyan women as "beasts of burden."[31] James Parker wrote that, "Although their women were held in low esteem by their men, Chipewyan women were economic assets because they were used as beasts of burden."[32] Sylvia Van Kirk, who is well known for her studies of Aboriginal women in the fur trade, stated that Chipewyan women "served as beasts of burden."[33] The anthropologist James G.E. Smith wrote that "The men would normally be accompanied by their families, for the women were essential as the beasts of burden."[34] In all of the above mentioned cases, each commentator supported his or her statements with references to Hearne's published journal.

These scholars, using Hearne's published journal, appear to have accepted the notion of Chipewyan women historically being portrayed as beasts of burden. However, if one examines how images of beasts of burden are used in the field notes, a more ambiguous picture is created as to whether this role belongs solely to the women. In the field notes there are two instances where men are referred to as carrying heavy loads. On 25 May 1772, Hearne wrote that "In the morning several of the Northern Indians turned back not being able to walk with their heavy loads and in great want of provisions, threw away the sleads [sleds] and each man took a bundle to carry.[35] The second instance occurred on 31 July 1771. It is particularly interesting because, contrary to the perception of the published text portraying women always carrying loads, leaving the men unencumbered, this passage suggests that this relationship was not absolute. After being separated for some time from part of his family, Matonabbee, upon learning that they were not too far away from his present position, "accordingly the Captain sent some of his young men that way to meet them and bear a part of their loads."[36]

In marked contrast to the field notes, the wording in the published version has been altered to omit these images of the men carrying things on the above dates. The 25 May entry stated that the bundles were left behind.[37] The 31 July entry stated that "Accordingly, the next morning, Matonabbee sent some of his young men in quest of them, and on the fifth, they all joined us."[38] Here images of Matonabbee's wanting to help his family are missing, as are the images of the men helping the women. The care and concern of men for women has been erased from the published text. Deliberate action has been taken, in the form of editing the journal, to demonstrate a uniform image of only women hauling heavy loads.

In the published journal, the men's will only penetrates so far, for women's minds still appear to be their own. It was written that the women are "kept so much in awe of their husbands, that the liberty of thinking is the greatest privilege they enjoy."[39] Indeed this seems to be a potential area where the text may be explored further to find resistance and strength in the women; there are places in the text where the images of the women contradict and resist the patriarchal and colonial ideologies which were attempting to mould them.

Another pattern of representations in Hearne's journal deals with attempts by Chipewyan men to control Chipewyan women. The suggestion that men can control women seems to be a consistent pattern in the published journal. This has been done by speaking of ownership. The degree of this ownership is demonstrated by implanting incidents of physical force upon women's bodies. Realizing that women's minds are not as easy to own and control, it is suggested that this adds a dangerous element to relations with women. The relations between the two sexes has been limited in the published journal to a use-oriented bond. Caring, love and friendship are elements which are not dwelled upon. Where the field notes may have implied these emotional ties, the published text diminishes them. There are places in the published journal where it is possible to perceive that there was more to the relationship between men and women in the published text. It is possible to see that the bond between them was not only one way, men taking services from women, but that reciprocity was a factor; men and women gave each other companionship and were unhappy when they were apart.

It is clear that an effort has been made to limit the importance of these relationships. From the beginning of the text, Hearne seemed to get upset when relationships took precedence over reaching his destination. He became disgruntled when his first guide, Chawchinahaw, insisted he share his meat with the women and children.[40] A few days later, on 26 November 1769, Hearne was frustrated when Chawchinahaw abandoned the search for Matonabbee. Chawchinahaw did this so that he and the other members of his group could rejoin their families.[41] Hearne's reactions to these events suggests he lacks understanding of the rationale for the Native peoples' actions. Another interpretation of Hearne's reaction is that he simply was uninterested in the Chipewyan rationale for their behaviour. Anything that detracted from helping him complete his mission was perceived as an obstacle. Hearne's difficulty in overcoming such obstacles resulted in the tone of frustration that is present in the text.

On 31 May 1771, a lengthy passage in the published text is devoted to describing the men leaving the women and children behind. Separations and reunifications had been briefly mentioned throughout the text up to this point; the event itself was not unique. When the men tried to leave, the women attempted to follow them. Matonabbee was "obliged to use his authority before they would consent." The women "set up a most woeful cry, and continued to yell most piteously as long as we were within hearing." Hearne noted that "This mournful scene had so little effect on my party, that they walked away laughing, and as merry as ever." If any of the men were upset, Hearne wrote that it was because of leaving their children behind, not their mothers.[42] Later on in the entry for that day, it was noted that once the excursion was about to set out, half the men decided not to accompany them because they did not want to be separated from their families. Hearne wrote that the "real" reason these men decided not to go was because they did not have as many European weapons as Matonabbee and the rest of the original group did.[43] Diverging from the manner of representation in the published journal, in the field notes the women and children did not factor in the men's decision to stay behind.[44] The women were angry and upset, but not "piteous," "woeful" and "mournful." The men were not "merry" and "laughing."[45]

There are places in the journal where it is possible to read other interpretations than that which seems to be the case in one's first encounter with the image. It is stated in the published journal that "the existence of a family depends entirely on the abilities and industry of a single man."[46] Yet Matonabbee and Hearne were both to have suggested that Hearne's first two attempts to reach the Coppermine River failed because no women had accompanied them. While the first statement places the responsibility of this society's existence with the men, the second statement indicates that women also played an important role, one that men relied upon. The entry for 3 January 1771 stated that when some of the women are left on an island for a while, there was no danger of starving due to the number of fish in the lake and because the women could take care of themselves, "even without the assistance of a gun and ammunition."[47] Again, in contrast to the published journal, the field notes for that day suggest very different reasoning; the words "gun" and "ammunition" in the published text have replaced the original word, "men."[48]

It appears that there have been significant transformations in the representations of Chipewyan women between the field notes and the published text. While some of these references and descriptions were present in the field notes, by the time the published journal had been formed they had been elaborated upon and made more numerous. Some images, generally negative, appear only in the published journal. Others, generally empowering or demonstrating an emotional bond between the men and women, were omitted from this form of the text.

While it is a difficult question to answer, one needs to ask why certain images have proliferated, been created or even been deleted. One may begin to suspect that the violent images of women as victims, brutalized, mistreated and expendable, may stem more from the creation of the published journal than from within Chipewyan society. That this seems to be a strong possibility is indicated by the differences in the representations of Chipewyan women between Hearne's field notes and the published journal.

The motive for the alterations to the published journal seems to be more than Hearne remembering extra things as he sat down to revise his papers. This would not explain why other descriptions have been deleted. The manner in which Chipewyan women are portrayed in the published journal suggests that these Aboriginal people are excellent candidates for involvement in the fur trade; the women have been positioned as dehumanized, hard-working, expendable labour. To those within the Hudson's Bay Company and back in Europe, this depiction of women serves to justify colonial efforts to establish the fur trade and to employ Native people.

Notes

1 This paper is based on excerpts from my MA thesis, "Studying under the Influence: The Impact of Samuel Hearne's Journal on the Scholarly Literature about Chipewyan Women" (Trent University, 1995).

2 A 1796 reprint (Samuel Hearne, *A Journey from Prince of Wales's Fort in Hudson's Bay to the Northern Ocean, 1769, 1770, 1771, 1772* [Dublin, 1796; Canadian Institute for Historical Microreproductions, 1985], CIHM #40172) of the original 1795 edition was compared with the 1958 edition (edited with an introduction by Richard Glover [Toronto: Macmillan, 1958] to check for differences between editions. None could be found. The 1958 edition was used for this study. The editor of the 1958 edition, Richard Glover, included a biography of Hearne and some historical background of the production of the published journal.

3 This document is kept at the British Museum. The National Archives of Canada has a handwritten copy transcribed in 1914. The field notes are officially known as "Samuel Hearne's Narrative" (National Archives of Canada, Ottawa, MG 21, Stowe Manuscript 307, ff. 67-89). In this paper they will be referred to as the field notes or the Stowe Manuscript.

4 Richard Glover, "Editor's Introduction," in Hearne, *Journey* (1958), p. xxxii. Glover notes throughout this edition places where the field notes and the published journal differ. For example, see the footnotes on pp. 58-59, 69.

5 Ibid., pp. li-lii.

6 Ibid., pp. xlii-xliii, and see footnote 125.

7 Hearne, "Preface," in *Journey* (1958), p. li.

8 Sylvia Van Kirk, *Many Tender Ties—Women in Fur-Trade Society in Western Canada, 1670-1870* (Winnipeg: Watson and Dwyer Publishing, 1980), p. 24.

9 James Parker, "The Fur Trade and the Chipewyan Indian," *Western Canadian Journal of Anthropology*, 3, 1 (1972): 43-57, at 49-50.

10 Robert M. Bone, Earl N. Shannon and Stewart Raby, *The Chipewyan of the Stony Rapids Region*, edited by Robert M. Bone (Saskatoon: Institute for Northern Studies, University of Saskatchewan, 1973), p. 13.

11 Hearne, *Journey* (1958), p. 80.

12 Ibid., p. 56.

13 Ibid.

14 Stowe Manuscript, p. 9.

15 Hearne, *Journey* (1958), p. 71.

16 Stowe Manuscript, p. 13.

17 Hearne, *Journey* (1958), p. 222.

18 Ibid., p. 75.

19 Ibid., p. 35.

20 Ibid., p. 80.

21 Ibid., p. 46.

22 Ibid., p. 200.

23 Stowe Manuscript, pp. 4-5.

24 Hearne, *Journey* (1958), p. 69.

25 Ibid., p. 70.

26 Ibid., p. 170-71.

27 Ibid., p. 100.

28 The field notes do not treat this incident concerning the Inuit girl the same as the published journal. For a detailed examination, see Ian MacLaren, "Exploring Canadian Literature: Samuel Hearne and the Inuit Girl" (in Peter Easingwood, Konrad Gross and Wolfgang Kloob, eds., *Probing Canadian Culture* [Augsburg: AV-Verlag, 1991], and Ian MacLaren, "Samuel Hearne's Accounts of the Massacre at Bloody Fall, 17 July 1771" (*Ariel*, 22 [1991]: 25-51).

29 Hearne, *Journey* (1958), p. 24.

30 J.D. Leechman, *Native Tribes of Canada* (Toronto: W.C. Gage, [1962]), p. 204.

31 Glover, "Editor's Introduction," p. xix.

32 Parker, "The Fur Trade and the Chipewyan Indian," pp. 49-50.

33 Sylvia Van Kirk, "Thanadelthur," *The Beaver*, 304 (Winter 1974): 43.

34 James G.E. Smith, "Local Band Organization of the Caribou Eater Chipewyan in the Eighteenth and Early Nineteenth Centuries," *The Western Canadian Journal of Anthropology*, 7, 1 (1976): 72-90, at 75-76.

35 Stowe Manuscript, p. 57.

36 Ibid., p. 35.

37 Hearne, *Journey* (1958), p. 189.

38 Ibid., p. 121.

39 Ibid., p. 200.

40 Ibid., p. 4.

41 Ibid.

42 Ibid., p. 73.

43 Ibid., p. 74.

44 Stowe Manuscript, p. 16.

45 Ibid., p. 15.

46 Hearne, *Journey* (1958), p. 200.

47 Ibid., p. 46.

48 Stowe Manuscript, p. 5.

14

Is This Apartheid? Aboriginal Reserves and Self-Government in Canada, 1960-82

Joan G. Fairweather

O n 3 March 1987, South Africa's ambassador to Canada, Glenn Babb, followed by a crowd of journalists and television camera crews, arrived at the Peguis Reserve 150 km north of Winnipeg. He was there as the invited guest of Peguis Chief Louis Stevenson. The main objective of the visit was to attract media attention to the dismal social and economic conditions on Canada's reserves. It was also intended to embarrass the Canadian government, in particular former Prime Minister Brian Mulroney, who was currently promoting international sanctions against South Africa while denying any parallel between conditions of the black population in South Africa and Canada's Indigenous peoples.[1] Ambassador Babb's visit, though controversial, is an example of the frequent analogies drawn between Canada's Native policy and South Africa's apartheid system.[2]

The purpose of this comparative analysis of Aboriginal reserves and self-government in Canada and South Africa is to examine the validity of parallels drawn between Canadian Aboriginal policy and the apartheid system, which ended with South Africa's first multiracial elections in April 1994. While the symbol of apartheid may have drawn attention to racial injustice in Canada, the distinctions between Aboriginal-state

---

Notes to chapter 14 are on pp. 295-99.

relations in Canada and apartheid South Africa have not been clearly defined and understood. The thesis to be argued is that the experience of Indigenous peoples in Canada differed in fundamental ways from that of Africans living under apartheid. Moreover, the goals and aspirations of Canada's First Nations and black South Africans testify to their contrasting histories as dispossessed and oppressed peoples.

Africans under apartheid (and under previous white governments) were voteless and were prohibited by law (under the *Natives Land Act* of 1913 and the *Group Areas Act* of 1950) from purchasing land, finding employment in or even entering the areas classified as "white" without government permission. First Nations in Canada, in the course of their history as colonized peoples, have also been confined to assigned areas in their own country, denied unconditional enfranchisement and refused the right to organize and protest.[3] However, to equate their experience of oppression to apartheid is to misunderstand the uniqueness of a system that received universal condemnation for its flagrant abuse of human rights.[4] The systematic silencing of all forms of resistance, including detention without trial, torture and death squads, has no parallel in Canadian history.

The difference between the treatment of Canada's First Nations under the *Indian Act* and the experience of Africans under apartheid can be summed up in one word: labour. Partly the direct legacy of slavery in the Cape Colony (where, unlike Canada, slaves were imported to perform menial labour and brutally treated) and partly due to the Calvinistic ideology espoused by Afrikaners, the African population came to be regarded as properly the hewers of wood and drawers of water, whose sole purpose was to serve the needs of white society. The experience of Africans under apartheid is therefore most clearly defined in the oppressive burden of racial laws which kept them in the thrall of white mine owners and industry.

Apartheid (meaning "separate-ness") represents both an ideology and the political system formally adopted by the National Party government when it gained power in the Union of South Africa in 1948. Under apartheid laws, which numbered in the hundreds, racial segregation was institutionalized. While apartheid deprived all South Africans of basic human rights, the African majority, which was the bedrock of the South African economy as the primary source of cheap labour, was both the target of apartheid laws and the most critically affected. In his biography of his brother President F.W. de Klerk, Willem de Klerk reveals the outcome of the systematic and incremental process of apartheid legislation:

"Each opening address [of parliament] added yet another strand to a tapestry of apartheid legislation that would become, under Dr. Verwoerd, a finespun mesh from which no black could hope to escape."[5]

This paper touches briefly on the colonial origins of Native policy in Canada and South Africa, but its primary focus is the period from 1948 (when apartheid became the official state policy in South Africa) to the early 1980s, when constitutional changes in each country brought about significant changes in Aboriginal-state relations. With Canada's *Constitution Act* of 1982, existing Aboriginal land and treaty rights were recognized. In direct contrast, the new South African Constitution of 1983 excluded the African majority from any form of political representation outside the so-called tribal homelands. The question "Is this apartheid in Canada?" is addressed by examining two of the core characteristics of African experience under the apartheid system: the lack of labour rights and the lack of democratic rights. Finally, the history and objectives of the resistance movements in both countries are contrasted and compared.

Labour Rights

As illustrated in the visit of South African Ambassador Babb to the Peguis Reserve in 1987, parallels between the treatment of Native people in Canada and South Africa frequently have focused on the abysmal conditions of reserves in both countries. What is seldom recognized is that Aboriginal poverty in these two countries in the postwar period stemmed from fundamentally different political objectives. In Canada, Aboriginal poverty was the by-product of European colonial expansion which led to the destruction of traditional Native economies and food sources. African poverty in apartheid South Africa, on the other hand, was the result of the double exploitation of land and labour.

In South Africa, land rights were based on the "empty land" myth: the belief that neither Europeans nor Africans had prior claim to the land since both groups had arrived in the country at roughly the same time.[6] As the Boers (farmers of Dutch and German descent) and the British penetrated into the interior, a series of wars, annexations and treaties eroded the land bases and powers of resistance of the Indigenous African nations they encountered. Wars of conquest were still being fought when new considerations attracted British Imperial attention: the discovery of diamonds (in 1867) and gold (in 1886) in the two Boer republics. The need for cheap African labour grew with the rapid industrialization that followed.

Unlike Canada, where the policy was to "protect" and "civilize" the Indigenous peoples in order to eventually assimilate them into the mainstream society, the official policy of the Cape Colony was to mould the African population into an accessible and submissive labour force. A hut tax was imposed by the British Imperial government to induce Africans to seek wage labour in the white-owned mines, farms and factories. Under John Cecil Rhodes' *Glen Grey Act* of 1894, the Transkei (annexed to the Cape Colony in 1885) became a labour pool for colonial needs. Although his policy was never fully implemented, Britain's diplomatic agent in Natal, Sir Theophilus Shepstone, set out to dismantle the Zulu military structure and transform its thirty thousand warriors into "labourers working for wages." Shepstone's policy has been seen by many historians as the forerunner to apartheid.

A critical factor in the development of land policies in South Africa was the success of African farmers before they were forced onto the inadequate and desert-like reserves. Not only did African farmers offer unwelcome competition to their Afrikaner counterparts but, when their own farms were producing well, there was no incentive for Africans to sell their labour to white farmers.[7] The *Natives Land Act* of 1913 put an abrupt end to this period of relative prosperity. Under this *Act*, 13 percent of the country was formally set aside for Africans, who accounted for 87 percent of the total population, and barred Africans from purchasing land outside the "scheduled native areas." The *Natives Land Act* and the 1936 *Natives' Trust and Land Act* laid the legislative and territorial foundations of apartheid. The two acts were in essence the precursors of the apartheid government's bantustans in making Africans homeless outcasts in their own country.

Thus, from their inception, reserves in South Africa were designed as breeding grounds for a cheap labour force essential to the South African economy. When the apartheid government's *Bantu Self-Government Act* was promulgated in 1959, creating ten fictitious African "bantustans" out of the former reserves, millions of African people were deported from South Africa to their newly designated tribal homelands as "surplus people" not needed by white industry. Responding to the new legislation, Nelson Mandela commented:

> The main object [of the *Bantu Self-Government Act*] is to create a huge army of migrant labourers, domiciled in rural locations in the reserves far away from the cities. Through the implementation of the scheme it is

hoped that in course of time the inhabitants of the reserves will be uprooted and completely severed from their land, cattle and sheep, and to depend for their livelihood entirely on wage earnings.[8]

Under the terms of the *Act*, a total of 13.9 million people were slated for removal; in the period 1960 to 1983 an estimated 3.5 million Africans were forcibly removed to the already overcrowded and impoverished bantustans.[9] No provisions apart from some sort of water supply greeted the truckloads of mainly women, children, the elderly and handicapped who were literally "dumped in the veld."[10]

As the report of a monitoring body, the Surplus Peoples Project, points out, what made the poverty and suffering on the bantustans totally unacceptable was that these conditions were the deliberate creations of government policy. Referring to a bantustan township named Sada in the bleak northeast Ciskei, the report states:

> When the government and its planners established the place in 1964, they knew how overpopulated the Ciskei already was. They knew that the people they were sending to Sada came from among the lowest income groups in the country and had no money of their own to develop the place. . . . And yet they sent them there. Sent them and millions like them, to Sadas all over the country.[11]

As citizens of designated African homelands, reserve-dwellers were eligible only for what their impoverished local governments could afford (or chose) to pay them.[12] As the deputy minister of Justice, Mr. S. Froneman, starkly stated in 1959, "The White State has no duty to prepare the homelands for the superfluous Africans because they are actually aliens in the White homelands who only have to be repatriated."[13] Migrant African workers were therefore excluded by law from the limited welfare services provided for white South Africans because they were regarded as "foreigners" or "temporary sojourners" in white South Africa.[14] Unlike Canada, where "Indianness" was never a racial definition (some whites became Indian by marriage or adoption) and was defined in order to distinguish who had a right to benefits accruing to special status,[15] racial classification under apartheid was designed to maintain white privilege at the expense of the other racial groups. Under this system, Africans were accorded the lowest position in the socio-economic hierarchy; the most poorly served being Africans forced onto bantustans.[16]

South Africa's pass laws were the linchpin which held the crippling system of migrant labour in place. Often brutally enforced, these laws and regulations monitored and controlled every movement of the black population. Not only did the hated "pass books" record and restrict movements from one area of the country to another, they determined and confined the kinds of work for which any given worker was eligible.[17]

The philosophical basis of the pass system was articulated in the Stallard Commission (1921), which investigated housing and labour conditions of Africans in the urban areas: "Africans should only be permitted within municipal areas in so far and for so long as their presence is demanded by the wants of the 'white' population."[18] This notion subsequently became law through the *Native Urban Areas Act* of 1923. Independent of any social function they may have served, pass laws were integral to the vast array of legislation employed by the white minority to absorb Africans into the economy while maintaining political domination. Writing in 1979, Philip Frankel observed: "Today, both locally and nationally, the notions of apartheid and pass laws are considered as virtually inseparable."[19]

Every policeman and numerous government officials had the right to demand the production of a pass at any time of the day or night. Under the euphemistic title of *The Natives' Abolition of Passes and Co-ordination of Documents Act* (No. 76 of 1952) the law to carry a pass was extended to African women, children and juveniles, and the name was changed from "pass" to "reference book." Thousands of Africans were convicted under the pass laws every day. Between 1948 and 1981, at least 12.5 million people were arrested or prosecuted.[20]

Closely related to the pass system was the iniquitous practice of prison labour. Both the pass laws and prisons played key roles in the subjugation of African people.[21] The options facing pass offenders were stark: a fine which most were unable to pay, eviction from the urban area and forcible removal to the bantustans, or a prison sentence which usually included hard manual labour—mainly on farms.[22] The practice of prison labour was condemned as a violation of its statutes by the International Labour Organization in 1964. During this session, apartheid policies were unanimously declared "degrading, criminal and inhuman," and South Africa withdrew its membership.[23]

Bantu education, reorganized under apartheid in 1955 to serve the interests of white industry, was a further millstone around the necks of people forced onto the bantustans. In place of the common curriculum which African schools previously shared with white schools, African education under apartheid was designed to maintain a labouring class. As Dr. Hendrik Verwoerd (then minister of Education, later prime minister) clearly stated in 1953, when Bantu Education was introduced:

Native education should be controlled in such a way that it should accord with the policy of the state. . . . There is no place for him [i.e., Africans] in the European community above the level of certain forms of labour. . . . For that reason it is of no avail for him [sic] to receive a training which has as its aim absorption into the European community. . . . What is the use of teaching a Bantu child mathematics when it [sic] cannot use it in practice?. . . . That is absurd.[24]

Finally, there were wide differences between the wages and working conditions of African and white workers.[25] Because of the smaller ratio of white workers, Kenneth Vickery argued, the "vast army" of non-white migrant workers was forced to accept wages below the value of their labour, while white workers were paid inflated salaries.[26] White industries and mines were ensured of a steady supply of cheap black labour through the state-run labour bureaus on the bantustans. All African men between the ages of sixteen and sixty-five were required to register at the bureaus in order to obtain work. As Stanley Trapido aptly expressed it, bantustans became the perfect breeding grounds for labour repression by keeping workers "insecure, replaceable and impoverished."[27]

Connections have been made by several historians between the permits or passes first issued to reserve Indians in the Canadian West in the late nineteenth century and South Africa's pass laws.[28] Imposed at the time of the Riel Rebellion in 1885, the Canadian pass system was legalized. It was enforced by the North West Mounted Police (later the Royal Canadian Mounted Police) and continued until well into the twentieth century. Although never effectively enforceable, the system was administered by the Department of Indian Affairs through the Indian agents who threatened to deprive the Indians of rations if they failed to obtain a permit before leaving the reserve. The purpose of passes was ostensibly to encourage agriculture on reserves and to discourage Indians from their "nomadic lifestyle" and from exercising their hunting and fishing rights.[29] These early measures to control the movements of western bands, however deplorable, bear little relationship to the pass laws imposed under apartheid to maintain a cheap source of labour. In his essay on the Canadian pass system, Laurie Barron understated the case by observing: "In practice, the pass system unfolded in a way that was only a weak reflection of what transpired in South Africa."[30]

Unlike South Africa, where land policies and labour were linked, British Imperial policy in North America did recognize the prior ownership of the Indigenous occupants, subject to the exclusive right of the Crown to purchase Indian lands with their permission. This principle was codified in the Royal Proclamation of 1763, ensuring the protection of "Indians and lands reserved for Indians" from any form of interference or alienation. The provisions of the 1763 Proclamation were effectively reaffirmed in the *British North America Act* (*BNA Act*) of 1867. The special rights, which set Indigenous people apart from the rest of the Canadian population, derive from the *BNA Act* and a series of Indian acts (consolidated with the *Indian Act* of 1876) and also from treaties entered into with certain Indian tribes and bands.

With the exception of British Columbia, Quebec and the Atlantic Provinces,[31] Native peoples were induced to surrender title to their lands under various treaties as immigrant settlement expanded across the Prairies to the Pacific coast. With the disappearance of the bison, the major source of livelihood for western tribes, the only hope of survival for the Indians was to enter into treaties. As an Indian Affairs official observed in retrospect, "While these treaties or agreements were bilateral in form, actually, of course, the Indians had to accept the conditions offered or lose their interest in the lands anyway."[32] As John Tobias points out, the exchange of land for promised hunting and fishing rights, annuities, education, health services and agricultural implements and training, would never be adequate compensation for what the Cree and other Plains Indians gave up: their traditional means of subsistence and their independence.[33] Moreover, many of the treaty promises were not fulfilled. In the 1880s Cree leaders demanded redress from the government, claiming they had been deceived by "sweet promises" designed to cheat them of their heritage.[34]

When reserves were established in the late nineteenth and early twentieth centuries, Native lands were considered worthless and expendable by Europeans. It was only after World War II, when land became a precious commodity and minerals and other natural resources were vital sources of national revenue, that renewed interest was taken in the potential development of Indian lands. The coveted resources on Native lands ranged from valuable deposits of uranium at Lake Athabasca, Saskatchewan, to provincial parks and recreation areas of the Teme-augama Anishnabai in Northern Ontario.[35] As J.R. Miller has pointed out, the inevitable confrontation between developers and Aboriginal peoples who had lived on these lands for centuries had both negative and positive consequences for First Nations communities. The Hobbema Band near Edmonton, Alberta, became relatively wealthy (a mixed blessing in itself) on the compensation it received for oil found on its reserve. Others were less fortunate.[36] The general pattern, however, was one of land reduction and the destruction of traditional lifestyles and livelihoods. Forest industries, the construction of huge hydroelectric dams and chemical plants disrupted the habitat of fish and wildlife and irrevocably destroyed the primary food sources of northern communities.

Between 1954 and 1959, one hundred square miles of Mohawk territory was destroyed by the St. Lawrence Seaway project. The coming of the Seaway spawned new industries along the shoreline close to the Mohawk territory of Akwesasne. The pollution and environmental damage caused by the huge power dams and plants deprived Native communities of their two principle sources of survival: fishing and farming. Ronald Wright contends that Mohawk militancy had its genesis in the St. Lawrence Seaway project. Angered by the high-handed exploitation of their natural resources, the highly skilled ironworkers, famous for their "high steel" work on bridges and skyscrapers, reintroduced the "Warrior Society."[37]

Kermot Moore, president of the Native Council of Canada between 1974 and 1982, strongly criticized Canada's human rights record in its treatment of Native peoples. First Nations have been consistently denied the right to a standard of living adequate for their health and well-being and their homelands have been pillaged and spoiled, flooded and polluted in the interests of the dominant society. One of many examples Moore cited is the experience of the Grassy Narrows and White Dog reserves near Dryden, Ontario. Contamination of the waterways in the vicinity of Reed Paper Limited, a pulp and chemical mill on the Wabigoon River, seriously endangered the lives of the Native communities in the area who relied on the fish and drinking water they provided. Moore laid the blame on government inertia and apathy towards the needs of First Nations: "The mercury poisoning of the English-Wabigoon system is the sad tale of a provincial government that accepts development at any price and callously ignores the plight of its [Aboriginal] victims."[38]

Industrialization and government insensitivity towards Aboriginal communities only partly explain reserve impoverishment in Canada. In his analysis of the causes of poverty on Canadian reserves, Bernard Pelot points to the contradictory effects of preserving certain aspects of special status while pursuing an assimilationist goal. To take advantage of tax breaks under provisions in the *Indian Act*, Indian businessmen were kept behind what he terms the "buckskin curtain" of the reserves, rather than establishing themselves close to wider markets where they had a better chance of succeeding.[39] Thus the economic development of reserves was inhibited in many instances by the special status accorded to Native peoples.

In her perceptive article on Canadian Native policy, Marie Smallface Marule drew attention to the ways in which the Department of Indian Affairs manipulated the system and its position as trustee of reserve funds to feather the nests of the wealthy at the expense of poorer reserve communities. Despite the Liberal government's pronounced intention to help "those who are furthest behind" in its 1969 White Paper, it was frequently governments and large (white) corporations which benefited most from these schemes. In 1969, a fund was established devoted to Indian economic development. Prerequisites for loans to Indian businesses required incorporation and a lease surrender of reserve land. The effect was to further reduce the land bases of Native communities.[40]

The fact that Indian Affairs had been placed for many years under various ministries associated with resources or northern development is indicative of where the focus of Canadian policy lay: on Aboriginal land and resources, not the people.[41] Even in terms of social assistance programs, it was only after the Hawthorn study that parity with non-Indian programs became a policy goal. Not until 1966 was a specific Native services office located with the newly created Department of Indian Affairs and Northern Development (DIAND). As Jeanne Guillemin observes, the absence of a Canadian Bill of Rights until 1960 permitted the development of a "vertical mosaic" of diverse minorities under British Canadian rule, with Indians, as the least "Europeanized" group, relegated to the lowest social order.[42]

For Canada's Native peoples, residential schools run by Roman Catholic and Protestant churches until the late 1970s were an integral part of their experience as dispossessed and oppressed peoples. The history of abuse (psychological and physical) sustained by successive generations of Canada's Aboriginal people remains a bitter legacy of the residential school system. Although there is evidence of discrimination in both job training and in the range of employment available to Native people throughout Canada, the systematic subjugation of African people through the education system in South Africa has been largely absent in the Canadian experience. Indian students have been increasingly integrated into the provincial school systems and federally approved Indian language instruction and community control of education gained ground in most provinces in the 1970s. Opportunities were provided for both vocational and university education, and First Nations communities increasingly assumed greater responsibility for the education of their own children. The basic change in policy meant that Indians were recognized as residents of provinces with equal rights and privileges with respect to Indian education.[43]

Parallels drawn between the poverty of Canada's First Nations and black South Africans fail to recognize the significance of apartheid's primary aim: to maintain control of its cheap black labour force. Poverty on South African bantustans was a matter of policy; this was not the case in Canada. While conditions on Canadian reserves have deservedly been called a national disgrace, First Nations have had access to government subsidies and a welfare safety net. Moreover they were free to work and live where they chose. This was not apartheid.

Democratic Rights

In Canada, colonial notions of segregating Aboriginal peoples and treating them as perpetual wards of state gradually grew out of favour after World War II. In South Africa, on the other hand, colonialism merely took on a new, more potent form. Under the *Bantu Self-Government Act* of 1959, designed to convince the outside world of the legitimacy of the apartheid regime,[44] the heavy yoke of wardship was locked firmly in place. While fostering the illusion of self-determination, the *Act* denied the very presence of Africans in "white" South Africa, where 60 percent of them lived, and even the most rudimentary human rights.

While the advancement of Canada's First Nations towards self-determination laboured under the heavy hand of paternalism, the history of Aboriginal relations in South Africa was one of political regression and the diminishment of civil rights for South Africa's black majority. The lack of any meaningful participation of Africans in decisions affecting their daily lives was a hallmark of the apartheid administration in the 1960s and 1970s and further evidence of the oppression of Africans as a voiceless and voteless people.

The significant difference in the size of African and white populations in South Africa was a major factor in the denial of political rights to the Indigenous population which vastly outnumbered the dominant white society. While Canada's Indigenous population (representing 1.3 percent of the total population) amounted to a minority among many other minorities, in South Africa the situation was reversed. In 1983, of a total population of 31 million people, 24.1 million (85 percent) were classified as Africans.[45] The primary significance of the disparity between black and white populations lies in what Kenneth Vickery called the "Herrenvolk democracy" of apartheid South Africa, where the exercise of power and suffrage is restricted to the dominant group and democracy exists only for the "master race."[46]

In contrast to Canada's attempts to assimilate its Indigenous population into the common society, political exclusion rather than inclusion lay behind the regressive history of democracy in South Africa. When Britain granted representative government to the Cape Colony in 1853, the franchise was extended to all male subjects of the Crown, subject to certain conditions but regardless of "race." Successive regimes imposed stiffer qualifications to reduce the number of African voters and removed property and educational qualifications in the case of white voters. Finally, under the terms of the *South Africa Act*, by which Britain agreed to the union of its two former colonies with the Boer republics in 1910, the Cape vote for Africans was all but eliminated. In 1951 the recently elected National Party passed the *Separate Representation of Voters Act* to remove Cape Coloured people from the common voters' roll and, in 1959, under the misnamed *Promotion of Bantu Self-Government Act*, the last tiny wedge of African representation (the right to elect four white representatives to the Senate through a system of electoral colleges) was removed.[47]

Between 1976 and 1981 more than eight million Africans were made citizens of the ten newly assigned bantustans. As "aliens" in South Africa they ceased to qualify for South African passports and could be deported at any time to their assigned "homeland." As law professor Leonard Gering noted at the time, there were marked similarities between the apartheid law of 1976 (*Status of the Transkei Act*) which stripped 1.3 million Transkeians of South African citizenship and the Nazi decree of 1941 which deprived Jews of German citizenship. Both made ethnic and racial origins the criteria for deprivation of citizenship.[48] Far from advancing towards a recognition of democratic rights for its Indigenous population, apartheid entrenched the principle of white supremacy at the expense of the inherent civil rights of Native South Africans.

The height of political exclusion was reached in 1984 when the new *Constitution Act* of 1983 established a tri-cameral parliament, providing separate parliamentary chambers for whites, Coloureds and South Asians. Africans were excluded because they were not deemed to be citizens of South Africa.

In Canada until the 1950s, local autonomy on reserves was minimal. The *Indian Act* of 1876 (revised in 1927) defined who was and was not legally an Indian in Canada and empowered government officials to control virtually everything done on the reserves. According to the *Act*, Indians were childlike wards who needed to be "protected" from the corrupting influences of non-Indian society.[49] Under the *Indian Act*, so-called hereditary chiefs were unilaterally deposed and replaced by elected band councils.[50] Before the demise of the Indian agent in the 1960s, or superintendent as he came to be called in later years, local government and administration was centred in the position and person of the agent himself. His powers, which included the role of justice of the peace, extended over every aspect of reserve life from granting permission for "Indian dancing" to the leasing of reserve lands to white farmers.[51]

After a period of neglect of Indian issues in general between the two wars, public interest was awakened in the 1950s to the fact that full citizenship had been denied Aboriginal people, many of whom had fought side by side with white Canadians in the war. Veterans' organizations, churches and citizens' groups rallied to the call for a royal commission to investigate the administration of Indian affairs. Although no commission was appointed, a Joint Committee of the Senate and the House of Commons was appointed in 1946 to examine and consider changes to the *Indian Act*. The Committee invited presentations from Indian leaders, a significant departure from previous government practice. The subsequent revision of the *Indian Act* in 1951 (which remains in effect) was designed "to facilitate the gradual transition of the Indian from a position of ward up to full citizenship."[52] Claiming to be the Magna Carta for the Indian people, the new *Act* attempted to reduce the degree of intrusion into the lives of Indians. The prohibition of the potlatch was lifted, as were the 1933 provision that allowed an Indian to be enfranchised without his or her consent and the section of the *Indian Act* (1927) prohibiting political organizing.

In spite of its reforms, the revised *Indian Act* (1951) was essentially the same policy redefined. The objectives of the *Act* remained the eventual assimilation of the Indigenous population into the general society.[53] As an opposition Member of Parliament declared when the amending bill (Number 267, Respecting Indians) was debated in the House:

> We have cavalierly assumed, as white people in this country, that it is a completely desirable thing that the Indians mingle with us, become whites, be submerged and lose their identity. . . . The whole object of our policy in Canada seems to be to submerge the Indians and to assimilate them out of existence.[54]

Until 1960, when Indians were granted the franchise without the penalty of losing their Indian status, enfranchisement was an instrument to bring reserve populations from their status as a separate group into the fold of Canadian society. Unlike South Africa, it was never part of the official plan for reserves to remain Indian homelands (although treaties with First Nations in Ontario and the Prairies promised just that). Through compulsory enfranchisement, reserve lands were gradually whittled away, forcing Native people off the reserves and placing their ancestral lands into the hands of non-Indians.[55] Under Section 12, (1)(b) of the *Indian Act*,[56] women who married non-Indians or non-status Indians, as well as their children, were automatically enfranchised and forfeited their Indian status and the right to live on a reserve.[57] Although very few Indians accepted the franchise before World War I, it was the firm intention of successive governments to reduce the number of status Indians and to entice those who remained on reserves to move into the cities.[58]

In contrast to South Africa's entrenchment of racial segregation under the bantustan system, the Liberal government's White Paper in 1969 proposed the abolition of the *Indian Act* and the current system of Native administration. Prime Minister Pierre Trudeau asserted that Indian treaties and reserves could no longer be tolerated in a society which espoused the liberal principles of equality and democracy. A number of factors, both internal and external, influenced this new direction in Native policy. Inside Canada, the pressure of Quebec's "quiet revolution" for special status as one of Canada's founding peoples, the development of a new multicultural vision for Canada in which Aboriginal Canadians were seen as yet another ethnic group in Canada's multicultural mosaic, profoundly affected the direction of Native policy. The Civil Rights movement in the United States, the formulation of a Declaration of Human Rights by the United Nations and the growth of Red Power among the Indigenous peoples of North America gave impetus to the termination of former systems of administration, including reserves, and the substitution of more subtle forms of social control over the lives and lands of Indigenous peoples.

Although some progress was made in the 1970s in extending the input of reserve leadership and band councils in the decision-making process, the Department of Indian Affairs and Northern Development (DIAND) and its officials were reluctant to relinquish complete control. Even on reserves that are now self-governing, such as Walpole Island in southern Ontario, official power was only yielded under extreme pressure from local communities.[59] Even in the 1980s priorities were still being set by the government and the design and implementation of programs had not yet been handed over to Native leadership.[60]

Government funding of Native organizations, beginning in the 1960s, provided avenues of control over their priorities and programs.[61] In one sense, as Donald Purich points out, the funding of Native organizations gave struggling provincial and national associations the boost they needed to organize effectively. However, in her analysis of the "hidden agenda" of Native policy directions in the 1970s, Sally Weaver drew attention to the inherent costs of government aid.[62] Native writers like Howard Adams and Maria Campbell support Weaver's conclusions. Campbell's powerful metaphor of "the blanket" eloquently describes the debilitating effects of state paternalism and the widespread tentacles of state power:

> My Cheechum [grandmother] used to tell me that when the government gives you something, they take all that you have in return—your pride, your dignity, all the things that make you a living soul. When they are sure they have everything, they give you a blanket to cover your shame.[63]

While paternalistic perceptions of Aboriginal peoples in Canada inhibited equality of political rights, Canada's First Nations today possess a whole range of rights and options which were systematically and strictly denied black South Africans under apartheid. In direct contrast to South Africa's bantustan policy, which denied South Africans citizenship in the land of their birth, the basic underpinnings of democracy and constitutional rights offered the hope of full political and legal recognition to Canada's First Nations. This was not apartheid.

History and Objectives of Resistance

The transformation of Canadian reserves to battlefronts of political resistance took place over the decades following the announcement of the Trudeau government's White Paper in 1969. The policy direction proposed by the White Paper flew directly in the face of both the Hawthorn Commission's recommendations and the year-long consultation process on revisions to the *Indian Act* which had involved band leaders across the country. The immediate outcome of the proposal was to force Native leaders to regroup and organize a counterattack. In 1970 the Indian Association of Alberta published *Citizens Plus*, a statement of Native demands based on the premise of special status articulated in the

Hawthorn Report.[64] In its rejection of the abolition of the *Indian Act*, *Citizens Plus* reasserted the constitutional basis of their rights as Canada's First Nations and stressed the government's legal obligation to fulfil the terms of its treaties.

A series of court decisions in the 1970s brought about change, or at least a challenge to the status quo. In 1973 the protest action of the Nisgas of British Columbia, under the leadership of Frank Calder, became an important political catalyst as well as a symbol of the struggle for land rights. The Supreme Court of Canada declared in *Calder v. Attorney General of British Columbia* that Aboriginal title existed in common law, but the court was split on whether Aboriginal title had been extinguished in British Columbia. The issue the Nisgas were fighting was the pre-existence of Aboriginal title and rights before colonization. This point was eventually won in November 1984. In the case of *Guerin v. The Queen* pre-existing Aboriginal title—long recognized in principle by the Imperial powers—was finally established in Canadian law.[65]

In April 1971, the Cree and Inuit of the James Bay region challenged the announcement of a massive hydroelectric project by the Quebec government. The legal case of the Cree and Inuit was based on the assertion that Aboriginal rights had never been extinguished. As a result of their successful legal action, the province was forced to negotiate. A wide-ranging agreement was signed in November 1975 which included special benefits in education, health and economic development. The James Bay Agreement was given legal force by the Parliament of Canada in July 1977 with the passage of the *James Bay and Northern Quebec Native Claims Settlement Act*.[66]

The most significant assertion of Indigenous rights in Canada can be seen in the movement for constitutionally entrenched Aboriginal rights and self-government. The aggressive campaign for constitutional recognition launched by the National Indian Brotherhood was accompanied by a new spirit of militancy. In 1973 Indian youth staged a "sit-in" at the Department of Indian Affairs offices in Ottawa and the occupation of Anishnabe Park in Kenora followed. Indian protest reached a peak in Ottawa in the fall of 1974 when the Native Caravan from Vancouver staged demonstrations on Parliament Hill. The protesters demanded that "the hereditary and treaty rights of all Native peoples in Canada including Indian, Métis, non-Status and Inuit must be recognized and respected in the Constitution of Canada." Although the Caravan never got to present its demands to Parliament (barricades were erected and a

Royal Canadian Mounted Police tactical force removed the Native delegation from the Hill), the first bill (Bill C-60) to amend the Constitution in 1978 included some limited protection for Native rights. The following year the National Indian Brotherhood took its campaign to Britain and appealed to the Queen to refuse patriation of the Constitution until Aboriginal rights were fully recognized.

The determined efforts of Aboriginal groups both in London and Ottawa in the year leading up to the patriation of the Constitution were finally rewarded. In response to fierce lobbying by Aboriginal and non-Aboriginal groups and individuals, the final version of the new *Constitution Act* (1982) recognized the "existing aboriginal rights and treaty rights" of Aboriginal peoples. In addition to the inclusion of Métis and Inuit (as well as Indians) as "Aboriginal peoples of Canada," the *Act* provided for consultation with Aboriginal leaders in future constitutional conferences. The guarantee of Aboriginal and treaty rights in the 1982 *Constitution Act* thus opened the way for the reaffirmation of the rights of First Nations to govern themselves.

In South Africa, Africans responded to a political climate which was entirely different to the situation in Canada. Instead of the Anglo-French duality of Canadian nationhood, South Africa's Indigenous majority confronted what Archie Mafeje called the "two nations thesis," in which an oppressing nation and an oppressed nation lived side by side in the same territory. The "group feeling" on either side of the colour line produced an increasing sense of solidarity among the victims of apartheid; mainly among the African population, but Coloured and Asian groups also saw themselves as "black South Africans" in their shared oppression with the African people.[67] Thus African nationalism is explained as a response to white oppression and racial discrimination, not as a political bid to establish an independent nation or state in the same way as African nationalism did elsewhere in Africa—or as Canada's Native peoples have done. As Mafeje explains it: "It is a move to establish a more inclusive state in which the processes of national integration which have already taken place despite apartheid can continue unimpeded."[68]

Reserves in South Africa became battlefronts of resistance when the Verwoerd government pushed forward its bantustan policy in 1961. Although earlier protests had been launched against unpopular soil conservation schemes, increased taxation, and other official policies, grass-roots anger in the 1970s focused on the government-appointed and salaried chiefs in the Legislative Assemblies.[69] The status of "independence" was imposed on the Transkei, Bophuthatswana and Venda bantustans in the face of massive opposition. Legislative buildings were burned down and bantustan officials attacked. A major uprising which preceded the Transkei's reluctant acceptance of independence was quickly and brutally crushed by the apartheid government. Special legislation (Regulation 400 and 413) was imposed, which provided for detention without the right to habeas corpus and a ban on all meetings. Large areas were sealed off from the media and specially trained riot police and heavily armed troops moved into the area.[70]

After the banning of the two most powerful organizations, the African National Congress and the Pan-African Congress in 1960, a new spirit of militancy emerged in the resistance movements. Encouraged by the collapse of Portuguese colonialism in Mozambique and the victory of the liberation party, Frelimo, the armed wings of the ANC and PAC (both in exile in the neighbouring southern African states) carried out widespread sabotage and armed attacks on strategic and economic targets. Railway lines, bridges and power stations and symbols of apartheid policy such as pass offices, commissioners courts, bantustan offices, military bases and police stations were attacked by ANC and PAC activists.[71] Mass arrests followed and thousands of people were imprisoned.

In the face of brutal police action and the use of armed military personnel carriers to intimidate and control the township residents, mass action continued throughout the 1970s and 1980s. In 1976 the confrontation between the masses and the apartheid regime entered a new phase when police opened fire on a demonstration of schoolchildren in the township of Soweto who were protesting the enforcement of Afrikaans as the medium of instruction in African schools. The uprising that followed spread to other parts of the country. Children now moved into the forefront of the struggle and were brutally dealt with by the police. Trade unions, civic and community organizations, women's organizations and university student bodies launched concerted and effective campaigns to bring down the apartheid regime. Between 1979 and 1983 widespread, sustained and, in many cases, intense campaigns were directed against specific manifestations of apartheid. Trade union rights, high rents and transportation costs, racially segregated and inferior education, and enforced removals and resettlement in urban or rural areas were all identified as deriving from the injustice of the apartheid system.

Strengthened by the mass action campaigns across the country, political organization against the apartheid state gained new momentum and unity with the launching of the government's constitutional proposals for a segregated tri-cameral parliament which excluded the black majority in 1982. From late 1984 to the end of the decade, a phase of continuous and often violent resistance deepened the economic and political crisis of the apartheid regime.

Having failed to destroy the popular organizations or to impose a reformed apartheid Constitution, and seriously affected by international sanctions and military losses in Angola, the regime of P.W. Botha was forced to remove some of the central pillars of the apartheid system in the late 1980s. However, the structure of apartheid did not collapse that easily. It was not until 1990, when the leader of the African National Congress, Nelson Mandela, was released from prison (having served twenty-seven years of his life sentence) and the restricted organizations were unbanned, that negotiations were able to take place paving the way for the country's first democratic elections on 27 April 1994.

The struggle for the recognition of Aboriginal rights by Canada's Indigenous peoples stands in direct contrast to the liberation struggle in South Africa. The fundamental differences between the aspirations of Canada's First Nations and Africans under apartheid are clearly illustrated in the Dene Declaration of 1975, a statement by the Native peoples (Indian and Métis) of the Northwest Territories, and the Freedom Charter of the African National Congress of 1955. The Dene Declaration stated that

> We the Dene of the Northwest Territories, insist on the right to be regarded by ourselves and the world as a nation. What we seek then is independence and self-determination within the country of Canada. This is what we mean when we call for a just land settlement for the Dene Nation.[72]

The preamble to the Freedom Charter, adopted by a multiracial gathering known as the Congress of the People[73] at a meeting held at Kliptown near Johannesburg on 26 June 1955, expresses the entirely different objective of the mass democratic movement in South Africa:

> We the people of South Africa, declare for all our country and the world to know: that South Africa belongs to all who live in it, black and white, and that no government can justly claim authority unless it is based on the will of all the people; that our people have been robbed of their birthright to land, liberty and peace by a form of government founded on injustice and inequality[; and] . . . that only a democratic state, based on the will of all the people, can secure to all their birthright without distinction of colour, race, sex or belief.[74]

Conclusion

The era of apartheid has finally ended in South Africa. Institutionalized racism—and the system of terror which kept it in place—has been replaced by a multiracial government of National Unity headed by the once-outlawed African National Congress. The sham homelands created by the apartheid regime have been absorbed into a new, regionally structured South Africa where all its people—black and white—have equal rights to the resources and riches of the country.

Canada's Indigenous peoples have not experienced apartheid, but their demands for justice and political independence are no less valid. Three hundred years of cultural denial and paternalistic administration under the *Indian Act* have produced a generation of First Peoples who are determined to reclaim their lost birthright. First Nations are no longer prepared to be passive victims. Looking back over two decades of protest, Georges Erasmus observed in 1990: "Right now, we're leading fairly peaceful, non-violent protests. We may find that, in ten or fifteen years, people like [Peguis Chief] Louis Stevenson and I are not very radical at all. There isn't going to be the patience among our people."[75]

Four years after the revelations of poverty and destitution on the Peguis Reserve, media reports of yet another "apartheid-like" situation were flashed around the world: the Oka crisis of 1990. Determined to protect their ancestral land from being taken over for the extension of a golf course by the municipality of the town of Oka, the Mohawk of Kanesetake confronted first the Sûreté du Québec and then the Canadian Armed Forces. In television sequences reminiscent of the military occupation of South African townships under the apartheid regime (albeit on a vastly reduced scale), armoured vehicles and heavily armed soldiers were shown pushing their way into the majestic pine forests of Kanesatake. Low-flying helicopters and high-powered search lights scarred the night skies above the tiny group of Mohawk men, women and children holed up in an isolated treatment centre. The shock of seeing Canadian troops in one-on-one confrontations with armed Mohawk Warriors shattered the self-perception of Canadians as a peaceful and tolerant nation. When the neighbouring reserve of Kahnawake built a barricade across the Mercier Bridge (in solidarity with the people of Kanesatake), obstructing commuter traffic to and from Montreal, any illusions Canadians might still have harboured about themselves as non-violent and non-racist were seriously challenged. News coverage showed chilling images of angry white Canadians stoning the cars of Mohawk residents leaving the reserve under police escort.

Canadians joined the world community in denouncing apartheid and responding to the call of the Indigenous peoples of South Africa for liberation and democracy. It is time to put our own house in order.

Notes

1 *The Ottawa Citizen*, 7 March 1987, 84. "Chief Stevenson said in an interview: 'Prime Minister Mulroney doesn't have to fly half-way around the world to find poverty and disease and substandard conditions and oppression. . . . If he spent ten days on an Indian reserve, he'd find the same things here.'"

2 This action by Peguis Chief Stevenson was condemned by many anti-apartheid groups as well as prominent Native organizations as insensitive to the plight of South Africa's black majority and counter-productive to the cause of Native rights. See Ron Bourgeault, "Canada's Indians: The South Africa Connection," *Canadian Dimension*, 21, 8 (January 1988).

3 First Nations in the Prairie provinces were confined to reserves under pass laws set up in 1885. An unconditional franchise was granted by the federal government to First Nations citizens in 1960. The Parliament of Canada included a provision of the *Indian Act* of 1927 making it an offence punishable by law to raise funds for the purpose of pursuing any Indian land claims.

4 The United Nations Declaration of 1989 characterized apartheid as "a crime against the conscience and dignity of mankind, [which] is responsible for the death of countless numbers of people in South Africa."

5 Willem de Klerk, *F.W. de Klerk: The Man in His Time*, translated by Henri Snyders (Johannesburg: Jonathan Ball, 1981), p. 4.

6 The fallacy of the "empty land" theory is revealed in T.R.H. Davenport, *South Africa: A Modern History*, 3rd ed. (Toronto: University of Toronto Press, 1985), p. 7: "Radiocarbon dating . . . has produced evidence of negroid iron age settlement in the trans-vaal as early as the fifth century AD."

7 Colin Bundy, *The Rise and Fall of the South African Peasantry* (London: Heinemann, 1979), p. 210.

8 Nelson Mandela, *The Struggle Is My Life* (London: International Defence and Aid Fund for Southern Africa, 1978), pp. 61-62.

9 *Survey of Race Relations in South Africa* (Johannesburg: South African Institute of Race Relations, 1983), pp. 298ff. These statistics were based on the findings of the Surplus Peoples Project in 1983.

10 Laurine Platzky and Cherryl Walker, *The Surplus People: Forced Removals In South Africa* (Johannesburg: Ravan Press for the Surplus Peoples Project, 1985), p. 40: "In practice even these regulations [the provision of transportation and a water supply] are not followed. For example, people [removed] from farms have to provide their own transport and do not receive rations."

11 Ibid., p. 327.

12 *Survey of Race Relations in South Africa* (Johannesburg: South African Institute of Race Relations, 1984), p. 734. In 1984 KwaZulu reported a backlog

of 18,000 aspirant pensioners and the administrations of Ciskei, Lebowa and Bophuthatswana reported similar difficulties in paying their pensioners. "It has also been alleged that pension payments vary, apparently because of corruption and theft."

13 Cited in Desmond Cosmas, *The Discarded People: An Account of African Resettlement in South Africa* (Harmondsworth, England: Penguin Books, 1971), p. 33.

14 *The South African Yearbook, 1985*, p. 649, cited in Roger Omond, *The Apartheid Handbook: A Guide to South Africa's Everyday Racial Policies* (Harmondsworth, England: Penguin Books, 1986), p. 75.

15 In the federal government's definition of "Indianness," only Indians belonging to registered bands (i.e., "Status Indians") are included. Status Indians comprise approximately 30 percent of the total Indigenous population. Other categories of Native people are treaty and non-treaty Indians (many of these are also status Indians), and non-status Indians. Non-status Indians, Inuit and Métis peoples are not included under the terms of the *Indian Act*. See Brad Morse, "Australia and Canada: Indigenous Peoples and the Law," *Legal Service Bulletin* (June 1983).

16 Omond, *The Apartheid Handbook*, p. 77. The ratios for old-age pension payments in 1984 were: Whites: R166; Coloured and Indians: R103; Africans in white areas: R65; and Africans in bantustans: R40-49 per month. (In 1993 a Rand was equivalent to fifty Canadian cents.)

17 Philip Frankel, "The Politics of Passes: Control and Change in South Africa," *The Journal of Modern African Studies*, 17, 2 (June 1979): 199-218, at 205.

18 E.S. Sachs, *The Anatomy of Apartheid* (London: Collet's Publishers, 1965), p. 74.

19 Frankel, "The Politics of Passes," p. 201.

20 *Apartheid: The Facts* (London: International Defence and Aid Fund for Southern Africa, 1983).

21 Allen Cook, *Akin to Slavery: Prison Labour in South Africa*, Fact Paper on Southern Africa, No. 11 (London: International Defence and Aid Fund for Southern Africa, 1982), p. 2.

22 Ibid., p. 52. In 1982 South Africa's prison population was the highest per capita in the world, with 0.44 percent of South Africans in prison. The United States is the next highest with 0.19 percent. This is largely because of the pass laws.

23 Brian Bunting, *The Rise of the South African Reich* (London: International Defence and Aid Fund for Southern Africa, 1986), p. 171.

24 Cited in ibid., p. 260.

25 Stanley Trapido, "South Africa in a Comparative Study of Industrialization," *Journal of Developmental Studies*, 7 (1971): 309-20, at 312-14.

26 Kenneth P. Vickery, "'Herrenvolk' Democracy and Egalitarianism in South Africa and the U.S. South," *Comparative Studies in Society and History*, 16 (1974): 309-28, at 328. See also Bernard Magubane, "The Political Economy of the South African Revolution," in Bernard Magubane and Ibbo Mandaza, eds., *Whither South Africa?* (Trenton, NJ: Africa World Press, 1988), pp. 74-75.

27 Trapido "South Africa in a Comparative Study of Industrialization," p. 319.

28 See Donald Purich, *Our Land: Native Rights in Canada* (Toronto: James Lorimer, 1986), p. 130, and Bourgeault, "Canada Indians: The South African Connection," p. 8. Bourgeault erroneously claims that "[In 1913] the first of many pass laws were . . . implemented based on Canadian experience."

29 Purich, *Our Land*, p. 131.

30 F. Laurie Barron, "The Indian Pass System in the Canadian West, 1882-1935," *Prairie Forum*, 13, 1 (Spring 1988): 25-42, at 39.

31 British Columbia refused to recognize Aboriginal title to lands even after it entered Confederation in 1871. In the provinces of Quebec and the Atlantic region, treaties did not involve land surrenders.

32 T.R.L. MacInnes, "History of Indian Administration in Canada," paper presented at the annual meeting of the Canadian Political Science Association, Toronto, 1946.

33 See John L. Tobias, "Canada's Subjugation of the Plains Cree, 1879-1885," in J.R. Miller, ed., *Sweet Promises: A Reader on Indian-White Relations in Canada* (Toronto: University of Toronto Press, 1991), pp. 212-42.

34 Ibid., p. 225.

35 See Bruce W. Hodgins, "The Temagami Indians and Canadian Federalism: 1867-1943," *Laurentian University Review*, 11, 2 (February 1979): 73-100.

36 J.R. Miller, *Skyscrapers Hide the Heavens: A History of Indian-White Relations in Canada* (Toronto: University of Toronto Press, 1989), p. 406.

37 Ronald Wright, *Stolen Continents: The "New World" through Indian Eyes* (Toronto: Penguin Books, 1992), p. 328.

38 Kermot A. Moore, *The Will to Survive: Native People and the Constitution* (Val d'or, QC: Hyperborea Publishing, 1984), p. 84.

39 Bernard J. Pelot, "The Buckskin Curtain: Canada's Indians from Government Wards . . . to Feudal Lords?" a discussion paper on Aboriginal Rights in the Constitution, 1985, pp. 35-36. The policy also inhibits university graduates and professional people from seeking positions off the reserve, and deprives employed Indians from the benefit of the Canada Pension Plan which is limited to taxpayers under the *Income Tax Act*. The policy also prevents Indians from seeking the benefits of incorporation of their businesses because "corporation" is not equivalent to "an Indian" under the *Indian Act* and is therefore liable to taxation.

40 Marie Smallface Marule, "The Canadian Government's Termination Policy: From 1969 to the Present Day," in Ian A.L. Getty and Donald B. Smith, eds., *One Century Later: Western Canadian Reserve Indians Since Treaty 7* (Vancouver, BC: University of British Columbia Press, 1978), p. 108.

41 Jeanne Guillemin, "The Politics of National Integration: A Comparison of United States and Canadian Indian Administrations," *Social Problems*, 25, 3 (1978: 319-32, at 325.

42 Ibid., p. 323.

43 Stan Cuthand, "Native Peoples of the Prairie Provinces in the 1920s and 1930s," in J.R. Miller, ed., *Sweet Promises*, pp. 387-88.

44 The events that most seriously damaged South Africa's image in the eyes of the international community (with the accompanying withdrawal of eco-

nomic investment) was the killing by state police of protesting Africans in the township of Sharpeville in 1960.

45 Omond, *The Apartheid Handbook*, p. 21.

46 Vickery, " 'Herrenvolk' Democracy and Egalitarianism in South Africa and the U.S. South," p. 310.

47 Omond, *The Apartheid Handbook*, p. 111.

48 *The Star* (Johannesburg), 4 June 1976, quoted in Patrick Laurence, *The Transkei: South Africa's Politics of Partition* (Johannesburg: Ravan Press, 1976), p. 13.

49 Dave De Brou and Bill Waiser, eds., *Documenting Canada: A History of Modern Canada in Documents* (Saskatoon, SK: Fifth House Publishers, 1992), p. 19.

50 Wright, *Stolen Continents*, p. 317.

51 Peter Carstens, *The Queen's People: A Study of Hegemony, Coercion, and Accommodation among the Okanagan of Canada* (Toronto: University of Toronto Press, 1991), p. 223.

52 John Leslie and Ron Maguire, "The Historical Development of the *Indian Act*," DINA, Treaties and Historical Research Centre, P.R.E. Group, Ottawa, 1978, p. 142.

53 The term "integration," which implied economic and political integration and the recognition of cultural identity came to be used in place of the term "assimilation," which implied the absorption of Aboriginal peoples into the dominant society.

54 Canada, *House of Commons Debates*, 21 June 1950, vol. 2, p. 3947.

55 Canada, Indian and Northern Affairs, Saskatchewan Region, *The Indian Act: A Simplified Version* (December 1982): "Section 109-113, 40, 111(1). Once he is enfranchised an Indian can sell or give away any piece of reserve land which he owned, to the band or another band member. If he has not disposed of it thirty days after the enfranchisement order then the superintendent shall offer the land for sale to the highest bidder and pay the money to the enfranchised Indian. If no bid is made and the land is still unsold six months after it was put up for sale then the land goes back to the band."

56 This section of the *Act* was revoked in 1985. See Janet Silman, *Enough Is Enough: Aboriginal Women Speak Out* (Toronto: The Women's Press, 1987). The passage of legislation to amend the *Indian Act* marked the culmination of a long campaign by Native women to regain their full Indian status, rights and identity.

57 Sally M. Weaver, "Recent Directions in Canadian Indian Policy," a paper prepared for the annual meetings of the Canadian Sociology and Anthropology Association, London, Ontario, 1978, p. 9.

58 John L. Tobias, "Protection, Civilization, Assimilation: An Outline History of Canada's Indian Policy," in Miller, ed., *Sweet Promises*, p. 137. In the period from 1857, when the enfranchisement process was first enacted, until 1920 only slightly more than 250 persons were enfranchised.

59 Nin.Da.Waab.Jig., *Walpole Island: The Soul of Indian Territory* (Walpole Island, ON, 1987), p. 102. Walpole Island action in seizing the reins of self-government also pushed the Indian Affairs Branch faster than it would otherwise have moved.

60 Purich, *Our Land*, p. 226.

61 Ibid., p. 186.

62 Weaver, "Recent Directions in Canadian Indian Policy," p. 10.

63 Maria Campbell, *Halfbreed* (Toronto: McClelland and Stewart, 1973), p. 159.

64 *Citizens Plus*, a presentation by the Indian Association of Alberta to the Right Honourable P.E. Trudeau and the Government of Canada, 1970, pp. 19-20.

65 Olive P. Dickason, *Canada's First Nations: A History of Founding Peoples from Earliest Times* (Toronto: McClelland & Stewart, 1992), p. 354.

66 In de Brou and Waiser, eds., *Documenting Canada*, p. 590.

67 Archie Mafeje, "South Africa: The Dynamics of a Beleaguered State," in Magubane and Mandaza, eds., *Whither South Africa?*, p. 31. Mafeje argues that tribal culture was not a factor in South Africa. The so-called tribal faction fights in the mines are more a result of ghetto mentality fostered by the South African government than a reflection of deep-seated tribal antagonisms. From 1912 Africans projected themselves as "Africans," not as separate "nationalities" or "national groups"—as the chosen names of organizations indicate: African National Congress, the All-African Convention, Pan-African Congress, the Cape African Teachers' Association.

68 Ibid., p. 33.

69 Barbara Rogers, *Divide and Rule: South Africa's Bantustans* (London: International Defence and Aid Fund for Southern Africa, 1980), p. 55. One example cited concerns the Venda bantustan where a crowd of 16,000 demonstrating students stoned the car of Venda's chief minister; the minister was forced to flee for his life.

70 Gwendolen M. Carter, Thomas Karis and Newell M. Stultz, *South Africa's Transkei: The Politics of Domestic Colonialism* (London: Heinemann, 1967), p. 25.

71 Frances Meli, *A History of the ANC: South Africa Belongs to Us* (Harare, Zimbabwe: Zimbabwe Publishing House, 1988), p. 190.

72 *Dene Declaration* (1975), reprinted in J. Rich Ponting and Roger Gibbins, *Out of Irrelevance: A Socio-political Introduction to Indian Affairs in Canada* (Toronto: Butterworths, 1980), pp. 351-52.

73 Meli, *A History of the ANC*, p. 124: "The Congress of the People was the beginning of the Congress Alliance of the African National Congress, the South African Indian Congress, the Coloured People's Congress, the Congress of Democrats and the South African Congress of Trade Unions."

74 Ibid., p. 125.

75 Cited by Geoffrey York, *The Dispossessed: Life and Death in Native Canada* (London: Vintage U.K., 1990), p. 261.

15

The Sechelt and Nunavut Agreements: Evolutionary and Revolutionary Approaches to Self-Government

---

Cameron Croxall
Laird Christie

Introduction

The issues of land claims and self-government have been central concerns in discussions and negotiations between First Nations and the federal government for the past two decades. However, in another sense, self-government, which in the federal view is some form of local administrative autonomy, has been a part of government Indian policy since shortly after Confederation. This paper examines two case studies involving the development of some form of self-government for Native peoples: the Sechelt Salish of lower British Columbia, and the Inuit of the Eastern Canadian Arctic. Of the several self-government agreements and proposals currently under development in Canada, we feel that these two cases provide striking and significant contrasts. More importantly, these two cases have both provoked a

---

Notes to chapter 15 are on pp. 318-19.

measure of controversy both in their origin and throughout their development. As we will demonstrate, the patterns of political development which these two groups illustrate, reflect differing concepts of Indigenous political autonomy, and at the same time suggest models which may prove applicable in the development of future First Nations governments.

Background

The pattern of federal government/First Nations relations was established during the eighteenth and nineteenth centuries. With the creation of Indian superintendencies in her American colonies and the promulgation of the Royal Proclamation of 1763, the British government laid the framework for Crown relations with First Nations people and the legitimate acquisition of Indian lands. These developments provided the basis of the treaty-making process. However, these arrangements were not sufficient to avoid conflict between the Crown and the Indians. By the end of 1814 problems arose as a result of the influx of American settlers into Upper Canada, in particular, displacing resident Indian peoples (Smith 1981). In an effort to clear land for loyalist settlers, the Crown signed a series of agreements with Upper Canadian Indian groups. The resultant loss of hunting lands and lake and river access left many Indian groups in a destitute state. In an effort to ameliorate the conditions of Indian groups and develop an administrative apparatus which would manage their affairs, an enlarged and civilianized Indian Department was created.[1] While reserves were established under terms of most signed treaties, it was not until the 1830s and after, that the Indian Department made efforts to collect Indians on the reserve lands where their housing and material needs could be supplied. The reserve system, Indian administration and legal enactments concerning Indians were in the process of evolution by 1839.

The reserve system of administration was applied in successive western regions as the colony of Canada expanded.[2] An essential feature of this organization process was the creation of the Indian band: basically a group of Indians resident on a reserve. In legislation passed between 1839-76, the band and the reserve became increasingly the focus of Indian law and administration. The social consequence of this system was the breakdown of hereditary tribal and intertribal customary and social bonds which frequently led to the fragmentation of Aboriginal groups. To the present time, the band has been the legal sociopolitical entity in the Canadian system of Indian administration, though in many instances it had no Aboriginal cultural roots.[3]

The history of the early period of the reserve system illustrates the manner in which the Indians of Upper Canada were grouped together for reserve settlement to create administratively feasible entities out of existing scattered and fragmented Indian peoples (Christie 1976). This fragmentation of Indian groups was compounded by various Indian movements, notably Ojibwa, Potawatomi, Oneida, and Moravian Delawares in Upper Canada in the eighteenth century. Hence recommendations made by Sir James Kempt in 1830 were designed to gather groups of Indians together into villages, creating artificial boundaries between Indians and colonists. This was to protect Indian lands and morality and to ensure the commencement of Crown assimilationist policies.[4]

The key to the reserve system was the band; however, the basis for its establishment was the legal transfer of land. The colonial government, on behalf of the Crown, negotiated for title to great tracts of the North American wilderness in exchange for guaranteed reserve lands and the annual allocation of annuities. However, herein lay the basis for later conflict: the reserve model, born of the unique situation that existed in Upper Canada, was not necessarily applicable to the many diverse nations of peoples upon whom it was thrust. The "band" was in most applications outside of Upper Canada an alien social unit, far removed from any existing Indigenous social order. The band was incorporated solely for administrative convenience, and in the long run its consequence has been to further Indigenous political fragmentation.

In 1869, the *Indian Advancement Act* was passed by Parliament. The *Act* provided for the first time arrangements for the establishment of local band governments. The minister and Governor in Council had the power to set the regulations for and oversee band elections. They were also empowered to determine eligibility for elected offices. The elected councils themselves were in fact administrative units with powers that related almost solely to the maintenance of the reserve itself. Thus, the *Indian Advancement Act* did not provide for the creation of government in any real sense. The principal concerns of the band council related to property management on the reserve and the maintenance of order and decorum in the Indian community.

No notable changes to self-government were made into federal legislation regarding Indian bands until the 1951 *Indian Act*. In the 1951 *Act*, section 83 increased a band's fiscal responsibilities. As the *Advancement Act* of 1869 offered some fiscal power to a band, the legislation of 1951 was the liberalization of fiscal control that offered participating bands increased powers. However, this *Act* served to increase the visibility of the "line organization of administration": a unidirectional line of authority beginning at the top with the minister and continuing down through deputy ministers, district officials, Indian agents and finally band councils. As R.W. Dunning has pointed out, the elected band council still (after 1951) represented the terminal end of a line that through various levels of the Indian Affairs bureaucracy, only ensured that Indians remained under the strict regulation of the Department. Thus one has to make a distinction between "responsible municipal government" as provided for under Indian legislation since 1869 and self-government—the acquisition of authority—beyond that allowed for under the terms of the *Indian Act*.

Band Administration and the Sechelt

The Sechelt are members of the Coastal Salish linguistic community. Traditionally the Sechelt were divided into four subgroupings, each having its own recognized hunting and fishing areas (Etkin 1988: 78). They had a sophisticated system of internal government and an economy based primarily on the abundant salmon supply of the area. They occupied small villages or communities spread out over the area today called the Sunshine Coast, and it was the social interaction existing between these communities that formed the basis for the Sechelt social structure. In the late nineteenth century, a smallpox epidemic all but extinguished the Sechelt population and today they still number fewer than one thousand.

During the colonial period of 1850-71, many Natives of British Columbia were deprived of traditional lands and relocated in small settlements (Fisher 1977). Since the village was an easily recognizable social unit, it was utilized in the creation of bands in the Salish area.[5] However, Suttles has pointed out that in traditional times, local villages were not autonomous or independent. He argued that intervillage kinship and social linkages have persisted through the period of the reserve system. In fact, he argued, they have strengthened in recent years.[6]

In British Columbia, especially among the Coastal Salish people, the reserve administrative system contributed to a breakdown of intercommunity linkages, and led to social encapsulation and physical isolation. Here as well as in the rest of Canada the reserve system had no provisions for Indigenous political organization outside of the band. Moreover, the weakening of the traditional social fabric of the Coastal Salish contributed to the breakdown of their self-sufficiency as they were administered as self-contained band units and not as intervillage communities (Suttles 1962: 665). For the Sechelt, legislated municipal self-government has offered opportunity for local political efficacy. The desire to accept this form of political settlement arguably stemmed not only from the natural intervillage social structure of the Sechelt, but from the sense of supra-community, or the "consciousness of kind" which bound pre-contact village communities to one another.

Arctic Administration and the Inuit

Prior to the imposition of European political structures, Inuit peoples congregated in small familial groupings. Leadership within the social group was restricted to general direction or advice as offered by *isumataaq*—those with great maturity or wisdom. Considerable emphasis was placed upon consensual and egalitarian relations. Contact over and above the familial unit occurred seasonally, when game harvesting both demanded and permitted larger social groupings. Band and tribal groupings did not exist. Regional populations (typically characterized by the Inuktitut suffix *-miut* or "people of") occupied contiguous regions of coastline or island areas and engaged in similar exploitive patterns. Both popular and scholarly literature includes frequent reference to Inuit "tribes" (e.g., the Copper Inuit, Caribou Inuit, Central Inuit, etc.). For the most part, such regional groups included several *-miut* populations (e.g., the Caribou Inuit included inland *Aharmiut* and coastal *Paddleimiut* peoples). There is no evidence that large tribal political structures ever existed.

Radical economic and socio-political change did not come to the Arctic until the twentieth century. Sporadic visits by Europeans are recorded from the sixteenth century onward, and whaling in both the Eastern and Western Arctic was established in the latter half of the nineteenth century. While Scottish and American whalers frequently established seasonal factory posts and both employed and traded with the Inuit, significant reorganization of their economic life did not occur until the permanent posts of the Hudson's Bay Company appeared in the Arctic after 1900.

After World War II and with increased intensity after 1950, the Canadian government became involved in the Canadian Arctic; initially with a focus on Inuit health, subsequently in major social and population reorganization. In the early 1950s, under the Northern Service Officers Program (NSO), local federal administrators were placed in Arctic communities to represent federal government interests and facilitate to the interests of the Inuit. At the same time, the establishment of medical clinics and elementary schools created nuclei which along with churches and HBC stores provided the basis for the contemporary Arctic centres. In a number of instances, Inuit populations were encouraged to relocate in these centres. In other cases they were relocated for various purposes.[7] In effect these communities were northern "reserves" in that they were almost exclusively ethnic enclaves and had been created for purposes of administration and service delivery.[8]

Political Development

Tribalism and the Coastal Salish

Many scholars have argued that the tribe is in fact the fundamental unit of Indian identity and loyalty.[9] Tribalism might be said to include patterns of thought and action based upon language and/or cultural traditions. In contemporary nation states such as Canada, tribalistic tendencies and movements seem to arise as a form of opposition to the large-scale bureaucratic management patterns such as those represented by the Department of Indian Affairs; in certain cases they seem to be counterfoils to pan-Indian movements as well (i.e., the tendency of Iroquoians to resist involvement in the Assembly of First Nations).

Tribalism became an overtly visible political movement among the Coastal Salish in the early 1970s perhaps as a direct response to existing provincial pan-Indian organizations (Tennant 1990: 180). Salish peoples, including the Sechelt, Squamish and Musqueam, formed the Alliance of British Columbia Indian Bands in 1974, a political organization based on the traditional Salish bi-kindred system.[10] Through the later 1970s this small alliance of bands grew to include nine bands and acquired recognition as a new provincial Indian organization. However, unlike such organizations as UBCIC, this organization retained its tribalistic political structure, based on principles of popular equality and participation, and all members were exclusively Coastal Salish peoples (Tennant 1990: 181). Throughout this period of interregional political organization, the Department of Indian Affairs (DIAND) continued to administer through their agents. Neither interregional, provincial nor national pan-Indian organizations have ever been incorporated into the DIAND administrative structure. The reserve system was neither designed, nor was it capable of, dealing with Indian political organization beyond that of the band and reserve. As a result, elimination of Indian Department control at the band level became a priority. As Tennant observed: "District and tribal political organization was in every sense motivated in good part by the benefits of common action on the part of communities in seeking more local control" (1990: 182). Through tribal association, communities could pursue political mandates through a strong unified front without eclipsing the fundamental importance of the smaller community group. Such action was not feasible within the system created by the reserve and band political structures.

The success that the Coastal Salish people have experienced with this system of association demonstrates the importance to the Salish of the intervillage community structure. Tribalism as an intercommunity, integrative movement was in effect already present among the Coastal Salish as we have noted previously. There was an ongoing traditional system of community linkages which here, as elsewhere in Canada, reflected the failure of the band and reserve system to meet the social and political needs of First Nations groups.[11]

Inuit and Arctic Politics

The decade of the 1960s was characterized by significant political changes in the North. Largely as a result of the recommendations of the Carrothers Commission (1965-67), the devolution of power from Ottawa to the new northern capital of Yellowknife brought not only the Northwest Territories administrative centre to the North but also a localized or regionally based political infrastructure. On the surface, this system fit well into the political development process of the Eastern Arctic. The emergence of the co-operative movement during the late 1950s had already familiarized the Inuit with concepts of local business development, communal consultation and the foundations for local level Inuit politics. Further, the tendency towards regionalization during the 1960s and early 1970s helped to promote Eastern Inuit political aspirations. Ironically, the new Yellowknife administrative apparatus created many of the same problems for communities in its far-flung constituency (particularly the Eastern Arctic) as had the earlier Ottawa-based administration. Like the line organization in Indian administration, the government of the Northwest Territories/municipality relationship in the Arctic represented a unidirectional flow of power. Local councils exercised little in the way of real political power outside the areas of hard services (e.g., the maintenance of physical facilities, water delivery, sewage disposal). The situation created what Dickerson has called a "crisis of legitimacy" among the Inuit population (Dickerson 1993). The Yellowknife government was seen as both alien and insensitive to Eastern Arctic Inuit needs.

Northern issues were further complicated with the Trudeau government position on Native affairs. The White Paper of 1969 effectively laid out a plan for the dismantling of all Native administration in Canada. The outcry from Indigenous people as well as the public at large led the federal government to retrench on its plans for dismantling the Indian Affairs apparatus. After 1973, reversing its earlier position on Native rights, it began funding Indigenous political organizations and research on land claims and treaties. In the north, Indigenous mobilization was reflected in the founding of two Arctic political organizations: the Committee for Original Peoples Entitlement (COPE), and the Inuit Tapirisat of Canada (ITC). Indeed northern Indigenous political organizations such as the ITC and COPE provided the catalyst for the creation of an Indigenous ethnonational identity for such peoples as the northern Métis, Dene, and Inuit.[12]

COPE was founded in direct response to the northern expansion of industrial economics. COPE represents those people most affected by resource exploration and development. Resource exploration was uneven across the Arctic and, perhaps for this reason, regional rather than partisan politics emerged as the means towards active political formation. COPE itself was regionally based, but more interestingly, this regionalization brought with it new regional ethnic identifications. Following the formal ITC/COPE split (1976), the Western Arctic land claim "Inuvialuit Nunangat" became more than a comprehensive claims proposal. It was in fact a claim for recognition of an ethnic entity (the Inuvialuit) which had not previously existed; the land claim had created a new ethnocultural entity (Dahl 1988).

In almost direct juxtaposition to the organizational components of COPE, the ITC was predominantly ethnically exclusive from its inception. The organization and agenda of this political body was reflective of the uneven nature of Arctic resource development. With limited exploration and development occurring east of Keewatin, the ITC focused more on the settling of Eastern Arctic territorial claims, and ultimately, the creation of an Inuit homeland within the fabric of the Canadian Constitution. From 1972 until 1976, the ITC managed to incorporate COPE as well as several other regional organizations from the Eastern and Western Arctic, Kitikmeot, Quebec, Labrador, Keewatin and the Baffin region. However, the 1976 Nunavut proposal put forth by the ITC brought forth an underlying ethnic schism. When COPE withdrew from ITC, and the Quebec Inuit independently signed the Quebec agreement, the creation of a pan-Arctic identity had given way to the realpolitik of state-Native relations. Moreover, in the aftermath of the split, the ITC, which was organized to assert the cultural interests of its membership, shifted its emphasis increasingly towards political and economical concerns. For the Inuit, the Indigenous "renaissance" of the 1970s was not characterized by the "tribalism" of many other Native peoples. Here political organization emerged at the regional level. Unlike the Sechelt, the Inuit embraced large-scale political organization of a sort that bore no semblance to traditional political structures. Such organization in itself has created socio-political dilemmas for the Inuit in that it has no real approximate parallel in tradition.

Self-Government

Self-Government and the Sechelt

Michael Asch stated that: "At its most basic level, self-sufficiency is the ability to set goals and act on them without seeking the permission of others" (Asch 1992: 50). Asch claims that Aboriginal Nations have been denied their right to self-government and to act in a manner that would more closely represent true self-sufficiency. This problem stems from the federal government regarding Aboriginal self-government as a contingent right and not an inherent one. On this assumption, the federal government presents changes in the *Indian Act* providing for increased band council powers as both liberal and progressive. However, even the most autonomous forms of legislated self-government under the *Indian Act* still remain under the ultimate authority of the minister and hence lack constitutional entrenchment. Native self-government remains at the legislative mercy of parliament. Therefore, so long as bands operate within the parameters of the *Indian Act* they are restricted in terms of land tenure and political organizational freedom. The government's ultimate jurisdictional authority over reserves gives it the power to dictate the terms by which an Indian group is to operate politically. Under the ambiguous terms of the *Indian Act*, the band again remains subject to judicial interpretation. In light of this jurisdictional situation, the Sechelt Band has attempted one approach to the goal of greater local political autonomy.

The Sechelt Indian Band has opted for legislated self-government outside of the confines of the *Indian Act*. This was achieved through special enabling legislation at both the federal and provincial levels. The Sechelt case is significant in that it represents one model for the attainment of local self-government for other First Nations groups. The creation of Sechelt self-government culminated a decade of efforts to attain a greater measure of local political autonomy. The "Sechelt Indian Band" is the new entity which shares certain legal rights with its forerunner. Its members retain their Indian status and as such may pursue land claims.

Legislation that legitimized Sechelt self-government included Bill C-93, the *Sechelt Indian Band Self-Government Act* (proclaimed 9 October 1986), and Bill 4-1987, the *Sechelt Indian Government District Enabling Act* (proclaimed 23 July 1987). In addition to this legislation, the band itself created its own constitution. Together, these three documents outline the rights and privileges of the government of the Sechelt Indian Band.

The *Sechelt Indian Band Self-Government Act* (referred to hereafter as *The Sechelt Act*) established a comprehensive scheme for the self-governance of the band. This legislation includes (1) the replacement of the *Indian Act* "Sechelt Band" with the "Sechelt Indian Band"; and (2) the recognition of the Sechelt Indian Band as "a legal entity" with "the capacity, rights, powers and privileges of a natural person"(R.S., ca. 1986, c. 27). In fact, the Sechelt Indian Band achieved, through provincial legislation, the legal powers of a corporation and operates in a manner similar to other municipalities within British Columbia. The band may "enter into contracts . . . acquire and hold property or any interest therein . . . borrow money . . . [and] do such things as are conducive to the exercise of its rights, powers and privileges" (ibid.). These are privileges not offered under the terms of the *Indian Act*. In numerous case decisions it has been held that a band does not possess the legal powers and capacities of a natural person. Such judicial decisions have denied bands the right to own real property or hold legal custody of children (Woodward 1994: 164). Under the terms of the Sechelt agreement, the band's fiscal autonomy has been radically increased. While the *Indian Act* allows for "advanced bands" (s. 83) to exercise a measure of fiscal independence, such powers remain subject to the minister's prerogative of disallowance.

The Sechelt Indian Band Council received its municipal powers through provincial enabling legislation even though the Sechelt Indian Government District and the District Council were created through federal legislation. Under the terms of s. 19(2) of *The Sechelt Act*, the District Council is identical to the band council. In fact, the Sechelt Indian Band Council is the District Council and as such holds the powers and benefits of a municipality and may pass laws that carry the authority of the province (Woodward 1994: 131). The Sechelt Indian Government District holds the right to make and enforce laws relating to zoning, taxation, law and order, traffic, roads and "the good government of the community" (ibid.: 98). These laws, passed by the District Council, are published in the *Canada Gazette* (R.S., ca. 1986, c. 27, s. 13).[13] Thus, the Sechelt Indian Government District Council is not only freed from the restrictions of the *Indian Act*, but it operates with the powers of a municipality.

The Sechelt Indian Government District is located fifty kilometres northwest of Vancouver on the Sechelt peninsula. The district itself, thirty-three Sechelt Indian reserves that comprise a total 1,000 hectares, includes the majority of the Sechelt population (fewer than 1,000) as well as 500 non-Sechelt residents who rent Sechelt lands. To afford representation to those peoples occupying lands who are not band members, the provincial statute provides for the creation of an Advisory District Council. The responsibilities of this council focus on the planning and budgeting of "hard service" delivery in the district (Etkin 1988: 96). Such services include the physical maintenance of roads and other facilities necessary for the daily operation of the district. This council has no political mandate. In fact, the council's powers closely resemble those exercised by band councils under the *Indian Act*.

The Sechelt Indian Government District and the District Council are both creations of federal legislation. In effect, the Sechelt Indian Band was stripped (through federal legislation) of its status as a reserve community and came to resemble a municipality under the jurisdiction of the province. The District Council became a representative body of the district and was formally empowered by the British Columbia legislature under the terms of the *British Columbia Municipalities Act*.

Concerns of land ownership are an integral part of the negotiation process between First Nations and the federal government. The Sechelt agreement is no exception. *The Sechelt Act* transferred to the Sechelt Indian Band in fee simple, all Sechelt lands which have been surrendered but have not been sold.[14] The Sechelt Indian Band thus obtained corporate fee simple ownership of its reserve lands. With Aboriginal title erased through the acquisition of fee simple ownership, the Sechelt Indian Band may mortgage their lands or use of them for collateral in financing developmental projects. However, Sechelt lands are not in fact entirely free from Indian legislation. Section 24 of *The Sechelt Act* stipulates that both the *British Columbia Indian Reserves Mineral Resources Act* and the *Indian Reserves Minerals Resources Act* still apply to Sechelt lands. Further, section 31 states that all Sechelt lands remain "lands reserved for Indians" under the meaning of the 1867 *Constitution Act*. Therefore, Sechelt lands have been transferred in fee simple to the band, but remain within the Reserve Land Registry and as such may not be expropriated without the consent of the Governor in Council. The process of expropriation must occur in accordance with the procedure established in the band's constitution (R.S., ca. 1986, c. 27). Until such time as it is expropriated, Sechelt lands remain registered with the federal, and not the provincial, government.

The Sechelt agreement is a culmination of federal and provincial legislation which, together with the band's own constitution, offers the possibility for a significant measure of political autonomy. At the same time, the preservation of the separate Sechelt reserve communities legitimates the existence of traditional Salish intercommunity linkages. Guided in part by a 1986 Department of Indian Affairs policy directive, the Sechelt agreement may, while well recognizing the diversity of First Nations communities across Canada, offer solutions applicable to similar First Nations proposals elsewhere in Canada.

Self-Government and the Inuit: Nunavut

Boldt has pointed out that "A fundamental reciprocal and interdependent relationship exists between a society's social organization and its cultural philosophies and principles" (Boldt 1993). He goes on to argue that contradictions exist between many traditional Native cultural philosophies and those imposed upon them by colonial authorities. On the other hand, encapsulated societies, such as those of Canada's First Nations, must perforce formulate structures for self-government consonant with the state environment in which they are located. Nunavut, in its currently proposed state, is modelled after existing "colonial" political structures (in that it is to be recognized by the Canadian Constitution as a political division within the Canadian state), yet it will almost certainly become permeated with the salient qualities of Inuit tradition (cf. Bell and Phillips 1995).

We have dealt with Nunavut as a land claim earlier. Now we must examine it as a plan for self-government on behalf of the Inuit of the Eastern Arctic. When the Nunavut proposal was first put forth in 1976, the federal government perceived the plan as contributing further complications to the problem of an administrative split in the Northwest Territories. The notion of splitting the NWT had been under consideration since the previous decade and was the focus of the Carrothers Commission. The federal government's arguments against division stemmed primarily from economic concerns focusing on the increased expense of duplicating northern administrative apparatus. As the Nunavut land claim constituted most of the Eastern Arctic, the federal government perceived this as an attempt to allocate legislative authority and governmental jurisdiction on the grounds of "race," hence the governmental response:

> Legislative authority and governmental jurisdiction are not allocated in Canada on grounds that differentiate between the people on the basis of race. . . . Jurisdiction is placed in the hands of governments that are responsible directly or indirectly to the people—again without regard to race. (Purich 1992: 66)

The federal government could not equate a land claim with public government. In a political era plagued with impending or threatened separation and fragmentation, the Nunavut proposal did not mesh with federalist policies and initiatives. Further, constant pressure for territorial division was applied to the Territorial Legislature from the mostly Inuit Eastern Arctic members of the Legislative Assembly (MLAs). This pressure managed to initiate a further study on the issue, and in 1978 the Drury Commission was created. Drury's report asserted that territorial division was not the solution to the increasingly conflicting interests of Inuit, Dene and whites. Instead, it recommended the continuation of the existing territorial political apparatus with further devolution of powers to the outlying communities. "A new administrative centre in the north," it said, "would only be a further economic burden on the Canadian taxpayer." The ITC's proposal to finance the new government through their control of natural resources involved in the land claim was muted by Drury as too expensive to start up.

The Drury Report did not diminish Inuit hopes to create for themselves a homeland in the Eastern Arctic. In the 1979 territorial elections tremendous Aboriginal participation resulted in a Territorial Assembly dominated by Aboriginal MLAs. In November of 1979 this Assembly appointed a committee on unity to determine, gauge and report on support for the status quo. It argued that support for the maintenance of a unified territory was indeed low, if not non-existent and recommended a vote on the issue. The Legislative Assembly voted unanimously for a territorial plebiscite on division.

During the lead-up to the plebiscite a lobby group was initiated by MLAs and other Inuit representatives to promote territorial division and the constitutional reconstruction of the Northwest Territories. Known as the Constitutional Alliance, this group continued to play a major role in territorial politics for the next decade. In April of 1982, the returns of the plebiscite showed a 56 percent vote in favour of division.[15] When the federal government's response was to accept the results of the plebiscite, provided a southern and western boundary could be agreed upon, the Constitutional Alliance then created two forums to deal with this task. The forum for the east was the Nunavut Constitutional Forum (NCF) and in the west it was the Western Constitutional Forum (WCF). Together these two forums developed a new boundary, created proposals for new constitutions for the intended territorial governments and ensured public participation in each of these developments.

The boundary question was the most critically disputatious issue. By 1990 the Western Arctic had become so politically fragmented due to cultural sensitivity, inevitably arising from the delineation of political boundaries on the basis of ethnohistory, that only in opposition to the proposals put forward by the appointed claims negotiation body, Tungavik Federation of Nunavut (TFN), could there be found any degree of unity. Concomitantly, economic concerns were also a factor. Early TFN proposals included the Mackenzie Delta-Beaufort Sea in Nunavut. This would have placed 90 percent of the known NWT oil and gas reserves in the new eastern territory (Purich 1993: 84). Thus, cultural and economic factors combined to create almost a decade of boundary disputes. Indeed final agreement was only reached as a result of arbitration efforts of John Parker, former commissioner of the Northwest Territories.[16]

Nunavut was negotiated in the Eastern Arctic through the Nunavut Constitutional Forum and the ITC with their appointed claims negotiators, the TFN. The Nunavut agreement calls for the establishment of public government in the Eastern Arctic. This is a point of considerable significance. Nunavut was not conceived of as a "mega-reserve" but as a provincial/territorial political division within the Canadian state. It was and is dominantly Inuit in demographic terms; however, as a political subdivision it cannot be structured so as to maintain ethnic exclusivity. It must be observed that the deal was negotiated, with minor exceptions, through ethnically elected representatives.[17] Whether the administrative structure itself will incorporate distinctively Inuit values or legislate into existence cultural safeguards for Inuit traditions remains to be seen. However, with deft ability, Inuit leaders themselves have managed to create what they hope will be a political future that will see the continued existence of their traditions.

Conclusion

The Sechelt and Nunavut agreements differ significantly in many ways. Most striking is the scale of the lands involved. Nunavut covers more than three-and-a-half million km^2 of the Canadian Arctic of which 350,000 km^2 was transferred in fee simple ownership to the 21,000 Inuit within the region and 36,000 km^2 include subsurface mineral rights. This enormous land mass will be the largest administrative area in Canada. In fact, had the initial Nunavut proposal been accepted, and the Inuvialuit remained in accord, most of the Canadian Arctic would have been included in Nunavut. In almost direct contrast to this, the Sechelt agreement involves only 10 km^2, with another 5,000 km^2 outstanding in comprehensive claims. The population involved numbers fewer than 1,500 (750 Sechelt and 500 renters). However, areas contiguous to Sechelt lands hold a population in excess of one million. Where Nunavut is a large land mass with a scattered sparse population, the Sechelt lands are densely populated with both Native and non-Native inhabitants.

An examination of the political structures and the distribution of powers in these agreements reveals several significant differences. While the Sechelt hold powers roughly equivalent to those of a municipality, similar to the surrounding provincial jurisdictions, the Nunavut agreement proposes the creation of another Arctic territory, similar to the Yukon or Northwest Territories. The Sechelt settled for "supra-municipal" status, whereas Nunavut looks ultimately towards the attainment of provincial status. In essence, the Sechelt agreement remains modeled on the reserve system; it involves lands under the jurisdiction of a single band, and the lands involved remain in fact within the federal Reserve Registry.

Legislative powers granted to the Sechelt through the agreement include those typical of municipalities: zoning, local taxation, public order, etc. In addition to these powers the Sechelt have the right to legislate on matters concerning health services, preservation of natural resources, matters pertaining to the good government of the band and the education of band members on Sechelt lands. These additional powers allow for a measure of autonomy in social services and education that actually give the band the power to create their own school curricula. This offers a built-in in safeguard through the inclusion of Salish cultural knowledge and activities in school programs. In direct contrast to the Sechelt legislative powers, the Nunavut government will have legislative authority at the territorial level. Inuit education and social

service interests will no doubt be reflected within the Nunavut legislature through sheer demographic domination. However, unlike the
Sechelt, the Nunavut government is public government and contains no
true ethnic safeguards. Inuit ability to influence education in their own
cultural interests exists only so long as they dominate the legislature.
Mass migration of *Qallunaat* (non-Aboriginal) into the Eastern Arctic
will pose perpetual threats to Inuit demographic and hence political
domination of Nunavut.

When one compares and contrasts these two agreements in terms of
legislative powers, the marked differences appear to stem from legal
status based on ethnicity. The Sechelt have the ability to determine band
membership and, concomitantly, political participation within the Sechelt
Indian Government District through terms of the agreement. Membership in the Sechelt Band allows for land rights as well. In contrast, Inuit
status within Nunavut is significant only in relation to the land claim.
Within this agreement, the "beneficiaries"—persons enrolled as Inuit
claimants—will be recipients of additional privileges in land use and
monies as they are transferred to the Tungavik Federation of Nunavut.
However, as a territorial political jurisdiction Nunavut cannot be restricted to Inuit alone. Thus, unlike the Nunavut agreement, the Sechelt
agreement simply perpetuates on a somewhat higher political level the
basic mono-ethnic enclave identical to existing reserves. The Sechelt are
left with a given territory in which they alone determine residency.

The radical political differences between these two agreements
immediately raises the issue of "sovereignty" and culture and the nature
of their relationship. Is culture to be maintained through "sovereignty"
or is sovereignty to be achieved through cultural assertion? Long before
the Sechelt or Nunavut agreements were achieved as solutions for First
Nations autonomy, the Dene Declaration of 1975 likened the people to
an emergent third world nation and argued that only through the creation of "Denendah" as a sovereign territory could they realize their
goal of cultural protection. Since that time, the term "sovereignty" has
frequently recurred in First Nations political rhetoric as well as in social
science writings (Etkin, Boldt). However, the notion of sovereignty and
its relationship to autonomy and self-government deserves some consideration.

Clearly, within the Canadian nation state, all jurisdictions operate
with less than sovereign power. This is sometimes termed or called a
form of "domestic" sovereignty. First Nations would simply call it
sovereignty. Asch's comment (p. 8) must be tempered with the realiza-

tion that within the nation state the exercise of "sovereign" power must be construed metaphorically. The degree of autonomy which is realizable for any First Nations group will be in direct relation to its population and the size of its territorial claim. In discussions of sovereignty and culture, Boldt has recently argued that current First Nations agendas in which political autonomy (or "sovereignty") is given pre-eminence are short-sighted in the point of view of Native cultural preservation:

> the survival of "Indians" as "Indians" depends primarily on cultural realization within a framework of traditional philosophies and principles, not on political autonomy. . . . [R]evitalized "Indian" cultures are a prerequisite for political sovereignty rather than the reverse. (Boldt 1988)

Boldt buttresses this argument with the instance of the Jewish people whose culture has survived without the benefit of political autonomy or a national homeland. Without the persistence of that culture, no Jewish state would ever have been attainable. Boldt suggests that in Canada a charter of collective rights, entrenched within the Constitution, might be a means whereby Indian cultural preservation could be attained.

While the Sechelt agreement has built-in cultural safeguards (primarily control over band education), the Inuit deal offers prospects of cultural survival instead. The government of Nunavut may very well act in a quasi-provincial manner to promote culture through policies of language, education and heritage conservancy. In both instances, a measure of political autonomy will provide the means for a measure of cultural preservation. However, in the final analysis, the Nunavut "revolutionary" approach to self-government entails risks for Inuit culture that are not present in the Sechelt solution. The Eastern Arctic Inuit are gambling on a "Quebec solution" to the preservation of their culture and language. Nunavut cannot be, as the Sechelt reserves are, exclusively Inuit territory. It will be trilingual and will be subject to the same principles of accessibility that apply across Canada. There will be the risk (indeed almost the necessity) of increased *Qallunaat* settler populations. As their numbers rise through northward migration or recruitment of skilled labour and bureaucratic service personnel, the Inuit voice in Nunavut will of necessity be diminished. Indeed some distant future may see a minority Inuit population in a land they created for themselves.

Much of the Native population in Canada lives within small isolated, scattered communities. For these people the "supra-municipal" model is a possible solution to political problems that stem from their demographic distribution. For example, the Anishnabek of Ontario

might secure increased political power through a government district
with municipal powers comparable to the Sechelt.

The Nunavut solution is unlikely to be duplicated. In size and
nature the area resembles that of the Inuvialuit and Alaska claims: territories where the Native populations outnumber the non-Natives. However, in an outstanding claim such as that of the Council of Yukon
Indians (Yukon) or the James Bay claim, Indigenous populations do not
make up the majority and for this reason it is improbable that the
Nunavut pattern of self-government will be achieved. The likelihood is
that when self-government for Indian peoples is developed, it will be
based upon regional groupings of reserve communities with an assembly
or legislature comparable to the present AFN. It will in effect be a third
order of government over territorially non-contiguous settlements.

Notes

1 British Indian affairs had been administered since 1755 partly by an Indian
  superintendent and partly by colonial governments.
2 The Robinson-Huron and Robinson-Superior treaties of 1850 were the first
  of the large-scale land treaties obtained through this process.
3 The *Indian Act* (1876) defines a band as any "tribe, band or body of Indians" who hold a reserve or an annuity (Woodward 1994: 12).
4 Sir James Kempt made these suggestions to secretary of state for war and the
  colonies, Sir George Murray, for "improving the condition of the Indians."
  These suggestions were passed by the Secretary of State and by the Lords of
  the Treasury and thereby "provided the essence of the Indian reserve policy
  in Upper Canada" (Surtees 1967: 7-8).
5 As well as elsewhere in British Columbia.
6 In contemporary times these ties manifest themselves more in intervillage
  ceremonialism rather than as economic bonds.
7 Widely publicized examples included the rescue of the inland Caribou peoples (1950s) and the Grise Fiord/Resolute Bay relocations.
8 They were, of course, not reserves under the terms of the *Indian Act*. While
  for purposes of administration Inuit have been treated as Indians since 1939,
  the *Indian Act* is not actually applicable.
9 One should be careful to distinguish between contemporary political organizations and traditional social groupings. Technically only Iroquoians and
  some of the Plains groups were politically structured as "Tribes" in the
  anthropological sense of the term. British Columbia First Nations peoples
  were traditionally "chiefdoms" (see Service 1962).
10 The provincial Indian organizations referred to here are the Union of British
   Columbia Indian Chiefs (UBCIC) and the British Columbia Association of
   Non-Status Indians (BCANSI). Both of these groups faltered and nearly collapsed in 1975. However, BCANSI came to embrace a political structure
   based on the aspects of tribalism and for this reason, among others, it

quickly rebounded to become the United Native Nations (UNN) (Tennant 1990: 181).

11 Indeed it could be argued that regional political organizations, such as those identified with treaty and linguistic groups (e.g., Treaty #9 peoples, Quebec Cree), emerged to provide not only the political strength but the recognition of existing cultural/linguistic ties for which the band/reserve system makes no provision.

12 Dahl pointed out that these groups were "artificially" ethnic in that, before the claims process, the idea of these people banding together as a single entity was not possible: " We are dealing with ideas and ideological constructions, not with political realities nor with ethnic groups rooted in early history" (Dahl 1988).

13 By-laws enacted under the *Indian Act* come under the *Statutory Instruments Act* and are not published in the *Canada Gazette*. This leaves them as instruments of which judicial notice is not required (Woodward 1994: 178).

14 These surrendered lands fall within the definition of "surrendered lands" within the *Indian Act*, s. 2(1). This does not imply the existence of a formal surrender treaty for Sechelt lands.

15 An analysis of the vote shows that of the 18,962 eligible voters, 9,891 actually voted; 5,560 voters supported division. The turnout was considerably higher in the Eastern Arctic (75 percent) than in the west (45 percent). Eighty-two percent of the voters in the east favoured division while in the west there were only 44 percent in favour. This was indicative of the importance of Nunavut to the population of the Eastern Arctic, more so than in the west (Purich 1993: 70).

16 Actually both the WCF and the TFN agreed upon a boundary by 1987; however, the WCF was not able to gain approval for the boundary from all of its constituent communities (Purich 1993: 84).

17 The guidelines of the Constitutional Alliance allowed for at least one non-Aboriginal MLA in both the NCF and the WCF to represent the non-Aboriginal population (Purich 1993: 71).

References

Asch, Michael
  1993 *Home and Native Land: Aboriginal Rights and the Canadian Constitution*. Vancouver, BC: University of British Columbia Press.
Bell, James, and Todd Phillips
  1995, 12 May "Footprints in the Snow: The NIC Report." *Nunatsiaq News*, 23, 15: 1.
Boldt, Menno
  1993 *Surviving as Indians*. Toronto: University of Toronto Press.
Brody, Hugh
  1991 *The Peoples Land: Inuit, Whites and the Eastern Arctic*. New ed. Vancouver, BC: Douglas & McIntyre.

Canada. DIAND
  1969 *Statement of the Government of Canada on Indian Policy.* Ottawa: Queen's Printer.
  1981 *In All Fairness: A Native Claims Policy.* Ottawa: Queen's Printer.
  1984 *Report of the Special Committee on Indian Self-Government.* Ottawa: Minister of Supply and Services.
  1993 *Agreement between the Inuit of the Nunavut Settlement Area and Her Majesty the Queen in Right of Canada.* Ottawa: Minister of Indian Affairs and the Tungavik Federation of Nunavut.
Cardinal, Harold
  1969 *The Unjust Society.* Edmonton: Hurtig.
Christie, Laird
  1976 "Reserve Colonialism and Social Change: A Case Study." Unpublished PhD dissertation, University of Toronto (Anthropology).
Craig, Gerald
  1963 *Upper Canada—The Formative Years: 1784-1841.* Toronto: McClelland and Stewart.
Cserepy, F.A.E.
  1980 "New Styles in Arctic Administration Since 1945." In Morris Zaslow, ed., *A Century of Canada's Arctic Islands: 1880-1980.* Ottawa: Royal Society of Canada.
Dahl, Jens
  1988 "Self-Government, Land Claims, and Imagined Inuit Communities." *Folk*, 30.
Dickerson, Mark
  1992 *Whose North?* Vancouver, BC: University of British Columbia Press.
Diubaldo, Richard
  1993 *A Historical Overview of Government-Inuit Relations, 1900-1980's.* Ottawa: DIAND [original prepared 30 July 1992, revised 1 January 1993].
Duffy, Quinn
  1988 *The Road to Nunavut: The Progress of the Eastern Arctic Inuit Since the Second World War.* Kingston: McGill-Queen's University Press.
Engelstad, Diane, Tim Schouls and John Olthuis
  1992 "The Basic Dilemma: Sovereignty or Assimilation." In D. Engelstad and J. Bird, eds., *Nation to Nation: Aboriginal Sovereignty and the Future of Canada*, pp. 12-27. Concord: House of Anansi Press.
Etkin, Carol
  1988 "The Sechelt Indian Band: An Analysis of a New Form of Self-Government." *Canadian Journal of Native Studies*, 8, 1: 73-105.
Fisher, Robin
  1977 *Contact and Conflict: Indian-European Relations in British Columbia, 1774-1890.* Vancouver, BC: University of British Columbia Press.
Frideres, James
  1983 *Native People in Canada: Contemporary Conflicts.* Scarborough, ON: Prentice-Hall Canada.

Gough, Barry
   1984   *Gunboat Frontier: British Maritime Authority and Northwest Coast Indians, 1846-1890.* Vancouver, BC: University of British Columbia Press.
   ————, and Cameron Croxall
   1994   "Canadian Arctic Communities: Their Recent Administrative History—Baffin Perspectives." Paper presented at the Western Regional Science Conference, Tucson, AZ.
Irwin, Colin
   1989   "Lords of the Arctic, Wards of the State." *Northern Perspectives*, 17, 1 (January/March).
Knight, Rolf
   1978   *Indians at Work: An Informal History of Native Indian Labour in British Columbia, 1858-1930.* Vancouver, BC: New Star Books.
Mathiasson, John
   1992   *Living on the Land: Change Among the Inuit of Baffin Island.* Peterborough, ON: Broadview Press.
Nunavut Constitutional Forum
   1983   *Building Nunavut.*
Purich, Donald
   1992   *The Inuit and Their Land: The Story of Nunavut.* Toronto: James Lorimer.
Service, Elman R.
   1962   *Primitive Social Organization and Evolutionary Perspective.* New York: Random House.
Surtees, Robert J.
   1967   "The Development of Indian Reserve Policy in Canada." *Ontario History*, 60, 2 (June 1968): 87-98.
Suttles, Wayne
   1962   "The Persistence of Intervillage Ties Among the Coastal Salish." *Ethnology*, 2 (October 1963): 512-25.
Tennant, Paul
   1990   *Aboriginal Peoples and Politics.* Vancouver, BC: University of British Columbia Press.
Vallee, Frank, Derek Smith and Joseph Cooper
   1984   "Contemporary Canadian Inuit." In David Damas, ed., *Handbook of North American Indians*, vol. 5: *Arctic.* Washington: Smithsonian Institution.
Woodward, Jack
   1994   *Native Law.* Scarborough, ON: Carswell.

Statutes

Indian Act, R.S., c. 149, s. 1 (1951).
Sechelt Indian Band Self-Government Act, R.S., c. 27 (1986).
Sechelt Indian Government District Enabling Act (S.B.C.) (1986).

Retrospect

A Meeting Ground of Earth, Water, Air and Fire

David T. McNab

$\int$even years ago, in his path-breaking study of the "middle
ground," Richard White posited a new way of examining
the relationship between Aboriginal peoples and the European newcomers. While his study was largely confined to the "pays d'en
haut," the geographical area of the Great Lakes in the seventeenth and
eighteenth centuries, White emphasized that the "middle ground" was
the "place in between: in between cultures, people, and in between
empires and the nonstate world of villages." He went on to define this
concept as a place where "diverse peoples adjust their differences
through what amounts to a process of creative, and often expedient,
misunderstandings. People try to persuade others who are different from
themselves by appealing to what they perceive to be the values and practices of those others. They often misinterpret and distort both the values
and practices of those they deal with, but from these misunderstandings
arise new meanings and new practices—the shared meanings and practices of the middle ground."[1] However, in defining the "middle ground"
as an abstract concept, but a specific geographical space, White has
missed the real significance of the physical space and the Aboriginal peoples special understanding of place, as part of the circle of life and time,
as part of Mother Earth. It is also a spiritual place.[2] And it encompasses
all of Turtle Island.

Notes to the Retrospect are on p. 327.

In this context, from the perspective of Aboriginal people and their oral traditions,[3] the historiographical concept of the "middle ground" reflects the written record of the European newcomers to Turtle Island and not the Aboriginal oral traditions. In this sense, it is, at least in part, wishful thinking. It is a hope that accommodation can be made among diverse peoples on the North American continent. But Turtle Island was given by the Creator to the Aboriginal peoples to protect and it is an Aboriginal place. And in this sense it is a part of Aboriginal sovereignty. Thus, there is really no "middle ground." However, there has been always a time and a place for a Council between Aboriginal peoples and the Europeans on Turtle Island. Parallel and yet separate, this is a place of fire—a meeting ground.[4] And this meeting ground occurs still today— not just in the Great Lakes or the "pays d'en haut"—but throughout the continent.

All too often we see history as change, rapid change as a result of progress in the development of European and Canadian societies in the twentieth century. As we enter the twenty-first century, we should stop to ponder this concept of history. Our perspective of Canada's history reflects the immediacy of seemingly dramatic changes in the structure of Europe and North America. The difficulty is that this view may well in time be seen to be exaggerated in terms of the impact of change. It may also contradict the essential continuity and integrity of Aboriginal history in what we now know as Canada.

Too often in the past the continuing power and presence of the Aboriginal oral traditions in Canada's history have been either overlooked, ignored or dismissed. This history has been written and viewed only through the lens of written history based on documents left by Euro-Canadian visitors about what they believed they saw for a fleeting moment in time within the framework and the context of European Imperial history. This approach, a linear perspective, has frequently left us with a highly distorted portrayal of Aboriginal people. It is epitomized by pen or ink. Nevertheless, we must never forget that Clio is by her nature flexible and diverse; this is not the only way to perceive the history of the geographic entity called Canada.

The Elders of the Walpole Island First Nation have reminded us of this fact: "When we were created we were made without those advantages; we have no pen or ink to write, we have nothing but a little piece of flesh called a heart, to remember by." This metaphor of the heart binds together Aboriginal people, their languages and their cultures. It is altogether different than just historical facts with the written documents left out. First Nations oral traditions are a powerful cultural force. It is part of their tool-box of survival. Aboriginal people have a holistic, non-linear view of history within which they see circles of time which are ever expanding and infinite. It is their way of knowing and comprehending their spiritual place in the world of the Creator. In their oral traditions, the landscape, or Mother Earth, is seen as inseparable from their memory of that landscape. This is one of the beginning points for understanding Aboriginal oral traditions. It is important to see the inside of events, through the eyes of the sacredness of Mother Earth. Put another way, Aboriginal oral traditions see the history of humankind as one with, and inseparable from, nature.

Without "pen or ink," First Nations remember and understand, through their stories, their internal and external landscapes of being and becoming. There are no boundaries and there are no beginning or end points. Their history is both separate from and parallel to the history of Canada, as understood by non-Aboriginal people—the history of the newcomers. In this way, Aboriginal oral traditions evoke the European past and have much to teach us about ourselves. They provide a necessary corrective, a balance, if you like, as well as a deeper understanding of what we know today as Canada.

Notes

1 Richard White, *The Middle Ground, Indians, Empires, and Republics in the Great Lakes Region, 1650-1815* (Cambridge: Cambridge University Press, 1991), p. x.

2 See Basil Johnston, *The Manitous: The Spiritual World of the Ojibway* (Toronto: Key Porter Books, 1995). See also his *Ojibwa Ceremonies* (Toronto: McClelland and Stewart, 1982), especially "The Council Zuguswediwin," pp. 155-75.

3 For another example see Dean Jacobs, "'We have but our hearts and the traditions of our old men': Understanding the Traditions and History of Bkejwanong," in David McNab and S. Dale Standen, eds., with an "Introduction," *Gin Das Winan: Documenting Aboriginal History in Ontario*, Occasional Papers of The Champlain Society, no. 2 (Toronto: The Champlain Society, 1996), pp. 1-13.

4 The meeting ground is also part of the circles of time. See David T. McNab, "Making a Circle of Time: The Treaty-Making Process and Aboriginal Land Rights in Ontario," in *Co-existence? Studies in Ontario-First Nation Relations* (Peterborough, ON: Frost Centre for Canadian Heritage and Development Studies, Trent University, 1992), pp. 27-49. An earlier version was published as "Aboriginal Land Claims in Ontario," in Ken Coates, ed., *Aboriginal Land Claims in Canada: A Regional Perspective* (Toronto: Copp Clark Pitman, 1992), pp. 73-100.

Contributors

Thomas S. Abler is a professor of anthropology at the University of Waterloo. He has written widely on the Haudenosaunee and on Aboriginal people in Canada generally.

Laird Christie teaches anthropology at Wilfrid Laurier University. He is continuing his research on self-government in the Canadian North.

Janet E. Chute is a research associate with the School of Resource and Environmental Studies at Dalhousie University. She is the author of a forthcoming study entitled *The Legacy of Shingwakonse* which is scheduled to be published in the spring of 1998.

Cameron Croxall is currently completing a Master of Arts degree at Trent University, Peterborough, Ontario.

Olive Patricia Dickason, a member of the Order of Canada, is Professor Emeritus in history at the University of Alberta as well as adjunct professor at the University of Ottawa. Professor Dickason is well known for her *Canada's First Nations: A History of Founding Peoples from Earliest Times*. In 1997 Professor Dickason received the Aboriginal Lifetime Achievement Award.

Joan G. Fairweather currently resides in South Africa and works at the Centre for History and Culture at the University of the Western Cape. An archivist at the National Archives of Canada in Ottawa, she is currently on leave for two years and is continuing her research on the history of apartheid.

E. Reginald Good is a historian who currently is working as a historical research consultant for the Saugeen Ojibways in Ontario.

Elizabeth Graham, an anthropologist, resides in Waterloo, Ontario. She is completing a study on residential schools in southern Ontario.

Sidney L. Harring teaches law at the City University of New York Law School and the Graduate Center, City University of New York. He has published widely on Aboriginal legal history in North America and is the author of *Crow Dog's Case* (1994).

Bruce W. Hodgins is a professor of history at Trent University in Peterborough, Ontario. Author of numerous books and articles on Canadian history, he is an authority on the history of Northern Ontario and the Lake Temagami area in particular.

Dean M. Jacobs is the executive director for Nin.Da.Waab.Jig., the Walpole Island Heritage Centre, Bkejwanong Territory. He has published a number of articles on the history of Bkejwanong and co-ordinated the publication of the award-winning *Walpole Island: The Soul of Indian Territory* (1987) for Nin.Da.Waab.Jig. In the spring of 1998 he received an honorary doctorate from Bowling Green State University.

David T. McNab is a claims advisor for Nin.Da.Wab.Jig. and an Honorary External Associate in the Frost Centre for Canadian Heritage and Development Studies at Trent University. Author of numerous articles on Aboriginal land and treaty rights as well as on Métis history, his *Circles of Time: Aboriginal Land Rights and Resistance in Ontario* is forthcoming from Wilfrid Laurier University Press.

Jim Miller resides in Port Lambton. He is Professor Emeritus at the University of Western Ontario and former priest-in-charge of St. John the Baptist Anglican Church on Walpole Island. Professor Miller has recently completed, with Professor Ed Danziger, Jr., a study of residential schools in partnership with the citizens of Bkejwanong.

Theresa Redmond is currently Litigation Project Manager for the federal Department of Indian and Northern Affairs in Hull, Quebec.

Heather Rollason currently resides in Toronto and is completing work on Samuel Hearne's Journal and the Chipewyan people for her PhD in history at the University of Alberta.

Rhonda Telford is a Toronto-based historical research consultant on Aboriginal rights for First Nations in Ontario. A PhD graduate from the University of Toronto in 1996, she has written on Aboriginal and treaty mineral rights as well as on the nineteenth-century Indian Department.

Index